WTO and Environment Development

WTO and Environment Development

Edited By

TALWAR SABANNA

SERIALS PUBLICATIONS
NEW DELHI (INDIA)

First Published - 2011

ISBN: 978-81-8387-363-5

Published by

SERIALS PUBLICATIONS
4830/24, 1st Floor, Ansari Road
Darya Ganj, New Delhi-110002 (India)
Phone : 23245225. Fax : 91-11-23272135
E-mail: serials@satyam.net.in

CONTENTS

PREFACE

A big section of planners and policy makers think that there are no serious environmental problems in the developing countries. According to them, if however, there by, any variety of solutions exist, they often are of the opinion that government should come forward to implement the solution. As a remedial package minimization of public sector interference and maximization of government intervention, ensuring suitable prices for infrastructure and urban amenities through removal or reduction of subsidies, generating employment directly through anti-poverty programs, easing private and joint sector projects, are being prescribed. However, the ultimate solution is being sought through competent and transparent management of environmental projects. Although the desirability of growth is globally accepted and recognised, recent years have provided testimony to raising anxiety about whether environmental problems are already very serious and call for immediate attention. Environmental threats evolve because of both resource depletion and negative externalities caused by development process and projects. With a view to achieving the object of sustainable development it is inevitable to do with both types of problem adequately. In this context as editor I feel privileged to present this book to the reader on WTO and Environment Development.

Chapter–1

ENVIRONMENT VS DEVELOPMENT: CAN WE HAVE EQUILIBRIUM?

Rameshwari Pandya

The man on the street does not feel "bothered, directly and personally, by farmer suicides and melting Himalaya glaciers", then let us understand well that no amount of structural or policy changes can truly help us face these trials. It will take large number of courageous, creative and caring citizens who feel personally responsible for the state of society and ecology, and are charged with the agenda for transformation.

There are two over arching narratives. The first narrative is of "Emergent India" - a nation growing in confidence and willing itself to become an economic powerhouse. The second theme is that of the "other India" where socio - economic development still remains a distant reality. Paraphrasing a renowned journalist, it is the story of booming sensex and of a hundred thousand farmer suicides. There are several challenges which we are facing today. The most important challenge is environmental. It is estimated that, given the speed of glacier melt, the major rivers will become seasonal, Rising sea levels will threaten our coastal communities and monsoon will become more erratic. Global warming is reality and will begin to impact the most basic necessities food and water– sooner than we might imagine. The challenge is even greater for India given the stage of economic development we are in. The coming years will see a significant surge in our energy consumption most of which will be met by burning increasing quantities of fossil fuels.

If climate experts are to be believed, we are on the verge of losing all the economic gains made over the past couple of decades because India's economy ultimately sits on a bedrock of the subcontinent's ecology.

Environment and development are two sides of the same coin. The development of science and technology and ever increasing world population brought about tremendous changes in the earth environment. These changes upset the ecological laws, thereby disturbing the balance of human life. Any one of these cannot be sacrificed for the other. In the mad race for development, developed and developing nations alike are tremendously surging towards rapid industrialization at the cost of destroying the natural ecology of the environment. Since Development and environment pollution are inevitable and interdependent phenomenon, judicial attitude is geared around for drawing up of a line of control over both these contingencies.

Developmental attitudes causes increasing impact on the ecosystem, which is essential for well being of mankind. Stiglitz (2002) uses apt metaphor of dilapidated boats when he says "small developing countries are like small boats. Rapid capital market liberalization, in the manner pushed by the International Monetary Fund holes in their hulls have been repaired, before the captain has received training, before life vests have been put on board. Even in the best of circumstance, there was a high likelihood that they would be overturned when they were hit broadside by a big wave"

The current environmental crisis is world wide, among the most serious issues are the destruction of tropical rain forests, the depletion of the ozone layer, acid precipitation, soil erosion and depletion and global warming. In 1993, almost 1700 of the world's top scientists, including 104 Nobel Laureates, signed a "Scientists Warming to Humanity", which argued that current methods of production and consumption are unsustainable, that "human beings in the natural world are on a collision course' and that "a great change in our stewardship of the earth and the life on it is required, if vast human misery is to be avoided and our global home on this planet is not to be irretrievable mutilated".

Economic growth and development of a country or region may be realized through the optimum utilization of available resources and the state of technology, which in turn depends on the quality of institutional arrangement or structure that is being the force in production and distribution. Because there is a close connection between the institutions and technology employed and the efficiency of a market economy is directly shaped by the institutional framework. In the whole process of the economic progress, various types of institutions are to function and they work at various levels interdependently. It is evident that institutions are as important as technology for economic development and they evolve together interactively during the development process. The role of institutions in economic activity is that defining the parameters and processes through which agents use technology, natural and human resource are to increase the level of production and income. However, it should be noted that all the time all the institutions would not be equally effective.

Whenever some external substance interferes with the original one and deteriorates or destroys its quality then it is known as pollution. Environment pollution happens when external factors deteriorates the natural environment in any form. These human activities are like use of automobiles, combustion engines, industrial wastes, household wastes, fertilizers and others. When this environment pollution reaches to a great extent it takes the form of environmental crisis.

It is at this stage, when a balance between biotic and abiotic substances gets imbalance and resulted into adverse effect on the lives of living being.

During the twentieth century, people have put a heavy burden on the earth's environment by giving priority to economic development, mass production, mass consumption and mass disposal. Population explosion, industrialization, unplanned urbanization, depletion of natural resources, deforestation, generation of sewages, liquid and solid waste materials, technological advancement etc are the major cause of poor quality of environment in metropolitan cities.

India is one of the fastest (3rd) growing economies of the world. It achieved a commendable growth rate (9%) in 2006 and the average growth rate in the Xth five year plan period (2002-03 to 2006-07) is about 7%. This is the highest rate achieved in any plan period. For the XIth plan the target is to achieve 9% growth rate. But there are several constraints in the way to sustainable growth.

'Industrial Revolution' gave mankind both luxuries and evils of push button living. Industries generate, use and discard toxic substances that lead to the generation of enormous wastes possessing hazardous characteristics scientifically proven to have adverse effect on human health and environment. The hazard industrial development and the anarchic operations of the world economy have had a disastrous impact an the global environment this has, also led to the generation of huge quantities of hazardous wastes that includes all kind of toxic materials such as pesticides, nuclear waste, bio medical waste etc. Development today is no longer only a comfort but also a liability. The reason: development brings in as many problems as it solves. The common scene across Asia today, to name a few consists of over flowing streets, lack of integrated planning.

For about Six decades, since independence, we have adopted a growth strategy, aiming at achieving the highest possible growth rate through exploitation of environment. Heavy and basic industries were located mainly with a view to reducing regional disparities rather than increasing environmental pollution.

Model of Growth

The old Paradigm of directed and regulated economic growth was replaced by a new paradigm of market - oriented growth, guided by profit motive, leading to flow of industries to areas where economies were available abundantly. The objective underlying this strategy is to maximize growth rate caring little for preservation of natural resources and bio - diversity. Private sector thus never calculates social costs.

Thus in our both models of growth, one of the direct growth and the other of market oriented growth, the economists did not assign any place to natural resource conservation and pollution abatement. We have to ensure higher growth rate without increase in environmental pollution. For this purpose, we have to change our approach as well as strategies in regard to higher economic growth and better environment, in such a way that one reinforces the other.

Table 1
Impact of Development Activities on Environment

Development Activities	*Impact on Environment*
Forest clearing and land selltement	Extinction of rare species of flora and fauna, create breeding grounds for mosquito.
Shifting cultivation in upland agriculture	Soil erosion in upland areas. Soil fertility decline. If shorter cultivation cycle, flooding of low land areas.
Agro-industries e.g. Sugar and tapioca	Air pollution due to burning of bio gas as fuel in mills, large amount of highly polluting organic with surface water pollution.
Use of pesticides	Organisms develop resistance & new control methods needed. Leads to complex and widespread environment problems. Biological magnification, poisoning.
Timber Extraction	Degrades land, destroys surface soil, reduces production potential of future forest.
Urbanization and industrialization	Concentration of population, making huge dent on rural environment, air and water pollution.
Water resources projects	Human settlement and resettlement spread of e.g. extensive irrigation, waterborne disease reduction of fisheries, physical changes, e.g. temperature, humidity.

Environmental Problems in Developing Countries

The rapid industrialization in developing countries results in irreparable contamination of surface, ground water, air and soil, the depletion of forests the discharge of hazardous effluents from industries, the uncontrolled dumping of contaminated solid waste, over -exploitation of natural resources, increasing number of unknown diseases caused by pollution, and new phenomenon like acid rain and so on. The situation existing in many developing countries is the complex growth of environmental pressures is the rapid population growth, unprecedented rates of urbanization and the urgent need to pursue economic development at whatever cost.

Proper management of the natural resources base is especially important in developing countries, because these countries can least afford the opportunity costs of irreversible loss of their renewable natural resources, or efforts to remedy environmental damage. But despite their increasing attention to environmental management many developing countries still cannot deal effectively with serious environmental problems they face. Important among these are the need to conserve and manage renewable natural resources (including forests, crop lands, grazing land, marine and fresh water fisheries and wild life) control of industrial and urban air, water and land pollution, public health aspects of developmental projects, occupational health and safety, involuntary resettlement of people living in project areas, the well being of tribal peoples and the preservation or salvage of unique cultural properties such as archaeological sites. Many environment losses are either completely irreversible or reversible only over a very long time. Among the more urgent environmental problems of developing countries are those relating to land and water resource. Other serious environmental problems also contribute to problem of human health and well being in developing countries. The costs of add on pollution control technologies are usually prohibitively expensive and do not resolve the basic deficiencies in the industrial processes, moreover such facilities are most often operated very inefficiently and with many health and safety hazards. The economies of many developing countries depend heavily on their natural resources base, especially in agriculture, forestry and fisheries.

Urban India began to colonise India, thousands of dams were constructed without once pausing to establish whether or not the nation was profiting from them, mines were dug indiscriminately pesticides such as DDT were sprayed in such massive doses that instead of insects, human began to die from the poisons. Nuclear reactors were built without worrying about the fact that there was no place to dump the lethal waste they would continually produce. As for our forests, almost anyone with an axe, bulldozer or servants at their disposal began to cut unprotected timber for sale to the highest urban bidder.

Similarly the slums are the result of urbanization. The urban population has grown 5 fold from 1951 - 2001. People come to urban area in search of employment. Urban areas are reeling under increasing pollution, traffic congestion making urban life unbearable. On going fast - paced urbanization under the influence of increasing globalization especially in developing countries of Asia is like a twin edged sword with multiple risks, and consequences of several kinds.

Slums by definition, are heavily congested residential settlements in which one find bad housing and poor family life, over crowding, crimes, insanitary conditions, begging, pollution, drug abuse, human abuse, lack of basic service, endangering public health, safety and morals. The steep rise in slum growth has led to grave threats mainly to the environment, law and order and to public health. As a consequence of environmental crisis, problems like excessive heat, excessive humidity, adverse effect on physical and mental development of human beings, danger to health of living beings. Extensive industrialization has resulted into polluted world. Three Indian cities are amongst the 15 most polluted cities of the world.

Urbanization promotes the influx of population from rural areas to urban centers because of push and pull factors operative in the respective area. This has resulted into urban poverty, fast growth of informal sector, and acute pressure on basic services which ultimately deteriorates urban environment. But we must not forget that the world's future is largely an urban future. Our ability to incorporate the urban poor in the development processes and assist in their growths will be highly significant if we are to achieve sustainable development.

Development comes through industrialization which in turn the main factor behind the degradation of environment. To resolve the issue, the experts worldwide have come up with a doctrine called 'Sustainable Development' i.e there must be balance between development and environment. The doctrine of 'Sustainable development' resolves the issue of such development at the cost of the environment by adopting an anticipatory measure to tackle the future hazards. Development and Environment must co-exist and go hand in hand. Economic growth is needed to realize development; it should be of Sustainable growth mode so that it does not result in the depletion of capital or environmental assets beyond the rate of regeneration of these assets. Not surprisingly, galloping soil sterility has overtaken millions of hectares of once fertile farmlands. And there is not one river in India whose water we can safely drink. For millions, landslides, floods and droughts make a mockery of the delusive projections of economists and politicians.

Sustainable development in a global economy requires a delicate long-term balance between human activity and nature's ability to renew itself. Future prosperity depends both on preserving ecological treasures for the benefit of future generations and on continued economic growth and innovation. For smooth running of society several legislations are passed. The law relating to environment has seen a paradigm shift over the concept of right to environment in India since 1980s; primarily after a series of global co-operative initiatives. The nation has not only enacted specific legislation on environmental protection, but has also created a new fundamental right to clean environment in the constitution.

The environment (protection) act 1986 provides for single focus in the country for the protection of environment and aims at plugging the loopholes in the existing legislation. In the developing countries like India, exploitation of natural resources is essential for economic progress for development. Right to wholesome environment is also a fundamental right under article 21 of the Indian Constitution.

To achieve the equilibrium between both, Hon'ble Supreme Court in series of landmark judgment has evolved some fundamental principles. The important principles evolved by the highest court of the country focuses on concept of :

'Sustainable development'

'Polluter pay'

'Precautionary'

'Strict liability'

With growing environment concerns in India policy makers have evolved the system of Environment Impact Assessment which seeks to bring about a balance between industrialization and environmental conservation. As hazardous industries become a characteristic of 21st Century world, and India is in the race of rapid industrialization which is accompanied with massive environment and social burdens, monitoring tools like Environment Impact Assessment (EIA), assumes great significance in ensuring sound economic development without compromising on environmental and social costs.

Some Significant Features of the Act are:

- Making top Management responsible for environment protection and liable for prosecution.
- Providing stringent punishment and penalties.
- Empowering enforcement agencies to effect closure of polluting industries.

New Policy for Discouraging Acquisition of Farmland for SEZs.

In the backdrop of controversies over setting up of SEZs, the Central Government unveiled on November 25 2007, a new policy which provides for discouraging acquisition of agricultural land for non-farming purposes and setting up a commission to look into resettlement aspects. The National Rehabilitation and Resettlement Policy 2007 also entails setting up of a committee to review and monitor the progress of implementation and resettlement schemes across the country.

"Acquisition of agricultural land for non-agricultural use in a project may be kept to the minimum 3 multi-cropped land. Land may be avoided to the extent possible for such purposes, and acquisition of irrigated land, if unavoidable, may be kept of the minimum". The policy states. "Waste land, degraded land or un-irrigated land should be the option for acquisition." This assumed significance as acquisition of farming land for SEZs has triggered violent protests all over India. The new policy envisages setting up a Rehabilitation Commission at the national level to look into the Settlement issues of the families displaced from their land following its acquisition for projects.

Problems in implementing the Policies

The Environment Protection Act, 1986 has always remained a paper tiger because of enforcement authorities in India could not effectively implement them it can be a powerful tool but has many loop holes and weaknesses. Law is a regulator of human conduct but no law can indeed effectively work unless there is an element of acceptance by people in society. There are certain problems such as:

- Deficiency of environmental education knowledge among enforcing authorities
- Lack of responsibility due to ecological illiteracy on part of community.
- Lack of provision for training of professional manpower in the field of environmental education
- Lack of coordination among the administrative institutions and educational institutions on environmental activities.
- Shortage of human and financial resources.

- Improper technology
- Lack of overall proper planning

ECO–FRIENDLY WORK SOLUTIONS

Developing Countries are in need of 'home grown' solutions which are in harmony to live well can not achieve high standards of living at the expense of environmental and ecological integrity. The situation is alarming and requires immediate action, legislation, execution and planning so that we may justify ourselves.

Therefore the need of a comprehensive approach to the problem of environmental protection is required. They can be

- Innovative strategies to address the problems are necessary.
- People's participation is very helpful and urgent need here (NGOs, SHGs)
- Development of minor irrigation and utilization of created irrigation potential
- Rainwater harvesting and conservation for the development of rainfed areas water shed approach.
- Reclamation or development of problem soils / lands.
- Encouragement to the private sector for effective extension services.
- Encouragement to organic farming.
- Detailed indigenous knowledge and greater skills in blending modern and traditional technologies to enhance productivity efficiency of farming Community.
- Encouraging sanitary landfills, biogas generating technologies and vermicomposting.
- Offering good incentives for the local bodies and the government, to drive benefit by utilizing the wastes.
- There are two major areas on which research and development efforts are needed.
  (i) Genetic resource management and biotechnology.

(ii) Natural resource management and agro ecology.

- The local body with the help of Govt. should chalk out the plan to divert and dispose of sewage.
- Proper drainage system be developed to get rid of water logging problem.
- Help more in pollution prevention than pollution control.
- Use eco friendly products
- Save electricity by not wasting it when required because, electricity saved is electricity generated without polluting the environment.
- Promote reuse and recycling wherever possible and reduce the production of wastes.
- Use rechargeable batteries. Rechargeable batteries will reduce metal pollution.
- Environment education should result in the development of an ecological ethics a change in attitude of man towards man, society and nature, in realization of man as a part of nature, not alien to it.
- Adequate funds should be provided by the UGC, Dept of science and Technology Central and State Governments for effective implementation of environmental education programme.
- Developing forest cover in the urban areas will result in reducing the air and sound pollution in cities and people living there will have benefits like purification of air, recreation etc available locally.
- The existing regulations and laws to protect forest and wild life should be implemented by the concerned government agencies vigorously and in spirit.
- People dependent on the forest should be trained to use the resources in self sustainable and viable manner.
- Provide green cover along the main roads, railway tracks and so on.

- Provide thick foliage between road dividers.
- The public carriers like buses and autorickshaw's should compulsorily use fuels like CNG in place of petrol and diesel so as to reduce the pollution.
- Nuclear power plants should be developed to generate power on large scale.
- The Government should install equipment to measure the pollution and presence of particles and harmful gases in the atmosphere. So that the corrective actions are taken on a timely basis.
- Legislation, though in place, should be implemented in letter and spirit for disposal of effluent by the industries. Pollution industries should be controlled in the vicinity of the large water bodies.
- An in-depth study of impact of large dams and reservoirs on the ecology should be studied before construction.
- The mass means of transportation should be developed like metro railways, buses etc in order to reduce the traffic and use of private vehicles in the cities. This will drastically reduce the pollution caused by vehicles.
- Use of windmill to generate power.
- Use of solar energy in lighting, heating and running small domestic appliances.
- Use of biogas in households.
- Use of nuclear power to generate electricity in place of coal, naphtha or lignite.
- Teachers, parents, doctors, engineers, planners, administrators and scientist and general public should be involved in environmental education programme.
- The interdisciplinary research projects on environmental problems should be undertaken.
- The Govt. should establish environmental research centers in every state. A data bank and eco systems

information base / system should be developed, so that the required information is available at a central place.

- Seminars, conferences and workshops should be organized from time to time on environmental education.
- The general public should be educated about the environmental degradation and improvement of the environmental quality through mass media by incorporating them through regular programme of AIR, TV and visual aids etc, documentary films should be prepared on these themes and exhibited for the benefit of the people.

Conclusion

Development and Environment are interrelated to each other, as one hand development affects the environment and on the other, more stress on environment protection would close the door to development. The two are so significant that one of them cannot be compromised for the growth of the other. To achieve the objective of sustainable development lies with technological know-how and social commitment of research institutes, environmental regulating agencies, as well as the government's determinations in devising scientifically sound, pro-active or preventive strategies and policies for sustainable development. Sustainable rate of growth is that rate of growth which can be continued over a long period of time, for making growth sustainable in India, we have to make growth inclusive by tackling the problems of poverty, inequality and improving the environment. Proper planning, implementation, management of policies and public participation can ensure a sustainable system.

In matter of ecology and environment and considering the principle of sustainable development, no person or organization, however, high and mighty they man be cannot be permitted to flout the law of the land. The variations in the environment include the following aspects like urban and rural industrial and the agricultural, the slum dwellers and the sophisticated. Education at different levels should take cognizance of these factors and if they are ignored, it will not be meaningful. Education programmes and courses should be planned and implemented, taking into consideration, the very vital role played by the environment in the life of learner.

The United Nations Conference on environment and development held in Rio de Janeiro in 1992 and popularly known as 'Earth Summit' followed by the world summit on sustainable development at Johannesburg in 2002, just 10 years after the first summit, have highlighted the key issue of global environmental concern and have attracted the attention of the general public towards the deteriorating environment. Any government at its own level cannot achieve the goals of sustainable development until the public has a participatory role in it. Public participation is possible only when the public is aware about the ecological and environmental issue. A drive by the government to ban the littering of polythene cannot be successful until the public understands the environmental implications of the same. The public has to be educated about the fact that if we are degrading our environment we are actually harming our own selves.

This is because we are a part of the complex network of environment where every component is linked to one another. It is all the more important to educate the people that sometimes the adverse impact of environment are not experienced or noticed until a threshold is crossed. There is a Chinese proverb. "If you plan for one year, plant rice, if you plan for 10 years, plant trees and if your plan for 100 years, educate people".

In the present era, the human race is faced with the danger of environmental hazard. This has belittled the freedom to live in clean environment. We are to balance or coordinate properly between environment and development should be synonymous to each other when we talk about human being, we will have to include ecosystem.

The society shall have to prosper, but not at the cost of the environment and in the similar vein, the environment shall have to be protected but not at the cost of development of the society. It is important to strike a balance between the two i.e. development on one side and pollution free environment on the other.

References

Adam, D. (2000), Planning between Cultural Paradigms: Traditional Knowledge and Transition to Ecological Sustainability, Dissertation Abstract International. Vol. 60(7). Jan.

B. N. Neelima, Communication for Environmental Education, JRF, Deptt. of Journalism, Sri Padmavathi Mahila University, Tirupathi.

B. R. Kukreti (1993), Environmental Education- A Blue Print, University News, August 16.

Bharat B. Dhar (2000), Environmental Education in India, University News, 38(6), February.

Bhatia, A. (2000), Women's Development and NGO's, Rawat Publications, Jaipur and New Delhi.

Francois, N. (2000), Cultivating the Human Environmental for the Adoption and Use of Information Technology, Dissertation Abstract International Vol. 60(7), Jan.

G. R. Chhatwal (1998), Encyclopaedia of Environmental Education, Anmol Publications Pvt. Ltd. New Delhi.

lyer S. (1996), Blue Print for Environmental Action. Social Welfare 40(8) June.

Jain, R. (1997), Sustainable Development, Policy and Practices 1st ed. New Age International Publishers. Australia.

K. B. Powar. (1993), Environmental Issues and University, University News, November 22.

Onkar N. Srivastava (1992), Environment and Sustainable Development, University News, January 13.

Prakash, J. Srivastava, S. K. (1999), Environmental Problems, Policies and Strategies, Mohit Publications. New Delhi.

(1990), Rs. 60 Crore for Environmental Studies. University News, November 12.

S. Lakshmi (1991), Challenges in Indian Education.

Sharma, S. (2001), Managing Environment: A Critique of "The Tragedy of Commons", Journal of Human Ecology. Vol. 12(1).

Subramanyam. V. and K. R. Rama Moham (2001), Tribal Ecology and Food Scarcity. Journal of Human Ecology. Vol. 12(5) pp. 351-356.

Vishwanandha K. R. (2000), Environmental Impact on the Economic Life of Yeruka Tribe. Journal of Human Ecology Vol. 12(4) pp. 267-270.

Yogendra K. Sharma (2001), History of Problems of Education (Volume - 2), Kanishka Publication.

Ali, sabir, S. N. Singh (1998), Major Problems of Delhi Slums Uppal Publishing House, New Delhi.

D. Bhugra and Anastasia Mastrogianni, Globalization and Mental Disorders. British Journal of Psychiartry 184. PP 10-20.

Desh Bandhu and N.L. Ramnathan (1982), Education for Environmental Planning and Conservation. Indian Environmental Society, New Delhi.

M.A. Farok (2005), Issue in Environmental Education. Arise Publishers and Distributors, New Delhi.

Asthana D.K. Asthana M, (2001), Environment Problems and Solutions. S.Chand and Company, New Delhi.

Chhokar K.B. and Pandya N. Raghunathan (2004), Understanding Environment, Sage Publication, New Delhi.

Deb S.C. (2003), Environmental Management Jaico Publishing House, Mumbai.

Ghanta R. Rao D.B. (1998), Environmental Education Problems and Prospects. Discovery Publishing House, Delhi.

Ghosh A. (2000), Environment ad Development. A.P.H. Publishing Corporation, New Delhi.

Kaushik A. Kaushik C.P. (2004), Perspectives in Environmental Studies. New Age International Publications, New Delhi.

Singh P.P. Sharma S. (2004), Teaching of Environment. Deep and Deep Publication, New Delhi.

Prabhakar V.K. (2002), Environmental Pollution, Ammol Publication, New Delhi.

Honley Nick, Robert Colin (2002), Issues in Environmental Economics, Black Well Publishers, UK.

Webliography

http://www.scacobgy.org/gclid

(New 3 nig, 7ko8cfsuy about kxdrv)

http://www.gisdevelopment.net/application/environment/pp/envp 1001 .htm

http://www.unrptie.org/ozonactin/events/ozoneday/2006-events.htm

http://www.m-w.com/difinary/environment

http://www.infochangeindia.org/analysisl35.jsp

http://envfor.nic.in/report/report/html

http ://www. inforchangeindia.org/environmentbp.jsp

http://www.indiabudget.nicin/es98-99/environ.htm

CHAPTER–2

DEVELOPMENT IN INDIAN ECONOMY THROUGH COOPERATIVE SECTOR

Muzamil Jan

Introduction

Indian cooperative movement was organised against the exploitation of unscrupulous money-lenders to exonerate the farming community from the web of poverty and indebt. The Government took lot of measures to improve the conditions of the farming sector and as such promoted cooperative credit societies in the light of Raiffeisan model credit societies because of recommendations of Sir Fredrick Nicholson in 1889. Now cooperatives and formal legal entities under a statute have been existence for more than hundred years (International Cooperative Alliance. 1995). Today cooperative movement in India is one of the largest movements in the world. Initially it was started with a limited spectrum of activities or dispensation of rural credit has now entered in all fields of economic activity with social content. It has been playing a significant role in disbursing agricultural credit, distribution of agricultural inputs, providing market support, processing, etc. Over the last more than hundred years (1904-2007), cooperatives have made substantial contribution to the country, particularly to the rural poor. Notwithstanding their achievements and phenomenon growth, cooperatives are beset with several issues and confront with challenges in the era of economic reforms (Department of Agriculture and Cooperation, 2006). The employment generated through cooperatives is 15 per cent at national level, in addition to 14.79 million self employed persons via cooperatives (Nation Resource Centre, 2004).

The importance of cooperative movement cannot belittle. It reminds the findings of the All India Rural Credit Survey Committee, 1954 that "Cooperation has failed but it must succeed" and the comments of Royal Commission on Agriculture "if the cooperatives fail, this will be a failure for best hope of India". It is, therefore planners of post-independence era who gave thrust to the cooperative movement and the then Prime Minister Pandit Jwaharlal Nehru wanted India to be convulsed with cooperatives. In the new millennium, a serious challenge, which is being faced by cooperatives, relates to WTO Agreement on Agriculture. Cooperatives are closely attached with agricultural and agro-based activities in the rural areas. Members of cooperative fraternity are expressing concern that the implementation of various provisions of Agreement on Agriculture will seriously affect the farming community in terms of their income levels, levels of living and quality of life. This aspect is particularly important as 70 per cent of our population is dependent on agriculture and agro-based activities: whereas, only 4 per cent of population is dependent on agriculture and allied activities in case of developed countries. Further, it has to be ensured that food security in terms of providing minimum food for various sections of Indian population does not get adversely affected by the WTO Agreement on Agriculture and hence there is the need for providing a separate "Food Security" under WTO provisions with emphasis on encouraging on food production and per hectare productivity of various crops. Various segments of cooperative movement should be encouraged for improving their operational challenges of competitive culture.

Cooperatives have lost their democratic character and have become the government controlled bureaucratic organisations. The cooperative societies must evolve as independent, self-reliant, autonomous and member-driven institutions. Capoor Committee (2000) has recommended on these lines besides professionalism, human resource development (HRD), business diversification, recovery management, fund mechanism and getting up of a cooperative rehabilitation and development fund. The committee also cautions against excessive control and regulation. Central government along with its state counterparts has taken initiative to strengthen infrastructure facilities and to develop professional skills in the cooperatives. The cooperative education and training programmes are being implemented by National Cooperative Union (NCUI) and National Council for Cooperative Training (NCCT) and junior level cooperative training centres. Still there is a feeling all over the need for professionals. The cooperatives professional may have to redefine their roles in the light of the emerging knowledge society. Information technology (IT) has assumed such high importance that ICMs should now turn their focus on e-Business, e-Commerce, e-Governance, CRM, etc. To enable them to acquire competitive ability in terms of quality, cost, timeliness, availability, service and support, total quality management (TQM) are the specific areas that would improve cooperative during the dawn of new millennium (International Cooperative Alliance. 1995).

Related Literature

Roy (1998) evaluated the *'Kushmandi Cooperative Marketing Society'* situated in South *Dinajpur* district of *West Bengal*. During the year 1965-66, this Society started with a meagre share capital of Rs.6,340 i.e. beginning with zero. The Society has become hero of Agricultural Cooperative Movement in *West Bengal,* as their share capital for 1997-98 swelled to Rs. 31.42 lakh. The Society has not restricted its area of operation in the West Bengal State only, but it works throughout India. The main activities involve procurement and sale of agricultural commodities produced in their area which are paddy, wheat, *urad, arhar*, mustard seeds, raw jute, garlic etc. The Society has a consumer shop for selling various kinds of shirting/suiting clothes, sari, bed sheet, woollen garments, etc. which is running profitably; besides, the Society sells fertilizer to the local farmers with bare minimum margin. The Society is authorized dealer of *Konark Cement* and sells cement to local consumers. 'Indian Oil Corporation' has set up a diesel-cum-petrol pump of the Society that is running successfully. It encourages the local students by providing financial assistance regarding to the meritorious poor students.

Rao (2000) studied *'Cooperative Tea Industry'* in *Tamil Nadu—INCOSERVE;* which is the apex body for the seventeen *Industrial Cooperative Tea Factories* in the *Nilgiris,* serving 21,326 acres of tea gardens through the *Industrial Cooperative Tea Factories.* The annual production of the tea factories attached to *INCOSERVE* is about 167 lakh kilograms. It is the largest *Tea Cooperative* in India functioning under the control of Government of *Tamil Nadu.* Its major weakness is that tea growers are having small-holdings and there is absence of technical field staff to render technical adviser to the tea growers. In order to encourage the tea farmers, tea board should develop basic infrastructural facilities and financial support to the tea factories through *INCOSERVE.* Government should extend financial support in respect of promotion of packet tea sales through reasonable advertising budget.

Sharma (2000) found that the Cooperatives in *Gujarat* and *Maharashtra* are laying great emphasis on developing infrastructure facilities in the form of schools, hospitals, entertaining centres, rural roads, drinking water facilities for the common masses. Social forestry programmes are being arranged by *'Indian Farmers Fertiliser Cooperative Limited'* (IFFCO) for protecting the rural environment. The interest of the weaker sections of society like unskilled labour, illiterate fishermen and landless labourers are also being promoted through setting up of Cooperatives for weaker sections. The latest innovation of Farmers Credit Card in the field of rural finance is helping the farmers in getting working capital for enabling them to purchase inputs like fertilizers, seeds etc. All these efforts are a pointer towards the positive role of Cooperatives in the empowerment of people in India.

Kalamkar et al. (2001) investigated the progress of *'Agricultural Credit Societies and Non-Agricultural Credit Societies'* in *Vidarba*. The study reveals that the number of Societies increased by 3.64 and 14.60 percent during 18 years period registering a growth rate of 0.36 and 5.87 percent for *'Agricultural Credit Cooperative Societies and Non-Agricultural Credit Cooperative Societies'* in *Vidarbha* respectively. The membership has increased by 49.46 and 32.39 percent during the study period registering a growth rate of 2.23 and 8.24 percent for *'Agricultural Credit and Non-Agricultural Credit Cooperative Societies'*, respectively. Growth in advances accompanied by poor recovery have kept the over dues at significantly high level. This increase in over dues shows poor performance of the Credit Societies.

Kulkarni et al. (2001) examined the growth of *'Lead Bank Credit'*. Growth parameters of the total deposit, total advance and total branches showed highly significant and positive growth rate. The growth rates of total priority sector advance, agricultural advance, small-scale industry advance, other priority sector advance, and 'Integrated Rural Development Programme' (IRDP) advance are positive and significant at 5 percent level. The growth rates of total deposits, total advances, agricultural advance and small-scale industry advance reveal more than 10 percent during 11 years. There is positive and considerable correlation between total advance of the lead bank and moderate correlation between total advance and advance to agricultural sector and negative correlation with other priority sector advances of the lead bank. There is moderate correlation between total advance of all institutions except lead bank and advance to small scale industry and the correlation between total advance of all institution except lead bank and advances to total priority sectors, agriculture, other priority sector and IRDP are non significant.

Behera and Dash (2001) assessed the district-wise growth of Cooperative Societies, i.e. *'Primary Agricultural Cooperative Societies'* (PACS), *'Large Adivasi Multi-Purpose Cooperative*

Societies' (LAMPS) and *'Farmers Service Society'* (FSS), over the period of 1984-85 to 1996-97, covering all the districts (undivided) in *Orissa.* In *Orissa,* in the year 1996-97, the number of *Primary Agricultural Cooperative Societies* including *Large Adivasi Multi-Purpose Cooperative Societies* and *Farmer Service Societies* stood at 2,806 with a total membership of 34.44 lakh and a working capital of Rs.371 crore. It is found that there exists inter-district variations in the growth rate of different selected indicators, namely, number of Societies, number of members, number of borrowing members, working capital, share capital, deposits, loan advanced (short-term loan and medium-term loan), total loan outstanding, total over due and amount of consumer goods sold. In certain cases, as the development of Cooperatives has been in a negative direction, this hampers the Cooperative Movement in the state. Share capital per member has significant impact in the net earning per Cooperative Society, whereas, loan advanced per member has no significant impact on the net earnings per Society. Hence, in order to increase the net earnings per Cooperative Society, which includes *Primary Agricultural Cooperative Societies, Large Adivasi Multi-Purpose Cooperative Societies* and *Farmers Service Society,* in *Orissa,* advancement of loan to borrowing members, deposits of the member and total loan outstanding of the Cooperative Societies have to be decreased.

Dharmarujan (2001) undertook a case-study of *'Kerala Dinesh Beedi Workers Central Cooperative Society'* that was organized and registered in February 1969. At the time of unit's inception, the total number of members stood at 3,000. But, gradually the Society increased the membership to 39,000 and by the year 1998, it reached to 42,185. The structure of the Society is two tiers in nature. At the top 'Central Society' is functioning and at the bottom level, there are 22 'Primary Societies', operating with 42,000 beedi workers, 50 percent of them are females. The 'Central Society' purchases beedies made by the 'Primary Societies' every week on an agreed price, after adjusting the advances the 'Central Society' purchases the beedies and besides the advances, they are not allowed to make any outside borrowings. The future vision of this Cooperative enterprise will have to be based on the efficient management in strategic way of functioning with some parameters relating to management excellence, business diversification, improvement of operational efficiency, cost reduction and cost control, productivity development and strengthening of financial resource base.

Duggal (2001) made an attempt to study *'Cooperative Marketing'* in *Uttar Pradesh.* In *Uttar Pradesh,* Cooperatives play a vital role in distribution of agriculture inputs like fertilizer, pesticides, and seeds agriculture implements. During 1997-98, Cooperatives' network of *Uttar Pradesh* distributed 10.30 lakh tones of fertilizer, in nutrient from which is around 23 percent of total fertilizer distribution by the Cooperatives in the country i.e. around 45 lakh tones in nutrient form. In *Uttar Pradesh,* the marketing of fruits and vegetables is done in haphazard manner and is mostly controlled by the private party. There are three Apex Federations in the Cooperative Sector; these are: 'Apple and Fruit Federation', *Haldwan;* 'Potato Federation', *Ferukhabad;* and 'Uttar Pradesh Horticulture Marketing and Processing Federation', *Lucklnow.* Besides, there are more than 200 Societies registered in the state, but very few of them are doing marketing of fruits and vegetables successfully. As a result, during 1997-98, the Cooperatives in *Uttar Pradesh* marketed fruits and vegetables worth Rs.5.8 lakh only. Therefore, farmers should be motivated to organize Cooperatives and confederation of Cooperatives is Apex Federation should ensure remunerative price to the horticulture produce of the farmers.

Ramesh (2001) enumerated 13 milk unions of *'Karnataka Milk Federation' (KMF),* throughout the state. The *KMF* also have 'Mother Dairy' at *Yelahanka, Bangalore;* 'Nandini Milk Products', *Bangalore;* 'Four Cattle Feed Plants' at *Rajankunte, Gubbi, Dharwad* and *Hassan; 'The* Bull-Breeding Farm' and 'Frozen Semen Bank' at *Hassaraghatta, Bangalore;* 'The Central Training Institute' at the KMF complex in *Bangalore* and 'Centralized Testing and Quality Control Laboratory' at the *KMF, Bangalore.* The *KMF* is playing pivotal role in both rural and urban milk marketing by propelling tough competition to the private milk traders. On the other hand, it is acting truly as an apex body for the promotion of milk unions. In spite of an impressive growth of the Dairy Cooperative Movement in the state, there is need to strengthen the Milk Cooperatives further so as to make milk production activity a successful venture by eliminating the malpractices committed by private milk traders. This will go a long way in helping the dairy farmers to realize better prices for their produce and in turn consumers will be benefited by way of getting quality milk at reasonable prices.

Objectives of the Study

The Study is carried out with following objectives in view:

1. To Study the different types of Cooperatives in India
2. To evaluate the sustainability of Cooperatives in India.

Methodology

The study is based on primary as well as on secondary data. The primary data was collected from 50 per cent (n=266) of Cooperatives in Jammu and Kashmir State of India. Such sample was selected through Disproportionate Stratified Random Sampling Technique, using the Random Number Table, constructed by Miller; in 1996. However, secondary data was collected from National Resource Centre, New Delhi. Content analysis using quantitative as well as qualitative approach was done to understand the research study. Data are scrutinised and analysed, keeping the objectives in order to determine inherent facts and meanings. Appropriate statistical techniques were employed in order to understand the problem under consideration and attempt is made to draw right inferences out of it. Such statistical analyses were done with the help of software programmes namely Minitab 2000 and S-Plus 2000. Cross tabulation made possible cross analysis of data computing, counts, percentages and Kearl Pearsons' Levels of Significance (p-value) on Chi-square values (c^2) along with its degrees of freedom (d.f). Level of significance is considered highly significant at less than or equal to 0.01 level, significant or less than at 0.05 level and insignificant at above

0.05 level. Kearl Pearsons' correlation (r) was calculated wherever necessary, to facilitate better information along with its Level of Significance (p-value) on actual numerical data.

Results and Discussion

The cooperative sector in India had more than 5.49 lakh societies of various types with membership of more than 22.95 million and working capital of about Rs. 3,827,496,000 thousand as on 31st March 2003. The membership in cooperatives has risen from 142.1 million in 1984-85 to 229.4 million in 2002-2003 (Figure 1). The movement has covered 100 per cent villages and 75 per cent rural households (Table 1). Modern cooperative movement has made

Table 1
Indian Cooperative Movement: 2002-03

(Value Rs. in Millions)

Sl. No.	*Particulars*	*Value*
1	Number of Cooperatives	549,119
A	Primary Agricultural and Credit Cooperatives	145,928
B	Primary Non-Credit Cooperatives	399,934
2	Membership of Cooperatives (Millions)	229.510
A	Membership of Primary Agricultural and Credit Cooperatives (Millions)	150.553
B	Membership Primary Non-Credit Cooperatives (Millions)	64.827
3	Share Capital (Rs.)	223,944.0
A	Share Capital of Primary Credit Cooperatives	102,791.8
B	Share Capital of Primary Non-Credit Cooperatives	56,655.5
C	Government Share Capital in Primary Agricultural Cooperatives (in per cent)	5.76
4	Working Capital: Credit and Non-Credit (Rs.)	3,827,496.4
5	Reserves (Rs.)	300,504.0
6	Deposits (Rs.)	1975,633.1
7	Coverage of Rural Households (per cent)	71
8	Villages Covered by Cooperatives (per cent)	100
9	Number of National Level Cooperative Federations	19
10	Number of State Level Cooperative Federations	367
11	Number of District Level Federations	2,890
12.	Total Loans Advanced	319,297.3
A	Agricultural Short Term Credit Advanced (Rs.)	235,436.2
B	Agricultural Medium Term Credit Advanced (Rs.)	52,833.8
C	Investment Long Term Credit Advancement(Rs.)	31,027.3

Source: National Resource Centre.

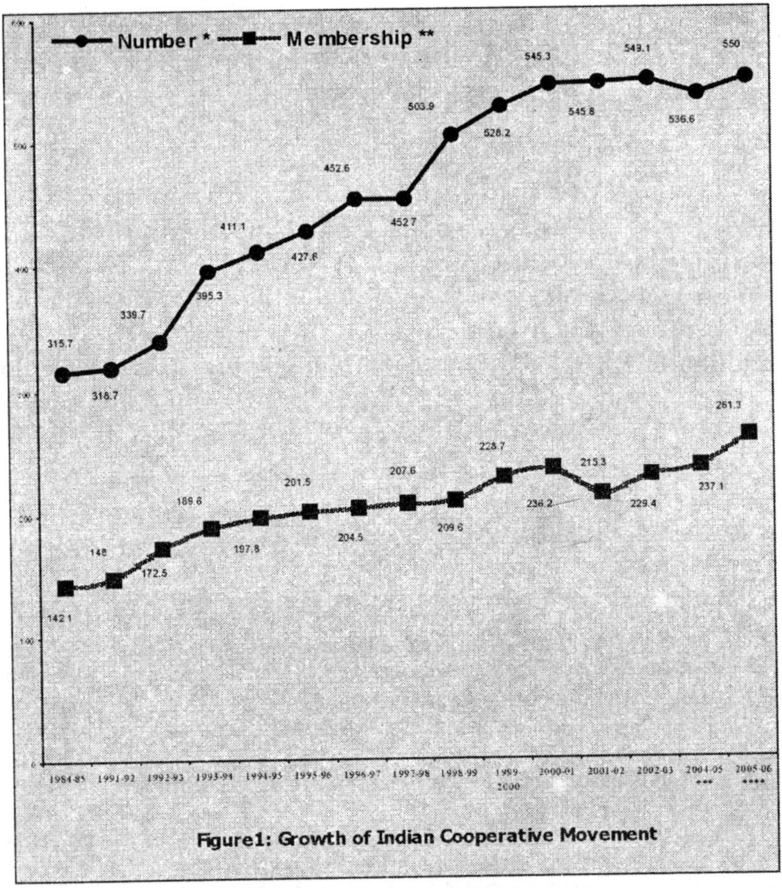

Figure1: Growth of Indian Cooperative Movement

tremendous progress in every walk of its activities and occupies a major place in the share of the national economy (Table 2). In India, there are separate cooperative institutions for short term loans on the one hand and long term loans on the other. For the former, there is a three-tier structure. At the village level, there is the Primary Agricultural Credit Society (PACS). At the intermediate level, there is the Central Cooperative Bank (CCB) at the district level. At the Apex level, there is a State Cooperative Bank (SCB) in each state. For long term credit, some states have a unitary structure with State Level Cooperative Land Development Banks, while some other states have a two-tier structure consisting of a State Cooperative Land Development Bank at the apex and Primary Cooperative Land Development Bank at the village level

Table 2

Share of Cooperatives in National Economy: 2002-03

(In per cent)

Sl. No.	*Particulars*	*Value*
1	Agricultural Credit Disbursed by Cooperatives	42.8
2	Fertiliser Disbursed	36.17
3	Fertiliser Production Nutrient	25.0
4	Sugar Production	50.5
5	Capacity Utilisation of Sugar Mills	99.8
6	Wheat Procurement	33.5
7	Animal Feed Production and Supply	50.0
8	Retail Fair Price Shops (Rural and Urban)	20.3
9	Milk Procurement to Total Production	7.44
10	Milk Procurement to Marketable Surplus	10.5
11	Ice Cream Manufacture	45.0
12	Oil Marketed (Branded)	50.0
13	Spindling in Cooperatives	9.7
14	Handlooms in Cooperatives	54.0
15	Fishermen in Cooperatives	21.0
16	Storage Facility	64.5
17	Rubber Procurement and Marketed	18.5
18	Areca-nut Processed and Marketed	15.0
19	Salt Manufactured	7.6
20	Direct Employment Generated*	1.15
21	Self Employment Generated*	14.79

* In Millions

Source: National Resource Centre.

(Table 3). In addition to the district and state level cooperative societies, central apex cooperative institutions or federation of cooperatives have been established in India. National Cooperative Union of India (NCUI), National Agricultural Cooperatives Marketing Federations, National Federation of Indian Cooperatives, National Federation of Cooperative Sugar Factories, National Cooperative Dairy Federation, National Consumers' Cooperative Federation (NCCF), Indian Farmers' Fertilisers Cooperatives (IFFCO), National Cooperative Land Development Banks are some of the examples of such apex bodies of cooperatives at the national level (Gupta, 1993).

Table 3
Indian Cooperative Movement at Primary Level (2001-2002)

(Rs. In Lakhs)

Name of Cooperative	*No. of Societies*	*Total Membership*	*Working Capital*	*Total Employment*
Credit Cooperatives				
Primary Agricultural Cooperative Societies	95670	102816003	4937290.54	208593
Primary Cooperative Agriculture Development Bank	726	7569246	1278880.41	16148
Primary Urban Cooperative Banks	2053	17791358	9268815.00	77594
Employees Credit Societies	47479	22377134	1400651.29	NA
Credit Total	145928	150553741	16885637.24	302335
Non- Credit Cooperatives				
Marketing Cooperatives	10581	5269389	138948.06	41616
Consumer Cooperatives	26765	6870338	33576.25	41184
Students Cooperatives	7880	14697082	4318.12	NA
Agro- Processing Cooperatives	1941	1406246	106381.63	9429
Dairy Cooperatives	103938	11565255	185549.86	112263
Women Cooperatives	11622	1024709	13997.02	NA
Housing Cooperatives	920000	6500000	607830.00	59740
Farming Cooperatives	7065	351276	4971.40	1532
Irrigation Cooperatives	8105	605930	82704.85	8161
Electricity Cooperatives	52	974638	35763.49	5209
Industrial Cooperatives (Other than Weavers)	45017	2439291	44256.12	17993
Weavers Cooperatives	20764	1927964	80116.39	81627
Fisheries Cooperatives	13884	2166422	16756.91	6083
Poultry Cooperatives	4879	472233	12822.76	NA
Labour Cooperatives	30234	1696285	25698.80	152239
Forest Labour Cooperatives	3278	707793	18150.28	4852
Transport Cooperatives	10634	160292	22070.03	4691
Sugar Cooperative Mills	313	5059000	873661.00	50318
Spinning Cooperative Mills	159	771192	177561.25	69331
Tree Growers Cooperatives	633	49618	61.35	NA
Hospital Cooperatives	190	112878	3740.83	1308
Non-Credit Total	399934	64827831	2488936.40	667576
Credit Total	145928	150553741	16885637.24	302335
Grand Total	545862	215381572	19374573.64	96911

Source: National Resource Centre, 2004.

Primary Agricultural Credit Societies (PACS)

These societies came into existence with the passing of Cooperative Credit Societies Act in 1904. They perform a number of functions at the village level like meeting short term and medium term credit needs of farmers, supplying production requirements like seeds, kerosene, etc. The also endeavour to inculcate the habit of thrift and saving among the villagers. A primary Agricultural Credit Societies (PACS) is the basic unit that provides direct assistance to the borrowers. It forms a link between final borrowers on the one hand and the higher financing agencies like State Cooperative Bank and RBI on the other. Up to June 1985, there were 92,000 PACS covering about 90 per cent of villages with the membership of 69 million. It covered about half the total estimated population of about 140 million rural households (IGNOU, 1997). In 1990-91, PACS covered 99.8 per cent villages of India, comprising the population of 6359 million. The total number of PACS during the period reached to 88167 thousand, out of which 51.8 per cent were found viable. Such cooperatives comprised 84.77 million members. The share capital accounted Rs. 12966.3 million, with the working capital of Rs. 124653.1 million (Suresh and Joseph, 1990). However, the number of PACS decreased from 15.38 thousands in 1973-74 to 9.56 thousands in 2001-02. The year 2003 marked 102.816 million members in PACS, covering 100 per cent villages, with 37.4 per cent Scheduled caste members, 9.85 per cent Scheduled tribe members and 2.52 per cent women members (Kapoor, 1992).

Numerous committees and reports have reviewed the working o PACS and have generally found that PACS to be the weakest link. They suffer several weaknesses in organisational efficiency. There are also regional disparities and gender disparities in PACS. Areas in north-east India are not adequately covered by PACS Moreover, the proportion of borrowing members in the total membership, then four states (Punjab, Haryana, West Bengal and Tamil Nadu) make up 50 per cent of effective coverage of PACS. In case of borrowing members or the proportion of total rural households and proportion of loan given to weaker sections, a few states like Gujarat, Punjab, Haryana and Tamil Nadu are found to have done better than others. Moreover, there are a meagre percentage of women members in PACS (Puri, 1992).

Farmers Service Societies (FSS)

Although the existing cooperative credit structure went a long distance in meeting the credit requirements in rural areas, there were still some sections which were not adequately helped by PACS. The National Commission on Agriculture in its Fourth Interim Report (1971), too, pointed out that the prevalent institutional structure did not meet the entire needs, particularly of the weaker sections, small and marginal farmers, agricultural labourers and artisans. Hence, on the recommendation of the Fourth Interim Report of the commission, Farmers Service Societies (FSS) were started in 1972 to provide integrated credit service to the farmers. The commission further recommended that the agricultural credit service should be structured at three levels—Farmers Service Society at the block level dealing with credit disbursement as well as supply of the inputs and services; a bigger version (in scale) of these societies at the district level and other district organisations for related activities; and the Lead Bank in the district for providing overall guidance and organisation for agricultural credit services. The FSS is a registered society with byelaws which give it an autonomous status. Efficient management and independence from official intervention is also sought. The FSS's perform a number of functions such as supply of short, medium and long term advances for agriculture, supply of various types of inputs for subsidiary occupations like dairy, poultry, fishing, etc., arranging marketing of agricultural produce; and encouraging thrift and saving habits among the rural masses. FSSs are conceived as local institutions geared to meet the needs of the local people. FSSs were launched in areas where Small Farmers Development Agencies (SFDA) and Marginal Farmers and Agricultural Labourers Development Agencies (MFAL) were in operation. Only those who were eligible to receive assistance under SFDA and MFAL were eligible to become members of FSS. Their main finances come from share capital, loans and funds from various sources. The Lead Bank of the district assists the FSS in various ways—for instance by contributing to the share capital of FSS, lending to the FSS for developmental financing in the area initiating and assisting the functions of the FSS, providing guidelines for grant of loans etc. The FSS revealed the high rate of growth from the initial level of 30 FSS in 1973-74 in SFDA areas. The number of FSS increased to 2,517 by the end of June 1985. However, the spread across regions has not been even. The four states of Uttar Pradesh, Assam, Karnataka and Bihar accounted for 2.062 societies out of the total of 2,517 for the entire country. The total membership of the FSS in June 1985 was 5.8 million out of which 21.1 per cent was accounted for by Scheduled Castes and Scheduled Tribes (Misra, 1999).

In 190-91 the number of FSS reached 2410; out of which only 15 per cent were found viable. The membership in such FSS comprised 6,774,000, with 30 per cent borrowing by members and 30.2 per cent over dues to demand. The number of FSS in profit accounted only 7.5 per cent [113]. However, there was an increase in government share in FSS from 18.2 per cent in 190-91 to 23.7 in 1995-96. In spite of this, the membership decreased from 6774.4 in 1990-91 to 4218 in 195-96. Similarly share contribution declined from Rs. 974.9 million in 190-91 to Rs. 730.7 million in 1995-96. Nevertheless an increase in profitable FSS was found in 1997-98 by 68.5 per cent with agricultural produced marketed by Rs. 245.2 million and agricultural inputs distributed worth Rs. 742.1 million. The women membership in FSS was found only 85354 in 1995-96 and 1,46423 in 1996-97 (Nation Resource Centre, 2004).

Large Size Multipurpose Cooperative Societies (LAMPS)

These are also known as *Large Size Adivasi Multipurpose Societies*. For provision of institutional finance in tribal areas, LAMPS were set up in 1971 on the recommendations of a Study Team appointed by the Government. The main functions of LAMPS were considered to be:

- Provision of all credit—long term, medium term and short term including consumption loans under one roof in tribal areas.

- Provision of technical assistance for the intensification and modernisation of agriculture
- Arranging to market agricultural produce in tribal areas.

Membership of LAMPS is open to all residing in its areas of operation. It is designed to serve areas larger than those served by primary agricultural cooperative societies (PACS), possibly a block. But in areas where credit and other requirement are greater, their area of operation may be as a tehsil. The major sources of LAMPS are share capital entrance fees, depositions from members and non-members, loans from Central Cooperative Banks, State Cooperative Banks and Government share.

At the end of June 1985, there were 2,863 LAMPS mainly in tribal and hilly areas. Five states viz., Madhya Pradesh, Bihar, Maharashtra, Rajasthan and Orissa accounted for 78 per cent of LAMPS in the country. The total membership of LAMPS in 1985 was 4.07 million of which 2.48 million belonged to the scheduled tribes and 0.62 million to the scheduled castes (IGNOU, 1997). However, the number of LAMPS decreased in 190-91 by 2646; out of which only 1201 were found viable and only 13.7 per cent LAMPS in profit. The membership in LAMPS during the same period was recorded as 39,31,000, with 20.5 per cent borrowers and 66 per cent over dues to demand. The year 1995-96 further showed declined in LAMPS by 3615, with only 37.3 per cent viable LAMPS comprising the meagre women members by 2.2 per cent only. The paid up capital was found Rs. 1115.0 million in LAMPS during the same period, with 52.8 per cent government share. However, the year 196-97 marked a slight increase in LAMPS up to 3621 with a double increase in its viability by 60.9 per cent. The women membership also showed a slight increase up to 4.6 per cent. The paid up capital of Rs. 1191.5 million marked a decrease in government share by 51.6 per cent. Fifty per cent of LAMP was found in profit during the same period (Nation Resource Centre, 2004).

Marketing Cooperatives

The beginning of Cooperative Marketing Societies was made in Hubli in Bombay province in the year 1915 when a society was formed to market cotton. After this, the second marketing society was started at Gadag (Bombay) in the year 1917. The development of cooperative marketing commenced in India after 1935 with the constitution of the Directorate of Marketing and Inspection at the Centre and States on the recommendation of the Royal Commission on Agriculture. But the progress was not encouraging. Even after independence i.e. during the second five year plan, serious efforts were made to organise and strengthen the Cooperative Marketing Societies. A Committee on Cooperative Marketing under the chairmanship of Prof. M. L. Dautwala was appointed to study the problems in this area. In 1958, National Agricultural Cooperative Marketing Federation (NAFED) was set up to promote inter-state and external trade.

Cooperative Marketing Structure has been developed n the form of a NAFED as the national apex marketing society, state cooperative marketing federations at the state level, central marketing society as the intermediary and taluka block level marketing cooperative at the primary level. The structure of marketing cooperatives is different in different states. In Kerala and Meghalaya, the structure is two tier, primary level, district level and state level. Thus, there is no uniform organisational structure of marketing cooperatives in the country. Up to March 1991, 2933 General Purpose Primary Marketing and 4398 Special Commodity Marketing Societies were working in India with 5.04 million members. The paid up capital of these societies was Rs. 1245.3 million of which government participation was 58 per cent. The total working capital of these societies was Rs. 7186.6 million. The total business turnover of these societies was Rs. 38689.4 million. However, many societies were not viable and they were not able to market the agricultural produce especially food grains (Dev, 1998). However, the number of Marketing Cooperatives in India rose from 6.872 thousand in 1984-85 to 10.581 thousand in 2001-02 with 5.269 million members. The government share in

Marketing Cooperatives was observed by 46.75 per cent in 2001-02, with 4356 profitable Marketing Cooperatives (Nation Resource Centre, 2004).

Consumer Cooperatives

The consumer Cooperative Movement has taken root in India in 1904 with the establishment of Triplicane Urban Cooperative Societies (TUCS) in Madras. The government showed considerable interest in the growth o consumer cooperative movement during the First World War and Second World War for distributing the scare commodities like sugar, cloth, food grains, etc. After independence, the consumer cooperatives had growth but after the establishment of National Consumer Development Cooperative (NCDC) in 1959 and after the Chinese attack in 1962, consumer cooperative movement got a boost. The Government of India sponsored a scheme for establishing consumers' Cooperative Societies in all cities having a population of more than 50,000.

A country wide net work of consumer cooperative movement has been built up under a four tier structure. The primary consumer stores at the primary level, wholesale/ central consumer cooperatives at the district level, state consumer federation at the state level and national consumer federation at the national level. The federal pattern was adopted after 1962. Some states adopted unitary pattern. Where in the wholesale/central stores have direct links with individual members and other states have adopted primary societies and individuals. After 1966-67, a determined shift towards unitary pattern of organisation in the interest of business efficiency and viability was made. The states which had a federal set up had also changed into unitary pattern and he wholesale/central consumer societies had set up departmental stores besides opening a number of large sized retail outlets known as mini-departmental stores. In the year 1990-91, there were 24190 primary stores. Of them 16 per cent were defunct. The total number of members of these stores was 7.57 million. The paid up share capital of primary stores was Rs. 7662.5 million of which 13.6 per cent was contributed by government. The total working capital of these stores was Rs. 22392 million. The total business turnover of these stores was Rs. 10568.53 million. Of these sales, 62.7 per cent was in the form of controlled goods and 37.2 per cent was non-controlled commodities. Of the total 24190 stores were in profit. During the same period, 627 District Wholesale/Central Stores were working. The total number of members was 23.38 million. The paid up share capital of these stores was Rs. 449.9 million. Of which the government share capital account for 77.4 per cent. The total working capital of the stores was Rs. 1526 million. The total sale of these stores was Rs. 11577.3 million. Of the total sales, 55.3 per cent was controlled goods and 44.7 per cent was non-controlled goods. Of the total number of wholesale stores 46.7 per cent were in profit. There were also 30 state cooperative consumer federations during the same period working with 1.89 million members. The paid up share capital of these federations was Rs. 498.25 million, of which the government contributed 77.3 per cent. National Cooperative Consumer federation which was organised in 1965 recorded 108 members in 1991-92, with total paid up capital of Rs. 109.4 million (Dev, 1998). In 1993-94, the primary consumer cooperatives comprised the working capital of Rs. 2715.0 million with 52 per cent government share. This increased up to Rs. 3357.6 million in 2001-02, with 60.7 per cent government share. The number o consumer cooperatives reached 26,426 in the same year with 10,305 branches, Rs. 1098.1 million share capitals and a decrease in government share by 29.81 per cent (Nation Resource Centre, 2004).

Industrial Cooperatives

The term Industrial Cooperatives is used, in India, to cover some specific type of societies. These are societies for traditional artisans and craftsman as well as for industrial workers and mechanisms within which there are numbers of several types. Most of the industrial cooperatives formed by traditional artisans like weavers, tanners, carpenters, blacksmiths, potters, oilmen, etc are those in which artisans carry o production in their homes with the help of the members of their family.

Industrial Cooperative Societies are also formed by artisans working on a piece-wage basis under a master craftsman or under a private entrepreneur. The agricultural processing cooperatives promoted by farmers and others, Cooperative Sugar Factories, Spinning Mills, graining mills, etc are not considered as Industrial Cooperatives in India; but in other countries they are also considered as Industrial Cooperatives. Further, Industrial Cooperatives have been formed by working (modern labourers), but quite often in these types of cooperatives, all employees are not members. Industrial Cooperatives are generally divided into two categories i.e. Weavers Cooperatives and Non-Weavers Cooperatives. Among Weavers cooperatives, in 1991-92 National All India Handloom Fabrics Cooperative Society recorded 19325 members, State Handloom Cooperative Federations accounted 11138 member and 24 in number, Regional/District Weavers Cooperative Societies with 4153 members and 86 in number, and Primary Handloom Weavers Cooperative Societies with 1.70 million members. In case of Non-Weavers Industrial Cooperatives, in 1992-93, its primary cooperatives accounted for 2.74 million members.

The Industrial Cooperatives also receive financial assistance in the form of working capital from NABARD and investment finance from other financial agencies like State Industrial Development Banks, etc. NCDC helps only coir cooperatives for constructions of work sheds, setting of processing units and purchasing of tools and equipments. The Government through its industries department and through promotional agency like District Industrial Centre helps the Industrial Cooperatives to raise their resources like share capital participation, share capital loan, managerial subsidy, furniture grant, training fund, etc. The Industrial Cooperatives are also assisted by the government in marketing their produce i.e. government agencies are required to purchase even if the rate is higher up to 15 per cent than the private merchants. Thus, the Industrial Cooperatives are being assisted in many ways by the government (Dev, 1998).

The number of Weavers Cooperatives has increased from 10396 in 1984-85 to 20764 in 2001-02. Similarly, the number of Non-Weavers Cooperatives has shown an increase from 27531 to 45017 between 1984-2002. The membership comprises 1.9279 million in Weavers Cooperatives and 2.439291 million in Non-Weavers Cooperatives, with a government share of 19.2 per cent and 33.8 per cent respectively (Nation Resource Centre, 2004).

Dairy Cooperatives

Dairy cooperatives are giving a fresh lease of life to Indian farmers in drought-prone areas. Milk production and un-exploitative marketing through the cooperatives is providing an assured source of income to farmers helping them sustain themselves against recurring drought. The migrating population is settling down. About Rs 2,000 crores is being paid to the farmers in their villages daily—morning and evening—which constitutes a large portion of their income. Operation Flood has, therefore, emerged in India as the largest rural employment scheme. It has been able to modernize the dairy sector to a level from where it can take off to meet not only the country's demand for milk and milk products in the next century, but can also exploit global market opportunities and thereby capitalizing on the inherent production advantages that India has provided that the right policy options are exercised to overcome some already visible signs of market disorder in the post-liberalization period.

During the pre-independence era, public and private agencies dominated the dairy industry, although government policy did not favour any one organizational form. Early efforts to organize dairying along cooperative lines were made immediately after the enactment of the Cooperative Societies Act, 1912. The Kaira District Cooperative Milk Producers' Union (AMUL) was established in 1946 (Indian Dairy Industry, 2007) at Anand in 1946 under the direction and guidance of Sardar Vallabhbhai Patel. The dairy farmers of the then Kheda District of Gujarat organized themselves to form a dairy cooperative in order to directly undertake sale and processing of milk collected from member dairy farmers of the district.

The government of India took some steps to improve the quality of milch animals and their productivity through the Key Village Scheme, launched as part of the First Five-Year Plan (1951-56) and the Intensive Cattle Development Plan, launched under the Third Five-Year plan (1961-66). However, in the absence of a stable and remunerative market for milk, production remained more or less stagnant. During the two decades between 1951 and 1970, milk production grew by barely one per cent annually, while per capita milk availability declined by an equivalent amount.

During the 1960s, various state governments tried different strategies to develop dairying, including establishing dairies run by their own departments, setting up cattle colonies in urban areas, and organizing milk schemes. Almost invariably, dairy processing plants were built in cities rather than in the milk sheds where milk was produced. This urban orientation to milk production led to the establishment of cattle colonies in Mumbai, Calcutta, and Madras. The objective was to meet the demand for milk and milk products in big cities through improvements in milk collection, processing, and distribution.

The Operation Flood (OF) programme implemented by the National Dairy Development Board (NDDB) from 1970 to 1996 played the key role in bringing about the transformation in dairy development in the country. The OF programme established milk producers' cooperatives in villages and made modern technology available to them. The broad objectives were to increase milk production ("a flood of milk"), augment rural incomes, and transfer to milk producers the profits of milk marketing that were hitherto enjoyed by well-to-do middlemen.

The importance of Operation Flood lies in its focus on small rural producers. Lucrative alternate employment opportunities are often not available in Indian villages, making dairying an attractive option for many villagers. Low capital intensity, a short operating cycle, and steady returns make dairying a preferred activity among marginal (less than one hectare of land holding) and small farmers (those having 1-2 hectares of land holding), who make up about 57 per cent of rural households in India. Dairying is feasible even for the landless, which depend for fodder on common grazing and forest lands. Nearly 70 million Indian households hold a total of 98 million cows and buffaloes. A majority of milk producers have one or two milch animals, and these small producers account for some 70 per cent of the milk production. On average, 22.5 per cent of the income of rural households is contributed by milk. The Operation Flood programme is based on what are known as Anand Pattern dairy cooperatives, referring to their origin in Anand District in the state of Gujarat (AMUL, 2006).

The National Dairy Development Board was created in 1965. In the late sixties, the Board drew up a project called Operation Flood (OF) - meant to create a flood of milk in India's villages with funds mobilized from foreign donations. Producers' cooperatives, which sought to link dairy development with milk marketing, were the central plank of this project. Operation Flood which started in 1970 concluded its third phase in 1996 and has to its credit these significant results:

- The enormous urban market stimulus has led to sustained production increases, raising per capita availability of milk to nearly 200 grams per day.
- The dependence on commercial imports of milk solids are done away with.
- Modernization and expansion of the dairy industry and its infrastructure, activating a milk grid.
- Marketing expanded to supply hygienic and fair priced milk to some 300 million consumers in 550 cities and towns.

A nationwide network of multi-tier producers' cooperatives, democratic in structure and professionally managed, has come into existence. Millions of small producers participate in an economic enterprise and improve the quality of their life and environment (Indian Dairy Industry, 2007). Starting in 1970, NDDB replicated the Anand Pattern cooperatives through the OF programme all over India. Under the Anand Pattern structure, individual farmers are joined in village-level dairy cooperative societies (DCS), which are joined to form district-level unions, which in turn are joined in state-level marketing federations. In each state, the Anand Pattern features:

- Decentralized milk *production* by the small milk producers;
- Milk *procurement* by the village-level dairy cooperative societies;
- Centralized milk *processing* by the district-level unions; and
- *Marketing* of milk and milk products by the state-level federation.

The primary milk producers democratically govern this entire federal cooperative structure to ensure that the higher-tier organizations serve the purpose of the lower levels and that the gains at all levels flow back to the milk producers in significant measure. The core feature of the Anand Pattern model is farmer control of the three stages following production, that is, procurement, processing, and marketing of milk and milk products. The value added at the procurement and processing stages can be realized by the cooperatives only through control over marketing, which is therefore an essential requirement for success. In contrast, many dairy cooperatives worldwide end up as suppliers of raw material to private companies that own the brands and control marketing. By cutting out the need for middlemen in procuring and selling milk, the Anand Pattern cooperatives have helped to reduce seasonal price variations and have enabled the farmers to enjoy the fruits of their labour instead of surrendering most of the profit to corrupt and exploitative middlemen. Consumers too have benefited. In 2003, dairy cooperatives accounted for the major share of processed liquid milk marketed in India. Milk reaches consumers in 750 towns and cities through the National Milk Grid network. Over the years, brands of dairy products created by the cooperatives have become known for quality and value (AMUL, 2006).

Today in India, there are 75,000 dairy cooperative societies, spread all over the country with a membership of 10 million. In 2004-05, average daily cooperative milk marketing stood at 156.28 lakh litres; annual growth has averaged about 3.9 per cent compounded over the last five years. During the last decade, the daily milk supply to each 1,000 urban consumers has increased from 17.5 to 54.8 litres. Dairy Cooperatives now market milk in about 200 class cities including metros and some 550 smaller towns. Dairy cooperatives generate employment opportunities for around 12.3 million farm families [133]. The farmer in the village is now assured of a better future thanks to these cooperatives. Recently one of the European Embassies in Delhi requested us for information on the five biggest "companies" in the dairy business. The first three are in the cooperative sector - The Gujarat Cooperative Milk Marketing Federation (GCMMF). The Kaira District Cooperative Milk Producers' Union Limited and The Mehsana District Cooperative Milk Producers' Union. The Kaira District Cooperative is the second best in the country. It helped to create GCMMF, the apex body of all cooperatives in Gujarat (Indian Dairy Industry, 2007).

Now milk is processed and marketed by 170 district-level cooperative unions, which are federated to 22 state-level marketing federations. Over the years, cooperative brands have earned the reputation of being known for quality and value. Some of the brands that have earned consumer confidence are Amul (in Gujarat), Vijaya (Andhra Pradesh), Verka (Punjab), Saras (Rajasthan), Nandini (Karnataka), Milma (Kerala) etc. Each of these brands has become market leader in its own state or traditional area of operation and gradually expanding its presence in other states. Presently, the Gujarat Cooperative Milk Marketing Federation (of Amul brand) is the largest food company in India. The success of Amul proves that cooperatives can successfully compete with even multinational companies. Cooperative dairying also empowers people at another level. The village dairy cooperative is a clean, well-lit, and orderly place. The villages have gone through a similar transformation ever since the cooperatives began to operate.

When the people of a village see cleanliness, sanitation, hard work, and discipline in the cooperative, and when they know that the cooperative serves them well, it probably inspires them to bring more of these qualities into their own lives (AMUL, 2006). Some of the major Dairy Cooperative Federations (National Dairy Development Board, 2007) include:

- Andhra Pradesh Dairy Development Cooperative Federation Ltd (APDDCF)
- Bihar State Cooperative Milk Producers' Federation Ltd (COMPFED)
- Gujarat Cooperative Milk Marketing Federation Ltd (GCMMF)
- Haryana Dairy Development Cooperative Federation Ltd. (HDDCF)
- Himachal Pradesh State Cooperative Milk Producers' Federation Ltd (HPSCMPF)
- Karnataka Cooperative Milk Producers' Federation Ltd (KMF)
- Kerala State Cooperative Milk Marketing Federation Ltd (KCMMF)
- Madhya Pradesh State Cooperative Dairy Federation Ltd (MPCDF)
- Maharashtra Rajya Sahakari Maryadit Dugdh Mahasangh (Mahasangh)
- Orrissa State Cooperative Milk Producers' Federation Ltd (OMFED)
- Pradeshik Cooperative Dairy Federation Ltd (UP) (PCDF)
- Punjab State Cooperative Milk Producers' Federation Ltd (MILKFED)
- Rajasthan Cooperative Dairy Federation Ltd (RCDF)
- Tamil Nadu Cooperative Milk Producers' Federation Ltd (TCMPF)
- West Bengal Cooperative Milk Producers' Federation Ltd. (WBCMPF)

Fisheries Cooperatives

The beginning of cooperation among fishermen is traced back to 1930, when the Kerala Machnimar Cooperative Society was organised in Maharashtra. It is still in existence. However, in the inland sector, the real start was given after independence as a result of inclusion of fisheries development in the five year plan. Over the years, the fisheries structure continues to grow into multifunctional units at the primary level. There were 1599 societies with 1.71 lakhs member with capital of Rs. 50 lakhs in 1948. The growth of fishery cooperatives was phenomenal after independence. There were 5331 primaries, 72 district unions, a state level federation and one national federal in 1980 with 5,97,000 fishermen at primary level. The share capital of primary societies was Rs. 587.50 lakhs. However, the fishery cooperatives faced a lot of problems like lack of institutional support both in respect of infrastructure and finance adversely affected their working. Further, the fishery cooperatives were organised and controlled by middle men and traders who exploit the poor fishermen. The dominance of vested interest in the fish trade and the enormous assistance provided by the state and financial institutions, has led to a mushroom growth of fishery cooperatives during the seventies. However, most of the societies registered turned out to be on paper or became dormant after a few year of their existence. In Marine sector, the fishery cooperatives are traditionally three tier in structure in different states with the exception in Andhra Pradesh with four tier and Maharashtra with five tier. In Kerala, an entirely new structure has been created by liquidating all existing primary societies. In inland sector, broadly three tier structure is operating but in most states the apex federation or the district federations are either dormant or non-functional. The activities are mostly controlled by development of fisheries. The National Federation of Fishery Cooperatives "Fishcopped" was registered in 1980. Since its inception, it arranges supply of fisheries inputs and equipment to the members. They also procure pond/lake on lease basis for development of fish breed and sale o fish at reasonable price. It is coordinating the centrally sponsored Group Accident Insurance scheme for active fishermen which came in to force since December 1982. The "Fishcopped" has been also helping cooperatives in inter-state sales of fish and exporting them to the potential markets.

By 1990-91, there were 72 fishery societies functioning in the country at central/district level. The primary fisheries cooperatives have been organised in inland as well as marine sectors. At the end of 1990-91, there were 6612 societies functioning in the marine as well as inland sectors. The total membership of these societies were 0.75 million. The share capital in these societies was Rs. 122.8 million. The working capital was Rs. 589.4 million the total business/sale turnover of these societies was Rs. 743.6 million. The major agencies financing fishery cooperatives are NCDC and NABARD (Dev, 1998). The number of Fisheries Cooperatives increased from 13,649 in 1999-2000 to 13884 in 2000-2001. Out of the total membership of 2.166 million, 9.3 per cent 7.5 per cent are scheduled Castes and 9.85 per cent are scheduled tribes. The share capital has reached to Rs. 350.936 in these societies, with 29.26 per cent government participation (National Resource Centre, 2004).

Housing Cooperatives

The National Cooperative Housing Federation operates through 26 apex cooperative housing federations in the states. There are nearly 90,000 primary cooperative housing societies with 6.5 million individual members. Up to 31 March 2001, the apex federations have mobilised Rs. 6,407 crore from LIC, NHB, HUDCO commercial and cooperative banks etc., and disbursed loans of Rs 6,800 crore to housing cooperatives and individual members. This has led to the construction of approximately 2.13 million dwelling units (completed and under construction). Housing cooperatives have been given a target of construction of one lakh houses each year under the 2 million housing programme for the EWS/LIG, and they have been able to construct a total of 2.92 lakh units in the 1998-2001 period (Planning Commission, 2007). In 2001-2002 the number of housing cooperatives reached 92,00, out of which

22,024 are established in urban India. The number of scheduled caste and scheduled trite housing cooperatives has reached 779. The total membership of 6.5 million has been observed in housing cooperatives, with the working capital of Rs. 60,783.0 million and share capital of Rs. 3689.42 million (National Resource Centre, 2004).

Sugar Cooperatives

The very first sugar cooperative, which was established by Vithalrao Vikhe Patil, was a reaction to the plight of cane-growing peasants who were trapped by landlessness, moneylenders and the exploitative policies of private sugar mills. In the mid-1940s peasants struggled to market their sugarcane. Extracting sugar from cane was expensive and uneconomical. So the cane was made into jaggery. But as there was a surfeit of raw sugarcane and jaggery prices invariably reached rock bottom. In 1948, Vikhe Patil organised the sugarcane growers of 44 villages in Ahmednagar district in western Maharashtra. The outcome was Asia's first cooperative sugar factory, which was commissioned in 1950 (Bavadam, 2005).

The number of Cooperative Sugar Factories in India has accounted 281 in 2000-01, which increased to 313 in 2002-03., with the membership of 5.059 million, comprising 90.45 per cent growers' members and 5.7 per cent Non-growers' members. The share capital in such cooperatives has reached Rs. 29,728.2 million, with Rs. 87,366.1 million working capital (Beniwal, 1981).

Sustainability of Indian Cooperatives

Functioning of Cooperatives as per their Economic Conditions in Table 4, Figure 2.1 and Figure 2.2 reveal that among profitable Cooperatives, almost all of them (97.60 percent) are viable; whereas only 2.40 percent have the possibility of non-viability. Among Cooperatives bearing loss, 8.51 percent have the possibility of viability if revived; whereas, 91.49 percent Cooperatives which are functioning in loss, are non-viable and can be considered for wind up. These differences between economy and functioning of Cooperatives are statistically highly significant at 0.01 level.

Table 4
Functioning of Cooperatives as per their Economic Conditions

	Functioning			
	Viable		*Non-Viable*	
Economy	*N*	*%*	*N*	*%*
Profit	122	97.60	3	2.40
Loss	12	8.51	129	91.49
Total	134	50.37	132	49.62

Based on Field Survey
N=266
P-Value <0.01
Row percentages in parentheses

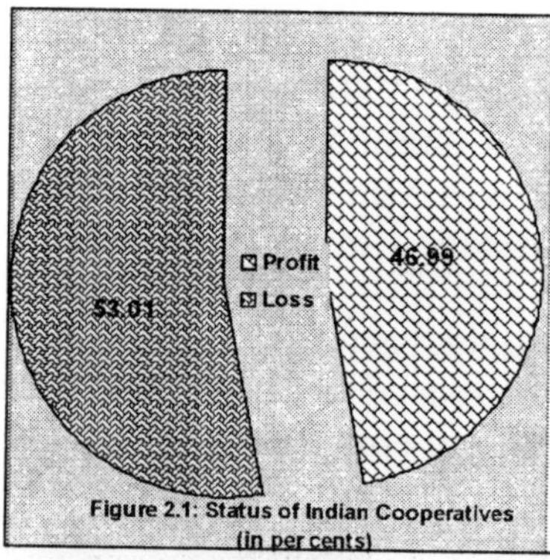

Figure 2.1: Status of Indian Cooperatives (in per cents)

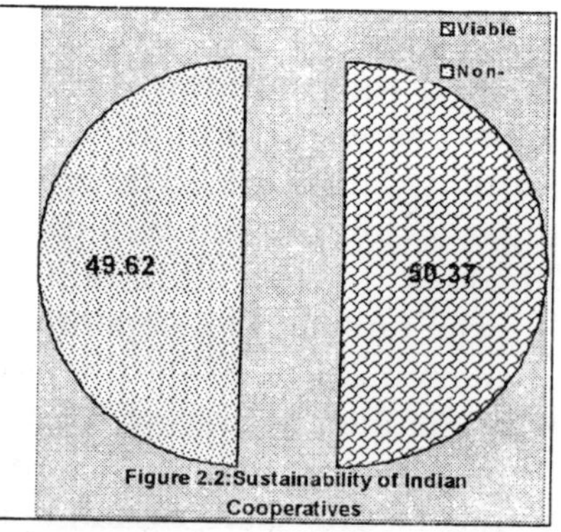

Figure 2.2: Sustainability of Indian Cooperatives

Based on Field Survey
N=266
In per cents

Correlation Analysis between Economic Status and Working Capital among Indian Cooperatives (Table 5) shows positive and highly significant relation ($p<0.01$) of business turn over with Government share capital. Individual share capital is not influenced by business turn over of the Cooperatives. Interest free loan is negatively influenced by the business turnover of the Cooperatives. But such influence is not found statistically significant ($p>0.05$).Similarly, business turn over of Cooperatives is insignificantly and positively influenced by their bank borrowings. Profit of Cooperatives has shown positive and significant influence ($p<0.05$) on individual share capital, Government share capital and managerial subsidy provided to Cooperatives; whereas, insignificant ($p>0.05$) and negative influence of profit is noted on special assistance, interest free loan and bank borrowings. Profit of Cooperatives has shown more relation with other types of financial assistances provided to them. Loss of Cooperatives is not significantly correlated with any variable of working capital. Negative influence of interest free loan is observed on losses incurred by the Cooperatives. The assets of the Cooperatives have positive and highly significant ($p<0.01$) effect on Government share capital. Bank borrowings have also influenced the assets of Cooperatives and such influence is also significant ($p<0.05$).

Table 5
Correlation Analysis between Economic Status and Working Capital in Cooperatives

	Dimensions of Economic Status			
Working Capital	*Y i* *[r]*	*Y ii* *[r]*	*Y iii* *[r]*	*Y iv* *[r]*
Individual Share Capital	-0.00	0.28**	-0.04	0.05
Government Share Capital	0.42**	0.24**	0.06	0.54**
Managerial Assistance	0.06	0.24*	-0.06	0.15
Special Assistance	-0.07	-0.19	-0.04	-0.06
Interest Free Loan	-0.20	-0.60	-0.24	-0.08
Other Assistances	-0.05	0.00	-0.03	-0.08
Bank Borrowings	0.12	-0.03	-0.02	0.13
	Business Turn-Over	Profit	Loss	Assets

Based on Field Survey
N=266
* Significant at 0.05 level
** Significant at 0.01 level

Correlation Analysis of Economic Status with External Dimensions among Indian Cooperatives (Table 6) brings forth that hired and owned infrastructures pertaining to

Cooperatives are negatively influenced by the business turnover of Cooperatives. Total infrastructure and capacity including hired infrastructure capacity, trained employees of Cooperatives and branches of Cooperatives have positive and highly significant influence (p<0.01) on business turn over of Cooperatives. Total number of infrastructures in Cooperatives are also positively and significantly (p<0.05) influenced by business turn over of Cooperatives. But owned infrastructure capacity has insignificant (p>0.05) positive influence on

Table 6
Correlation Analysis of Economic Status with External Dimensions of Cooperatives

	Dimensions of Economic Status			
Variables	*Y i* [r]	*Y ii* [r]	*Y iii* [r]	*Y iv* [r]
Branches	0.30**	0.21**	0.06	0.26**
Number of Employees	0.60	0.20	0.13	0.65
Trained Employees	0.60**	0.21**	-0.21**	0.68**
Hired Infrastructure	-0.03	-0.20*	0.00	0.11
Own Infrastructure	-0.03	-0.20*	0.00	0.11
Overall Infrastructure	0.13*	0.06	0.04	0.36**
Hired Infrastructure and Capacity	0.30**	-0.01	0.60**	0.46**
Own Infrastructure and Capacity	0.14	0.13	-0.02	0.29**
Overall Infrastructure and Capacity	0.18**	0.13	0.05	0.35**
	Business Turn Over	Profit	Loss	Assets

Based on Field Survey
N=266
* Significant at 0.05 level
** Significant at 0.01 Level

business turn over of Cooperative. Profit incurred by Cooperatives is positively and highly significantly related with branches and trained employees of Cooperatives; whereas, hired infrastructures and owned infrastructures of Cooperatives have negatively significant (p<0.05) effect on Cooperatives. Number of employees in Cooperatives, total infrastructure capacity excluding hired infrastructure capacity are also positively but insignificantly (p>0.05) influenced by

Cooperatives. Trained employees and hired infrastructure capacity in Cooperatives have highly significant correlation with loss of Cooperatives. No relation of hired and owned number of infrastructures is observed with loss of the Cooperatives. 'Owned Infrastructure and Capacity' is the only variable having negatively insignificant and meagre effect on loss. Number of employees in Cooperatives are insignificantly ($p>0.05$) and positively influenced by loss of Cooperatives. Assets of the Cooperatives have positive and highly significant relation ($p<0.01$) with branches, trained employees, total number of infrastructures and their capacity including hired and owned infrastructure capacity in the Cooperatives. Number of employees and hired and owned number of infrastructures are also found influenced by assets of the Cooperatives, but such influence is not found significant ($p>0.05$).

The Correlation Analysis of Economic Status within Internal Dimensions among Indian Cooperatives (Table 7) reveals that assets of the Cooperatives have highly significant ($p<0.01$) and positive influence on profit, loss and business turn over of Cooperatives. Business turn over of Cooperatives is also positively effected by profit and loss of Cooperatives. But such effect is not seen statistically significant, where p-value is greater than 0.05.

Table 7
Correlation Analysis of Economic Status within Internal Dimensions of Cooperatives

	Economic Status		
Variables	*Y i* [*r*]	*Y ii* [*r*]	*Y iii* [*r*]
Assets	0.24**	0.33**	0.64**
Business Turn Over	0.14	0.15	-
	Profit	Loss	Business Turn Over

Based on Field Survey
N=266
** Significant at 0.01 level

Summary and Conclusion

Cooperatives provide sufficient infrastructure to carry out the programme of economic development. The aim of any developmental programme is to achieve rapid growth, reduction of disparity in income and wealth, removal of poverty and achievement of egalitarian society based on social justice. The Cooperative Organization is an effective means in realizing all these objectives. All most all types of economic activities can be organized through the Cooperatives. Cooperative's many fold activities and self-employment schemes could go a long way to help unemployed youth to run their own ventures instead of running after the white collar jobs. Housing shortage is increasing every year. But Cooperative Sector aims to provide houses to their members or help them construct their housing units by providing financial assistance or construct houses for their members. The Cooperative Sector of the sugar industry has also played a significant role in the overall development of rural areas. Sugar Cooperatives have made much impressive progress and it now occupies the top position both in respect of number and capacity of sugar units. The problem of equitable distribution of water can also well be tackled by the Cooperative Societies of the irrigation users. It is in this area that Cooperative Movement can involve itself intensively by taking over the administration of water-supply below the outlet level. Cooperative Stores and Outlets are also established in the rural as well as urban areas with special emphasis on the sale of essential commodities of life, whose demand is highly inelastic, despite rise in prices. The Cooperative Institutions play important role in holding the price line by supplying essential goods at the doorsteps. At the same time, the Consumer Stores in Cooperative have to deal with the same form of work as in private sector.

The main reason for the non-resilience of the Cooperative Sector is interference and over-regulation of the movement by authorities, especially at the state level. State governments are interfering in the internal managements of Cooperative Institutions and in many states; government has appointed administrators in key institutions. Cooperatives being democratic institutions, efforts should be made to nurture and strengthen their democratic contents. Cooperative Education only can prepare the members to run their Cooperatives as service institutions on democratic lines [25]. Cooperative Organizations cover all most all activities of our economic life and they, therefore, need leadership for all tires of management in different areas of their operations. Development of leadership should be stresses, ideally between values, ethos, ideas, socio-economic objectives and competitive strengths of the Cooperatives. A regular and expanded programme of seminars and conferences planned and executed by the State and District Cooperative Unions with imagination can go a long way in enabling the leaders in learning from each other, in giving them orientation regarding changes in Cooperative Policies and Programmes and in discussing the common problems and devising strategies for solving them.

References

AMUL (2006), A Note on the Achievements of the Dairy Cooperatives, Challenges being Faced by them and Policy/Legislative Changes required to ensure Democratic, Autonomous and Professional Functioning of the Dairy Cooperatives, Available at: http://www.amul.com.

Bavadam, L. (2005), Cooperatives: A Movement in Decline, Frontline, Volume 22-Issue 08, Mar. 12-25, India's National Magazine, Mumbai, from the Publishers of THE HINDU

Behara, M., and Dash, T.R. 2001. An Economic Analysis of the Growth and Performance of Cooperatives in Orrisa, The Maharashtra Cooperative Quarterly, LXXXV (1), July-Sept., Pune, Maharashtra Rajya Sahakari Sangh.

Beniwal, K. (1981), Women in the Indian Cooperative Movement, Cooperative News Digest, XXXII (8), Aug., Bombay, Reserve Bank of India.

(2006), Department of Agriculture and Cooperation. Cooperation, New Delhi, NCUI.

Dev, J. S. (1998), Emerging Challenges to Cooperative Movement in Jammu and Kashmir State and Future Strategy, Co-operator's

Bulletin, XXXXI (4&5), April & May, Jammu, Jammu and Kashmir Cooperative Union Limited.

Dharmarujan, S. (2001), Business Diversification of Kerala Dinesh Beedi: A Journey towards Strategic Management, The Maharashtra Cooperative Quarterly, LXXXIV (4), April-June, Pune, Maharashtra Rajya Sahakari Sangh.

Duggal, K. (2001), Cooperative Marketing in Uttar Pradesh, The Maharashtra Cooperative Quarterly, LXXXIV (4), April-June, Pune, Maharashtra Rajya Sahakari Sangh.

Gupta, C.B. (1993), Business Organisation and Management, 2nd Edition, New Delhi, Sultan Chand and Sons.

IGNOU (1997), Development of Rural Women: Rural Social Development, RD.D.4, I, New Delhi, Indira Gandhi National Open University.

Indian Dairy Industry (2007), Cooperatives: Cause and Effect, Indian Dairy .com/Facts and Figures/Operation Flood/Cooperatives. Available at: http://indiadairy.com.

International Cooperative Alliance (1995), Dimension of the International Co-op Movement, Fourth World Conference on Women: Action for Equality, Development and Peace, Beijing, China, 4 - 15 September.

Kalamkar, S.S., Alshi, M.R., Shende, N.V., and Atkare, V.G. (2001), A Study of Credit Cooperative Movement in Vidarbha, The Maharashtra Cooperative Quarterly, LXXXIV (3), Jan-March, Pune, Maharashtra Rajya Sahakari Sangh.

Kapoor, D.R. (1992), Prospective Planning for the Development of Agricultural Cooperative in India, Co-operator's, Bulletin, XXXV (3), March, Jammu, Jammu and Kashmir Cooperative Union Limited.

Kulkarni, H.S., Patil, H.K., and Bhosale, S.S. (2001), Growth of Lead Bank Credit in Ratnagiri District of Maharashtra State, The Maharashtra Cooperative Quarterly, LXXXV (1), July-Sept., Pune, Maharashtra Rajya Sahakari Sangh.

Miller, J. (1996), Statistics for Advanced Level, 2nd Edition, N. York, Cambridge University Press.

Misra, R.V. (1999), National Policy on Cooperatives, Co-operator's Bulletin, XXXXII (4), July-Aug., Jammu, Jammu and Kashmir Cooperative Union Limited.

National Cooperative Agriculture and Rural Development Bank's Federation (1997), *Statistical Bulletin,* Mumbai, NAFCARD.

NCUI (2005), Cooperatives in India, available at: http:/// www.ncui.nic.in

National Dairy Development Board (2007), Facts at Glance: Dairy Cooperatives in India, Available at: http://www.indiadairy.com.

National Resource Centre (1998), *Indian Cooperative Movement: A Profile,* New Delhi, National Cooperative Union of India.

National Resource Centre (1999), *Indian Cooperative Movement: A Profile,* New Delhi, National Cooperative Union of India.

National Resource Centre (2001), *Indian Cooperative Movement: A Profile,* New Delhi, National Cooperative Union of India.

Nation Resource Centre (2004), Indian Cooperative Movement—A Profile, Centenary Celebrations, New Delhi, National Cooperative Union of India.

Planning Commission (2007), Tenth Five Year Plan, Urban Development, New Delhi.

Prakash, D. (2006), Cooperatives and Agricultural Extension Services, NCDC Bulitin, Dec., XXXX (5), New Delhi, National Cooperative Development Corporation.

Puri, S.S. (1992), Cooperative Sector in India: Directions of Changes, Co-operator's Bulletin, XXXV (11), Nov., Jammu, Jammu and Kashmir Cooperative Union Limited.

Ramesh, R.S. (2001), Growth of Dairy Movement in Karnataka: A Case Study of Karnataka Milk Federation, The Maharashtra Cooperative Quarterly, LXXXIV (4), April-June, Pune, Maharashtra Rajya Sahakari Sangh.

Rao, Y.V. 2000. Incoserva: A Success Story of Cooperative Tea Industry in Tamil Nadu, The Maharshtra Cooperative Quarterly, LXXXIII (4), April-June, Pune, Maharashtra Rajya Sahakari Sangh.

Roy, T.K. (1998), Kushmandi Cooperative Marketing Society Proves it's Worth, NAFED Market Review, XXVIII (8-10), Aug-Oct., New Delhi, National Agricultural Cooperative Marketing Federation.

Sharma, P.S. (2000), Cooperatives for Empowerment of the People, The Cooperator, XXXVIII (3), Sept., New Delhi, National Cooperative Union of India.

Suresh, K.A., and Joseph, M. (1990), Cooperatives and Rural Development in India, New Delhi, Ashish Publishing House.

CHAPTER–3

PHYSICO CHEMICAL AND BIOLOGICAL CHARACTERISTICS OF SOILS AMENDED WITH DAIRY WASTES IN WYRA, KHAMMAM DISTRICT OF ANDHRA PRADESH.

B. Lalitha Kumari

Introduction

Rapid industrialization and urbanization is introducing potentially harmful chemical and biological substances in soil. The soil contamination around cities causes changes in biological populations in an ecosystem. Now a days disposal of dairy effluents and sewage sludge on agricultural land is becoming a wide spread practice and these contain large amounts of toxic pollutants and they could be retained and accumulated in soils. Substantial work has been done on chemistry of toxic elements and heavy metals in soils and their toxicity to their biological systems. The toxic substances in the sewage accumulated soils are absorbed by the crops (cereals, vegetables, leafy crops) and cause damage directly and indirectly due to enzymatic hydrolysis within the plant cells. In this regard, an attempt was made to investigate the physico-chemical and biological characteristics of dairy effluents of sewage irrigated soils in Wyra, Khammam Dist.

Sampling Site

Vaishnavi Dairy situated in Wyra, on State highway from Hyderabad to Rajahmandry. It is 24 kms away from Khammam city. It was started in the year 1990 with handling capacity of 50,000 liters per day. It has twelve milk routes and 35 milk collection centers and 4361 milk producers in Wyra, Khammam District is resourceful and having good potential of milk. In order to develop the dairy activities and enhancement of milk production and procurement in district, the national cooperative development corporation has came-up for financial assistance with an out lay of Rs.12 crores. The processes of dairy industry include fat tests, acidity tests etc. with various chemicals such as H_2SO_4, HNO_3 amylalcohol, caustic soda etc, excess amount of milk sugar lactose and casein. Approximately 125 kg of polythene paper is used to prepare Sackets per day. During all these processes enormous amounts of effluents were released and without any treatment these are drained into near by soils causing an unhealthy situation around this industry causing damage to agriculture soils (paddy, cotton, chillies). In view of this , soils adjacent to this industry were analyzed.

Materials and Methods

The dairy effluents through the sewage amended soils adjacent to sewage canals at dairy industry were selected and collected for analysis. For comparison the road side soil served as control. The soils were air dried and crushed to parts in 2mm screen. The physical, chemical and biological characteristics were analyzed following methods suggested by Trivedy et al. (1987).

Results and Discussion

The physical properties of the soils from July 2006 to June 2007 are presented in Table -1. The maximum soil temperature was recorded in May and June. The pH was 7.0 in control site while it ranged between 7.0-7.5 in polluted sites. Ajmal and Khan 1984 Effects of Industrial dairy effluent on soil and crop plants. The colour of the soils in dairy effluents, flooded soils varied from light red to dark brown, while the control soils were always red.

Table 1
Physical Characteristics of Polluted and Unpolluted Soils at Dairy Industry in Khammam 2006-07

Month/Yr	*Site*	p^H	*BD*	*%PS*	*%WHC*	*CD*	*PWC*
July 06	1	7.0	1.31	50.6	22.9	0.98	7.89
	2	7.0	1.19	55.1	24.2	0.62	8.35
Aug 06	1	7.5	1.29	51.3	20.1	0.8	6.93
	2	7.0	1.23	53.6	23.4	0.46	8.07
Sept 06	1	7.5	1.41	46.8	22.9	0.84	7.89
	2	7.0	1.26	52.5	22.8	0.17	7.85
Oct 06	1	8.0	1.26	52.5	21.8	0.32	7.52
	2	7.1	1.39	47.6	20.3	0.37	7
Nov 06	1	7.0	1.17	55.9	20.4	0.26	7.04
	2	7.2	1.26	52.5	21.9	0.19	7.55
Dec 06	1	7.0	1.16	50.2	20.8	1.59	7.12
	2	7.1	1.36	46.7	19.7	0.2	6.79
Jan 07	1	7.5	1.36	48.7	20.6	2.48	7.13
	2	7.0	1.42	46.4	20.2	0.68	6.96
Feb 07	1	7.1	1.32	50.2	22.6	4.68	7.19
	2	7.1	1.41	46.7	21.8	0.72	7.59
Mar 07	1	7.4	1.21	54.3	25.4	1.79	8.76
	2	7.0	1.23	53.6	20.6	1.02	7.79
Apr 07	1	7.5	1.26	55.1	24.3	0.98	8.38
	2	7.0	1.32	50.2	20.3	0.98	8.38
May 07	1	7.1	1.19	55.1	25.6	4.28	8.8
	2	7.0	1.38	47.9	24.8	0.44	8.89
June 07	1	8.0	1.36	48.7	25.9	0.94	9.62
	2	7.0	1.28	51.7	24.9	1.28	8.93
Mean	1	7.33	1.28	51.6	22.8	2.85	7.86
	2	7.0	1.31	50.4	22.4	0.49	7.84
SD	1	0.39	1.81	2.95	2.12	4.28	1.55
	2	0	1.72	3.16	1.92	1.08	0.91
SE	1	0.12	0.54	1.13	0.64	1.29	0.47
	2	0	0.52	0.95	1.73	0.33	0.28

BD: *bulk density (gm cm*$^{-3}$*),* ***%PS:*** *percentage of pore space,* ***WHC:*** *water holding capacity CD: conductivity,* ***PWC:*** *permanent wilting coefficient*

The bulk density of the soils was maximum during winter season with a range of 1.12–1.43. Jeevan Rao et al 2003 Physical properties and elemental analysis of urban solid waste. The percentage of water holding capacity was high during the month of March (26.27%) low in July (19.9%). The percentage of pore space was maximum in March, (57.4%) minimum in February (42.8%).Electrical conductivity was measured and found to be the maximum in December (3.90mMho/cm) and minimum in July (0.15) and permanent wilting coefficient was maximum in April (8.48) and minimum was in September (6.55.) Chakravarthy and Sharma 2006 Impact of shifting cultivation on physico chemical properties and microbial population in soils.

Table 2
Chemical Characteristics of Polluted and Unpolluted Soils at Dairy Industry in Khammam District 2006-07

S.No	*Parameter*	*Concentration*	*Site*	*Range*		*Mean*
				Min.	*Max.*	
1	Total Alkalility	mg/100g	1	0.6	3.6	2.09
			2	0.2	2.2	1.04
2	Chlorides	mg/100g	1	18	60	31
			2	14	24	19.6
3	Calcium	mg/100g	1	12	60	30.3
			2	14	28	18.8
4	Magnesium	mg/100g	1	18	60	30.5
			2	16	26	18.7
5	Calcium carbonate	%	1	24	46	35.3
			2	20	44	31.5
6	Sulphates	NTU	1	12	182	
			2	12	90	
7	Phosphates	mg/100g	1	0.3	2.4	1.2
			2	0.2	1.4	0.7
8	Nitrates	mg/100g	1	0.28	0.76	0.5
			2	0.26	0.90	0,5
9	Nitrites	mg/100g	1	0.12	0.34	0.2
			2	0.10	0.34	0.2
10	Ammonia	mg/100g	1	0.24	0.56	0.4
			2	0.18	0.90	0.4
11	Organic matter	%	1	2.6	6.6	5.4
			2	2.4	7.4	4.5
12	Aluminium	mg/100g	1	0.3	1.5	0.93
			2	0.14	1.02	0.59
13	Silicates	mg/100g	1	300	800	103.6
			2	200	740	54.2
14	Potassium	ppm	1	2	18	6.25
			2	4	8	5.5
15	Iron	ppm	1	0.08	0.7	0.29
			2	0.1	0.9	0.25

Site 1= polluted; site 2= un polluted

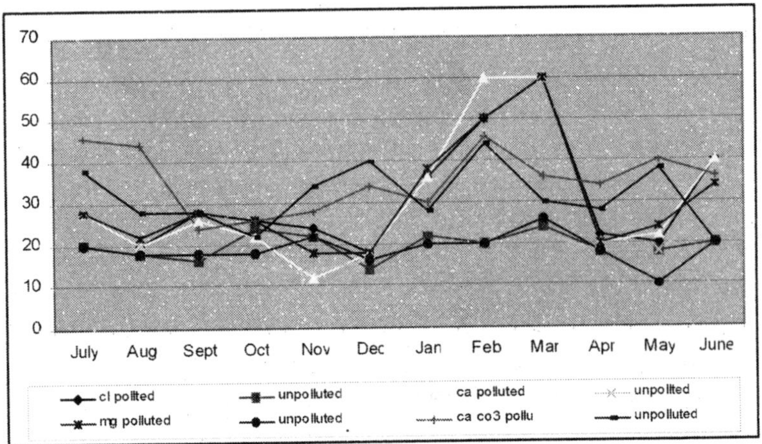

Figure 1: Chloride, Calcium, Magnecium,Calcium Carbonate Concentration in Polluted and Unpolluted Soils at Dairy Industry Khammam Dist. 2006-07

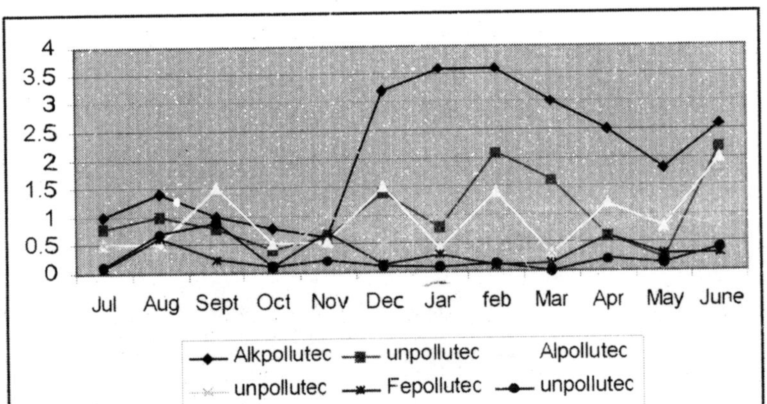

Figure 2: Total Alkalinity, Aluminium, and Iron Concentration in Polluted and Unpolluted Soils at Dairy Industry Khammam Dist. 2006-07

The chemical features of soils were analyzed and the data were given in Table.2. The total alkalinity was maximum (3.60mg/100g.) in the month of February in winter. Chlorides were maximum (60mg/100g) in the month of March in summer. Plant nutrients calcium range was 22-60mg/100g. Magnesium was high in the month of March, 60mg/100g. Calcium carbonate percentage was high in the month of

February (46 %). Potassium content was also maximum during summer, in the month of May, while the amount of iron was maximum in 0.7 ppm. The basic nutrients in the soil, sulfates were found to be maximum 182mg/100g in April and phosphates were maximum (24mg/100g) in the month of May. Chhonkar and Tarafdar 1984 stated in Accumulation phosphates in soils. Marwaha 1998, Manivikasam 2002, Sharma and Minhas 2004. Nitrite content was high during summer months (0.76mg/100g). Ammonia content was high in summer in April and marginal variation in these chemical constituents was recorded between dairy industry, polluted sewage and control soils. The organic matter was maximum during the month of November (winter), the amount of organic carbon was maximum in dairy effluents, polluted sewage than in control soils. Silicates were high in the month of August 800 mg/100g. Aluminium was high in winter (1.4 mg/100g). Hitoichishiga 1997 stated in the Decomposition of fresh and composed organic materials in soil.

Table 3
Bacterial (1X 10^6g), Fungal (1X 10^5g), Actinomycetes (1X 10^5g) Colonies in Polluted and Unpolluted Soils at Dairy Industry in Khammam 2006-2007

Month / yr	*Site 1*	*Site 2*	*Site 3*	*Site 4*	*Site 5*	*Site 6*
July - 2006	148	42	11	9	14	11
Aug - 2006	132	61	74	14	13	7
Sept - 2006	156	46	7	6	9	5
Oct - 2006	142	28	17	9	25	23
Nov - 2006	64	34	11	11	16	12
Dec - 2006	96	62	9	7	27	15
Jan - 2007	62	69	8	16	11	6
Feb - 2007	154	41	9	13	14	9
Mar - 2007	56	34	12	11	12	7
Apr - 2007	84	123	19	9	15	6
May - 2007	164	46	24	13	19	11
June - 2007	239	94	29	17	16	13
Mean	124.7	56.6	19.1	11.2	15.9	10.4
S.D.	51.9	27	18.5	3.44	11.9	5.43
S.E.	15.5	8.39	5.6	0.96	3.46	1.63

Site 1 & 2: polluted and unpolluted (bacterial colonies)
Site 3 & 4: polluted and unpolluted (fungal colonies)
Site 5 & 6: polluted and unpolluted (Actinomycetes colonies)

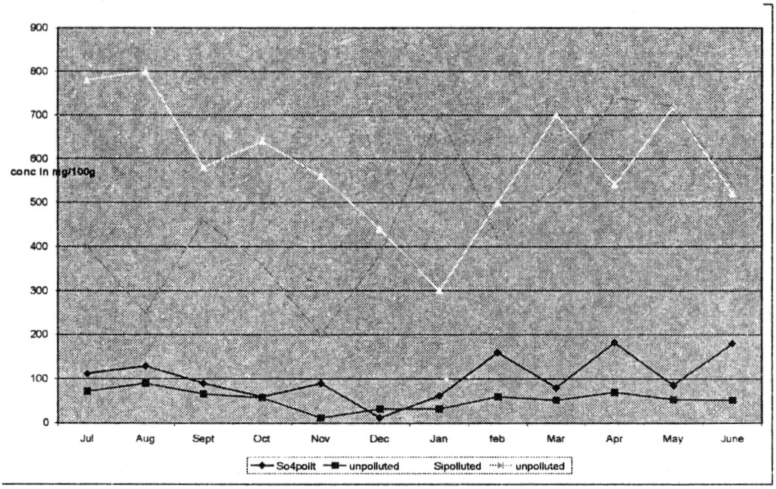

Figure 3: Sulphates and Silicate Concentrations in Soils at Diary Industry in Warangal During 2006-07

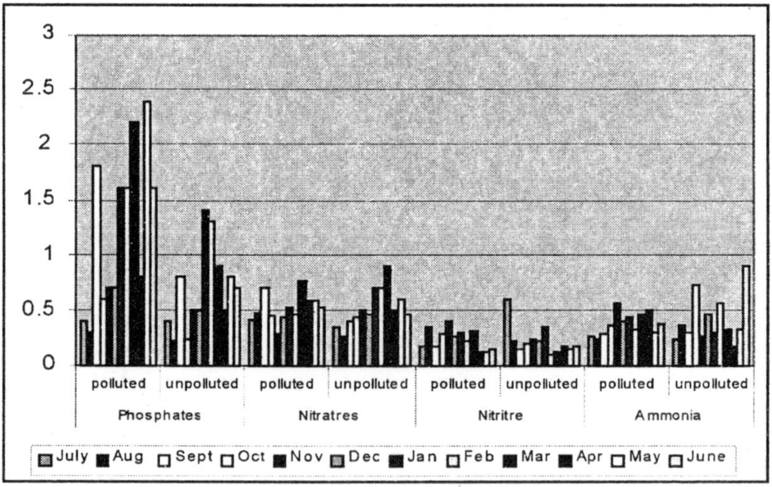

Figure 4: Phosphates, Nitrates, Nitrites, Ammonia Concentration in Polluted and Unpolluted Soils in Khammam Dist. 2006-07

The soil micro organisms which determine the arrangement of the soils were enumerated and presented in Table -3. The bacterial populations were maximum during May in dairy soils, while they were maximum in March in control

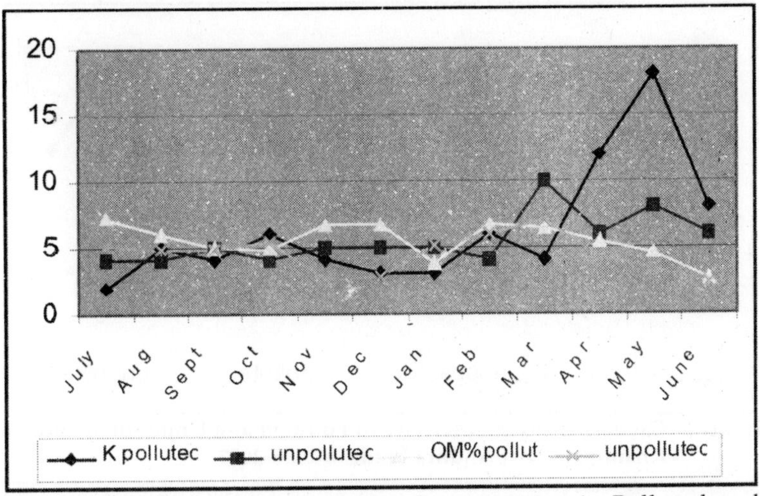

Figure 5: Potassium, Organic Matter Concentration in Polluted and Unpolluted Soils at Dairy Industry in Warangal District 2006-07

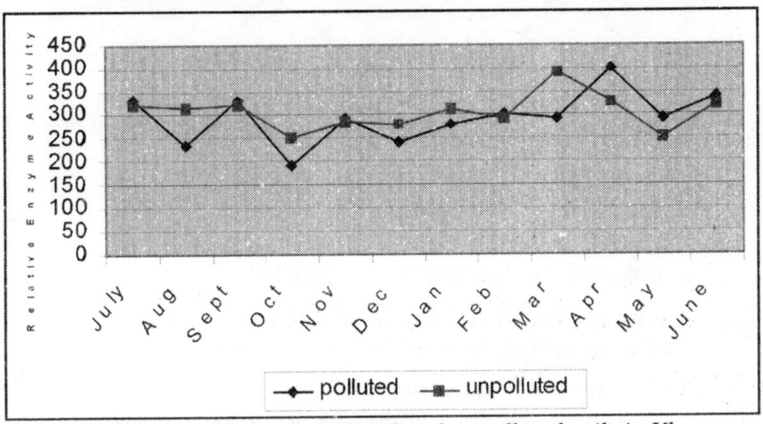

Figure 6: Cellulase Activity in Polluted and unpolluted soils in Khammam Dist,Andhra pradesh 2006-2007

soils. Chang 1984, Kulkarni 1992, Noorjahan et al. 2003, Noojahan et al. 2004. Isolation and Identification of Microbes in dairy effluents. The fungal colonies were maximum in October and actinomycetes ranges were maximum in August.

The soil enzymes which determine physiological status of the soils were estimated and presented in Figures. The cellulose (Relative Enzyme Activity REA) in polluted soils was

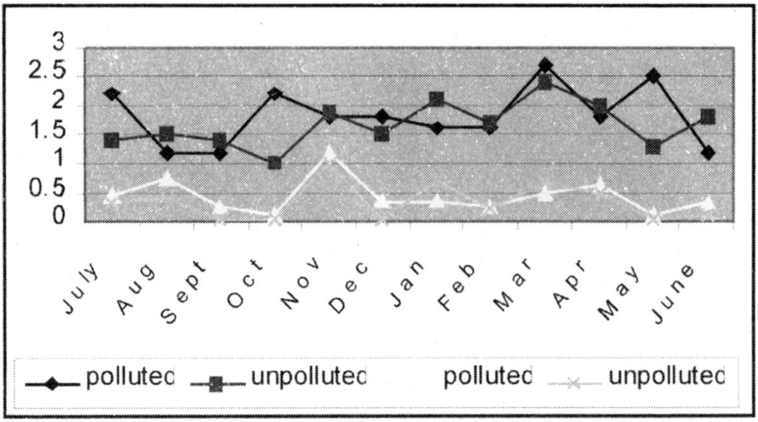

Figure 7: Catalase, Amylase Activity in Polluted and Unpolluted Soils in Khammam Dist Andhra Pradesh 2006-2007

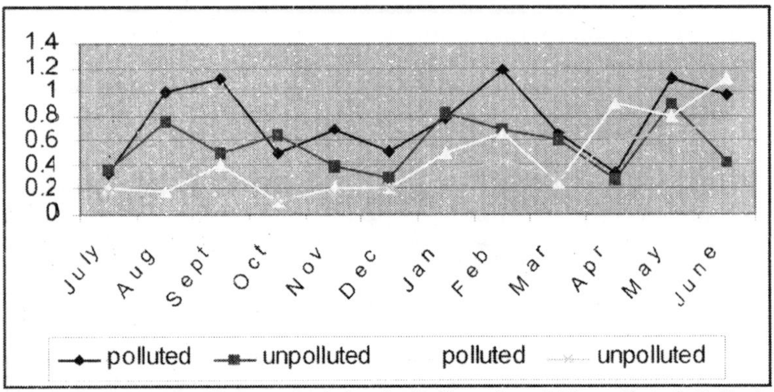

Figure 8: Protease, Urease Activity in Polluted and Unpolluted Soils in Khammam Dist, Andhra Pradesh 2006-2007.

maximum (400 REA) in April and in control soil it was 390 REA in March. Dick 2004 stated in Soil enzyme activities an indicator of soil quality. Kiss 1975 also stated in Biological significance of enzymes accumulated in soil; Chaturvedi 2004 Microbial sources of cellulase and their screening. The maximum values of catalase enzyme activity were 2.7 units in polluted, 2.4 units in control soils in the month of March. The protease activity ranged between 0.34 to 1.18 units in polluted soils, and 0.28 to 0.82 units in control soils. The urease activity ranged between 0.1 to 1.1 units in the soils amended with dairy effluents range and was 0.1 to 0.72 units in the control soils.

REFERENCES

Ajmal, M, M.A. Khan and A.A. Noman (1984), Effects of Industrial Dairy Effluent on Soil and Crop Plants. Envirion. Pollut Ser. 33: 97-106.

Chakravarthy M. Sarma JU (2006), Impact of Shifting Cultivation on Physico Chemical Properties and Microbial Population in Soils of Nagaland, Adv. Pl. Sci. 190,189-92

Chang,A C., Warn KC, J.E. Page, A.C. and Lund, L.T. (1984), Accumulation of Heavy Metals in Sewage Sludge Treated Soils J. Environ Qual. 13:87-91

Hitoichishiga (1997), The Decomposition of Fresh Composed Organic Materials in Soil. Food and Fertilizer Technology Center extension Bulletin. 44:1-14

Jeevan Rao,K.Y.S.S.Vimala Devi and A.Sreenivasa Raju (2003), Physical Properties and Elemental Analysis of Urban Solid Wastes of Hyderabad. Indian J. Environ. & Ecoplan.7:543-548.

Kul Karni, R.T. (1992), Source and Characteristics of Dairy Wastes from a Medium Sized Effluent on Micro Organism's Plant Growth and their Microbial Change. Life Sci Adv.3: 76-86.

Manivasakam, N. (2002), Physico Chemical Examination of Water, Sewage and Industrial Effluents, Pragati Prakashan. P 234.

Marwaha, S.S., Panesar, P.S. and Singh, B. (1998), Studies on the Isolation of Efficient Yeast Strain for the Dairy Waste Water. Poll. Res. 17: 56-57.

Noorjahan, C. Dawood Sharief, S. Namsheen Dawood and Jamal Mohamad, M. (2003), Isolation and Identification of Microbes in Dairy Effluent, National Conference of Envoriotech, Chennai. Proceedings. 161-163.

Noorjahan, C.M. Dawood Sharief, S. and Naurs Dawood (2004), Characterization of Dairy Effluent s. Jr. of Indus. Pollut. Cont 20: 131-136.

Sharma, D.R. and Minhas, P.S. (2004), Soil Properties and Yield of Upland Crops as Influenced by the Long Term Use of Waters having Variation Residual, Salinity, and Sodicity. J. Indian Soc Soil. 4: 52, 100.

Trivedy R.K., P.K. Goel and E.F Trisal (1987), Practical Methods in Ecology and Environmental Science. Environ Publications Karad, India.

CHAPTER–4

EDUCATION AND HEALTH STATUS OF INDIA: A STATE LEVEL ANALYSIS

D.N.Patil
M.B.Hiriyakkanavar

INTRODUCTION

Human resource development plays an importance role in economic development. Infact, effective use of physical capital itself is dependent upon human resources. This is due to this reason that if there is under investment in human resources the rate at which additional physical capital can be productively utilized will be limited, since technical, professional and administrative people are required to make effective use of material resources. Many economists in recent decades have pointed out that third world countries have remained under developed on account of under development of human resource. For instance the general masses in these countries are either illiterate or their education is very low most of them are unskilled and untrained and their general wealth is poor. Therefore, the issues of development of human resources such as education and health have acquired increased importance in recent time.

Education and health are the most important drivers of India's social and economic development. According to World Development Report 1996 entitled "From plan to Market" a-well-educated, healthy work force is essential for economic growth. But there is disparities in development of education and health in India. In this paper an attempt is made to examine the extent of disparities in development of education and health among the major states in Indian in post return period.

For this purpose of our study the 14 major states of India have been grouped into high income, middle income and low income states. States with per capita net domestic product above Rs. 23,000/- in 2001-2002 (at Current price) have been classified as high income states. States with per capita NSDP between Rs. 19000/- to Rs. 23000/- are classified as middle income states and states with per-capita NSDP below Rs. 19000/- are classified as low income states.

Objectives

- To study state wise education status in India during the post reform period.
- To compare the health status among the Indian states during the study period.
- To suggest the balanced development of education and health.

This paper is divided into three sections. Section I deals the trends of Education Status in India. Section II analysis development of health in India. The last concluding section presents a brief summary of the paper and suggestion for development of Education and Health.

SECTION - I

Trends of Education Status in India

Education plays a key role in the ability of a developing country to absorb modern technology and to develop the capacity for self-sustaining growth and development. The progress of India also largely depends on the education. The state of Kerala is most developed in India. But pace of expansion of education has been lagging behind in some other states.

Literacy Rates

Table 1 shows that the glaring level of inter-state variations in literacy. According to 1991 and 2001 census, Kerala and Bihar states respectively represent higher and lower literacy rates. Kerala had the highest literacy level measured in terms of two categories during 1991 and 2001, i.e., total literacy (89.8% & 90.9%) and female literacy (86.2% & 87.9%). The corresponding figures of Bihar 38.5% and 47.5%, 22.9% and 33.57%. The literacy level of as many as six states, i.e., Andhra Pradesh, Madhya Pradesh, Rajasthan, Uttar Pradesh, Orissa and Bihar, is below the all India average in terms of total literacy and female literacy.

Table 1
Educational Indicators

	Total Literacy Rate (%)		*Female Literacy Rate (%)*	
States	*1991*	*2001*	*1991*	*2001*
High Income				
1. Punjab	58.51	69.95	50.41	63.55
2. Maharashtra	64.87	77.27	52.32	67.51
3. Haryana	55.85	68.59	40.47	56.31
4. Gujarat	61.29	69.97	48.64	58.30
Middle Income				
5. Tamil Nadu	62.66	73.47	51.33	64.55
6. Karnataka	56.04	68.04	44.34	57.45
7. Andra Pradesh	44.09	61.11	32.72	41.17
8. Kerala	89.81	90.92	86.17	87.86
9. West Bengal	57.70	69.22	46.56	60.22
Low Income				
10. Madhya Pradehs	44.20	64.11	28.85	50.78
11. Rajasthan	38.55	61.03	20.44	44.34
12. Uttar Pradesh	41.60	57.36	25.31	42.98
13. Orissa	49.09	63.61	34.68	60.97
14. Bihar	38.48	47.53	22.89	33.57
All India	52.21	64.84	39.29	54.16

Source:
(1) CMIE, India's Social Sectors, February 1996.
(2) Manpower Profile, India, Year Book 2002.

Expenditure on Education:

Per-capita Expenditure on education is also higher in the middle and high income states as compared to low income states. The capacity to send on social services is dependent on the level of economic development of a state. However, it can be noticed that in spite of being a middle income state, Kerala manages to have an exceptionally high level of per-capita expenditure on education which is well above that of any other state in India. Bihar and Uttar Pradesh incur the lowest levels of per-capita expenditure on education then all major state in India in 1994-1995 as can be seen from table 1.2. During the 2001-2002 middle income state. Kerala again manages high level of per-capita expenditures on education, which is above that of any other states except Punjab. The lowest level of per-capita expenditure on education in Madhyapradesh, Bihar and Uttar Pradesh, which is less than all India average.

Table 2
State wise Per-Capita Expenditure on Education

(In Rupees)

	Per Capita Expenditure on Education	
States	*1994-1995*	*2001-2002*
High Income		
1. Punjab	385.4	951
2. Maharashtra	318.4	855
3. Haryana	302.8	724
4. Gujarat	349.4	785
Middle Income		
5. Tamil Nadu	341.4	781
6. Karnataka	353.5	673
7. Andra Pradesh	266.7	532
8. Kerala	457.3	902
9. West Bengal	301.7	519
Low Income		
10. Madhya Pradehs	222.4	250
11. Rajasthan	289.8	631
12. Uttar Pradesh	192.9	366
13. Orissa	245.5	410
14. Bihar	188.1	297
All India	312.8	365

Source: Various issues of RBI Bulletins, Currency and Finance (Vol. II)

Average annual growths in per capital expenditure major 14 states on education have been presented in table 1.3. Except Punjab, per annum growth in expenditure on education for other high income states has fallan in the post-reform period. For instance annual growth, in this connection for Punjab, Maharashtra, Haryana and Gujarat were recorded at 13.51 percent, 13.91 percent, 13.50 percent and 14.71 percent respectively during the pre-reforms period, while these respective figures were 13.73 percent, 13.33 percent, 13.20 percent and 12.46 percent for the post-reform period. Similarly, then all other states in the category of middle income and low income states have experienced poor results in this regard. Groups of economically poor states have also shown sluggish performance in this regard. For example, per annum growth, in this connection, for states like Bihar, M.P., Orrisa and Rajasthan were recorded at 12.66 percent, 14.32 percent, 13.51 percent and 14.05 percent respectively during pre-reform period which reduced onwards and were noted at 11.19 percent, 19.15 percent, 10.77 percent and 12.30 percent respectively during post-reform period.

Table 3
Average Annual Growth in Per-Capital Expenditure on Education

States	*Pre-Economic Reforms 1980-81 to 1990-91*	*Post–Economic Reforms*
High Income		
1. Punjab	13.51	13.73
2. Maharashtra	13.91	13.33
3. Haryana	13.50	13.20
4. Gujarat	14.71	12.46
Middle Income		
5. Tamil Nadu	14.87	12.43
6. Karnataka	14.14	7.91
7. Andra Pradesh	12.85	11.63
8. Kerala	11.09	11.77
9. West Bengal	13.22	12.01
Low Income		
10. Madhya Pradesh	14.32	9.15
11. Rajasthan	14.05	12.23
12. Uttar Pradesh	15.38	11.01
13. Orissa	13.51	10.77
14. Bihar	12.66	11.19

Source: Various issues of RBI Bulletins, Currency and Finance (Vol. I!)

SECTION-II

Health Development

Health plays important role in economic development. Improvement in the health of messes increases their productive capacity and leads to qualitative improvement in human capital. Therefore, expenditures on health are important in building and maintaining productive labour forces as well as in improving the lives of the people and quality of society. But in India wide disparities in health development.

Public Health Expenditure

Health care expenditure is a very necessary social expenditure for any country, whether it is a developing or a developed one, state's role in developing a good health infrastructure and assuring good health to everybody becomes very critical and improvement. It is important to examine inter-state differences in spending patterns.

Table 4
State wise per-capita Expenditure on Health

	Per-Capita Expenditure on Health (in Rupees)	
States	*1994-95*	*2001-02*
High Income		
1. Punjab	254.2	253.83
2. Maharashtra	113.7	189.39
3. Haryana	221.2	152.25
4. Gujarta	143.0	143.82
Middle Income		
5. Tamil Nadu	149.5	195.44
6. Karnataka	148.8	205.45
7. Andra Pradesh	102.2	179.45
8. Keral	158.6	237.45
9. West Bengal	91.7	176.26
Low Income		
10.Madhya Pradesh	97.9	84.77
11.Rajasthan	199.4	176.45
12.Uttar Pradesh	67.7	78.80
13. Orissa	112.8	122.15
14. Bihar	30.6	66.13
All India	133.5	184.92

Source: Various Issues of RBI Bulletins.

State wise per-capital expenditure on health during 1994-95 and 2001-02 are presented in Table 4. Per-capita expenditure on health during 1994-95 is found to be higher in middle and high income states as compared to low income states. Except Rajasthan the lowest levels of per- capita expenditure on health is incurred by the states of Bihar and Uttar Pradesh where the levels of expenditure are unacceptably low. In Uttar Pradesh, per-capita expenditure on health is only about half the national average while in Bihar it is less than one - fourth. During the 2001-2002 per-capita expenditure on health have been increased in higher income and middle income states except Haryana, but per-capita expenditure on health in poor states have been declined.

Health Status in India

Health status is generally measured in terms of life expectancy at birth, birth rate, death rate etc. According to WHO, health

Table 5
Health Status in India

States	*Life Expectancy at Birth 1998-2002*	*Birth Rate Per 1000 Person 2000-01*	*Death Rate Per 1000 Person 2000-01*
High Income			
1. Punjab	68.5	21.60	7.40
2. Maharashtra	66.2	21.00	7.50
3. Haryana	65.2	26.90	7.50
4. Gujarta	63.4	25.20	7.50
Middle Income			
5. Tamilnadu	65.2	19.30	7.90
6. Karnataka	64.5	22.00	7.80
7. Andra Pradesh	63.5	21.30	8.20
8. Keral	73.5	17.90	6.40
9. West Bengal	63.9	20.70	7.00
Low Income			
10. Madhya Pradesh	56.9	31.40	10.30
11. Rajasthan	61.1	31.40	8.50
12. Uttar Pradesh	59.1	32.80	10.30
13. Orissa	58.5	24.30	10.50
14. Bihar	60.8	31.90	8.80
All India	62.5	25.80	8.50

Source: WHO, 2003.

is a state of complete physical, mental and social well-being and not merely the absence of disease or in formation. The indicators of health status, the birth and death rates are more reflective of the demographic changes taking place in the country. State wise life expectancy, birth rate and death rate are presented in Table 5.

Birth Rates

The Birth Rate of a population is the number of child births per 1000 persons per year. All India average birth rate was 25.80 percent in 2000-01. The highest percentage of such rate in low income states like U.P [2.80%] followed by Bihar [31.90%] Rajasthan I.M.P [31.40%] while lowest percentage of birth rate in high and middle income states except Haryana.

Death Rates

All India average death rates were 8.50 percent in 2000-01. The highest percentage of such rate in poor states, like Orissa [10.50%] followed by U.P. [10.30%] M.P. [10.30%] and Bihar [8.80%] Remaining 10 states of there is major states had percentage lower than the national average.

Life Expectancy

Life expectancy is the average number of years remaining for a living being of a given age to live. "Life expectancy at birth is also called average life span or mean life span. India has made substantial progress in the health indicators over the past few decades. Life expectancy increased from 54 years in 1980 to 63 years in 2002. This increase in life expectancy is the result of an over all decline in mortalities; state wise life expectancy is presented in Table 5. Middle income state Kerala had high life expectancy [73.5 years], which is well above that of any other state in India. However, it can be noticed that high and middle income states had high Life expectancy than the national average [62.5 years]. The low life expectancy in poor states like M.P. [56.9], U.P. [59.1], Orissa [58.5] and Bihar [60.8], which is less than national average.

SECTION-III

Conclusion and Suggestions

Above mentioned fact and figures are sufficient to indicate the trends and issue related to the education and health sector in India. In the post-reforms period there has been an improvement in health facilities. The major Conclusion which emerge from the above Andy sis can be out lined as follows.

- Kerala and Bihar states respectively represent higher and lower literacy rates. Kerala had the highest literacy level measured in terms of two categories during 1991 and 2001.
- Per-capita Expenditure on education is also higher in the middle and high income states as compared to low income states.
- Except Punjab, per annum growth in expenditure on education for other high-income states has fallen in the post-reform period.
- During the 2001-2002 per-capita expenditure on health have been increased in higher income and middle-income states except Haryana, but per-capita expenditure on health in poor states have been declined.
- All India average birth rate was 25.80 percent in 2000-01. The highest percentage of such rate in low income states like U.P [2.80%] followed by Bihar [31.90%] Rajasthan I.M.P [31.40%] while lowest percentage of birth rate in high and middle income states except Haryana.
- All India average death rates were 8.50 percent in 2000-01. The highest percentage of such rate in poor states, like Orissa [10.50%] followed by U.P. [10.30%] M.P. [10.30%] and Bihar [8.80%] Remaining 10 states of there is major states had percentage lower than the national average.
- It can be noticed that high and middle-income states had high Life expectancy than the national average

[62.5 years]. The low life expectancy in poor states like M.P. [56.9], U.P. [59.1], Orissa [58.5] and Bihar [60.8], which are less than national average.

It's the high time, the planners and government authority is more on the path to make education and health within the reach of common man some suggestion and recommendation are as under: -

- Reduction of poverty should be the top priority.
- India needs to increase investment in education and health sector.
- Government should ensure equal opportunities of education for all girls. Girls education should be free and compulsory up to secondary level.
- Improve equity, efficiency and equality on education and health sector.
- Health and education policy should be decentralized and its changes from place to place.
- Government should implement health insurance schemes for the BPL people.

REFERENCES

Dr. A. K. Mukherjee (1998), Health Care: A Basic Input in Development, Yojana, Vol. 142, No. 8, August 1998.

P.V. Rajeev and C.K.G. Nair (1998), India The Emerging Economic Super Power, Deep & Deep Publications Pvt. Ltd., New Delhi, 1998.

Jaswinder Singh Brar (2002), Basic Education, Health Care and Economic Growth in Punjab, Man & Development, Vol. XXIV, No.1, March 2002.

Institute of Applied Manpower Research (2002), Manpower Profile India, Concept Publishing Company, New Delhi, 2002.

M.P. Todaro & S.C. Smith (2003), Economic Development, Published by Pear Education, Delhi, 2003.

Panchmukhi P.R. (2007), "Social Impact of Economic Reforms in India: A critical Appraisal". Economic and political weekly, March 2004.

Report on Currency and Finance (Vol.II), Various Issued (from 1980 to 2002).

Reserve Bank of India Bulletin: Bombay, various issues (from 1980 to 2002).

Dev S. Mahendra and Joss Mooji (2002), "Social Sector Expenditure in the 1990: An Analysis of Central and State Budget", Economic and political weekly, Vol. 37 No.9, March 2002.

CHAPTER–5

ENVIRONMENT DEGRADATION AND REMEDIES

Santosh Tikoo

Environment Degradation has come to be recognized as one of the major threats to the existence of humans and various other species of the planet.

The devastation of the natural environment and its flora and fauna domains far outweighs the achievement of man in the scientific and technological field. The threats has come from three quarters

1. Hungry and deprived people unaware of and indeed unconcerned with the implications of denuding forests, damaging soils and mounting pressure on the fragile ecosystem.
2. The rich and powerful segment of the population including industrialists which are defacing and defiling the environment.
3. The builders of roads, big dams, heavy engineering structure who have destabilized the slopes in mountains, terrains leading to a variety of unintended but harmful changes.

American colossus said, Man is gasping with both hands reaping what he had not sown, wasting what he thought would last for ever. Indira Gandhi once said that rich out of greed and the poor one out of the need have been reckless in plundering earth's assets.

These days even kids are aware of such terms as global warming, green house effect and ozone layer and in the last few decades the concern about environment has grown appreciably. So we all are aware of the degradation in our environment- be it on the surface of the earth, in the deep seas or in the skies above. How much we actually do to save and conserve our mother. We have to go much beyond mere bandying of these terms at wine and champagne dinners, global summits, cocktail circuit and get down to really changing the way we live to ensure that we do not add to the problems around.

FACTORS LEADING TO ENVIRONMENT DEGRADATION

Rapid Industrial Growth Without Consideration of Environment Effects

In the history of planet, the last two centuries have witnessed very rapid industrial growth. Various nations and states of the world have been competing with each other to achieve maximum possible levels of industrial production. Of course industrialization has helped in upgrading the economy of the country which benefited the society but it has created many environmental problems like forest destruction & denudation, climate change, soil erosion & desertification. The economic development is surfacing the problems of the ability to pay the price of pollution.

Industrial toxic pollutants and residential wastes released in fresh water lakes, rivers and streams eventually find their way to the coastal water and cause damage to marine ecosystems and coral bleaching. Synthetic organic pollutants such as pesticides, herbicides, polychlorinated biphenyls, wood preservatives, herbicide solvents and chlorofluoro carbons cause many types of diseases in human being.

A person breathes over 22,000 times a day, inhaling almost 70,000 pollutants in the process. This can damage the in nasal cilia or the microscopic hair lining in the nostrils and the wind pipe, making one prone to many respiratory problems (Sen., 1997).

Environmental pollution of sound, water & air is mainly caused by heavy industrialization. Development of agro industries specially in processing sector (Dal & rice milling, sugar production & oil seeds processing) can be undertaken in rural areas on decentralized basis & this will reduce the environment pollution.

Tremendous Increase in Population

The population of India would touch 140 crore by 2026 making us the world's most populated country. We have only 2.4% of world wide land and 16% of world's population (Khosla, 2005) A child is born every 1.2 seconds. The global population has doubled from three billions to over six billions in the last four decades (Singh. 2006). If the population will remain growing like this, then it will crowd schools, choke the transportation system, clog streets and jeopardize electricity, water and sewerage system. The growing population has caused large scale poverty, illiteracy, unemployment & hunger. Even our fundamental requirements are not being fulfilled.

This has resulted in tremendous pressure on our natural resources. For example, everyday on earth, we lose over 100 square miles of forest and about 70 square miles of productive land & at the same time we add quarter of a million people to the world population.

Natural resources are depleleted by high ratio consumption due to population increase. People have created a growing demand for household appliances, varieties of clothes & personal products. These are causing more development of technology & industries involving more utilization of natural resources such as minerals, metals & fossil fuels. Population when unchecked increases in geometric ratio where as substances increase only in arithmetical ratio.

Increase in population growth will increase diseases, economic inequity and environmental abuse. Hence there is no doubt that the explosion must end. If we fail to curb our population growth, nature will end in her own way by killing off a large portion of humanity. Population control by human beings must be moved to the top of the human agenda if posterity should enjoy the fruits of development.

Population control is possible only with the spread of education and awareness of contraceptives. Involvement of non- government organizations will have a positive impact in spreading awareness among men about family planning. For better dissemination of information, the role of gram panchayats, mass media, governmental agencies and voluntary bodies and NGOS will be important.

The government of India should adopt on area specific approach based on cultured and socio- economic situation. One can not use the same yardstick for all states. The growth of population should be checked by making the people aware of the small family norm. We should educate the masses.

Educated youth can easily understand the repercussion of having more children. Educated couples are satisfied with having two children or some are satisfied with one child only.

Moreover we should educate the rural and uneducated masses about the use of contracaptives. No authority or order can do anything so long as every couple is willing to limit the size. Couples can be made to understand the bad consequences of having a large family through education alone especially the education of women. Education changes one's attitudes towards family size & marriage. The people from the lower strata of society need to be educated so that they limit the sizes of their families and are able to provide their children better education. People should be educated about the relation between quantity and quality of population. Human capital formation to improve the quality of population can not be thought for a large family. The economics of small family & its benefits in terms of per capita availability of necessities, comforts & luxuries should be the subject of discussion all across the country. Government should provide exemptions or advantages for late marriages and small families.

The population bomb is ticking. Any delay in defusing it will bring about national disaster of unprecedented proportions. Our strategy should be to increase public understanding of how rapid population growth limits our chances of meeting our basic needs. It is essential for all of us to bring down the birth rate or nothing will be left for the coming generations. Proper planning should be done to curb poverty as the poor have no other way to entertainment but sex.

Wrong Orientation of Technology

Economic development of any kind will require technology. Excessive technology growth has created an environment in which life has become physically & mentally unhealthy. Polluted air, traffic congestion, irritating noise, chemical contaminants, radiation hazards and many other sources of physical & psychological stress have become part of everyday life for most of us. These manifold health hazards are not just incidental by products of technological progress but they are integral features of an economic system obsessed with growth & expansion, continuing to intensify its high technology in an attempt to increase productivity (Ramamurthy, 1996).

Military technology being such a large part of industrial activity particularly in economically developed countries is a major cause of global pollution & resource depletion. War & preparation for war are both directly related to environmental problems. With nuclear proliferation, both civil & military, the environmental hazard has become critical, arm control more difficult and nuclear war more probable. Exposure to ratio active wastes changes the way cells divide leading to mutated cells that retards the functioning of glands and organs. It can cause lung cancer, thyroid cancer, chromosomal abnormalities & genetic disorders.

There is need for use of appropriate technology. The environment soundness of any particular technology in the local condition for which it is intended should be fundamental element in deciding upon its appropriateness. The pressure on conventional sources of energy can be eased by use of non-conventional sources of energy. The solar water heater and solar cookers can be utilized on mass scale as the people are more receptive in urban areas. Energy conservation decreases the climatological threshold and also ecological deterioration.

Ecologically sound technologies such as with a stress on recycling will minimize stresses to the environment. Any new technology should be ecologically compatible and will be used for human survival & fulfillment. The enormous sums consumed in military expenditure may be applied directly to the task of global redistribution of resources and in environmental improvement.

As long as we tolerate the waste & the destructiveness of war itself, we can not achieve the stable environment on which the survival of all of us depends. It is absolutely essential to encourage use of indigenous eco - friendly technologies which are least harmful. Development is not merely achieving high rates of growth. It should be consistent with the promotion of higher quality of living for the masses. The highest profit is not in terms of money but is in terms of welfare all round.

Urbanization

The percentage of urban population which was only 10.84 in 1901 increased to 17.34 by 1951 and about 28 by 2001. Better health facilities, better education, better recreation, greater availability of electricity & employment & faster communication are the positive impacts of urbanization but it also leads to major problems of slums, sanitation, housing and water (Chauhan, 2006).

The ecology of urban and Indian is on the verge of collapse. One can find haphazard & chaotic growth of cities & towns, misuse of land, slums, jhuggies and jhonparies in all part of cities. Industries are established on political ground without consideration of pollutants. Most of the residential areas are having obnoxious & noise creating industries. Heavy traffic passes through residential colonies. There is also problem for electric energy, water supply, health & hygiene facilities. There are more contaminants, dusts, more cloudiness, more fog in winter, high temperature, less relative humidity, less wind speed & more unemployment in comparison to rural areas. But if there is water or air pollution in urban areas, it will certainly affect rural areas. Simultaneously, if there is a grain or vegetable pollution in rural areas, it will affect urban areas.

The demands for bricks, coal, cement, raw materials for industries and construction work have created derelict and waste lands in the rural areas. The reckless cuttings of tropical forest for fire wood construction activities in building are creating ecological disaster for rural and urban areas both.

Pollution in the modern cities are caused by the overloading environment with noxious substances contained in our daily consumption and production activities, they are the effluents of affluence in one sense discarded in the air, land and water , they become the wrong thing in the wrong place at the wrong time.

Urban ecological planning for both new & existing areas should recognize the ecological significance of the interaction of man not only with his physical environment but also with his socio economic, cultural and political environment. The ecological management must be people's movement. It has to be set right by the people and has to be for the people.

Over urbanization has today necessitated most of the cities to undertake renewal schemes. Urban renewal involves renewing the urban life where the process of degeneration or decline is set into motion due to the industrialization, modernization and their cumulative impact on the settlement pattern and social organization.

Laws formed by our government should be strictly enforced. There should be qualitative upgradation of local body administrations with high level of technical financial skill.

Threats of Environment Degradation

Soil Erosion & Soil Pollution

The soil erosion does not easily catch the eyes of public except when it causes calamities such as drought & flood. Huge pubic expenditure is incurred in fighting floods damage, desilting, protecting dams & repairing highways. Are we not silent spectators to this damage? Are we not losing our most valuable heritage that nature has taken million of years to build & that supported our nation for hundred of years. Do we know that each year world's finite capacity to grow food & fibre is being reduced by the loss & degradation of its soil. Many of the world's soils are losing the mineral and organic matter that makes them fertile and these materials are not being replaced in most cases nearly as fast as they are being depleted. Some soils are degraded in their salt or sodium content by water logging or by poisoning through indiscriminate application of agricultural & industrial chemicals.

In rural areas, the main sources of soil pollution are the residue of pesticides fertilizers crops & dirty water etc. while in the urban areas industrial wastes, garbage, cans, paper, bottle & junk wastes are responsible for polluting the land. Inadequate sewage system and slum household wastes are responsible for polluting the both rural & urban areas.

Every year pests damage crops worth billions of dollars in different parts of the globe. To prevent the damage caused by these pests, extensive use is made of pesticides. The use of pesticides started posing problems only because they were used with the short term benefits in mind. The harmful effects in the long run were not considered. Besides widespread poisoning of wild life and livestock, pesticides take a heavy toll on human lives both accidental & intentional. Contamination of ground water, food & food products are today global problem. Recent studies indicate that although we now use more than one pound of pesticide per person per year, only one percent or less of pesticide reach the targeted pests. The balance ninety nine percent of pesticide only add to the poisoning & pollution of land & water (Karpagam 2003).

Now a days UN bodies recommend integrated pest management methods these are

- Growing insect renstant varieties of crops.
- Cultivation practices like rotation of crops & early planting that would deter multiplication of pests.

- Nurture of natural enemies of the pests.
- Keeping the pests population below economically harmful levels through the use of chemicals but not eradicating them.

For saving the precious heritage of the soil, we should consider the following things.

- Soil should be considered a national asset and every land holder be considered its custodian and expected to use it according to its capability to realize its optimum potential.
- It should be recognized as a national policy to bring the deteriorated land back to normal condition and prevent its further deterioration
- Everyone should make an effort to return to the soil what he removes and improve it further so as to leave a better soil for the future generations.
- For solid waste disposal in all cities and towns, mechanical composting plants can be set up near the sewerage treatment plant where fermentable material can be used for composting. The compost can be sold in the city for kitchen gardening. The non fermentable materials can be either recycled or can be used for refilling. The cities night soil can be used for biogas generation & even for electric supply of colonies.
- The use of persistent pesticides such as DDT should be banned & its alternative to be developed. The pests can be controlled by adopting the measures like environmental control, sterile male technique & resistance breeding. At the place of chemical fertilizers, organic manure should be used and popularized to maintain the longievity of the carrying capacity of the soil.

Water Pollution

Water pollution is defined as a natural or induced change in the quality of water which renders it unusable or dangerous for consumption. Water being a universal solvent readily gets contaminated by the material with which it comes into physical contact. Agriculture, industry, irrigation, mining, power generation and the concentrations of millions of people in all cities contribute to a level of pollution that threatens to outstrip human ability to clean up afterwards. Water gets polluted by putrecible materials, heated effluents, toxic materials, inert wastes (Metal filings, dusts & oil films etc. which are not involved in chemical reaction) and also by radio active wastes.

Water is a significant vehicle in the transmission of disease when it contains water borne pathogens or disease producing organisms. These pathogens cause typhoid fever, dysentery, cholera and infectious hepatitis.

Polluted water also involves substantially high costs for industries- the cost of purifying the water, of repairing damaged equipment or of making extensive adjustments to industrial process themselves.

It is estimated that on account of pollution of our water, more than 60% of the diseases are water born & nearly 73 per million working days are lost due to these diseases. Also they account for a loss of productivity of the value of about 60 crores a year.

Although 70% of our planet is covered with water, only 3% of that is fresh water & most of the fresh water is tied up in ice caps, ice sheets & glaciers. Availability of fresh water in the rivers, lakes and aquifer is less than 1 percent. The water demand in 1995 was six times that of 1900 due to increased irrigation, intensive agriculture and industrial activity to meet the needs of over six billion people in the world. In the last 50 years aquifer depletion has caused the dropping of water table as much as over 20 ft. and salt water intrusion along the coastal areas. The Rio Grande of U.S, the Ganga's in India, the yellow river in China & Nile in Egypt are so much overexploited that some time, hardly make it to the oceans.

Today more than 21 millions Indian farmers tap underground reserves to water their fields & two third of India's crops are irrigated with underground water. This water is running & unlike the rivers, it will not be quickly replaced.

The international water management institute reported that in India 250 cubic kilometer of water are abstracted for irrigation each year. This is at least 100 cubic kilometer. more than the rains put back. But as every year passes the aquifers get emptied. The per cubic availability of water has declined from 5200 cubic meters in 1951 to 1820 cubic meters in 2001 & it is expected to decline to 1140 cubic meters by 2050 if urgent corrective measures are not taken.

For quality of drinking water, India occupies 120th slot on a list of 122 countries. About 37.7 billions Indian are effected by water born diseases every year. The government spends Rs. 6700 cr. on treating these people in rural India (Water A!D NGO). About 1.5 million children die of diarrhoea every year (World Bank). In ground water, there is an excess of nitrate, fluoride, iron & arsenic. An excessive use of fertilizer and pesticides in the field and an unchecked discharge of industrial waste into the rivers and canals result in water pollution. About 800 million people in India do not have access to clean drinking water.

The cost of environment damage in India is 4.5 % of GDP (World Bank). Our India has 15% of world's population and 4% of world's water availability. Realizing the growing menance of the problem, the government of India enacted the water (Prevention & control of pollution). Act. 1974 and formed central board for prevention and control of water pollution. It is necessary that strict actions should be taken against the polluter. The government agencies should see follows whether the industries adhere strictly to the norms prescribed

To bridge the gap between availability of water and future demands, water should be harvested in every form- rain water, ground water, stream & river & flood water. We should follow the following measures to conserve water:-

- Rainwater harvesting should be made mandatory so that water stored could be used for other than drinking purpose. It will also improve the moisture content of the soil.
- People should reconsider their life styles & make the rational use of water.

- Watershed development should be promoted.
- Some measures should also be taken for optimum production of crops & its sustainability.
- There should be improvement in water use efficiency appropriate technology in irrigation, households & industries.
- There should be further recycling & reuse of treated water.

Noise & Air Pollution

Noise is unwanted sound that interfere with human communication, comfort & health. The high levels (About 130 dB) of sound create intense pain, auditory fatigue or reduction of auditory sensitivity caused by exposure to prolonged & intense noise level & auditory trauma. It creates feeling of discomfort, distress, annoyance & reduced intellectual performance. It disturbs sleep, increases blood pressure, heart rate & muscular contradictions. Supply of oxygen to lungs is decreased due to air pollution. Heart patients appear to be particularly susceptible to the adverse effect of carbon monoxide and hydrogen and sulphide. In very high concentrations, hydrogen sulphide impairs that part of the brain that controls chest movement essential for normal breathing and causes almost instantaneous death. Lead poisoning attacks the blood forming mechanism, the gastro intestinal tract & in several causes affects the central nervous system.

Increasing industrialization and urbanization have created growing demand to use the atmosphere as a waste disposal medium. Thus the accumulation of waste gases and particles from combustion production and other economic activities exceeds the natural dispersion capacity of the atmosphere. When air movements are unable to disperse wastes at the rate they enter the atmosphere, air quality deteriorates and the seemingly infinite supply of clean air diminishes. Thus air is polluted.

The industrialized citics like Agra, Surat, Kanpur, Patna, Faridabad, and Ankleshwar had alarming are quality with 'SPM' raging from 384 micrograms per cubic meter to 412 micrograms per cubic meter. To curb the noise and air pollution we should apply the following things:-

- Automobiles are the major source of air pollution in the cities. To check it, public transport should be encouraged.
- Vehicles and roads should be maintained and adulteration of petrol and diesel should be thoroughly checked.
- No vehicle should be allowed to emit the pollutants above the maximum permissible limit. The central and state pollution control board should be develop instrumental & manpower competence for carrying out vehicular pollution monitoring to evolve and implement & control programs for vehicular emissions.
- Industries should not be allowed to set up without consideration of direction of wind, topo graphy etc. it should not be allowed to discharge its untreated pollutants in atmosphere or on the surface.
- To check the air pollutants in the thermal power stations, electrostic precipitators should be used.
- Cigarette and biri smoking must be banned at public places.
- Roads & vehicles should be so constructed and maintained as not to cause undue noise when in motion.
- In Bhajan, Kirtan & marriage procession, loud speakers should be avoided. There should be complete banning of use of loudspeakers in the night.
- The noise producing industries should use all the devices to reduce the level of noise inside the industries.

Climatic Change

Increasing concentrations of carbon dioxide result in an increase in the absorption & radiation of infrared rays which warms the lower atmosphere. The atmosphere absorbs a large percentage of the infrared radiation that is emitted by earth's surface. A portion of infrared radiation absorbed by the atmosphere is then re-radiated back towards the earth's surface. Re-radiation by the atmosphere makes it difficult for heat to escape into space, so the temperature of the lower atmosphere is not more hospitable for living being because it is warmer. This warming effect is also known as green house effect.

The temperature of earth is rising. This is affecting the health of human beings. This climatic change may have adverse impact on the ecosystems. Some species composition may change, some ecosystems might disappear and some species also become vulnerable to extinction. As farmers depends so heavily on a stable climate, this industry will struggle more than others to cope with more erratic weather, changes in growing season length and severe storms.

Environment & WTO

The countries normally restrict the imports of such products that do not meet the environmental needs, health and safety laws. The concern about the harmful effects of productive activity on natural environment which arouse 30 years back has come to include the undesirable effects also of trade in good and services which result from that of production, distribution and other value added activities. According to the world Development Report, Environmental damage is a matter of gıeat concern because it can undermine the future productivity. Soils that are degraded, acquifers that are depleted and ecosystems that are destroyed in the name of rising incomes today can Jeopardize the prospects of earning income tomorrow. Appropriate measures to prevent growing trade from harming the environment become necessary for sustainable development. Trade policies need to be formulated not only with a view to promote commerce but also growth and development on a sustainable basis.

The World Trade Organization (WTO) does not have a particular agreement that could deal with most burning issue of environment However a number of WTO agreements consist of steps dealing with environmental problems and its solutions. WTO have formed a committee known as WTO committee on trade and environment. This committee has considered the following aspects.

Environmental Steps with Significant Effects on Trade and WTO Provisions:-

- Use of process and production methods in environmental regulation.
- Packaging requirements.
- Environmental labeling.
- Consumption & other taxes imposed for environmental purposes.

Trade Provisions in Multilateral Environmental Agreements

Environmental Benefits of Trade Liberalization

WTO has also established a world's environmental centre at Geneva in Switzerland which keeps effective and efficient linkages between trade and environment.

WTO rules allows countries to prescribe trade barriers for environmental issues

A question does arise as to how widely are such sanctions applied for that product and what are their effects. Unless and until such questions are answered properly, WTO could not work effectively.

WTO aims at creating conditions of sustainability in the economic system of the country as it will add to the competition, productivity, cost effectiveness and a number of other benefits in the field of export, service sector and social environment.

There are three issues related to trade VS environment which are of particular concern to the developing countries like

- Interpretation of GATT Article.
- For providing further accommodation of trade measures pursuant to multilateral environmental agreements (MEAS).
- Accommodation of trade measures based on non product related PPM's on environmental ground in the context of eco-labeling.
- Greater scope for the use of precautionary principle.

The high cost of complying with external environmental regulation therefore poses a serious challenge to Indian exporters particularly those in the small sectors.

To resolve the conflict between environmental concerns and export promotions, WTO should incorporate the following things in its agenda (Tulapatia, 2005)

- Technology transfers under TRIPS (Trade Related aspects & Intellectual property rights) for environmentally sound technologies are to be made mandatory.
- Inclusion of process into the Agreement on technical barriers to trade must be resisted as it might lead to rejection of goods on the basis of the process of manufacturing.
- National standards should proximate as best as possible to the codex standards & in order to reduce the possibility of rejection of Indian goods in export market.
- There should be total transparency of environmental standards so as to avoid any confusion in any member country.

Global industry organization and government authorities in WTO membership should take some steps to make trade & environment mutually supportive.

Our government should also devise proactive policies both at the national as well as state level for attaining a harmonious balance between trade liberalization on the one hand & environment resource management policies on the other hand.

There is a need to address the developmental & environmental issues simultaneously. We should emphasis the sustainable development which aims at maximizing net welfare of economic activities along with maintaining or increasing the stock of economic, ecological & socio - cultural assets overtime. The sustainable development meets the needs of the present generation without compromising the needs of future generation.

- Market & policy distortions should be corrected at the source to promote growth with resource conservation & efficient allocation of resources.
- There should be internalization of the environmental costs so as to be fully reflected in the prices of produced goods & services. Making the polluter pay would prevent the polluter from polluting. Equally important is the need for policy makers to identify and correct whenever necessary the effects of economic activity on environment. If we fail to place a value on environment resources & to incorporate these into the prices of various produced goods and services can undermine the objective of sustainable development.

Government has to establish clear rules of how environmental costs are to be internalized and to punish polluters who fail to comply. Monitoring, measuring & enforcement all need government action and can not be left to private hands or the market mechanism only. Through regulation, governments set limits to the pollution emissions e.g. fuel efficiency norms for appliances, water discharge standards for factories and exhaust standards for automobiles.

An increase in economic well - being will help deprived countries preserve their own cultural heritages. Many people then in industrialized countries when faced with a reduction in their material possessions will need to find new definitions of progress in values compatible with environmental & social well being (Deoras, 1975)

If the global problems of environment & society are to be solved, then there should be rational distribution of industrial power. Such a redistribution would achieve at the same time a more equal apportionment of economic and political benefits among nations & individuals.

- The economic development, the foreign investments and technological practices of industrialized countries must be properly spent & altered by the basic claim of a region's people to the control of their resources. The resources must be allocated in such ways as to serve the needs of mankind in this & future generations.
- The authority of local people over resources and environment must include the obligation to recognize that the environment is an indivisible whole not subject to political barriers.

The government has made sustained efforts to halt the degradation of the environment and to preserve it for the future generations. India is the first developing country to label environment friendly products for marketing. For the award of ecomark, the manufacturers will have to apply to the bureau of Indian standards allowing the use of the label 'matka' on the payment of a fee. The labeling of environment friendly products is seen as Indian commitment to clean environment.

There are three Basic components of sustainable development-economic, social environment. The *economic component* of sustainability requires that societies pursue growth paths that generate optimal flow of income while maintaining their basic stock of human capital. There are three basic goals of *economic component.*

- Increasing production of goods and services.
- Satisfying basic needs or reducing poverty.
- Improving equity.

The *social component* of sustainable development built on twin principles of justice and equity. For the development path to be sustainable over long period of time, wealth, resources and opportunity should be equitably shared.

The *environment component* requires sustainable resource use, maintence of stock of natural capital. The environment should be able to perform its three functions efficiently. Unless transformation of society and management of the environment are addressed integrally along with economic growth, growth itself will be jeopardised over the long term.

Now the situation demands not one of the preventing or eliminating environmental deterioration totally but as to how much we could minimize our needs. Thus calls for natural resource accounting or valuation to be related to the type of resource whether it is a stock or flow, whether it is exhaustible or renewable.

There should be intra generational equity that is minimum wealth gaps between the developed and developing countries because today 18% of population are using 80% of resources enjoying high living standards at the expense of others with very low standards. As compared to rich nations, poorer nations are in great need of natural resources for the future

There is a conflict between preservation of the environment and traditional concepts of economic growth. Now a days uncontrolled continuous growth in the industrial production of environmentally harmful substances and products in some regions of the world has produced dangerous amount of pollution and has been responsible for inordinate waste of resources. At the same time, there has been an increasing centralization within a few nations of the benefits from the use of earth's natural resources and the international political influence flowing from the control of these resources.

The exploitation of Third World's national and regional resources by corporations with a consequent outflow of profits from the exploited regions, has resulted in a vast and growing economic disparity among nations and a monopoly of industrialized countries over production, energy technology, information and political power. Complimentary to this is the flooding of developing countries with surplus goods and capital, with a resultant distortion of their economics and the deformation of their environment into monocultures in the interest of further enriching the industrial states.

Developing Countries are facing Two Choices i.e

- These face a choices whether to preserve natural resources or destroy environment for pursuing economic growth. So knowledge about future damage is essential if a rational choice is to be made
- These countries are also confronted with a choice between satisfying basic needs of the people and between preserving natural resources which are required for maintaining quality of life.

Remedies to Save our Environment

Giving environment a chance means giving the whole human kind a chance. For if we do not do something soon to arrest the decline in environment at all levels, there is no future for the human race itself. That we recognize this in itself a big thing. For, if we do so much, then we can at least set ourselves on the path of rectifying our ways to ensure that the world at least exists in the way we know it for our heirs.

The economic value of ecosystem services for the entire biosphere (the thin zone of earth, water and air that is capable of supporting life) was estimated to be about $33 trillion which is minimum estimate.

India has one of the most degraded environments in the world. The real choice is therefore never one between growth and the environment. It is a choice between long term and sustainable economic gains derived by taking care of the environment and short term growth from its neglect. Unless our developmental plans are guided by our environmental needs, we will fail to achieve sustainable progress. Environmental problems like deforestation and unhygienic or poor sanitation are caused by poverty and lack of development. Lack of environmental safeguards could result in the pollution of air, water and soil. The paradox is that if we do not develop rapidly, such problems overtake us and if we develop fast and overuse energy, the problems overpower us.

India has a set back of three reasons not being able to do what the effluent developed countries were able to do i.e pollution control laws are difficult to implement, lack of education, awareness and poverty and cost of control requires heavy investments which is a great handicap in India.

Despite the wealth of technologies, human resources, policy options and technical scientific information at our disposal, humankind has yet to break decisively with unsustainable and environmentally unsound policies and practices. We need to protect ecosystems and resources on which all life depends and thereby merit more urgent attention and high level commitment. To confront the underlying causes of environmental degrading and poverty, we must integrate environmental considerations in the mainstream of decision making. We must also intensify our efforts in developing preventive action and a concerted response, including, international rule of law, environmental governance, environmental equation and awareness raising.

Environment is not a fixed asset. We inhibit a single planet but several worlds. There is a world of abundance where plenty brings pollution. There is a world of want where deprivation degrade life. Such a fragmented planet can not survive in harmony with nature and the environment or indeed with self. It can ensure neither sustained peace nor sustained development. The overwhelming reality that must be faced is that the resources of our planet would be able to sustain a given population within a given range of exploitations subject to a given rate of regeneration and maintenance for all to come. Any imbalance in any one or more of the above factors viz population, life style and extent of exploitation, regeneration and maintenance is sure to cut short the life of the planet.

The problem of environmental degradation can not be checked by prescription, technology or management alone but by people being helped to appreciate various improvements in the level of living and employment, to want to conserve their non renewable resource and promote their renewable resources in order to save the environment, we should keep in mind the following suggestions:-

- The need of the hour is avoidance of harmful chemicals in agriculture and industry.

- Production and use of eco-friendly manufactured items of mass consumption.
- Research on a continuing basis for finding out alternative sources of energy.
- Compulsory establishment by industries of pollution preventing measures like the effluent treatment plants.
- Dumping of hazardous wastes in places far removed from human and animal habitation or disposing of them in any other effective way.
- Strict vigilance over observance of environment regulations particularly by the multinational corporation.
- The non-government organizations can play great role in environmental conservation. They can foster the formation of pressure groups, environmental education and community improvement schemes. They can encourage the people's participation in environmental conservation. They can report the pollution problems in press, write to government, organize procession, cycle rally, meeting, seminars, force the government to choose the right way, oppose the construction of dams, selection of right trees and force the government to set up city refuse composting and sewerage treatment plants. They can ghearo factory manager discharging untreated effluents on land, water and atmosphere. They can help in cleaning rivers, lakes and beaches.
- NGOs can also campaign in favor of family planning, kitchen gardening. They can fight against unlimited urban expansion and sub standard housing. They can help in creating litter free zones, environment forestry zones, smokeless zones, noise fees zones. To give their own shape, they can raise funds for creating healthy environment.
- The people of the world must come to understand the environment, to preserve it and when altering it, to do it with care wisdom.

- Eradication of poverty is must to achieve sustainable development
- We should facilitate and encourage public awareness and participation by mankind environmental information widely available.
- There should be full participation of women to achieve sustainable development. The ideals, creativity and courage of youth and indigenous people are also needed.
- People should be made aware that healthy and productive life is possible only when there is harmony with nature.

Mikhail Grobachev once said that we are not masters but guests of our nature.

We must develop a new paradigm for development and conflict resolution, based on costs and benefits to all people and bound by the limits of nature herself rather than by the limits of consumerism and technology. We will be successful in building a sustainable environment only with the active participation of our society.

BIBLIOGRAPHY

Byravan, S. (1997), Environment is Good for Growth. The Times of India, New Delhi.

Chauhan, CPS (2006), Protection of Environment- A Serious Education Concern. University News 44(2), March 20-26.

Deoras P.J. (197), What Causes Pollution Safety Chronicle Vol IV No 4 PP 8-13

Khosla,s (2005), Empower, Educate Women. The Tribune Aug 15.

Mahawal, S (1992), Awareness for Environment Preservation, Yojna July 3, PP 13-4

Nair, SR, (1999), Let's Preserve our Environment. The Times of India, 10 June

Ramamurthi, (1996), Environment & Development, Nirnay, March-Dec. PP 27 to 37

Sen., S., (1997), A Pollution Industry, The Hindustan Times. December 20.

Shokand, J, (2007), The Earth is Dying, The Trubune 5th June PP9

Singla, S.P. (2006), Boi Centric Teaching Strategies for a Sustainable World University News 44(12) March 20-26.

Talaptra, A. (2005), WTO: Challenges & Dilemmas of Environmental Protection. in WTO & Development Opportunities Edited by Verma, S.B., Deep & Deep Publications, New Delhi.

Verma, S.B. (2005), WTO & Development Opportunities, Deep & Deep Publications, New Delhi.

Verma, S.B. (2005), Environmental Protection & Development. Deep & Deep Publications, New Delhi.

CHAPTER–6

IMPACT OF SOCIO-ECONOMIC CONDITIONS ON LIFE INSURANCE BUSINESS IN INDIA

M.V.S. Srinivasa Rao

Introduction

Since time immemorial we have been trying to achieve a perfect balance between the risk and the return for any investment decision. In the practical life also it is our constant endeavor to secure our assets and plan in such a manner so as to ensure fulfillment of current and future liabilities. One such tool for achieving the above condition is insurance[1]. The basic concept of insurance is not minimization of risk, but to arrange for compensation of risk. A person who opts for an insurance policy, be it life or general, is in a way trying to compensate the expected losses which he or she may face in case of happening of an event. Thus, the basic purpose of insurance is not to earn profits but hedging against expected losses[2]. However, in India, insurance is generally considered as a financial saving or tax-saving device instead of its other implied long-term financial benefits. Indian people are prone to investing in properties and gold followed by bank deposits. They also selectively invest in shares[3]. Therefore,

Life Insurance Business = Availability of Money for Financial Savings + the Insurable Population + to an extent the Micro Economic Indicators[4].

In the above equation, mainly three elements viz., availability of money for financial savings, insurable population and some micro economic conditions of life insurance business, which brings some dynamics in the life insurance sector.

Hence, this paper attempts to study the dynamics in the elements of business equation of Indian life insurance sector after its liberalization by stating the following objectives:

1. To understand the saving habits of Indian people in general and to trace out the saving rate in life insurance sector in particular,
2. To identify the insurable population by estimating the market potential for individual life insurance,
3. To analyze the micro economic conditions like supply, consumption and competition in life insurance sector and
4. To find the critical success factors of Indian life insurance business.

The subsequent sections will attain the stated objectives respectively. The conclusion and implications of the study are followed by the end notes and references. For thorough understanding of the analysis, more informative reference tables are appended last.

Saving habits of Indian People and Life Insurance Funds

The market for life insurance in India has evolved in the context of the specific socioeconomic and political environment that existed over the years[5]. After Globalization in 1991, the Indian economy has been growing rapidly and the growth impulses continued during 2005-06. Thus, the growth in real GDP was at 9.0 per cent during 2005-06 as against 7.5 per cent in 2004-05. Gross domestic savings as well as capital formation started increasing after 1996-97(Table 1). Within the services sector there has been an improved performance in finance, insurance, real estate and other business services. The reason behind this phenomenon is because of the improvement in the public sector savings and private corporate sector that reflected in the gross domestic savings[6] (Table 2).

Table 1
GDP Growth Rate, Money Supply and Gross Domestic Capital Formation in India for the Selected Years

Period	*Growth in GDP at Factor Cost at Constant Prices(real GDP)*	*Growth in Money Supply (%)*	*Gross Domestic Capital Formation as % of GDP*
1993-94	6.0	18.4	23.1
1994-95	7.0	22.3	26.1
1995-96	7.3	13.7	27.2
1996-97	7.5	15.2	24.6
2003-04	8.5	16.7	27.4
2004-05	7.5	12.3	30.2
2005-06	9.0	21.2	32.2
2006-07	9.2*	21.3*	NA**

Source:
1. Central Statistical Organization
2. Reserve Bank of India

* Estimated
** Not Available

Table 2
Composition of Gross Domestic Savings in India from 1980-2005

Item	*1980-81 to 1984-85*	*1985-86 to 1989-90*	*1990-91 to 1994-95*	*1995-96 to 1999-00*	*2000-01 to 2004-05*
Gross Domestic Saving	100.0	100.0	100.00	100.0	100.0
Household Sector	72.6	79.4	78.3	79.7	80.2
Financial Saving	34.9	38.8	39.8	44.5	43.0
Life Insurance Funds	3.2	3.9	4.2	4.9	5.95

Source: Reserve Bank of India, Report on Currency and Finance, 1999-2000.
Note: Data for the period 1980-81 to 1984-85 are based on 1980-81 series and data for the period 1995-96 to 2000-01 are based on 1999-00 series.

According to preliminary estimates for 2005-06, there has been a shift in the savings behavior of the households showing preference to deposits. As such, the currency and deposits constituted 45.5 per cent of the gross financial savings of the

Table 3
Composition of Gross Financial Saving of Indian Household Sector

(Per Cent)

Item	*2005-06#* (1)	*2004-05P* (2)	*2003-04P* (3)	*2002-03P* (4)	*2001-02P* (5)	*2000-01* (6)
Financial Saving (gross)	100.0	100.0	100.0	100.0	100.0	100.0
(a) Currency	(16.7)	(14.0)	(13.8)	(13.1)	(12.7)	(11.9)
(b) Deposits	8.8	8.5	11.2	8.9	9.7	6.3
(i) With banks	(1.5)	(1.2)	(1.5)	(1.2)	(1.2)	(0.7)
(ii) With non-banking	47.4	37.0	38.3	40.9	39.4	41.0
companies	(7.9)	(5.2)	(5.3)	(5.4)	(5.0)	(4.9)
(iii) With co-operative banks	46.7	36.4	37.4	35.5	35.3	32.5
and societies	0.8	0.8	1.0	2.7	2.6	2.9
(iv) Trade debt (net)	0.0	0.0	0.0	2.8	3.6	5.6
(c) Shares and debentures	0.0	0.0	0.0	-0.1	-2.1	0.1
(i) Private corporate business	4.9	1.1	0.1	1.7	2.7	4.1
(ii) Banking	(0.8)	(0.2)	(0.0)	(0.2)	(0.3)	(0.5)
(iii) Units of Unit Trust of India	1.3	1.4	1.1	0.8	1.5	3.1
(iv) Bonds of public sector	0.0	0.1	0.0	0.0	0.1	0.0
undertakings	-0.1	-0.7	-2.3	-0.5	-0.6	-0.4
(v) Mutual fund (other than	0.0	0.0	0.0	0.1	0.0	0.1
UTI)	3.6	0.4	1.2	1.3	1.8	1.3
(d) Claims on government	14.7	24.4	23.0	17.4	17.9	15.7
(i) Investment in government	(2.5)	(3.4)	(3.2)	(2.3)	(2.3)	(1.9)
securities	2.4	4.9	7.5	2.5	5.8	1.7
(ii) Investment in small savings, etc	12.3	19.5	15.5	14.9	12.1	14.0

Contd.

Item	*2005-06#*	*2004-05P*	*2003-04P*	*2002-03P*	*2001-02P*	*2000-01*
	(1)	*(2)*	*(3)*	*(4)*	*(5)*	*(6)*
(e) Insurance funds	14.2	16.0	13.7	16.1	14.2	13.6
(i) Life insurance funds	(2.4)	(2.2)	(1.9)	(2.1)	(1.8)	(1.6)
(ii) Postal insurance	13.5	15.1	13.0	15.5	13.5	12.9
(iii) State insurance	0.2	0.3	0.3	0.3	0.3	0.2
(f) Provident and pension funds	0.5	0.6	0.5	0.4	0.4	0.5
	10.0	12.9	13.6	15	16.1	19.3
	(1.7)	(1.8)	(2.3)	(1.9)	(2.0)	(2.0)

P : Provisional.

: Preliminary estimates.

Notes:

1. Figures in brackets are percentage at GDP at current market prices.
2. Components may not add up to the totals due to rounding off.

Source: The Reserve Bank of India Annual Report, 2004-05.

household sector in 2004-05. Provident and pension funds had a share of 12.9 per cent for the same period. On the other side, the share of deposits increased to 47.4 per cent, the share of insurance funds declined to 14.2 per cent in 2005-06. Specifically mentioned, there has been a notable decline of 1.6 percentage points in the savings in the form of life insurance funds (Table 3). This seems to be disturbing from the industry point of view as there has been a substantial increase in the life insurance business in 2005-06 (refer Table 10).

This disproportional is due to the huge amount of insurable population that exists in India. That is how, even the low rate of life insurance saving causes the increase in life insurance business. Let us identify the insurable population by estimating the market potential of the sector.

Market Potential for Individual Life Insurance in India

With a huge population of more than one billion and untapped market, life insurance happens to be a big opportunity in India. But, insurance penetration in the country continues to be low. Insurance penetration or premium volume as a share of a country's GDP, for the year 2005 stood at 2.53 per cent for life insurance (Table 4).

Table 4
Data on Life Insurance Density and Life Insurance Penetration in India

Year	*Population (Cr)*	*GDP (Cr)*	*Life Insurance Premium (Cr)*	*Life Insurance Density (Premiums Per Capita Income/ Population)*	*Life Insurance Penetration (Premium as % of GDP)*
2000-01	101.9	2104298	34898	342.5	1.66
2001-02	103.7	2296049	50095	483.1	2.18
2002-03	105.5	2451038	55738	528.3	2.27
2003-04	107.8	2659376	66653	750.7	2.26
2004-05	109.4	2858829	82858	851.0	2.48
2005-06	111.3	3116123	105875	904.3	2.53

Source: Insurance Regulatory and Development Authority Annual Reports, Various issues.

Table 5

Estimation of Market Potential for Individual Assurance on the Basis of Household Income

Income groups (Rupees in 1994-95 prices)	*Year 2001-02 (million)*	*Potential House-holds*	*Potential Policy per HH*	*No. policy (million)*	*Avg. Sum Assured per policy Rupees.*	*SA total (Rupees million)*	*Premium Income (Rupees million)*
Low (up to 22,500)	59.3	25%	1	14.825	10000	148,250.00	8,746.75
Lower Middle (22,501-45,000)	72.2	100%	1	72.2	50000	3,610,000.00	212,990.00
Middle(45,001-70,000)	23.5	100%	1.5	35.25	66666.67	2,350,000.00	138,650.00
Upper Middle (70,000-96,000)	13.6	100%	1.75	23.8	114285.71	2,720,000.00	160,480.00
High (Above 96,000)	12.1	100%	3	36.3	133000.00	4,827,900.00	284,846.10
Total	180.7			182.375	74,879.51	13,656,150.00	805,712.85
						13,65,615Cr	80,571.29Cr
Of which: Middle to High (above 45,001)	49.2		1.938008	95.35		9,897,900.00	583,976.10
Percentage	27.23			52.28		72.48	72.48

Assumptions:

1. Average sum assured based on sample studies.
2. Premium per thousand sum assured assumed to be Rs.59 based on the DD premium of LIC in the year 1996-97.
3. Premium income includes first year premium, renewal premium and single premium income.

Source: RBI report on Currency and Finance 1999-2000, pIII-10.

Obviously, the level of penetration tends to rise as income increases, particularly in life insurance[7]. India, with its huge middle to high class households of 49.2 million (27.2 per cent share to total house holds), has exhibited potential for the insurance industry. The trends depicts in the life insurance as shown in the Table 4 reveals in dawdling rate of growth primarily as against the expected in terms of insurance product to the insurable population. Evidence is that, the total market in life insurance was worth about Rs.35, 000 cr. in 2000-01. But estimated potential for this segment is Rs. 80,500cr for the same period (Table 5). So there is another 130 per cent potential to be tapped in this segment. Favorably, the growth rate of life insurance segment has been around 20-25% in 2001. If these growth rates are sustained, it is estimated that the market would grow to nearly Rs.2, 60,000cr by 2010.

Table 6
Rural Urban Divide of Indian Population, 2001

Rural-Urban Divide in India - 2001				
	Total	*Males*	*Females*	*Percentage*
Rural	741,660,293	381,141,184	360,519,109	27.78 -Urban
Urban	285,354,954	150,135,894	135,219,060	72.22 - Rural
Total	1,027,015,247	531,277,078	495,738,169	

Source: Census of India 2001.
Understanding: 72 % of people live in rural India.

To tap this potential, the life insurance business has to understand the asymmetric distribution of money, burgeoning population, rural urban divide and unbalanced regional development compared to developed nations[8]. Table 6 gives us a picture of diversity. According to industry observes, the biggest potential lies in the rural insurance market where the penetration of the insurance has been low. Often in rural areas, insurance is perceived as an additional burden rather than a means to combat risk. According to an independent survey conducted by a big private insurer, 18% of the rural population has an insurance cover. Considering the fact that, 72% of the Indian population lives in the rural area, the potential is highly attractive. Traditionally, the insurers have not found rural insurance attractive. While most of the insurers may find it unattractive to tap the rural insurance, it should be understood that relatively smaller amount of policies will be compensated by a large number of policies[9]. Rural insurance should be looked upon as an opportunity and not an obligation. It is important to take advantage of the immense potential that resides in the rural sector.

Table 7

Spread of Life Insurance Cover in Rural India (Selected Years)

(In Lakhs)

	Individual Insurance (No. of Policies)	
Year (at end of the year)	*Assurances*	*Rural Share*[1] *(in per cent)*
1961	85.77	36.5
1970-71	147.85	31.4
1980-81	228.12	29.62
1990-91	455.68	42.5
2000-01	1131.11	55.3/(18.18)[2]

Source:

1. Company Annual Reports, various issues.
2. RBI, Handbook of statistics on Indian Economy, 2001.

Notes:

1. Share of policies in rural areas to the total new policies during the year.
2. Though as per definition of rural/social sector as approved by IRDA this share comes to be 18.18 per cent.

Let us look at the spread of life insurance cover in rural India, share of rural policies in total new business in individual policies contracted during the same selected years is observed in Table 7. It is seen that, though rural share was fluctuating during the years under consideration, it has an increasing trend over the period. It was 36.5 per cent in 1961 which increased to 55.5 per cent in 2000-01, which is covered 18% of the total rural population. Thus it can be observed that the insurance cover is not only concentrated in urban areas, but also in rural areas. As depicted in the same table, number of policies of individual assurances increased more than 13 times from

Rs. 85.77lakh in 1961 (December end) to Rs.1131.11lakh by 2001 (March end). It may mean that on an average, one individual in every ten individuals is holding an individual policy. However, number of policies may not indicate exactly the number of individuals insured, as an individual may buy more than one policy[10]. Hence, in the absence of any other indicator this can be used as proxy for the number of individuals insured.

On the other side, the income of life insurance business is derived from life insurance sales, i.e., the premium income, but the estimates have only aggregate information of the quantity sold, i.e., the number of policies sold. Therefore, an estimate of the potential life insurance market is one thing and the actual consumption of life insurance is another. The former is already discussed; let us discuss about the latter. The actual consumption of life insurance is affected by micro economic conditions of the sector[11] and can be discussed in the next section.

Micro Economic Conditions of Indian Life Insurance Business

There are mainly three factors affecting the Indian life insurance business viz., supply, consumption and competition.

Supply

Insurance in India started without any regulations in the nineteenth century. The life insurance company was nationalized in 1956. Prior to 1956, life insurance business was done in a highly competitive and open market environment operating under the regulations lay down by the Insurance Act, 1938. At the time of nationalization, there were over 245 insurers, operating in India, of which 105 foreign companies operating then, only 15 transacted life businesses, with their share of total new life business being only 7 percent. Once the life insurance market is opened up in India in 2000-01; we do not have any appropriate reason to expect the Indian scenario to be different from the observed international experience where domestic companies dominate the market.

Because, till end of fiscal year 1999-2000, LIC (Life Insurance Corporation of India) was monopoly insurance provider in India. In fiscal 2000-2001, the Government of India lifted all entry restrictions for private sector investors. Foreign investment insurance market was also allowed with 26% cap. With the entry of private sector players backed by foreign expertise, Indian insurance market has become more vibrant. By end March 2006, out of total 16 (including public sector giant LIC), 15 private players are operating only in the remaining 20 per cent of the total market share.

Consumption

The country has witnessed the rapid growth of insurance services once the field has been thrown open. Given the fact that only a minuscule minority of the population in India today has access to insurance services; the potential for growth is clearly tremendous. On the supportive side, the private sector globally has shown the ability to innovate and offer a diverse range of products that matches the requirements of a wide variety of groups. It is more likely that the ushering in of competition in this sector will not merely expand the coverage, but also customize it in a manner that was far less evident in the days of monopoly in the sector[12]. Most of the private insurers venturing into the sector are highly attracted by the large middle class population of more than 300 million (Census of India, 2001), who are becoming increasingly sophisticated and are demanding new products and services[13].

Persistently, consumer awareness has improved. Competition has brought more products and better customer servicing. To manage this, intermediaries associated with insurance business like brokers, third party administrators (TPAs) and surveyors are playing a crucial role. The insurance agents, including corporate agents, represent the insurers, and play an important role in sale of insurance contracts.

Competition

Until the new players came along, what passed in the name of life insurance was a tax saving tool with insurance wrapped around it. But a true insurance product, experts say, must offer an optimal balance between protection and savings. And that is a formula that new life insurers have cottoned on to[14]. Offers from them is an array of products ranging from traditional term endowments and money back policies to contemporary whole life and pension plans. There is a clear shift from the one-size-fits-all strategy of yore to more flexible, customer-centric one[15] that the ICICI Prudential has adopted.

Table 8
Details of Premiums Underwritten by Life Insurers in 2004-05 and 2005-06

(Rs. Lakhs)

Insurer	*2004-05*	*2005-06*
First year premium		
LIC	1165823.94	1372803.17
	(-1.25)	(17.75)
Private Sector	422309.25	754772.99
	(106.46)	(78.73)
Total	1588133.19	2127576.16
	(14.65)	(33.97)
Single premium		
LIC	899482.42	1478784.14
	(62.32)	(64.40)
Private Sector	134148.09	272193.91
	(239.46)	(102.91)
Total	1033630.51	1750978.05
	(74.11)	(69.40)
Renewal premium		
LIC	5447422.62	6227635.05
	(17.95)	(14.32)
Private Sector	216293.48	481386.89
	(218.26)	(122.56)
Total	5663716.10	6709021.94
	(20.85)	(18.46)
Total premium		
LIC	7512728.98	9079222.36
	(18.25)	(20.85)
Private Sector	772750.82	1508353.79
	(147.65)	(95.19)
Total	8285479.80	10587576.15
	(24.31)	(27.78)

Source: IRDA Annual Reports
Note: Figures in brackets indicate the growth (in per cent)

Such aggressive planning of selling strategies is beginning to pay off for ICICI Prudential and other private life insurers. In the first two years after the life insurance was opened up in 2000-01, the new players have grabbed nearly 9 % of the total insurance market in terms of premium income and nearly 33 % of the pension products market. ICICI Prudential is the leader having sold Rs.3.5lakhs policies for the initial 3 years. The size of life insurance market increased on the strength of growth in the economy and concomitant increase in per capita income. This resulted in a favorable growth in total premium both for LIC (20.85 per cent) and to the new insurers (95.19 per cent) in 2005-06 (Table 8). The higher growth for the new insurers needs to be viewed in the context of a lower base in 2004-05. However, the new insurers have improved their market share from 9.33 per cent in 2004-05 to 14.25 per cent in 2005-06 in terms of total premium underwritten by private sector insurers to the total premium underwritten by the sector.

So, the premium underwritten[16] by the Indian life insurers in 2005-06, was increased by 27.78 per cent, which was higher than the growth i.e., 24.31 per cent in 2004-05. First year premium including, single premium accounted for 36.63 per cent of the total life premium. Renewal premium accounted for the remaining. First year premium including single premium recorded a growth of 47.94 per cent driven by a significant jump in the unit-linked business. The outlook for insurance in 2006 remains favorable.

Similarly, new policies underwritten by the industry were Rs.354.62lakhs in 2005-06 as against Rs.262.11lakhs during 2004-05 showing an increase of 35.29 per cent as against a decline of 8.44 per cent in the year before (Table 9). While the private insurers exhibited a growth of 73.37 per cent, (more than twice the growth reported in the previous year 34.62 per cent), LIC showed a growth of 31.75 per cent as against a negative growth of 11.09 per cent in 2004-05. The market share of the private insurers and LIC, in terms of policies underwritten, was 10.92 per cent and 89.08 per cent in 2005-06 as against 8.52 per cent and 91.48 per cent respectively in 2004-05.

Table 9
Market Shares of Life Insurers in terms of Premium Collections and the Number of New Policies Issued by the Insurers in 2004-05 and 2005-06. (Per cent)

Insurer	*2004-05*	*2005-06*
Premium Collections		*(per cent)*
First year premium		
LIC	73.41	64.52
Private Sector	26.59	35.48
Total	100.00	100.00
Single premium		
LIC	87.02	84.45
Private Sector	12.98	15.55
Total	100.00	100.00
Renewal premium		
LIC	96.18	92.82
Private Sector	3.82	7.18
Total	100.00	100.00
New policies issued		*(in number)*
Private Sector	2233075	3871410
	(34.62)	(73.37)
LIC	23978123	31590707
	(-11.09)	(31.75)
Total	26211198	35462117
	(-8.44)	(35.29)

Source: Reserve Bank of India Annual Report for the Year 2005-06.
Note: Figures in brackets indicate the growth rate (in per cent) of total new policies issued.

Besides, Life insurance industry recorded a premium income of Rs.105875.76 crore during 2005-06 as against Rs.82854.80 crore in the previous financial year, recording a growth of 27.78 per cent (Table 10). The contribution of first year premium, single premium and renewal premium to the total premium was Rs.21275.75 crore (20.09 per cent); Rs.17509.78 crore (16.54 per cent); and Rs.67090.21 crore (63.37 per cent), respectively. In the year 2000-01, when the industry was opened up to the private players, the life insurance premium was Rs.34,898.48 crore which constituted of Rs.6996.95 crore of first year premium, Rs.25191.07 crore of renewal premium and Rs.2740.45 crore of single premium. Post opening up, single premium had declined from Rs.9, 194.07 crore in the year 2001-02 to Rs.5674.14 crore in 2002-03 with the withdrawal of the guaranteed return policies. Though it went up marginally in 2003-04 to Rs.5936.50 crore (4.62 per cent growth) the year 2004-05 witnessed a significant shift with the single premium income rising to Rs.10336.30 crore showing 74.11 per cent growth over 2003-04, accounting for 12.74 per cent of the total premium underwritten in that year. Where as, the total pay-out by the life insurance industry on account of commissions in 2005-06 stood at Rs.8643.29 crore as against Rs.7104.46 crore in 2004-05.

Table 10
Total Life Insurance Premium Collected by the Insurers (2000-06)

(Rs. Cr)

Insurer	*2000-01*	*2001-02*	*2002-03*	*2003-04*	*2004-05*	*2005-06*
LIC of India	34892.02	49821.91	54628.49	63533.43	75127.29	90792.22
(Pub. Sector)		(42.79)	(9.65)	(16.30)	(18.25)	(20.85)
ING Vysya Life	–	4.19	21.16	88.51	338.86	425.38
HDFC Standard Life	0.002	33.46	148.83	297.76	686.63	1569.91
Birla Sun Life	0.32	28.26	143.92	537.54	915.47	1259.68
ICICI Prudential Life	5.97	116.38	417.62	989.28	2363.82	4261.05
Kotak Life	–	7.58	40.32	150.72	466.16	621.85
Tata AIG* Life	–	21.14	81.21	253.53	497.04	880.19
SBI Life	–	14.69	72.39	225.67	601.18	1075.32
Bajaj Allianz Life	–	7.14	69.17	220.80	1001.68	3133.58
Max New York Life	0.16	38.95	96.59	215.25	413.43	788.13
Met Life	–	0.48	7.91	28.73	81.53	205.99
Reliance Life	–	0.28	6.47	31.06	106.55	224.21
Aviva Life	–	–	13.47	81.50	253.42	600.27
Sahara Life	–	–	–	–	1.74	27.66
Shriram Life	–	–	–	–	–	10.33
Bharti AXA Life**	–	–	–	–	–	–
Private sector total	6.45	272.55	1119.06	3120.33	7727.51	15083.54
		(4124.31)	(310.59)	(178.83)	(147.65)	(95.19)
Total	34898.47	50094.46	55747.55	66653.75	82854.80	105875.76
		(43.54)	(11.28)	(19.56)	(24.31)	(27.78)

Source: Company Annual Reports, various issues.

Note:

1. *Figures revised for the year 2002-03.
2. – represents business not started.
3. ** Started business in the year 2006.
4. Figures in the bracket represent the growth over the previous year in percent.
5. 1 Crore = 10 Million.
6. Total premium income includes first year premium, single premium and renewal premium and excludes group life insurance premium.

In summary, the major increase in the consumption of insurance will be from the increase in the supply of insurance[17]. It is clear from the above that the major increase in the consumption of insurance in the post liberalization scenario is going to come from the shift in the supply. It is already proven that, the demand already exists. The extent to which it is tapped would depend on the extent to which the supply will increase. To increase the supply of life insurance, some of the critical success factors in life insurance business are traced in the following section.

Critical Success Factors of Life Insurance Business

The competition in the sector is so intense that it has become difficult to identify the critical success factors. While some argue that product innovation is going to be the crucial factor in the success of the insurance companies, others argue that service and quality of distribution will determine the success[18]. However, insurance companies will need to expand the markets rather than vying for the same customer base. It is understood from the above discussion that the critical success factors would be find management capability, distribution and good underwriting practices. Besides, technology plays an important role in providing competitive edge designing and administering products and services and building long-term customer relationship. Technology will help enhance service ensure effective and efficient service delivery and lead to greater customization of products and greater transparency[19]. Moreover, all the new entrants are promising to speed up the process right from bond issuance to claims settlement.

Consistently, it is already a buyers' market now. He can be benefited by new customized products to match his needs, better service and of course would be able to get the value for the money spend, both in terms of insurance coverage and returns[20]. The most important change would be that his claims would be settled faster. Thus the competition has brought cheers for the customers. Today the customers are offered products to meet their individual needs rather than mass customized products. For instance, a customer who had opted to go for life coverage had limited choice with only one player offering the services. But now with more players in the market his choice is unlimited. Similar is the case in the future.

Of course, the size of the market for life insurance would be mind-boggling. Technically a life insurance policy or a pension product could be sold from ages 0 to 79. Life insurance provides relief to the members of society from financial difficulties arising from premature death of insured or surviving to old age[21]. Hence, growth in insurance industry has been spurred by product innovation, sales and distribution channels being put in place by the industry coupled with targeted advertising and marketing campaigns launched by them. Innovations have come not only in the form of benefits attached to the products, but also in delivery mechanisms which have emanated from various marketing tie-ups both within the realm of financial services and outside. All these have taken life insurance closer to the customer as well as making it more relevant. The insurance companies are increasingly tapping the semi-urban and rural areas to take across the message of protection of life through insurance cover.

Conclusion and Implications

India has a population of more than a billion people. Of these, it is estimated that around 300 million make up the consuming class (India Census 2001). With a high savings rate of approximately 27% (RBI Report on Currency and Finance, 2001) and a very low insurance penetration rate of 2.5% (IRDA Annual Report, 2005-06) of the gross domestic product, the opportunities are enormous for the insurance business. In developed countries, the owners have insured even pet dogs, whereas in India, about 80 percent of human beings and major natural resources have not been insured in globalization era. The latest series of bomb attacks, attack on parliament, attack on Ayodya, attacks of the Maoists, nature calamities like tsunami, floods and drought, ragging are prevailed in the country and need not to say about the farmer who has been insecure about rains, seeds, crops and suitable price for his crop. Of course, life insurance market covers the entire age range of the population of 1000 million in India. However taking into account their economic conditions and their ability to pay the premium for some sort of life insurance cover or an annuity, the number of eligible prospects for life insurance may be put around 30 per cent of the total population viz., 300 million (Based on Profile of Housing Stock, Census 2001). It means only 21% of the total insurable population of India is covered under various life insurance schemes. With the entry of private sector players backed by foreign expertise in 2000-01, the year in which the sector was liberalized, Indian insurance market has become more vibrant. By end March 2006, out of 16 life insurers, the total number of private life insurers are 15, operating only in the remaining 20 per cent of the total market share. Therefore, the business equation of life insurance sector has shown lot of dynamics.

Although the data gathered for this investigation approach allowed only to examine the recent performance of life insurers in India, it could be interesting to obtain a dataset which would enable the approach examine the quantity demanded (However, some estimates of market potential are provided in section-III for mere understanding). This would require a different dataset that records more detailed life insurance purposes such as – the type of contracts, the monthly or yearly premium, amount insured for, etc. Further, research could also utilize the present data and data released after 2006 to evaluate the business equation of Indian life insurance sector.

Notes and References

1. Zelizer Viviana R. (1979), "Morals and Markets: The Development of Life Insurance in the United States," New York: Columbia University Press, p.53.
2. Donald E. Fischer, Ronald J. Jordan (2000), "Security Analysis and Portfolio Management," Tata McGraw Hill, p.7-11.
3. Ray P. K (1991), Reprinted 1998, "A Practical Guide to Multi-Risk Insurance for Developing Counties," Science Publishers Inc., USA, pp.132-46.
4. Narayan Chambers, Caul Shah, Petesch (1999), "*Global Synthesis Summary*," in Brown W, Churchill, "Providing Insurance To Low-

Income Households," Part 1: Primer on Insurance Principles And Products, Micro Enterprise Best Practice (MBP), p.21.

5. Bajpai.G. N, Jyothi Navara (1994), "Marketing of Insurance," Global Business Press, pp.12-14.
6. Haja Shareeff K. S. G (1999),"Indian Economy Challenges And Opportunities," Allied Publications Ltd., New Delhi, pp.47-48.
7. Wasaw Bernard (1986), "Determinants of Insurance Penetration: Cross-Country Analysis," In the Insurance Industry in Economic Development, Bernard Wasow and Raymond D. Hills, Eds, New York, New York University Press, pp.121-22.
8. Dickson G.C.A (1991), "Risk and Insurance," Chartered Insurance Institute, Study Text, p.4.
9. Boose M. A, Gokharn R. Karahan (1995), "An Empirical Estimation of the Market Demand for and Supply of Life Insurance," Paper Presented at the Annual Meeting of the American Risk and Insurance Association, pp.58-64.
10. Browne Mark J, Kihong Kim (1993), "An International Analysis Of Life Insurance Demand," *Journal Of Risk And Insurance, Vol.*60, pp.616-34.
11. Malhotra R. M (1994), "Report Of the Committee On Reforms In Insurance Sector," Ministry Of Finance, Government Of India, pp.78-97.
12. Sharma. S. P (1986),"Organization Of Indian Insurance," Allied Publications, Gwalior, p.13.
13. S. L. Rao, I Natarajan (1995), "Indian Market Demographic," Global Business Press, Delhi, p.8.
14. Brown W, Churchill C. (1999), "Providing Insurance To Low Income Households, Part 1: Primer On Insurance Principles And Products," Micro Enterprise Best Practice (MBP), p.36.
15. Berry L. L (2002), "Relationship Marketing-Emerging Perspectives of Services Marketing," Colombia University Press, pp.21-25.
16. Underwriting, the process through which insurers select what risks to insure and decide how much premium to charge for accepting those risks and by investing the premiums they have collected from insured population. Hence contract of insurance come in to force called underwritten.
17. George E. Rejda (2002), "Principles of Risk Management and Insurance," Pearson Education, Delhi, p.15.

18. Rao .D. Tripati (1999), "Life Insurance Business In India: Analysis Of Performance," *Economic And Political Weekly,* Vol. XXXIV, No.31, July 31-August 6, p.31.

19. Skipper Harold D. Jr. (1998), "The Structure Of Insurance Market," p.43, Skipper Harold .D. Jr. Eds., International Risk And Insurance Environment-Managerial Approach, Irwin McGraw Hill, pp.238-47.

20. Irkwu J. O (1991), "Risk Management In Developing Countries," Wither by And Co, London And Rolls Royce Pic (1996), Risk Management Strategy, p.13.

21. Pearson Professional Limited (1996), "Report on Insurance in Asia," London, pp.16-22.

Chapter– 7

AN ANALYSIS OF VARIATIONS IN WHEAT PRICES IN REGULATED MARKETS

S. R. Takle

Introduction

Agricultural production is of seasonal nature. It is now an established fact that both prices and arrivals of agricultural commodities are subjected to variation from one season to another within a year, due to the low capacity of the small and marginal farmers to hold stock and to obtain credit to postpone their sales, less storability of agricultural products etc. One of the most important aspects of agricultural prices is the wide range of seasonal variations, resulted many a times due to 'distress sales'. Acharya and Agrawal (1994) say that price variations are observed for agricultural commodities mainly because of the nature of agricultural production. The annual variation in prices also depends on size of the market. Mathur and Ezekeil have stated the hypothesis that there is an inverse relationship between marketed surplus (arrival) and prices of foodgrains, while Rajkrishan, Dantwala and Schutz have stated the hypothesis there that is a positive relationship between marketed surplus and prices. Thus we find two opposite views of different economists.

In this paper an attempt is made to study the seasonal and annual variation in arrivals and prices of Wheat. The specific objectives of the study are;

1. To study the seasonal variation in Market arrivals and prices of Wheat in regulated markets
2. To study the seasonal indices in Market arrivals and prices of Wheat.
3. To study the annual variations in Market arrivals and prices of Wheat

Data and Methodology

The study covers the period of ten years from 1997 to 2006. Eight regulated markets were taken for the study. The regulated markets were; Nanded, Manjlegaon, Latur, Hingoli, Manwat, Parbhani, Aurangabad and Jalna. The monthly data of arrivals and prices of Wheat were collected from the office record of the 'Agricultural Produce Market Committees'. The range between maximum and minimum, coefficients of variations and standard deviation have been worked out to study the variation in arrivals and prices

Result and Discussion

Seasonal Variation

The seasonal nature of agricultural production, low capacity of the small and marginal farmers to hold stocks of farm products and to obtain credit to postpone their sales and less storability of agricultural products are the factors which explain the variation in arrivals and prices of agricultural commodities from one season to another season within a year.

Wheat is the most important crop grown in India. The results of the obtained after analyzing the data on monthly arrivals and prices of Wheat at regulated markets are presented in Table. 1. They show that the range between maximum and minimum monthly arrivals of Wheat is the highest in Nanded (17367.10 quintals), followed by Jalna (13825.80 quintals), Aurangabad (12913.30 quintals) and Latur (10763.80 quintals)

Table 1

An Analysis of Seasonal Variation in Wheat Prices in Regulated Markets

Arrivals in Quintals
Prices in Rupees

Markets	Nanded		Manjlegaon		Latur		Hingoli		Manwat		Parbhani		Aurangabad		Jalna	
Month	Arrivals	Prices	Arrivals	Prices	Arrivals	Prices	Arrivals	Prices	Arrivals	Prices	Arrivals	Prices	Arrivals	Prices	Arrivals	Prices
Jan.	1793.70	777.50	510.60[a]	851.30	1215.80[a]	885.10	1807.50	776.70	310.40[a]	823.90	291.80[a]	844.20[b]	2402.30	855.10[a]	3273.70	828.40
Feb.	2690.10	750.40	827.80	762.80	8806.70	833.90	1829.50	781.50	931.00	780.40	583.60	793.80	5076.80	802.40	4975.50	777.60
Mar.	18921.00[b]	671.00[a]	3291.80[b]	728.70[a]	11979.60[b]	790.00[a]	6141.40[b]	714.10[a]	3792.20[b]	689.90[a]	2730.10[b]	699.50[a]	14657.00[b]	737.50	16594.50[b]	731.70[a]
April	11758.60	677.60	2761.60	798.60	10728.00	840.40	4805.60	728.10	3597.00	751.80	2701.90	779.80	11858.80	726.20[a]	16189.10	790.20
May	4374.70	695.70	1817.70	779.00	4787.90	835.50	4491.60	734.50	1416.10	743.40	1114.20	740.50	8000.70	771.20	8755.00	789.90
June	2884.70	701.60	1316.90	768.60	3683.30	808.00	2350.00	733.20	1034.00	703.90	898.20	712.60	5953.80	739.50	6970.10	773.50
July	2050.10	733.90	983.20	783.80	1559.90	819.50	1725.10	734.80	817.60	745.20	666.80	724.40	3974.90	763.00	5856.90	781.10
Aug.	2036.70	752.50	982.50	793.70	1659.10	801.90	1785.80	728.60	678.00	745.00	596.60	752.80	4441.00	771.90	5735.50	770.00
Sept.	1553.90[a]	739.20	802.40	788.50	1547.50	811.00	1646.90	783.00	565.70	742.80	454.60	756.50	4262.70	801.70	7560.10	774.30
Oct.	1626.60	736.50	917.80	800.50	1882.10	825.20	1096.90[a]	755.60	461.50	772.50	461.10	770.00	4591.10	793.20	4204.80	800.00
Nov.	1990.20	705.40	968.10	822.30	2398.60	849.50	1801.00	817.60	581.80	805.20	473.30	800.40	3887.70	827.10	3238.40	830.50
Dec.	1798.60	788.60[b]	663.40	900.40[b]	1496.10	897.40[b]	1446.40	852.00[b]	385.80	838.10[b]	359.40	815.90	1743.70[a]	802.90	2768.70[a]	879.30[b]
Avg.	4456.58	727.49	1320.32	798.18	4312.05	833.12	2577.31	761.64	1214.26	461.84	944.30	765.87	5904.21	782.64	7176.86	793.88
Range Bet. Max & Min	17367.10	117.60	2781.20	171.70	10763.80	107.40	5044.50	137.90	3481.80	148.20	2438.30	144.70	12913.30	128.90	13825.80	147.60
S.D.	5135.31	35.93	832.83	42.33	3765.16	30.77	1549.94	39.95	1147.90	42.72	821.60	41.52	3663.70	36.76	4474.65	36.01
C.V.	115.23	4.94	63.08	5.30	87.32	3.69	60.14	5.25	94.54	5.61	87.01	5.42	62.05	4.70	62.35	4.54

A = minimum level B = maximum level S.D. = standard deviation C.V.= co-efficient of variation

Source: The data monthly arrivals and average prices are compiled from the office records of regulated markets.

GRAPHS OF SEASONAL VARIATION

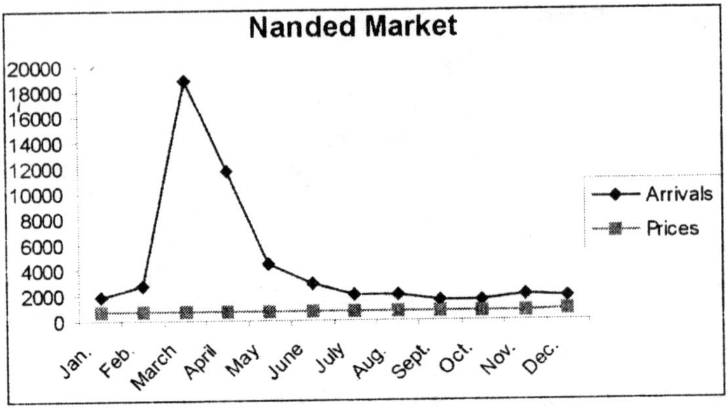

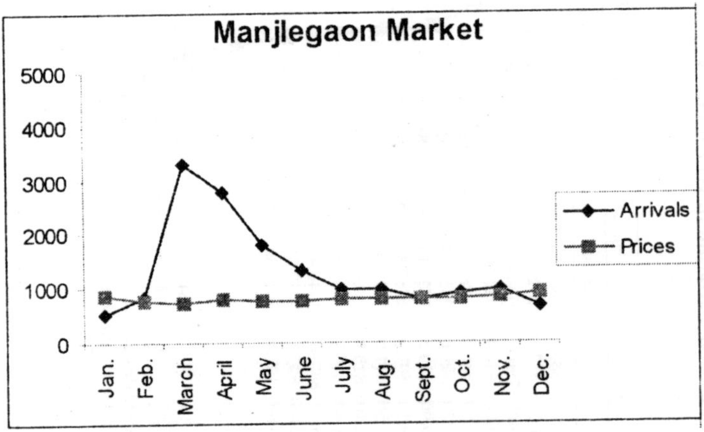

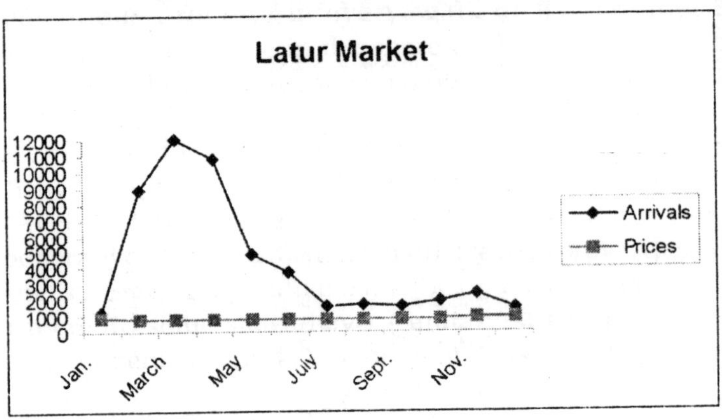

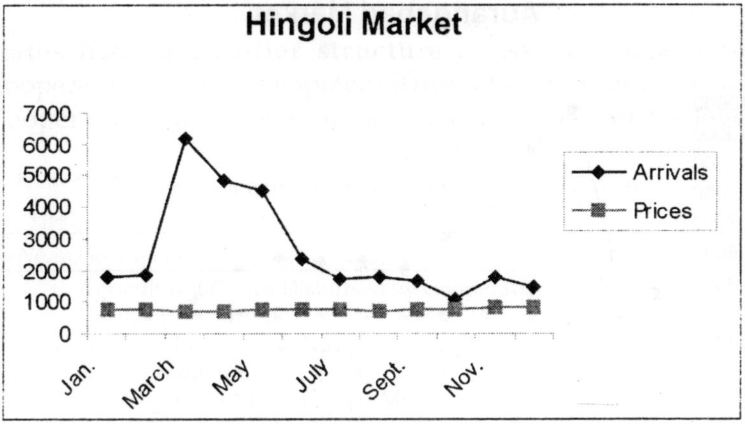
Hingoli Market
7000
6000
5000
4000
3000
2000
1000
0
Jan.
March
May
July
Sept.
Nov.
Arrivals
Prices

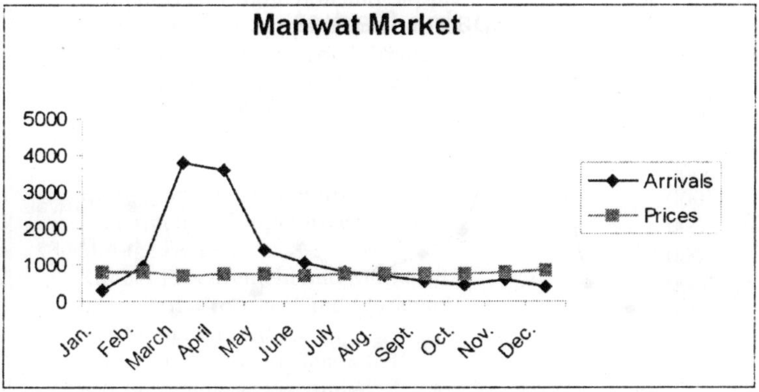
Manwat Market
5000
4000
3000
2000
1000
0
Jan.
Feb.
March
April
May
June
July
Aug.
Sept.
Oct.
Nov.
Dec.
Arrivals
Prices

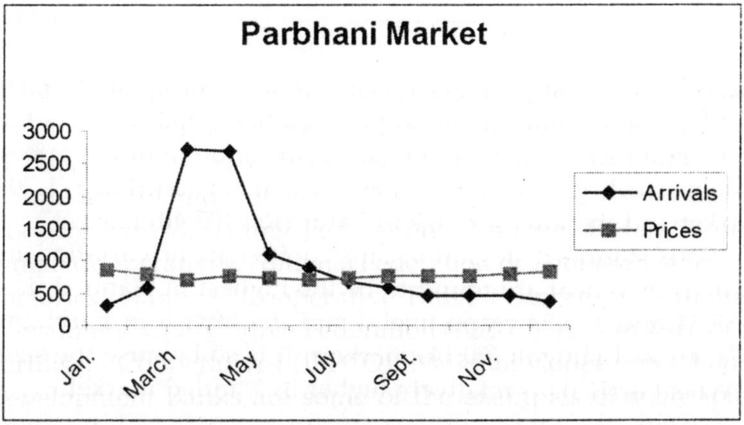
Parbhani Market
3000
2500
2000
1500
1000
500
0
Jan.
March
May
July
Sept.
Nov.
Arrivals
Prices

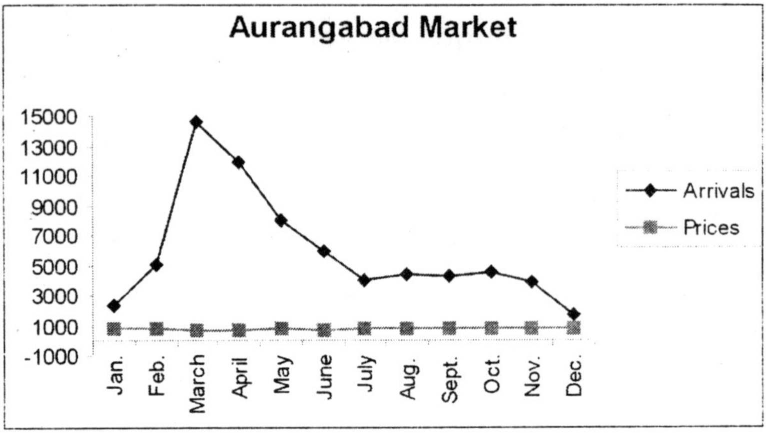

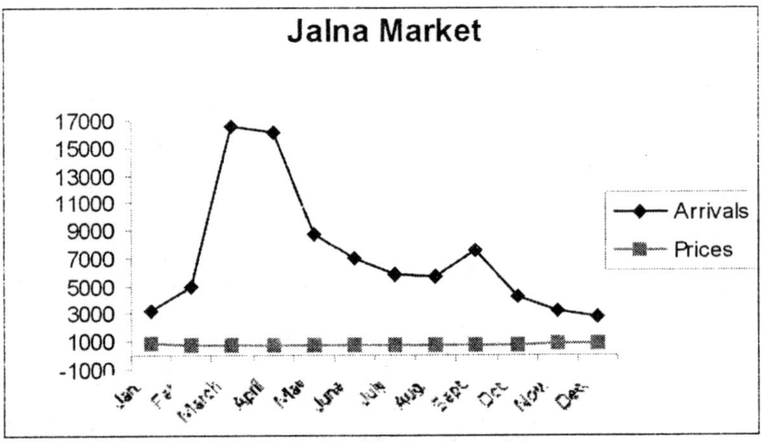

and the lowest range in arrivals is found in Parbhani (2438.80 quintals), and Manjlegaon (2781.20 quintals) markets. As far as the monthly range between maximum and minimum prices is concerned, it were the highest in Manjlegaon (Rs. 171.70) market and the lowest range in Latur (Rs. 107.40) market.

Both standard deviation and coefficient of variation in arrivals of Wheat are found to be the highest in Nanded (i.e. 5135.31 and 115.23 respectively) and the lowest in Parbhani (821.60) and Hingoli (60.14) markets. It is so because the size of Wheat arrivals is relatively higher in Nanded market.

As far as the monthly variations in prices is concerned, the value of standard deviations and coefficient of variations are found to be highest in case of the Manjlegaon (42.33) and Manwat (5.61) markets and the lowest in Latur (i.e. 30.77 and 3.69 respectively) markets. In Manjlegaon and Manwat markets arrivals of Wheat is low compared to Latur market because sugarcane and cotton is cultivated on large areas and therefore the price fluctuations are different. Further, the data in presented in Table 1 reveals that the degree of variations in monthly arrivals is highest than the monthly prices in case of Wheat. It means that the arrivals of Wheat have shown greater monthly variations than its prices

Seasonal indices of arrivals and prices of Wheat are presented in Table 2. The seasonal indices of arrivals of Wheat are found to be the highest in all markets during March, April and May and the lowest indices in July, August, September and October. But the seasonal price indices of this commodities are found to be the highest in the months of October, November, December and January and the lowest in March, April, and May. From this it is clear that when the arrivals indices of Wheat are the higher level at that time price indices of Wheat are at a lower level and vice versa. It means that the increase in arrival leads to reduction in prices and decrease in arrivals of Wheat which leads to increase in prices.

Annual Variation

Market arrivals and prices of Wheat also varied from to year. Standard deviation and coefficient of variation techniques were used to study the annual variation in arrivals and prices during the period under study.

The result presented in Table 3. shows that the range between the maximum and minimum annual arrivals of Wheat is the highest in case of Aurangabad (9498.08 quintals) market and the lowest in Manjlegaon (1727.83 quintals) market. As far as annual variations in prices concerned it is the highest in Manjlegaron (Rs. 402.75) and the lowest in Parbhani (Rs. 244.42) Market. Size of Manjlegaon market arrivals is relatively higher as compared to Parbhani market

Table 2
An Analysis of Seasonal Indices in Wheat Prices in Regulated Markets

Markets	*Nanded*		*Manjlegaon*		*Latur*		*Hingoli*		*Manwat*		*Parbhani*		*Aurangabad*		*Jalna*	
Months	*Indices of Arrivals*	*Indices of Prices*	*Indices of Arrivals*	*Indices of Prices*	*Indices of Arrivals*	*Indices of Prices*	*Indices of Arrivals*	*Indices of Prices*	*Indices of Arrivals*	*Indices of Prices*	*Indices of Arrivals*	*Indices of Prices*	*Indices of Arrivals*	*Indices of Prices*	*Indices of Arrivals*	*Indices of Prices*
Jan.	40.25	106.87	38.67	106.65	28.20	106.24	70.13	101.98	25.56	108.15	30.90	110.23	40.69	109.26	45.61	104.35
Feb.	60.36	103.15	62.70	95.57	204.23	100.09	70.98	102.61	76.67	102.44	61.80	103.65	85.99	102.52	69.33	97.95
March	424.56	92.23	249.32	91.29	277.82	94.82	238.29	93.76	312.31	90.56	289.11	91.33	248.25	94.23	231.22	92.17
April	263.85	93.14	209.16	100.05	248.79	100.87	186.46	95.60	296.23	98.68	286.13	101.82	200.85	92.79	225.57	99.54
May	98.16	95.63	137.67	97.60	111.04	100.29	174.27	96.44	116.62	97.58	117.99	96.69	135.51	98.54	121.99	99.50
June	64.73	96.44	99.74	96.29	85.42	96.99	91.18	96.27	85.15	92.39	95.12	93.04	100.84	94.49	97.12	97.43
July	46.00	100.88	74.47	98.20	36.18	98.37	66.93	96.48	67.33	97.82	70.61	94.59	67.32	97.49	81.61	98.39
Aug.	45.70	103.44	74.41	99.44	38.48	96.25	69.29	95.66	55.84	97.79	63.18	98.29	75.22	98.63	79.92	96.99
Sept.	34.87	101.61	60.77	98.79	35.89	97.35	63.90	102.80	46.59	97.50	48.14	98.78	72.20	102.44	105.34	97.53
Oct.	36.50	101.24	69.51	100.29	43.65	99.05	42.56	99.21	38.01	101.40	48.83	100.54	77.76	101.35	58.59	100.77
Nov.	44.66	96.96	73.32	103.02	55.63	101.97	69.88	107.35	47.91	105.69	50.12	104.51	65.85	105.68	45.12	104.61
Dec.	40.36	108.40	50.25	112.81	34.70	107.72	56.12	111.86	31.77	110.01	38.06	106.53	29.53	102.59	38.58	110.76

Source : Indices are based on data on monthly arrivals and average prices compiled from the office record of regulated markets.

GRAPHS OF SEASONAL INDICES

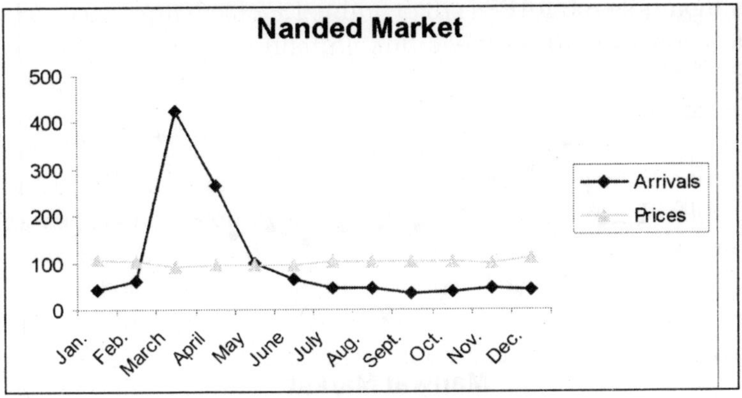

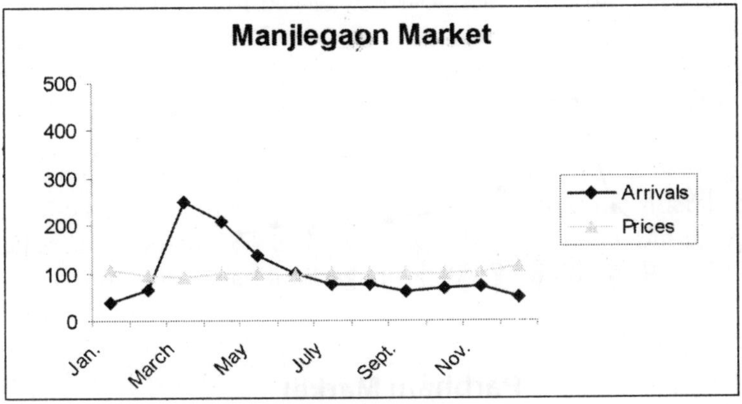

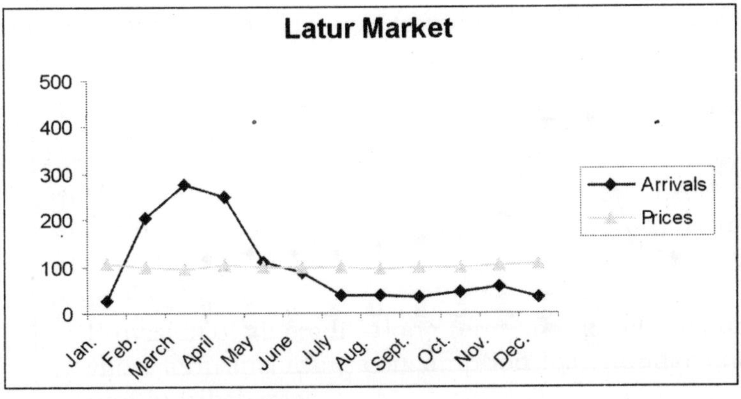

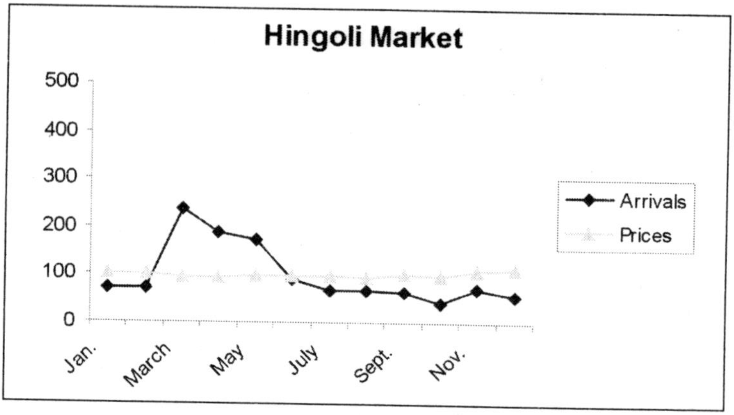
Hingoli Market
500
400
300
200
100
0
Arrivals
Prices
Jan.
March
May
July
Sept.
Nov.

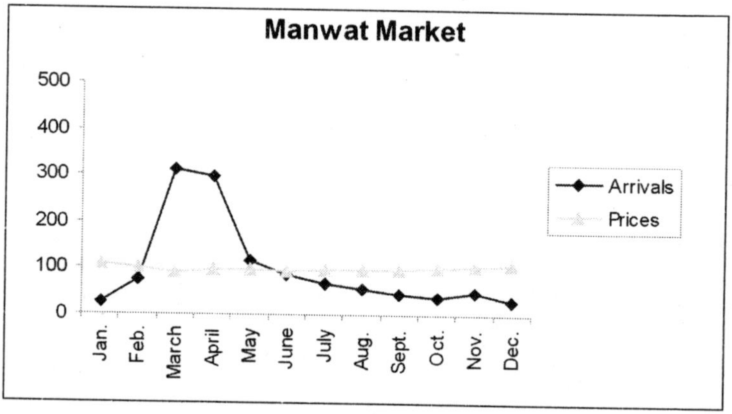
Manwat Market
500
400
300
200
100
0
Arrivals
Prices
Jan.
Feb.
March
April
May
June
July
Aug.
Sept.
Oct.
Nov.
Dec.

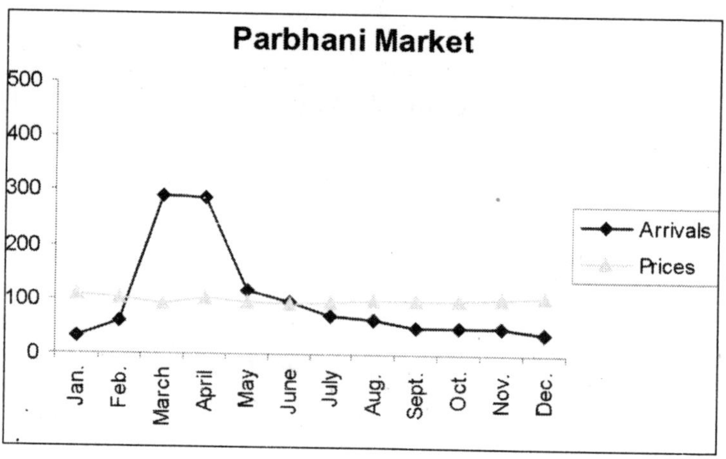
Parbhani Market
500
400
300
200
100
0
Arrivals
Prices
Jan.
Feb.
March
April
May
June
July
Aug.
Sept.
Oct.
Nov.
Dec.

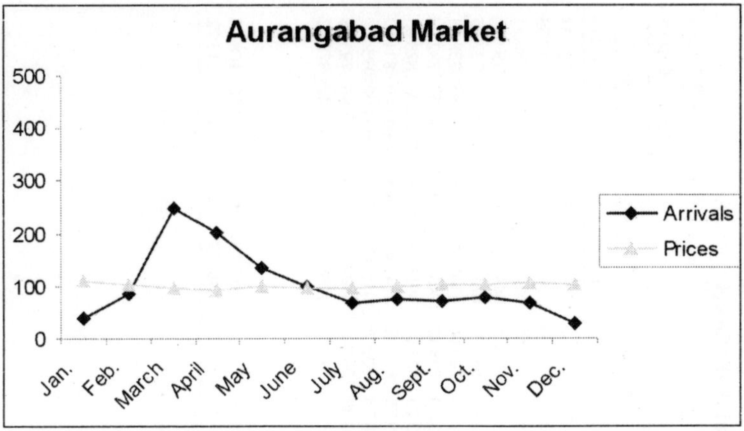

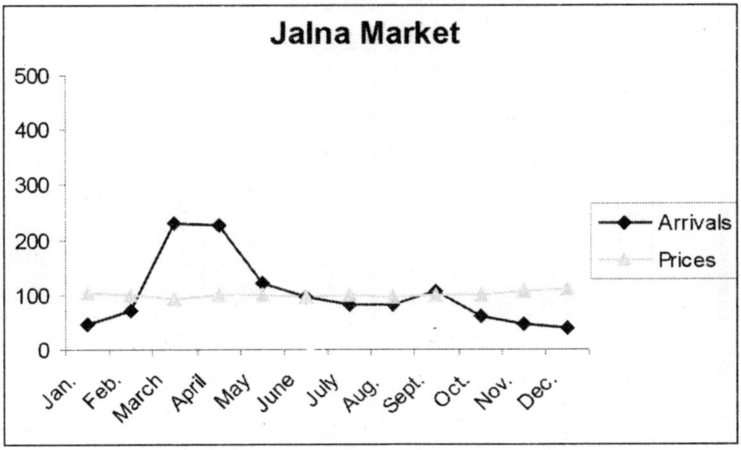

The standard deviation and coefficient of variations in arrivals were found to be the highest in case of Aurangabad (2782.29) and Parbhani (106.75) markets respectively and lowest in Manjlegaon (624.28) and Jalna (43.65) markets respectively.

The highest degree of variation in arrivals at Aurangabad and Parbhani Market may be attributed to larger variation in average and yield of this crop. But the interesting thing to note here is that both the standard deviation and coefficient of variation in annual prices of Wheat were found to be the

Table 3

An Analysis of Annual Variations in Wheat Prices in Regulated Markets

Arrivals in Quintals
Prices in Rupees

Markets	Nanded		Manjlegaon		Latur		Hingoli		Manwat		Parbhani		Aurangabad		Jalna	
Year	Arrivals	Prices	Arrivals	Prices	Arrivals	Prices	Arrivals	Prices	Arrivals	Prices	Arrivals	Prices	Arrivals	Prices	Arrivals	Prices
1997	1999.75	653.92	815.17	659.17[a]	5093.17	702.08[a]	1404.33	700.25	333.75	693.75	115.25[a]	702.00	2984.17[a]	707.83	3905.92	721.33
1998	1166.25	630.33[a]	811.33	702.08	986.08	766.25	1203.50	633.92[a]	634.67	753.00	584.67	753.00	1915.33	677.67[a]	2178.83[a]	730.58
1999	880.83[a]	719.75	892.33	726.83	3631.58	753.33	1177.67	702.50	538.33	749.58	419.67	749.58	5343.33	702.42	5635.50	730.33
2000	4343.08	679.67	980.75	709.67	5015.17	726.17	4417.25	667.00	1449.25	689.42[a]	1449.25	689.42[a]	8044.92	737.50	9380.17	718.92[a]
2001	4238.08	686.25	2481.17[b]	747.67	7224.00	824.17	2638.75	722.50	3683.83[a]	693.00	3686.58[b]	693.00	8747.92	777.17	10950.00	727.75
2002	3853.25	692.00	1534.83	791.67	3475.50	811.25	3396.25	712.42	2323.50	702.17	1384.33	745.00	4501.00	817.83	7445.83	757.58
2003	6925.42	739.08	2398.17	837.25	906.42[a]	907.83	3919.00	761.83	1751.33	761.25	593.50	758.42	7437.25	802.08	11624.25[b]	792.67
2004	7830.00	776.33	950.08	888.08	3161.00	874.08	1535.08	845.25	410.50	823.00	163.25	823.00	3911.33	770.92	3801.08	828.83
2005	5186.92	724.50	753.33[a]	857.50	8161.83[b]	871.83	1045.83[a]	857.58	243.00[a]	781.83	439.75	811.42	4743.42	834.67	6603.00	834.92
2006	8142.17[b]	973.08[b]	1586.00	1061.92[b]	5465.75	1094.17[b]	5035.42[b]	1013.17[b]	774.42	971.42[b]	606.75	933.83[b]	11413.42[b]	998.33[b]	10244.00	1095.83[b]
Avg	4456.58	727.49	1320.32	798.18	4312.05	833.12	2577.31	761.64	1214.26	761.84	944.30	765.87	5904.21	782.64	7176.86	793.88
Range Bet. Max & Min	7261.33	342.75	1727.83	402.75	7255.42	392.08	3989.58	379.25	3440.83	282.00	3571.33	244.42	9498.08	320.67	9445.42	376.92
S.D.	2483.24	91.11	624.28	112.59	2255.75	108.12	1433.74	107.68	1049.94	81.53	1008.08	70.50	2782.29	87.24	3132.58	108.95
C.V.	55.72	12.52	47.28	14.11	52.31	12.98	55.63	14.14	86.47	10.70	106.75	9.21	47.12	11.15	43.65	13.72

A = minimum level B = maximum level S.D.= standard deviation C.V.= co-efficient of variation

Source: The data monthly arrivals and average prices are compiled from the office records of regulated markets.

GRAPHS OF ANNUAL VARIATIONS

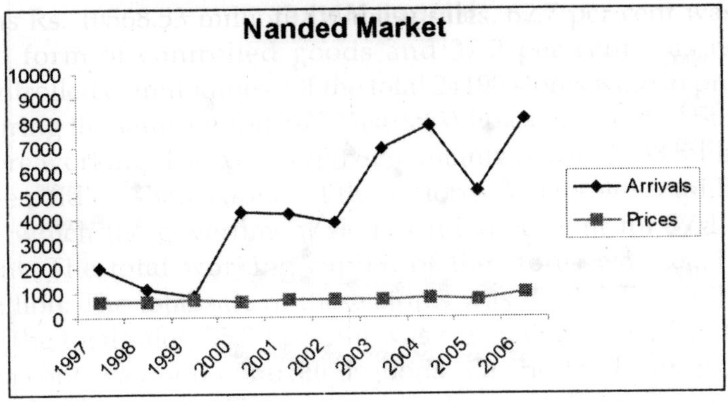

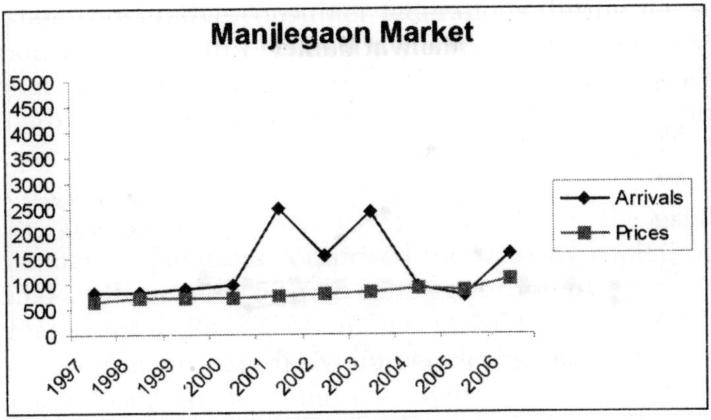

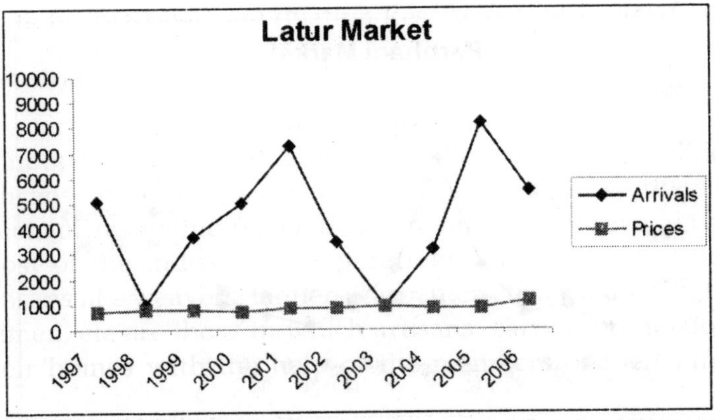

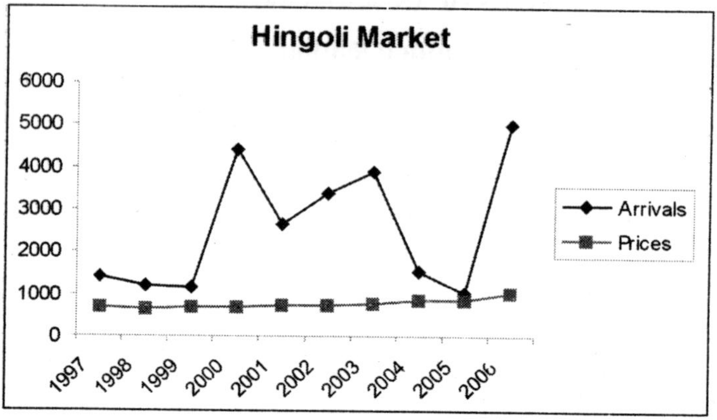
Hingoli Market
6000
5000
4000
3000
2000
1000
0
1997
1998
1999
2000
2001
2002
2003
2004
2005
2006
Arrivals
Prices

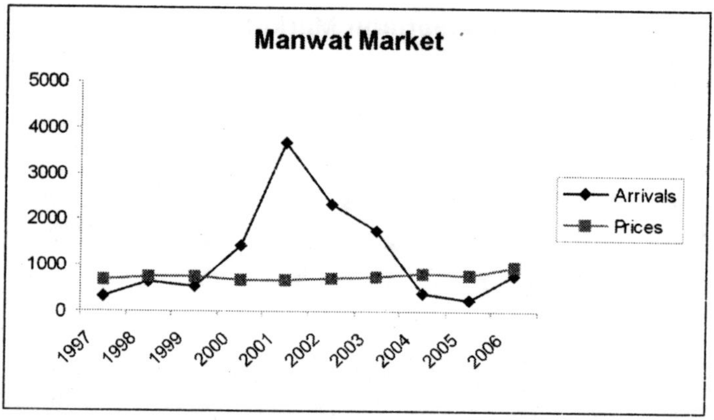
Manwat Market
5000
4000
3000
2000
1000
0
1997
1998
1999
2000
2001
2002
2003
2004
2005
2006
Arrivals
Prices

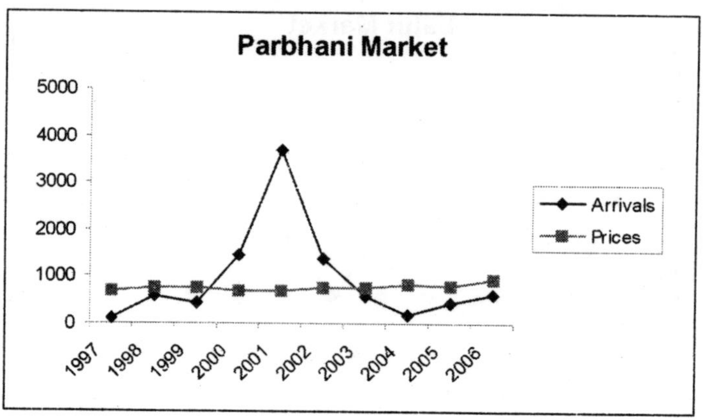
Parbhani Market
5000
4000
3000
2000
1000
0
1997
1998
1999
2000
2001
2002
2003
2004
2005
2006
Arrivals
Prices

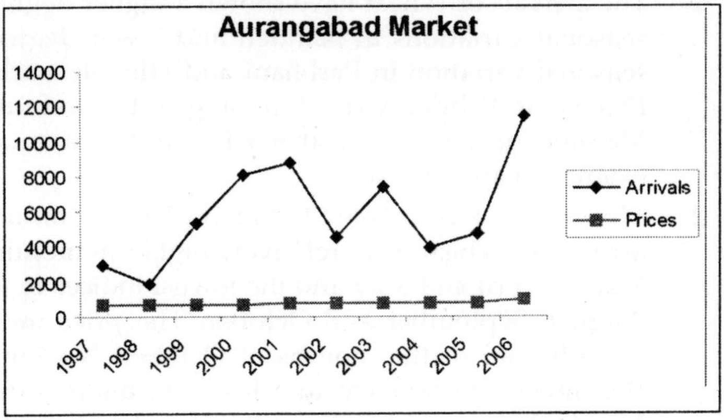

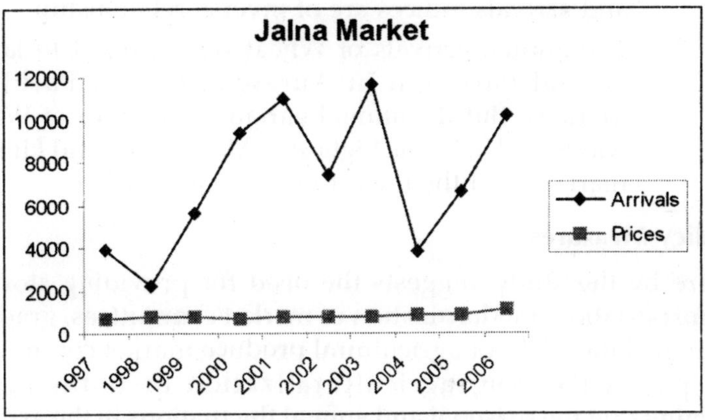

highest in case of Manjlegaon (112.59) market and Hingoli (14.14) Markets and the lowest for Parbhani (i.e. 7.50 and 9.21 respectively) Market. It means that the prices of Wheat have been subjected to lesser year to year variation in Parbhani market. On the contrary, they have varied to larger extent in Manjlegaon and Hingoli market. The larger annual variations in prices of Wheat at Manjlegaon and Hingoli markets may be due to greater fluctuations in arrivals by natural factor, and undeveloped market.

Conclusion

Form the above discussions, it is clear,

1. The arrivals of Wheat have shown a higher degree of seasonal variations in Nanded and lower degree of seasonal variation in Parbhani and Hingoli markets. Prices of Wheat varied to a greater extent in Manjlegaon and Manwat market and to a smaller extent in Latur market.
2. This study has revealed that indices of monthly arrivals of Wheat were relatively higher in months of March, April and May and the lowest indices in July, August, September and October. The price indices were higher in the months of October, November, December and January, and lower in the months of March, April and May. Form this it is clear that prices and arrivals indices are of inverse relationship.
3. The annual arrivals of Wheat were subject to larger annual variation in Aurangabad and Parbhani Markets. But the annual variation in prices of Wheat was found to be the highest in Manjlegaon and Hingoli markets and the lowest in Parbhani market.

Policy Measures

Here by the study suggests the need for providing storage, transportation, modernization of market committees, grading, loan facilities, role of agricultural produce market committees in prices fixation, agriculturalization of industry for minimizing the seasonal and annual fluctuations in the arrivals and prices of Wheat. It will definate help on stabilizing the Wheat income of the growers .

Reference

Achraya S.S. and Agrawal N.L. (1994), Agricultural Prices-Analysis and Policy, Oxford and IBH publishing Co. Pvt. Ltd. New Delhi.

Achraya S.S. and Agrawal N.L. (1996), Agricultural Marketing in India, Oxford and IBH publishing Co. Pvt. Ltd. New Delhi.

Brahma Prakash and Sushila Srivastva (1993), Analysis of Market Arrivals and Prices of Gram in Utter Pradesh, Indian Journal of Agricultural Economics Vol. 48, No. 3.

Indrasena Reddy (1995), Price Behaviour of Agricultural Commodities, Indian Journal of Marketing, Vol. 23, No. 6-7

Takle S.R. (2002), Behaviour of Market Arrivals and Prices of Rabi Jowar in Marathwada, Indian Journal of Agricultural marketing, Vol. 16 No. 2

Takle S.R. and Bhise V.B. (2007), Behaviour of Market Prices of Agricultural Commodities, Serials Publication, New Delhi. (India).

CHAPTER–8

REFORMS & HUMAN DEVELOPMENT

Lakshya Pal Singh Shekhawat
Protyaya Mukherji

Introduction

The globalization of economies and greater political alignment has seeded the conviction and commitment to human development as never before. There is now a clear realization that human development in its broadest sense must be achieved on a global scale. The Millennium Goals have been adopted on this basis, United Nations Development Programme (UNDP) and World Bank programmes support national initiatives and monitor progress and the global community of scientists, economists, agronomists et al are focusing their energies towards addressing the human development agenda.

This article attempts to put together for the lay person a basic understanding of the Concept of Human Development and identifies some of the fundamental implications of its use as a framework for development together with the Millennium Development Goals. It goes on to examine the standing of the large emerging economies in this landscape, the progress against some of the Millennium Development Goals and goes on to identify (a) India as the nation state that can potentially make the largest impact on Human Development in the shortest time and (b) South Asia and Sub-Saharan African as the regions which need to catch up on the Human Development scorecard. The policy directions in India as well as South Asia and Sub-Saharan African regions are then examined in detail from the perspective of the national government and the World Bank.

The Concept of Human Development

Human development is about creating an environment in which people can leverage their full potential and live with dignity. Economic growth and the rise of national incomes is an important element–a necessary but insufficient condition for human development. Fundamental to human development is building capabilities to improve the range of things that people can achieve. The most basic capabilities for human development are to lead long and healthy lives, to be knowledgeable, to have access to the resources needed for a decent standard of living and to be able to participate in the life of the community.

This way of looking at development, often forgotten in the immediate concern with accumulating commodities and financial wealth, has been propounded by philosophers, economists and political leaders for ages. People must be free to exercise their choices and to participate in decision-making that affects their lives. In this sense, human development shares complete alignment with human rights[1]

Origins of the Approach

The drive towards development in the 1980s was premised almost entirely on economic growth and the inherent assumption that such growth would automatically trickle down in an inclusive manner to benefit all sections of society. Researchers like the Pakistani economist Dr. Mahbub ul Haq and Nobel Prize winner Dr. Amartya Sen figured out that the human costs of Structural Adjustment Programmes were exceedingly high and contested this trickle down theory. They also pointed out that social ills such as crime, weakening of social fabric, HIV/AIDS, pollution and so on were still spreading despite strong and consistent economic growth. Consequently they urged for an alternate development model.

Meanwhile the trend towards democratization was getting increasingly stronger and political belief was progressively getting grounded on the basis of people's choices. This enabling environment and the conceptual framework provided by the economist fraternity gave impetus to establishing a human development framework–a process of enlarging people's choices, freedoms and capabilities.

There are many facets of human development. Priorities vary across and within countries and focus on different dimensions may emerge at different points of time. Some of the aspects that are currently considered most releavnt are:

- *Food security and shelter*–all of which are the fundamentals of human security but still very relevant in less developed countries.
- *Access to knowledge,* nutrition and health services and other *social infrastructure* coupled with *equity and equal opportunity* in participating in economic growth.
- *Economic growth and efficiency* in resource use as a means of bringing about greater equality and as tools for directing growth in a manner that benefits the poor, women and other marginalized groups.
- *Sustainability* for future generations in ecological, economic and social terms.
- *Participation, freedom and empowerment* through democratic governance, gender equality, civil and political rights, and cultural liberty, particularly for marginalized groups defined by urban-rural, sex, age, religion, ethnicity, physical/mental parameters, etc. [2]

It would therefore appear that the human development approach seeks to combine the socialist objectives of human security and equity with the empowerment and freedom inherent to democracies and use the capitalist principles of economic growth and efficiency in resource as leverage. The overlaying all of this with the theme of sustainability has no doubt created a very potent framework.

Reforms and Investments

The Human Development framework therefore calls for reform across many domains and imply inter alia:

- *Political Reforms*– to the extent of mandating democracy as the superior basis for national governance and as a guarantee of equity and equal opportunity for all but with priority for marginalized groups.
- *Social Reforms*– to ensure removal of all bias against rural folks, women, the elderly and the young, religious and ethnic minorities, those who are differently-abled or belong to the less favored castes. An agenda of this nature can only be progressed by committed political and constitutional support to social change driven by government as well as non-governmental organizations.
- *Economic Reforms* that not only drive growth but also direct it to achieve inclusiveness. This would call for market driven enterprises that compete on the basis of their superior competencies to satisfy consumer needs in the most efficient manner.
- *Land Reforms* that drive consolidation of agricultural land into larger holdings by mobilizing farmers to set up cooperatives or other forms of economic joint ventures to tap scale benefits and gain improved ability to access inputs, advice, technology and capital.
- *Infrastructure Creation* to ensure that the products of such competitive enterprises reach distant consumers. This calls for investment in infrastructure such as road, transport, communications, warehousing and markets as well as institutions that manage such facilities. It also calls for access to the benefits of information and communications technology.
- *Institutions* and social infrastructure in the areas of education, nutrition and health services to strengthen human capital and prepare people for market opportunities.

It is of course for national and sub-national governments at all levels to decide on their respective focus areas and accordingly plan for, fund and build the institutions to take the agenda forward. In the process, the governing institutions need to create the social momentum, adopt the legal framework, trigger the financial motivators that would be appropriate to their circumstances and best suited to bring about the development of the people, by the people, and for the people.

Global agencies have their role to play as well. Their role would be to convince national and sub-national governments to adopt the human development model, engage in and support research to aseess priorities for each region and nation state, catalyse the right public debate and encourage consequential policy recommendations.[3]

Measures of Human Development

The Human Development Index

The success or otherwise of the Human Development Model needs to be tested and appropriate measures need to be in place for this. The Human Development Index (HDI) developed by Amartya Sen and Mahbub ul Haq with help from several others has been used by the UNDP in its annual Human Development Report. HDI has its limitations but does address the wider aspects of development like life expectancy, literacy, education, standard of living and GDP per capita. It is therefore useful to determine whether a country is developed (HDI>0.8), developing (0.8>HDI>0.5) or under-developed (HDI<0.5).

According to the HDI classification, 70 countries are listed as high or developed, 85 as medium or developing and 22 countries as low or under-developed. The top half of the developed countries is largely from North America, Western Europe including Scandinavia, Oceania and a smattering of other countries like Japan, South Korea and Singapore. The HDI in such cases exceed 0.875. Most countries at the low end are from sub-Saharan Africa. The classification of HDI on the basis of regions is tabulated below:[4]

Region	*HDI*
OECD	0.916
Central, Eastern Europe & CIS	0.808
Latin America & Caribbean	0.803
East Asia and the Pacific	0.771
ASEAN	0.708
Arab States	0.699
South Asia	0.611
Sub Saharan Africa	0.493
World	0.743
Developing Countries	0.691

The Human Poverty Index

The Human Poverty Index (HPI) offers an alternative measure and enlarges the definition beyond mere economic poverty to other features of deprivation:

(a) Survival rights as represented by probability of not surviving to ages 40 and 60,

(b) Knowledge, measured by illeteracy and

(c) Living standards which, is measured for OECD countries by the percentage of the population below the income poverty line and for non-OECD countries by the percentage of the population without access to safe water and the percentage of underweight children.

The findings based on HPI have not been separately reviewed in this article as these are unlikely to differ from those based on HDI indicators.

The Gender-related Development Index

The gender-related development index (GDI), measures achievements using the same parameters as the HDI but captures inequalities in achievement between women and men. The greater the gender disparity in basic human development, the lower is a country's GDI relative to its HDI. The GDI for the BRIC countries is tabulated below:[5]

Bias of a significant magnitude is visible in India relative to the other selected countries with women lagging on education.

	GDI as % of HDI	Life Expectancy	Adult Literacy	Education Enrollment
		(Females as % of Males)		
Russia	99.8	123.1	99.5	110.2
China	99.8	104.7	91.0	98.6
Brazil	99.7	110.9	100.4	104.2
India	97.0	104.7	65.2	87.7

Millennium Development Goals

The UN Millennium Development Goals were agreed on at the United Nations Millennium Summit in September 2000 and nearly 190 countries have subsequently signed up.[6] The Millennium Development Goals are intended to drive Human Development globally. The objectives that are targeted to be achieved by 2015 are:

- Reducing Poverty & Hunger by half
- Achieving universal education by ensuring all Children get the benefit of primary education
- Empowering women by eliminating gender disparity at all levels of education
- Reducing Child mortality by two thirds, and Caring for Mothers and reducing mortality ratio by three quarters
- Combating Disease and reversing the spread of HIV/ AIDS, Malaria and other major diseases.

That apart, the Millennium Development Goals also have targeted many other specific goals within its broad ambit of operation like integrating the principles of sustainable development into country policies to reverse loss of environmental resources, reduce by half the proportion of people without sustainable access to safe drinking water among other targets

Millennium Development Goals-Progress

While writing this article, progress against three of the eight Millennium Development Goals has been examined.

Reducing Poverty & Hunger

The pursuit of human development and consequential reforms are showing positive results. According to World Bank data, the number of people in the world who lived in extreme poverty (living on less than $1 a day) fell from nearly 1.5 billion to just under 1 billion between 1981 and 2004. The Middle East, North Africa, Europe and Central Asia regions had essentially eliminated extreme poverty by 1981. The transition economies of Europe and Central Asia, which moved out of communist and socialist systems to adopt democracy and free market economies, saw poverty rates rise in the 1990s and then fall. Nearly 800 million poor people lived in East Asia—over half of the global total. By 2004, extraordinary progress, led by China, dramatically lowered poverty incidence. Consequently, 630 million people exited from extreme poverty and the region's share of total poverty declined from 58 per cent to just 9 per cent.

Concurrently, poverty fell in South Asia from 52 percent of the population in 1981 to 32 per cent in 2004, but absolute numbers have been persistent at around 470 million people. However, accelerating growth in India has put South Asia on track. While Latin America and the Caribbean has stagnated, with modest poverty reduction, Sub-Saharan Africa lags behind targets. Poverty incidence hovered around 46 per cent between the early 1980s and 1999, and declined to 41 per cent in 2004. Despite this better trend, the absolute number of poor is still around 300 million.[7]

Such optimism is founded on some major success stories. An example of this is NERICA, or New Rice for Africa–a hybrid between the Asian and African rice. This high yielding, drought resistant and protein-rich variety has contributed to food security and improved nutrition in several countries such as Congo, Ivory Coast, Kenya, Mali, Nigeria, Togo and Uganda and improved the standard of living of the farmers themselves. Prior to the introduction of NERICA, rice production in sub-Saharan Africa was being outstripped by rapid population growth by the mid-1990s. The resulting rice imports were taxing foreign reserves by nearly US$1 billion annually.[8]

Educating All Children

Globally, the primary completion rate has increased from 63 per cent in 1990 to an estimated 83 per cent in 2005. The pace of improvement has accelerated significantly since 2000 in the regions of North Africa, South Asia, and Sub-Saharan Africa consequent to the increasing focus given in these regions to universalizing primary education.

The surge in enrolment brings immense challenges to the entire learning infrastructure, from the physical building, to the class size, to the teachers. Despite this, countries such as Burundi, Congo, Ethiopia, Ghana, Kenya, Malawi, Mozambique, Tanzania and Uganda have abolished school fees, which have led to a surge in enrolment.[9] In Kenya, enrolment of primary school children increased dramatically with 1.2 million extra children in school in 2003 alone; by 2004, the number had climbed to 7.2 million, of which 84 percent were of primary school age.[10]

Latin America and the Caribbean, despite starting from a higher base, have also sustained an exceptionally strong rate of progress. The number of countries that have achieved universal primary completion increased from 37 in 2000 to 52 in 2005. What is extremely encouraging is that low-income countries such as Bolivia, Indonesia, and Kenya feature in this list.

Despite these positive trends, the goal of universal primary completion by 2015 will be difficult to reach as 57 of 152 developing countries unlikely to reach the goal on current trends. Reliable data is not available for 33 countries; they are unlikely to be on target. 65 per cent of African countries are seriously off track and are unlikely to reach the goal before 2040.Among fragile states, only 11 per cent have achieved universal primary completion or are on track to doing so, and 50 per cent are considered seriously off track.

Empowering Women

A country's mortality rates usually fall, fertility rates decline, and the health and education prospects of the next generation improve when its women are educated and better able to care for their children. Uneducated women also find it difficult to find employment and participate in governance processes. The resultant discrimination by the state, their community and family puts them at a disadvantage throughout their lives. The under performance of half the human capital limits progress for the country and society.

For many poor families, the economic value of girls working at home exceeds the perceived benefits from their schooling. The differences between schooling of boys and girls are greatest in regions with the lowest primary school completion rates and the lowest average incomes. Obviously, public awareness of the benefits of educating needs to be built up to overcome the social and economic obstacles that keep parents from sending their daughters to school. Improving the accessibility of schools and their quality and affordability is also necessary.

Globally, 55 per cent of countries achieved the first target of eliminating gender disparity in primary and secondary education by 2005. Latin America and Europe and Central Asia have achieved this goal and East Asia and Pacific are getting there. In Middle East and North Africa, girls are steadily overcoming the strong bias against them. But huge improvement is required in Sub-Saharan Africa and South Asia, where only 20 per cent and 35 per cent, respectively, of countries reached the 2005 target.

In these regions, where large numbers of children are out of school, girls are at a severe disadvantage. However, there is wide variation across states in terms of performance on the gender equality scorecard.[11] As usual, fragile states lag behind in achieving gender parity in enrollment, and more than 50 per cent of these countries do not have sufficient data to assess their progress. Although the gender gap in school enrollments has declined in most regions, the *gender gap* in labor force participation remains. Age patterns of labor force participation show that compared to young men, fewer young women make the transition from school to work, and this gender gap tends to persist throughout the life cycle. However, the size of this gap varies considerably across regions. The gender gap is the largest in South Asia and the smallest in Europe and Central Asia.

Nonetheless, several positive developments have been reported as well.[12] In Kuwait, women participated in parliamentary elections for the first time ever in 2006. Before and during the poll, Billboards, posters on buses and advertisements on television urged women to let their voices be heard. A leading expert on Islamic law came from Morocco to hold seminars on Islam and women's political participation. 35% of eligible women voted a participation rate higher than in some long-established democracies.[13]

Summary Findings

It would be apt at this point to summarize the discussions thus far. Very clearly, human development as a concept has been widely accepted and for good reason. The escape of 630 million people in East Asia from extreme poverty within a quarter of a century is abundant proof of the concept and evidence of the results that can be brought forth by focused attention to reforms synchronized with the Millennium Goals as in China. Nonetheless, the progress though laudable is falling short of targets by a significant distance and is not universal. The strong showing of the BRIC states - Brazil, Russia, India and China - is improving the global HDI indices; however, India in particular has serious distance to travel and can make a huge difference to human development in South Asia if it gets its act right. Not surprisingly, South Asia is lagging and generally Sub-Saharan Africa is seriously behind on all parameters of human development. The fragile states remain a problem set and promise little improvement.

Human Development in South Asia

The above discussion makes it imperative to take a closer look at what is happening in South Asia. More than one billion people live in South Asia and according to the Human Development Foundation, Schaumburg, Illinois, USA; the annual per capita expenditure on human priority areas of basic education, primary health care, family planning, safe drinking water, and nutritional programs is just $ 3 in Pakistan and $2 dollars in Bangladesh. To put this in perspective one might compare to other Asian nations such as Malaysia ($123) and Korea ($133).[14]

East Asian nations have invested in Human Development as a key strategy of economic growth. Obviously South Asia has not, as a result of which all countries in South Asia are at the lower end of Human Development. While South Asia' share in global income is only 2% its share in global arms imports is about 20%. In Pakistan, soldiers outnumber doctors by 10 to 1. This situation needs to change and serious money needs to be found in national budgets for agriculture, education, health and nutrition.[15]

	HDI Rank	*HDI*	*Life Expectancy*	*Literacy*	*Education Enrollment Ratio*	*GDP–PPP US $*
Maldives	100	0.741	67.0	96.3	65.8	5261
Sri Lanka	99	0.743	71.6	90.7	62.7	4595
Iran	94	0.759	70.2	82.4	72.8	7968
India	128	0.619	63.7	61	63.8	3452
Pakistan	136	0.551	64.6	49.9	40.0	2370
Nepal	142	0.534	62.6	48.6	58.1	1550
Bhutan	133	0.579	64.7	47.0	N.a.	N.a.
Bangladesh	140	0.547	63.1	47.5	56.0	2053

India, which is the big daddy of the region, has to take the lead. It has the financial capacity to do so on the back of its aggressive GDP growth (which has been of the order of 9% in the past three years), improving fiscal balance, strong capital flows. It has benchmark education institutions (Indian Institutes of Technology are as good as any) and a strong scientific and technology base (good enough for very credible nuclear, missile and satellite development programmes). It has a corporate sector that is demonstrating increasing commitment to CSR activities through Industry-Academia partnerships (Infosys), social development (Tatas) and induction of IT and Communications led benefits to the farming community (ITC). And all of this is backed up by a democracy that has now stood the test of time and a population that is young and will remain so all the way to 2050!

Fortunately, the national government is at least beginning to take notice. The Union Finance Minister Mr. P. Chidambaram was reported as "This country will hold together only if we give everyone in India a stake in the future of India ... We cannot build an inclusive society, unless every institution of governance consciously sheds its biases and prejudices that work for every section of the people." Again, sometime in May 2007 he said that the good news was that the working age population in India would grow to 500 million people and accept the downside that 50 per cent of these children would drop out by the time they reached Class V.[16] and has expressed his intent to raise the spending on education to 19 per cent of the Plan outlay during the Eleventh Plan

However, increased spending alone cannot be the panacea for all that is wrong. The system needs overhauling so that corruption is weeded out and the funding reaches its destination. This applies not only to India but to the region as a whole.[17]

Corruption Percentage Index (CPI)	*CPI Rank*	*CPI Score*
India	71	2.7
Pakistan	79	2.3
Bangladesh	91	0.4

The failure of Indian primary education is hard to escape. Sixty years after India's political independence, India was placed 126th out of 175 countries ranked in the 2006 Human Development Report. India's adult literacy rate was a dismal 61%, below Cameroon (68%), Angola, Congo, Uganda (67%), Rwanda (65%), and Malawi (64%). That 40% of today's Indian adults cannot even "both read and write a short, simple statement related to their everyday life" implies that they did not get the equivalent of the most basic of primary education. Compare that to China's 90% adult literacy.[18]

It is necessary to reverse the "talent-drain" that has taken place over the years. The human capital flight of this order is enormously expensive and is even more of a burden when the training is publicly funded. When a trained engineer migrates to the US, it is totally indistinguishable from a gift of US$ 100,000 from India to the US. Over the years, the total implicit subsidy from India to the US could be estimated to be of the order of hundred billion dollars. The need is therefore to create the right environment to retain superior talent.

A more comprehensive indication of the priorities for the national government came through on Jan.17, 2008 while the Finance Minister was speaking at a session entitled Indices for Development: Need for change at the Partnership Summit organized by the Confederation of Indian Industry. According to the Minister:

(a) Growth is undoubtedly the most important indicator of development and should remain the first priority of his government. It creates more employment, generates more opportunities in the hinterland and gives the state more resources to increase social spending,

(b) It is true that there is no one-to-one correlation between high income and a good quality life. Equally, there is no trade-off between economic growth and positive social outcomes.

(c) Development indicators other than growth certainly important. Poverty cannot be described just as the absence of income. Equally important are characteristics such as lack of education and healthcare, absence of skills for getting high value employment, no ownership of assets and no access to capital.

(d) Accordingly, the medium term objective is to increase government spending on health and sanitation in rural areas,

(e) In the longer term, more people have to be weaned away from agriculture. We do not need to have 65 million people engaged in agriculture in order to produce food for one billion people.[19]

This view on agriculture is broadly reflected in the approach of the *World Bank's* World Development Report 2008: Agriculture for Development in so far as South Asia is concerned. The report identifies agriculture as a vital unit for growth, food security and poverty reduction especially in South Asia and even more so in Sub-Saharan Africa and its diagnosis and recommendations are discussed in the next section.

Role of Agriculture in Development

South Asia

Asia's fast growing economies remain home to over 770 million people living on less than US$1 per day, and 80 percent of them live in rural areas. The top priority is to generate rural jobs by diversifying into labor-intensive high value agriculture and creating a viable non-farm sector in secondary towns. Investments in human capital are needed to prepare and migrate rural people to such jobs. Reducing the environmental backlash of intensive agriculture and confronting acute land and water scarcity are also areas of priority.

In these transforming countries, agriculture is no longer a major source of economic growth (e.g. In India it now accounts for less than 19% of the GDP). However, poverty remains overwhelmingly rural. Ninety eight percent of the rural populations in South Asia are in transforming countries[20] where the gap between urban and rural incomes is widening. The transition of people out of agriculture and rural areas is not keeping pace with the restructuring of economies away from agriculture due to lack of skills, rigidities in land and labor markets and social and community ties. These challenges, as discussed earlier have not been addressed well. With growing political attention to these widening income disparities, there are strong pressures to better use the powers of agriculture for development.

Common and diverse structural features that must be considered in designing an appropriate policy agenda are identified:

(a) In Asia, the average farm size is already quite small—a mere 0.4 to 0.5 hectares on average and *declining* due to *demographic pressures.* This together with growing landlessness puts huge pressures on rural jobs.

(b) Fresh water supplies are already fully used and escalating demands for industrial, urban, and environmental uses will reduce the water available to agriculture. *Water scarcity* is projected to worsen with climate change and rising demand in large parts of India.

(c) Some rural areas have prospered with overall economic growth, but others have stagnated with high levels of poverty. Lagging areas are found in several states in eastern and central India. But some of those areas, have good potential for agricultural growth and could be future breadbaskets.

(d) The *political pressure of farmers* to reduce the urban-rural income gap through protection and subsidies is increasing. This is exerting pressure on consumer prices of food buyers. Subsidies on inputs such as water and fertilizer distribute benefits to larger farmers and distort fiscal priorities away from investment in rural infrastructure.

The report therefore emphasizes on contract farming and the integration of small landholders to processors and retailers supported by technology and micro-finance. Reforms in irrigation and removal of water and electricity subsidies are advocated towards improving water productivity. The adverse environmental impact of intensive agricultural systems and agrochemical and animal waste pollution, is identified as a priority. More sustainable agricultural practices combining the right incentives through input and output prices, application of improved management technologies such as integrated pest and nutrient management, and better regulation are necessary.

Productivity growth in lagging regions rests on major investments in soil and water management, in agricultural research, and in new approaches to extension, supported by reforms in pricing and marketing for grains.

The consequential growth in agriculture can drive other sectors such as processed foods. Regional agricultural clusters for processing and packaging of high-value products can absorb subcontracting from urban-based industries. Investments in infrastructure and skills and improvements in the investment climate for the private sector are therefore the policy priorities. Developing land market to enable small farms to consolidate for efficient operation and to shift labor to non-farm activities and migration is also a priority. For migration to be effective, serious investment in education is a pre-requisite. However, some will be left behind and they need to be supported with well-governed rural employment schemes—including rural infrastructure, reforestation, soil conservation structures, small dams, and de-silting of canals and ponds. Significant monitoring, accountability mechanisms, and rigorous evaluations are needed to ensure effective and equitable resource use.

In India, the Union Cabinet on June 21, 2007 approved an Integrated Strategy for Promotion of Agri-business and has significant commonality with the World Bank's position on South Asia. With a view to trebling the size of the processed food sector; enhancing farmer incomes, generating employment opportunities and providing choice to consumer at affordable prices, by increasing level of processing of perishables from 6% to 20%, value addition from 20% to 35% and share in global food trade from about 1.5% to 3%, the strategy document calls for the following:

(a) Detailed mapping of the food cluster in country; with Clusterization of farming in the shape of contract farming or other formal/informal arrangements

(b) Strengthening backward & forward linkages and developing supply chains with cold chain mechanism

(c) Establishment of Mega Food Parks in identified Small Scale Industries, horticulture, meat, dairy and marine

Clusters, and the subsequent upgrading quality of street foods and food streets associated with local bodies and NGOs

(d) Enhancing capacity building in the areas of Human Resource Development/Research & Development and quality control labs and

(e) Adopting uniform and rationalized tax/duty structure for the entire food processing industry

Sub-Saharan Africa

The World Bank's *World Development Report 2008: Agriculture for Development* says that three of every four poor people in developing countries live in rural areas—2.1 billion living on less than $2 a day and 880 million on less than $1 a day—and most depend on agriculture for their livelihoods. Currently, while 75 percent of the world's poor live in rural areas in developing countries, a mere 4 percent of official development assistance goes to agriculture. In Sub-Saharan Africa, public spending for farming is also only 4% of total government spending and the sector is still taxed at relatively high levels.

The report argues that more needs to be spent on agriculture if international goals of halving extreme poverty and hunger by 2015 are to be realized and advocates a multi-sectoral approach is advocated to leverage synergy between improved technologies, sustainable soil and water management, institutional support, and human capital development. It finds that agricultural growth in Sub-Saharan Africa has accelerated from 2.3% in the 1980s, to 3.3% in the 1990s, and to 3.8% between 2000 and 2005. Concurrently *Rural poverty* has also started to decline in 10 of 13 countries analyzed over the period from 1990 to 2005.

Africa's low agricultural productivity features prominently in the 2008 report and the *common structural features* that must be considered in designing an appropriate policy agenda are identified:

(a) Sub-Saharan African agriculture is 96 percent rain fed and highly *vulnerable to weather shocks* and its diverse agro-ecological conditions produce a wide range of farming systems based on many food staples and livestock. Examples of new approaches for expanding irrigated areas such as Mali's institutional reforms for large-scale irrigation management and Nigeria's fadama schemes, based on small-scale technologies have good prospect.

(b) Most agriculture-based countries are *small and landlocked* and find it difficult to tap scale economies in research and training and face high and uncompetitive transport costs. This calls for better integration of regional markets.

(c) Vast *distances and low population densities* make trade, infrastructure, and service provision costly while representing untapped reserves for agricultural expansion.

(d) More than half the world's *conflicts* in 1999 occurred in Sub-Saharan Africa. Reduced conflict offers the scope for rapid agricultural growth as demonstrated by Mozambique's recent experience.

(e) The aging human capital base of the agriculture profession as a result of the *HIV/AIDS epidemic.* But major accomplishments in rural primary education are ensuring a future generation of literate and numerate African smallholders and nonfarm entrepreneurs.

In order to address these issues, better functioning input markets are needed as much as expanding product markets to increase agricultural productivity. This requires investments in roads and communications to link farmers to towns, and in price and weather risk management, market information, and organizing producers.

Infertile soil is a constraint. Ecological /organic farming methods need to be introduced; fertilizer consumption stepped up rapidly and approaches such as legumes and agro-forestry, which increase both soil fertility and soil structure need to be adopted as has been successfully done in Zambia. The widespread adoption green revolution/biotechnology methods would be an alternative strategy.

Accelerating adoption of new technologies to improve yields requires improved incentives, investments in agricultural research and extension systems, access to financial services and subsidies to stimulate input markets. Special efforts are also needed to tailor technologies and support services to women farmers who produce and process most of the food. Greater geographic labour mobility and improvements in skills of younger generations are central to reducing rural poverty. Because of HIV/AIDS and malaria, better health care and education must be an integral part of a broader set of safety nets that protect the assets of the poor from drought, disease, and the death in family.

Conclusion

The progress on Human Development has been substantial but not nearly enough. Speaking at the World Economic Forum, Professor Klaus Schwab, the Forum's founder said that so far the world had committed only 30% of the effort required to meet the United Nation's Millennium Development Goals and Gordon Brown was anguished that on current trends, the UN's health goals would not be hit in 2015, but in 2050, and the education goals in 2115. In this context it is vitally important that big business comes on board and supports the agenda through its world wide network, know-how, and management talent and money power.

The adoption of the Triple Bottom Line concept by companies is indeed a matter of satisfaction. Tim Weber of the BBC recently reported from the World Economic Forum at Davos that some of the leading firms will participate in a "public-private partnership" to fight extreme poverty and assist in the achievement of the Millennium Development Goals. Bill Gates of Microsoft and John Chambers of CISCO have voiced their commitment and these as well as other firms can be expected to pledge their specific contribution at a London summit in May 2008.[21]

Initiatives such as these are paramount, particularly in matters such as climate change, carbon and water positivist and so on, which are well beyond the resources and preparedness of poorer countries to address. The developing countries in general and BRIC economies in particular should focus on economic growth, modernize agriculture, invest in education and social infrastructure while Sub-Saharan Africa can look at improving the scale and productivity of agriculture to escape extreme poverty. For the fragile states, the starting point can only be political will and wisdom.

Footnotes

1. http://hdr.undp.org/en/humandev/
2. http://hdr.undp.org/en/humandev/origins/
3. The UNDP has taken by this role quite vigorously and the Human Development Report has emerged as a valuable enabler in this context. Human Development Reports are now being prepared widely at national and sub-national levels and together have created a nice hub-and-spoke model that feed information into and draw information out of each other.
4. Source:http://en.wikipedia.org/wiki/List_of_ countries_by_Human_ Development_Index
5. Source: UNDP: Human Development Report 2007
6. http://www.dfid.gov.uk/mdg/
7. Approximately 27% of the extreme poor in developing countries live in fragile states, which have grown more slowly than other low-income countries. Clearly, this will be, an obstacle to the achievement of MDG1 in those countries. Despite this, global poverty is projected to fall to 12% by 2015
8. http://www.mdgmonitor.org/story.cfm?goal=1
9. In Ghana, for example, public school enrolment in the most deprived districts and nationwide soared from 4.2 million to 5.4 million between 2004 and 2005.
10. http://www.mdgmonitor.org/story.cfm?goal=2
11. In Kenya, Madagascar, and Tanzania, girls' completion rates are over 5 per cent higher than boys' completion rates and give no evidence of gender bias. On the other hand, boys' completion rates are over 10% percent higher in Chad, Ethiopia, Nigeria, and Morocco. The varying outcomes are clearly a result of differences in priority given in different states to this important agenda item.
12. For example, the new constitution of Rwanda guarantees a minimum of 30% of parliamentary seats and other leadership positions to women. Consequently, Rwanda has the highest number of women parliamentarians in the world today with women constituting nearly 50%

in the Chamber of Deputies and about 35% in the Senate. The Government of Rwanda also has 34% of women in its Cabinet.

13. http://www.mdgmonitor.org/story.cfm?goal=3
14. http://www.hdf.com/hdf/newasp/whatIsHD/whatIsHD.asp?t=hdInSAsia
15. http://hdrstats.undp.org
16. http://www.thehindubusinessline.com/2005/05/25/stories/2005052502211700.htm
17. http://www.hdf.com/hdf/newasp/whatIsHD/what IsHD.asp?t = hdInSAsia
18. http://www.deeshaa.org/who-actually-paid-for-my-education/
19. http://209.85.175.104/search?q=cache:KM5p bR99qdUJ:www.khabarexpress.com/1/17/2008/No-chance- for-equity-without-growth-Chidambaram-news_9964.html+ chidambaram%2Beducation & hl=en&ct=clnk&cd=10&gl=in
20. World Development Report 2008: Agriculture for Development
21. http://news.bbc.co.uk/2/hi/business/7208990.stm

CHAPTER–9

THE CHANGING PHASE OF INTER-SECTORAL RELATIONSHIP IN INDIA: A JOURNEY FROM HEGEMONY TO PARTNERSHIP

V. S. Adigal

Introduction

The present paper is an Endeavour to explain the evolving pattern of inter-relationship between the First-Sector, i.e. the state, the Second Sector, i.e. economy and the Third -Sector, i.e. all those organization and individuals striving for the attainment of the cherished goal of 'civil society'. Before we venture in to the analysis of the evolving pattern of inter-sectoral relationship, it will be appropriate to state the core concepts in brief.

Hegemony

The term 'hegemony' is derived from the Greek word 'hegemonia' which means authority. Coilins English Dictionary describes hegemony as ' a ascendancy or domination of one power over others. In the present context hegemony implies domination of the state over economy and the voluntary sector.

Partnership

Collins English Dictionary describes partnership as "a contractual relationship between two or more partners carrying on a joint business venture with a view to profit, each incurring liability for losses and the right to share in profit." It further elaborates that partnership is "the deed creating a relationship between persons associated in such a relationship."

In the present context emerging pattern of relationship between the statutory sector (traditionally described as the state),the private sector (also described as the economy) and the voluntary sector (also described as the Third Sector) is labeled in the contemporary research as 'partnership' (also as collaboration). This description is based on the belief that partnership between the statutory, the private and the voluntary sector is the felt need of the new millennium. It is further maintained that the state has increasingly become aware of its inadequacy as the provider of social services. As a result, that state welcomes collaboration with the indigenous and foreign capital (private sector) in the development of infrastructure in the developing countries. At the same time, the state regards the voluntary sector as collaborator in the delivery of the social services.

On the other hand, the voluntary sector is aware of the fact that it is not in a position to tackle the wider socio-economic issues on its own to the inadequacy of the resources. As a result, the voluntary sector is willing to collaborate with the state and at the same time retain its independent identity, described as autonomy. The voluntary sector also strives to collaborate with the funding agencies, national and international, to enhance its financial capability. The voluntary organization, working at the grass-roots level, also try to involve the local community by means of active participation in the development process.

The trend in the direction of increasing cooperation, collaboration and participation is viewed as inter-sectoral partnership, and regarded as an appropriate strategy to meet the challenges of the new millennium. The Endeavour of the present paper is to identify and explain the issues and the challenges that the partnership initiatives face at the macro and micro-levels. It also discusses the implications of partnership for community development work at the grass - roots level.

Paradigm

The terms 'Paradigm' is derived from the two Greek works, viz. (a) *paradeigma* which means pattern and (b) *paradeikunal* which means to compare. Collins English Dictionary describes paradigm as a pattern or model. In the philosophy of science, the term paradigm, implies a very general conception of the nature of scientific endeavor within which a given enquiry is undertaken.

In our present context, the term paradigm implies (i) a very general conception of the pattern of inter-sectoral relationship (ii) an analysis of the shifts that have taken in this relationship (iii) a comparison of the patterns of relationship that existed at the different times and (iv) envisage the pattern of relationship in the times to came.

The Issues

The present paper deals with the following issues related with the terms of the paper:

(i) Nature and role of the state

(ii) Nature of relationship between the state and the voluntary sector

(iii) The positive outcome and the negative fall-out of partnership with the state

(iv) The ways and means to make the partnership workable (v) Partnership with the funding agencies and its implications (vi) Participation of community as a form of partnership.

The discussion of the principle and the related issue is attempted in the context of the Indian experience at the macro and micro-levels. The macro-level analysis pertains to the policy issues and the CAPART, the institutional device to facilitate partnership between the state and the voluntary sector. The micro-level analysis is the case study of successful voluntary organization, practitioner of this strategy.

Objectives

The modest objectives of the present work are as follows:

(i) To articulate a conceptually clear and concise thesis on the paper theme.

(ii) To present a preliminary research frame work and explore the possibilities of the cross-national studies in the region.

Research Approach

For preparing the present work, the existing theories regarding the nature and role of the state and its relationship with the society (associations/voluntary sector) were analysed and applied to the inter-sector partnership theme. The available published literature on the paper theme was analysed with a view to gain insight in the pattern of relationship and evolving partnership in the different parts of the world. The policy of Government of India regarding the voluntary sector and the emerging pattern of the partnership was also analysed. Finally the validity of the theoretical precepts was ascertained by undertaking case study of successful voluntary organization in India.

Theoretical Framework

Any meaningful discussion on the partnership between the voluntary sector and the statutory sector must take into consideration the nature and role of the state. This is due to the fact that the state is the 'senior partner' in this emerging partnership with the voluntary sector. The state has been described as the 'senior partner' because the state provides funds and regulates the activities of the voluntary sector. In fact the very existence and significance or insignificance of the voluntary sector is a direct outcome of the nature of the state, rather the government. Democratic form of government is the pre-condition for the very existence of the voluntary sector.

The emergence of the voluntary sector in the Eastern Europe in 1990s can be attributed to the collapse of the socialist regimes. Similarly the emergence of the voluntary sector in most countries of the Asia-Pacific region is a development of the post-colonial period.

Leslie Lipson has very ably summed up the evolving nature of the state that "The protective state.... the law and order state, the just state (and) the welfare state ....has been the upward evolution.... through four thousand years of efforts and commitment". We may add the further stage in this process as 'mixed economy welfare state' in the last two decades. The role of the state, too, underwent transformation. To quote Lipson again, " From the initial duty of providing protection, the responsibilities of the state expanded into a framework of the order that involves.... justice. The ideal (of justice)... did not mark the end of the quest for better life through political means.... The state has made progress from justice to the ideal of welfare, which is humanised justice,"

The relationship between the state and society, too, underwent many changes. The city states in ancient Greece were omnipotent as no distinction was made between the state and the society. The claim of the state to be Omni point was challenged by the medieval Church by advocating the doctrine of dualism that "Render unto Caeaser (state) the things that are Caeaser's and render unto God (personified by the Church) the things that are God's". The Church not only asserted it's authority but became hegemonic and subordinated the state. The hegemony of the Church was challenged during the Age of Renaissance and Reformation. This led to the emergence of strong unified nation-states, personified by absolute monarchy. The absolute authority of state was justified by John Austin and Thomas Hobbes. The absolute authority of the monarch and the result misuse of power was challenged towards the end of the seventeenth century. This led to the emergence of representative democracy in Europe and North America during the eighteenth century.

During the nineteenth century, pluralistic theory of sovereignty emerged as a sharp reaction to the absolute or unlimited power of the state. The pluralists argued that man's nature finds expression in numerous social, economic, political, cultural and religious associations. These associations are essential for an all-round development of individuals. De Tocqeville' while elaborating the significance of the associational life, had observed that, "absence of government and administration facilitates the emergence of associations".

In our content, an ideological interpretation of pluralism and associationalism would imply a reduced role for the state in order to facilitate the emergence and growth of voluntary sector. These ideas and their practical implications are now invoked and put forth with renewed vigor in the debate on inter-sectoral partnership.

The emergence of representative democracy coincided with the emergence of the ideology of classical liberalism and the doctrine of 'Leissez Faire' as a reaction against the evils of 'over government'. The non-interference of the state in the lives of its subject was advocated by John Stuart Mill and other liberals. They maintained that the greatest good of the greatest number can be realised by allowing the people to manage their affairs. While advocating limited government, J. S. Mill had observed that, "Every additional function means a new burden on body (the state) already overburdened with duties, the result is that most is not done at all, because the government is not able to do it without delay". It is significant to note our present context that the inability of the state to perform its duties is one of the significant reasons for the advocacy of inter-sector partnership, wherein the task of delivery of social services is not to be entrusted to the voluntary sector.

While advocating limited role for the state in the inter sectoral partnership, let us not overlook the self-defeating consequences of the excessive freedom to individuals and their associations. Lipson has pointed out that, "Despite its good intentions, the doctrine (of liberalism) paved the road to privileges. The presence of very rich and very poor side by side, the concentration of wealth and, with it of trusts and monopolies, the rise of holding companies and interlocking directorates.... negated the ideal of free competition among individuals."

The self-defeating consequences of the practice of laissez-faire doctrine accentuated miseries of the exploited masses. This led to the emergence of trade unions which demanded intervention of the state to save the poor from the exploitation at the hands of the rich. The state was expected not only to intervene but also play larger role in providing social services. The state took upon itself welfare functions towards the end of the nineteenth century. As a result, the state underwent transformation from the 'police state' to 'welfare state' in the twentieth century.

The advocacy of the welfare state led to the re-emergence of centrality, also described as hegemony, of the state. The state regulated economy to a lesser or greater extent. The state regulated, encouraged and provided funds to voluntary organizations and other associations engaged in social work. The weaknesses of welfare state became increasingly visible in 1970s. The critics pointed out the deleterious effect of the expanded, universal welfare state. As a result, the centrality of the state was questioned.

The Marxists like O'Connor and Gough pointed out the inherent contradictions in capitalist economies between the need to accumulate and the need for legitimacy. Capital accumulation requires policy mechanisms such as taxes and the need to sustain legitimacy in the eyes of the larger population requires larger quantum of spending on the expensive social beyond the financial capabilities of the state. The non-availability of larger quantum of funds and the huge administrative cost reduces the quantum of services and also undermines it's quality.

The neo-liberals like Robbinson, Le Grand and Glennerster point out the harmful consequences of universal welfare state on the economy. Their views were endorsed by the then British Prime Minister Margaret Thatcher. The ideas popularly described as Thatcherism' abandoned a number of state sponsored and financed social services. These developments led to the search for new ways and means of structuring welfare and social provision. The ideal of welfare state was substituted by the 'mixed economy of welfare 'in 1990's.

This new doctrine emphasises the multiple sources of welfare in society. This includes, besides the state, market, voluntary sector, community and family. It envisages a larger role for the voluntary sector. The role of the state is envisaged merely as 'the funder and regulator'. The 'non-state' sectors are looked upon as the agents for the delivery of welfare.

Strategy of Inter-sectoral Partnership

In site of the fact that the current debate on the inter-sectoral partnership as an effective strategy to tackle development issues owes its origin to the grave economic crisis faced by the welfare state, a defined relationship had existed in the form of state regulation of and funding to the voluntary sector. The state had sought cooperation of the voluntary organization in implementation of its community development oriented programmes in India and other countries. As the limitations of universal state became visible in 1970s and 1980s, the centrality of the state was questioned by the Marxists and the neo-liberals. The led to the search for new ways of structuring welfare and social service provisions.

The strategy of partnership was advocated and justified by the protagonists of the 'maxed economy of welfare' and associational democracy. Their arguments in the support of the strategy of partnership are briefly narrated.

(A) The 'mixed economy of welfare' emerged as the new paradigm. In essence, it emphasises the multiple sources of welfare in the society-state, Market, Voluntary Sector and Informal Welfare in the family and community. Specifically, it envisages a potentially larger role for the voluntary sector. In this approach the State is urged to adopt the role of founder and regulator, while increasingly seeing 'the non-State' sectors as agents for the delivery of welfare. Here the voluntary sector may be delegated certain welfare services, or may compete in a 'quasi-market ' with other providers to obtain State founded contracts for service provision. During the last two decades collaboration between the state and the voluntary sector has considerably expanded. The motivation on the part of the government was the realisation of it's own financial constraints

and the resultant difficulties in delivering its own development priorities. On the other hand, the voluntary sector emphasised the comparative advantages in terms of their closeness to community and their ability to foster participatory, cost-effective and flexible delivery. They emphasised that in such evolving

Partnership 'what' *(policy formulation)* was the core-business of the state, where as 'how' *(implementation)* has a direct-bearing on the recipients /beneficiaries of services and, therefore, delivery part is the core -business of the voluntary sector. The advocates of the inter-sector partnership also point out that users of services gain from the greater efficiency of providers who must complete to obtain State funding and that these efficiency gains are not at the cost of inadequate services. Welfare provided in this way, with the voluntary sector enabled by state, may enhance choice and facilitate greater responsiveness to recipients' varied needs. The advocates of partnership express hope that a dynamic, inter-active partnership will address sustainable development and redress inequalities, particularly rural inequalities. For this purpose they maintain that communication is key to promoting dialogue and understanding capabilities and limitations of each other, as well as encouragement to mutual capacity building. This will ensure effective implementation of policies and plans.

(B) Associational democracy viewpoint has also advocated a large role for the voluntary sector and a limited role for the State, in order to translate the concept of associationalism into an agenda for political and institutional reforms. *Paul Hirst, the* most eminent advocate of this view point, made a distinction between his plea for voluntary association from the neo-liberal strategy of simply 'rolling back the welfare state' and reducing state services. He suggests that new forms of democracy cannot be built "without ensuring a measure of social security", and acknowledges that this can only be achieved by" maintaining public funding and common minimum entitlements". For Hirst, the link between associational democracy and the welfare state is as follows:

Public funding combined with decentralised provision is the essence of associative democracy. Representative institutions continue to provide the basic rules and to set the fiscal framework, but associations are responsible for the provision of services to their members. Decentralisation of governance through voluntary self-governing associations would place individuals under the subsidiary governments they have chosen for the specific purposes in question and in which they have some voice. Associations would compete to provide definite services and to obtain public funds proportionate to membership for public purposes". The advocates of associational democracy believe that such a strategy would nourish, encourage and reward voluntary sector, as well as ensure speedy delivery of the social services.

Public policy in many countries has increasingly reflected this general approach. In the UK the role of voluntary and social housing has grown. In Continental European countries the provision of social care services to the elderly and the disabled operates increasingly within a mixed economy of welfare framework. In the USA, state and local governments increasingly look to contract human services, including welfare-to-work, case work services, to non-profit and for profit providers. In the USA, Clinton administration decided to undertake 'Empowerment Zone' and 'Enterprise community' initiatives to reduce persistent poverty in rural areas. This initiative envisaged participation of citizens and community based partnerships for building sustainable communities and developing economic opportunities for all residents in these communities. In the Republic of Ireland, social partnership has been advocated to tackle the problem of unemployment on a long term basis and that the Irish Government has formed twelve area-based partnership with the voluntary sector for this purpose. Similar initiatives have been witnessed in the Less Developed Countries (LDCs) of Asia-Pacific region too. Even in the erstwhile socialist states we witness the emergence of this pattern of relationship. The most notable has been the 'one percent' partnership between the state and the voluntary sector in Hungary.

Pattern of Relationship

The most significant issue in the inter-sectoral partnership is the pattern of relationship between the partners. The pattern of relationship is determined by the pattern of distribution of power between the state and the voluntary sector. Even while acknowledging that the role of state has diminished, to that extent, the role of voluntary sector has enhanced, the basic question that remains who wields the real power? There are two broad patterns of power distribution between the state and the non-state actors, viz. hegemonic pattern and distributive pattern.

Hegemonic Pattern

In this pattern the state continues to retain its central position vis-a-viz the non-state actors. The critics view its means of regulation and control over the voluntary sector as overtly oppressive. Even when the state pretends to be non-oppressive, it resorts to subtle means to ensure, to in the words of *Crag and Mayo* "the existing framework of economic and political power (is)... seen as both legitimate and non-contestable within (even) capitalist society." In the developing societies like India, the hegemony of the state is so pronounced that it does not require 'cover-up operations' in the form of subtle means.

Distributive Pattern

In the distributive pattern the power may be widely dispersed, yet it could be disempowering for the non-state actors. *Gilchrist and Taylor* have pointed out that, "Power works not just in overt exercise of power over another agent (voluntary sector), but also through creating the agendas and rules of engagement within which we see our world and the way things are, through unquestioning internalisation of values and ideologies." The state can partonise those voluntary organisation which are favorably disposed to the state and neglect those which are critical. Thus the distributive power may be accessible only on the basis of dominant norms and unequal competitions. The state possesses procedural powers to regulate the activities of the voluntary sector. The state that invite the nominees of the non-state actors for the deliberations on policy matters where, in the realist sense, collaboration becomes co-option and consultation becomes coercion.

The impact of the partnership model on the voluntary sector has generated a new research agenda; wherein the issues/problem-areas emerging out of inter-sectoral partnership are addressed. At the core of this research agenda is a concern that the nature of the voluntary sector is being transformed-and perhaps undermined-by this new context. *Taylor* has documented the challenges to voluntary organisations in the UK. Taylor points out that successive studies demonstrate how difficult partnership, particularly with local communities, is to achieve. They tell a story of continuing imbalances of power, conflicting interests, continuing frustration and an apparent failure to learn from past experience. Cost rhetoric about partnership with communities masks a number of persistent tensions-for example; between accountability and the flexibility required to involve communities effectively; between diverse interests within the community between political time imperatives and the real time required to work effectively with communities.

Chris Miller's comparative study of the voluntary sector in the UK and Canada points out the dangers, involved in the excessive dependence of the voluntary sector on the state funding and that the sector lacks capacity to resist the profound policy challenges which let to closure of several voluntary activities due to the lack of funds. Miller also points out that in the UK voluntary sector has been undergoing a process of professionalism. It is expected to focus on the provision of services previously delivered by the state. In acknowledgement of its growing importance, it is invited to sit as a partner in policy decision making. In addition, it confronts other pressures to conform to state priorities. This is likely to squeeze out members and wider constituents from the ownership of organisations and will enable professionals to consolidate their positions of influence. These links and local accountabilities need to be restored by creating public spaces for a new civic dialogue.

Similarly O'Sullivan has pointed to the growing reliance of the voluntary sector on State funding and on paid employees in the increasingly contractual relationship between the state and the voluntary sector in Ireland. In the US, Frumkin and Andre-Clark have noted the growing pressure on non-profit organisations to adopt commercial and managerial approaches to efficiency. Underlying these specific questions is a fear that voluntarism is losing its political autonomy and its capacity to act as an independent critic of public policy and an advocate for social change. There is also greater danger of the political agenda of the ruling party thrusted on the voluntary sector and voluntary organizations, especially largely funded by the state, succumbing to such pressures. In plain terms, there is eminent danger of loss of accountability and the voluntary sector becoming an extension of the state.

The critical analysis of the partnership theme is out of keen desire to strengthen associational life and to implement a mixed economy of welfare. This analysis differentiates between rhetoric and reality as well as suggests ways and means to tackle the problem areas. In the process of collaboration, the non-state actors should extend critical cooperation and retain critical edge in the process. There must be clarity as to their desired objectives and strategies to achieve these objectives. Gilchrist suggests formation and fostering of diverse and dynamic networks. She has listed their utility as under:-

(i) Parallel processing of information; updating and comparing knowledge from a range of sources;

(ii) The development and application of communal wisdom and collective intelligence;

(iii) Efficient mobilisation of support and resources towards a common cause.

(iv) Flexible experimentation with new combinations and organisational forms; and

(v) Inclusion and empowerment of marginalised groups in strategies for social transformation.

If there is some commitment on the part of those in authority to have meaningful engagement with those who are to be entrusted the responsibility of delivery of social welfare products, process and services, the areas of tensions and differences could be sorted out by evolving appropriate procedures and mechanisms. One of such mechanism suggested has been a strong and sustained social development planning at the gross-roots level undertaken by the NGO's with active participation of the local community. The experience in India, elaborated in the next section, in this regards has been very encouraging and the local-village communities have been capacitated to undertake development tasks in partnership with the state.

The Indian Experience

India attained political independence in 1947. The independent India had inherited a bloated and highly centralised colonial state, along with an impoverished economy and civil society. The organised voluntary sector, in the formal sense of the term was almost non-existence except for a number of charitable trusts and institutions. However, voluntary initiatives can be traced back to the pioneer experiments of Tagore and Gandhi in 1920s' There was no possibility of partnership of any sort with the colonial state as it was almost totally indifferent to the well-being of the people. The rules of some erstwhile princely states like that of Travancore-Cochin had encouraged and supported voluntary initiative, and those of Baroda, Kolhapur and Auundh had themselves initiated measures for the socio-economic upliftment of the weaker sections and promoted their welfare.

The Indian Constitution-makers were aware of the fact that political democracy would be incomplete without social and economic content and had embraced welfare state ideal, later described as the socialist pattern of society (1955). The state-centrist strategy was of mixed economy and centralised planning, with twin goals of economic development and social transformations. The Community Development Programme (CDP) was the most ambitious schemes undertaken by the Government of India in the early 1950s. The CDP was visualised as "Declaration of war on poverty, ignorance, squalor and diseases" and administrative machinery to implement the CDP was established in 5011 development blocks in the rural part of the country. The CDP had envisaged, active involvement of the voluntary groups at the local level as well as active participation of the people in this process. The failure of the CDP was attributed by the evolution team headed by late Balwanttrai Mehta (1957) to its failure to evoke popular initiative and owing to its state centrist nature, it had become an 'official programme' and not 'people's movement'. Even while admitting the fact that India did not have, a large voluntary sector in 1950s, the dominance of administrative machinery and it's distrust of people and their capability (a legacy of the colonial rule) indicated the limitations of the hegemonic state. The Government of India was earnest in its intention to bring about transformation in the rural segment and sought to induct the grass-roots leadership with the process by revising the administrative framework in the form of Panchayati Raj, the three-tier structure of local government in the rural area. The nascent voluntary sector did not figure any where in the revised strategy of 1960s. In other wards, the state-centrist strategy, in the form of democratic decentralization, had no room for partnership with voluntary sector.

A large number of voluntary organisations emerged in 1960s and undertook activities ranging from charity to economic relief. Some even venture into political mobilisation and struggle for social justice. These organisation were regarded as fringe entities whose activities were regulated by the state. The partnership, by far-fetched interpretation, between the state and the voluntary sector was in the form of state acting as a regulating and funding agency as well as monopolizing the welfare activities. These was not even a hint of the state giving up its control or even entrusting the task of delivering the welfare services to the voluntary organisation. This is in spite of the fact that there was considerable increase in the number of voluntary organisations. The state regulated and, to some extent, funded their 'social work'. There was no question of partnership with a localised, unorganised and scattered voluntary sector.

The decade of 1970 witnessed the growing disillusionment and dis-content among the masses owing to the failure of the state to deliver the goods. This gave birth to a large number of voluntary organistions, many of which were engaged in agitational activities. The response of the ruling elite was the slogan of *"Garibi Hatao"* (Eradicate Poverty) and launching of number of poverty alleviation, employment generation and welfare - oriented programmes. The task of delivering services and goods was entrusted to agencies like Small Farmers Development Agency (SFDA) and Marginal Farmers and Landless Labourers Development Agency (MFLDA) set up by the Government of India. In spite of the multiple programmes and multiple-agencies and financial provision of cores of rupees, the benefits of the poverty alleviation programmes did not percolate to the target groups. The review of the rural poverty-alleviation programmes indicated dismal results and Government of India decided to adopt integrated approach to rural development. Forty-odd poverty and employment generation programmes were merged a single programme, viz. the Integrated Rural Development Programme (IRDP) , to be implemented through a single agency, viz. the District Rural Development Agency (DRDA), Having an annual budget of Forty lakh rupees and headed by a project officer.

During this decade the voluntary organisations had become more critical and aggressive. Most organisations that emerged in 1970s 'neo-left' idological learning and disapproved 'status-quosm' of the earlier organisations. They advocated participatory methods of functioning. They launched frontal attack on the root causes of poverty and injustice. They strived to organise the mariginalised sections and provided leadership to their struggle against the semi-feudal rural elite as well as other vested interests . However, these organisations were localised and functioned in a couple of villages. The localised character of the voluntary activity restricted their overall impact but the national elite had to take a serious note of the growing number and significance of the voluntary organisations. At the same time, there was growing concern regarding enormous administrative cost, inordinate bureaucratic delay, inefficiency and rampant corruption in the delivery of welfare services. The political compulsions made it almost impossible for the government to launch a direct attack on the nexus between the semi funded rural elite and administrative machinery.

The neo-liberal ideology had influenced the decision making process in the developed world and India could not remain out of orbit. The state regulation was replaced by the de-regulation, the activities of the Public Sector Collaboration with foreign capital & Multi-Nationals was welcome Thus The Indian economy underwent transformation from welfare to new Liberal economy during the decade of 1990's

In spite of many hostile outcome, the negative impact was enormous. This paper endeavor to analyse the impact of LPG. The official thinking recognised that the voluntary organisations can play an important role infashining a capitalist civil society by collaborating with the state. This change in thinking of policy makers in mid 1990's was reflected in 7th five years economic plan which envisaged *voluntary organisations as partners in the implementation of rural development-oriented programmes. With a view* to encourage, promote and assist voluntary action in rural development and to inject new technical inputs to accomplish rural prosperity, the Government of India set up, within the Ministry of Rural Development, the Ministry of Rural Development, the Council for Advancement of People's Action and Rural Technology (CAPART) in September, 1986. This national body was to coordinate voluntary action and channelise funds for the activities of the voluntary organisation. The CAPART is a registered society, with an initial capital of one hundred crore of rupees. The CAPART has set up nine regional centers. The regional centers have been given power to scrutinize and sanction proposals received from the voluntary organisations within their respective jurisdiction up to an outlay of Rs. 10lakh. Since its inception in 1986, the CAPART has accorded a sanction to 18,126 projects and released an amount of Rs. 363.84 crores to the voluntary sector. The setting up of the CAPART could be viewed as a major policy initiative in direction of inter-sectoral partnership and to encourage the development of the voluntary sector.

In 1990s the scope of partnership between the state and voluntary sector has further enhanced at the micro-level due to the enactment of the 73rd Constitutional Amendment by Parliament which came into force on 24 April, 1993. Accordingly the Panchayati Raj institutions have been given powers and authority to function as institutions of self-government. The powers and responsibilities to be delegated to Panchayats at the appropriate level are:(a) preparation of plan for economic development and social justice, (b) implementation of schemes for economic development and social justice in relation to 29 subjects given in the Eleventh Schedule of the construction and (C) to levy, collect and appropriate taxes, duties, tolls and fees.

The 73rd Amendment Act gives constitutional status to the Gram Sabha. The Provisions of the Panchayats (Extension to the Scheduled Areas) Act, 1996 extends Panchayats to the tribal areas of eight States, namely Andhra Pradesh, Bihar, Gujarat, Himachal Pradesh, Maharashtra, Madhya Pradesh, Orissa and Rajasthan. This has came into force on 24 December 1996. Except Rajasthan and Bihar, all States have passed laws to give effect to the provisions contained in the Act 40 of 1996.

Under the Act, *Gram Sabha* has been vested with powers for ownership of minor forest produce, development plans approval, selection of beneficiaries under various programmes, consultation on land acquisition, manage minor water bodies, control mineral leases, regulate / prohibit sale of intoxicants, prevent alienation of land and restore unlawfully alienated land of STs, manage village markets, control money lending to STs, and control institutions and functionaries in all social sectors.

An another significant development in the direction of decentralisation of power and involvement of the grass-roots level voluntary organisations have been the launch of the Jawahar Gram Sanridhi Yojana (JGSY) on a April, 1999. The objectives of the Yojana are : creation of demand-driven village infrastructure including durable assets for increasing the opportunities for sustained employment, and generation of supplementary employment for the unemployed poor in the rural areas. The responsibility of the JGSY has been entrusted to the village Panchayats. The District Rural Development Agencies (DRDA) an Zilla Parishads (ZP) release the funds, including State marching share to village Panchayats. The Village Panchayat is the sole authority for preparation of annual action plan and its implementation with the approval of the Gram Sabha. The Village Panchayats have been given power to execute schemes up to Rs. 50,000 with the approval of the Gram Sabha. However, for schemes costing more than Rs. 50,000 the technical/administrative approval of appropriate authorities.

The village level voluntary organisations assist the Gram Sabha as well as the Village Panchayat in formulating the scheme, proposals and also in their implementation. this could be viewed as partnership between the state and the voluntary sector at the micro-level. It is also significant to note that the activists have also managed to get to get elected on the Village Panchayats and, as such, there is inter-locking of the two sectors.

The other most significant development was the launch of the *swarniayanti Gram Swarozgar Yojana* (SGSY) on 1 April, 1999 in place of the earlier employment generation-oriented programmes for the rural poor, which included the Integrated Rural Development Programme (IRDP), Training of Rural Youth for Self -Employment (TRYSEM), Development of Women and Children in Rural Areas (DWCRA), Supply of Improved Tool-Kits to Rural Development Artisans (SITRA), *ganga Kalyan Yojana* (GKY) And million Wells Scheme (MWS) The objective of the SGSY is to establish micro enterprises in the rural area. A significant aspect of SGSY is that every family assisted under this programme will be brought above the poverty-line in three years and as such the programme aims at creating substantial additional incomes for the rural poor. It proposes to cover 30 per cent of the rural households below the poverty line in all 5011 development blocks by 2004. The programme has been designed to provide proper support and encouragement to tap the inherent and capabilities of the rural poor. The SGSY is a holistic programme of micro-enterprises. The activity clusters have been formed on the basis of the availability of the resources in any village are decided by the Panchayat Samiti (PS)/the Zilla Parishad (ZP). The SGSY focuses on Group approach. This would involve organisation of the poor in to self-help groups (SHGs) and their capacity building. Efforts would be made to involve women members in each SHG. Group activity will be given preference and progressively majority of the funding will be for self-help groups. In each Panchayat Samiti, at least half of the groups will be exclusively women groups. The Gram Sabha will authenticate the list of families below the poverty-line identified in the BPL census.

The SGSY is a credit-cum-subsidy programme. Credit is the critical component in 'SGSY' subsidy being only an enabling element. Accordingly, SGSY envisages a greater involvement of the banks in the planning and preparation of projects, identification of activity clusters, infrastructure planning as well as capacity building and choice of activity of the SHGs, pre-credit activity and post-credit monitoring including loan recovery. It seeks to promote multiple credits rather than a one-time credit 'injection'. Subsidy under SGSY is 30 per cent of the project cost subject to a ceiling of Rs. 7,500 and for the SCs and the STs 50 per cent of the project cost subject to a ceiling of Rs. 1.25 lakh. There is no limit on the subsidy for irrigation projects. Special emphasis has been laid on skill development and attention to technology and marketing needs of the SHG are the hallmark of SGSY. SGSY provided for promotion of marketing of the goods products by the SHGs. The funds are provided by the central and state government in the ratio of 75:25. The quantum of the assistance to the states is determined on the basis of population under BPL. The additional parameters like absorption capacity and special requirement are also taken into consideration. The SGSY is implemented by the DRDAs through the Panchayat Samitis. The process of planning, implementation and monitoring integrates the banks and other financial institutions and the technical institutes in the districts. The voluntary organisations are- encouraged to take an initiative in forming the SHGs in the area of their operation. A large number of the voluntary organisation at the gross-roots level are involved in this partnership with the local government/administration.

This brief review of the Indian experience indicates the encouraging upward trend in the partnership between the state and the voluntary sector.

Lessons from Case Studies

The voluntary sector in India has perforated since late 1960s. and by a rough estimate there are more than 300,000 voluntary organisations at present . On these, it is estimated that about 100,000 voluntary organisations are actively engaged in activities ranging from charity to economic relief, rural development to environmental and gender issue, political mobilisation to struggle for social justice. In general, these organisations are formal, private, self-governing, non-profit and voluntary entities. Barring a few exceptions, these are local entries and their area of operation is confined to a city or town or a couple of villages. These are anomic entities as there are no federal or regional apex bodies. The efforts to bring them under the aegis of an umbrella entity have not succeeded as these entries are interested in remaining separate entries owing to their particularist and partronalistc character. In fact, the identity of most of these organisations is linked with their promoters and, in most cases, become the fiefdom of x or y or z. A veil of secrecy is maintained regarding their funds and funding agencies and, as result, there is lack of public accountability in most cases.

This prevailing scenario in the voluntary sector makes the task of a research in India unavailable. However, the author of this paper and many other engaged in the 'Third Sector Research' in India has ventured into in-depth case studies of the relatively better-known and successful experiments into voluntary actions. Keeping in view this basic limitation, the pattern of relationship, described as 'partnership' in the development literature, between the voluntary sector, that state, the International funding agencies and the indigenous donors, is as under.

Regulation and Control

The Indian state regulated the activities of the voluntary sector by making the registration of organisations a legal obligation. The voluntary organisations are registered under the provisions of the Societies Registration Act of 1862, the Bombay Public Trust Act of 1937 and similar Acts in other states. The state issues a certificate of registration which entitles the voluntary entities to conduct their activities, receive financial assistance from the state as well as to receive donations / contributions. The activities of those voluntary organisations which receive 'Foreign Funding' are regulated by the Foreign Exchange Regulation Act of 1976 which became more stringent after 1987. There was official thinking, vehemently opposed by the voluntary sector, to channelise the foreign funding through The government of India. The voluntary organisation are required to file returns on their financial transaction transactions, including their annual, audited statements of accounts to the government. They are also required to file the income-tax returns, although they are exempted from payment of income-tax. The government can institute inquiry into the activities and even order the closure of the organisation. The overwhelming regulatory power, has made the Indian state 'hegemonic' in relation to the voluntary sector.

Finance

The unequal pattern of partnership becomes more evident in the financial relationship; wherein the state is the 'donor' and the NGOs are the 'donees'. Three distinct patterns are visible in this regards\, viz.

(i) About 98% funds of 'Dilasa' are in the form of project grants from the state; which means almost total dependence on the state. the flow of funds from the state has enable the organisation to expand its activities in about 60 villages in 3 Talukas.

(ii) About 30% funds of 'Manav Lok' are in the form of project grants from the state, wherein the organisation has the option to accept the grants on its terms. About 40% of funds are in the form of Project funds from the international agencies/organisations. The organisation feels financial crunch, as many of these grants have expired. However, the organisation had prudently invested the foreign funds in the funds re-generating activities in the form of short and medium-term interest-free loans to the beneficiaries. The repayment of these loans enables the organisation to continue its own 'Employment for Community Development (EFCDP) Programme. In addition, it has set up a number of agro-processing units which also fetch sizable returns. Owing to the greater degree of financial self-sufficiency, the organisation deals with the state on 'equal footing' and is in a position to reject project grants. In fact, it had differences of perception regarding the rural health and sanitation awareness programme, jointly financed by the Government of Maharashtra and the World Bank which led to its withdrawal from the implementation of this programme in 49 villages in the area of its operation. The availability of substantial funds has enabled the organisation to expand its area of operation to about 150 villages in three districts.

(iii) The component of grants from the state and foreign funding is less than 20% in case of Yusuf Meheraly Centre. It has built up its own corpus from the funds of several public trusts and yearly donations from its well-wishers. It also undertakes its own production, research and development activities. The income from these activities, generates a sizable chunk of its funds. Although this organisation is financially almost self-sufficient but the limited funds at its disposal have confined its activities to a few villages.

Activities

The activities undertaken by 'Dilasa' could be described as *'Service role'* or *'delivery mechanism'*, wherein it implements the numerous rural development schemes of the Government of India and the Government of Maharashtra in the area of its operation. on the other hand, the lesser degree of dependence on the state has enabled 'Manavlok' to undertake advocacy role, in addition to the service role. It regards itself as a development pressure group'. Yusuf Meharaly Centre has more or less confined itself to the *"service role'* and the welfare-oriented activities are conducted out of its own funds. To a lesser extent, it also undertakes *'advocacy role'*.

References

Lipson, Leslie (1967), Great Issues of Politics, Jaico, Bombay, Indian Ed.

Mill, John Stuert (1975), On Libert (1859), Penguin, London.

O'Connor, J. (1973), The Fiscal Crisis of the State, St. Martin's Press,New York.

Gough, I. (1979), The Potential Economy of the Welfare state, MacMilan, London.

Le Grand, J and ribinson, R (eds), (1984), Privatisation and the Welfare State, George Allen and Unwin, London.

Glennerster, H., (1992), *Paying for Welfare:* The 1990's, Har vester Whearsheaf, london.

Hirst, P. (1994), Associative Democracy, Amberst, University of Massa-chusetts.

Hirst, P. (1995), *"Can Secondary Associations Enhance Demo cratic Governance?," in* Cohen, J and Gogers, J. (eds), Associations and Democracy, Verso, New York.

Hirst. P. (1998), Models of Democratic Governance in a Post-liberal Society, in Negotiated Economic and Social Governance and European Integration, Commission of the European communities, Brussels.

Craig, G. and Mayo, M.(eds), (1995), Community Empowerment: A Reader in Participation and Development, Zed Books, London.

Gilchrist, A. and Taylor, m. (1997), "Community Networking: Developing Strength Through Diversity", in *Hoggert,* P (ed.) Contested Communities, Policy Press.

Taylor. M. (1997), "Between Public *and Private Accountability in Volintry Organisations, in* Policy and Politics, *Vol. 24,* No. 1.

*Miller, C and Ahmad Y, (*1997), "Community Development at Cross Road: A Way Forward" in Policy and Politics, Vol. 25.No.3.

O'Sullivan, E. (1999), "Voluntary Agencies in Ireland-What Future Role?" in *Administration, Vol No.4.*

Frumkin, P. and Andre-Clark, A., Z (2000), 'When Missions, Markets and Politics Collide; Values and Strategies' in the *Non-Profit* and Voluntary Sector Quarterly, Vol 29, No.1.

*Government of India (*1957), Committee on Plan Projects: Report of the Team for the Study of Community Development and National Extension Service Projects, Four Volumes.

Chapter–10

SELF-HELP GROUPS AND POVERTY ALLEVIATION: A COMPARATIVE STUDY IN WEST BENGAL

Subrata Kumar Ray

Introduction

Over the years the poverty alleviation programmes have been implemented in India and a huge amount of social and financial investment has been made to achieve the sole aim and objective of poverty eradication. Considering the large number of persons still living below the poverty line , there is no doubt that the resources pumped down for poverty alleviation and provision of subsidies in the name of poor have not been much effective in achieving the goal of poverty alleviation.Generation of self-employment for the poor in rural areas is one of the most important components of anti-poverty and rural development programmes in India. Swarnajayanti Gram Swarozgar Yojana (SGSY) which came into being on 1st April, 1999 after merging the erstwhile Integrated Rural Development Programme (IRDP), Training of Rural Youth for Self-Employment (TRYSEM), Development of Women and Children in Rural Areas (DWCRA), Supply of Improved

Toolkits To Rural Artisans (SITRA), Ganga Kalyan Yojana (GKY) and Million Well Scheme (MWS) is the major on going programme for self-employment generation for marginalised sections of rural communities. This programme is entirely different from erstwhile programmes of self-employment in terms of strategy envisaged for its implementation. One of the drawbacks in the earlier version of self-employment programmes was their concentration on the inputs rather than output (finished products) and their marketing. To rectify this situation, SGSY provides avenues for promotion of marketing of the goods produced by the swarozgaries by way of involvement and participation of them in exhibitions/melas at international, national, state and sub-state levels (Pal, 2002). The SGSY focuses on group approach by organizing the poor into self-help groups (SHGs) through social mobilization. This is a single cell self-employment programme for rural poor aimed at establishment of large number of micro-enterprises. The policy expectation is to ensure that the group members or swarozgaris (self-employed) come out of poverty clutches through incremental income. The group approach stems from the underlying assumption that the poor will help themselves, their own organisation will help them by taking steps for their upliftment. The SHG is the surer way in reaching the poor and assisting them in terms of credit, technology, market, etc. Building capacity to manage own resources (as well as subsequent external credit), developing saving habit and community orientation, the members will have economic emancipation, self-identity and assertiveness (Mandal, 2005). The failure of the formal credit institutions in effectively meeting requirements of rural poor has been the major reason for innovations in micro finance. The SHG-Bank Linkage Programme, launched by NABARD in 1992, is a landmark in the field of micro-financing in India. On the basis of their saving pattern, SHGs are given the bank loans to fulfill the loan requirements of its members (Naithani, 2001). Independent studies of micro credit programmes show that providing easy and affordable access to credit and other financial services to poor families can have a host of positive impacts on their livelihoods (Yunus, 2004). In this context, the present paper makes a comparative study of panchayat-led and non-governmental organization (NGO) -led SHGs for highlighting the progress and problems of SHG activities and impact of SHG activities on poverty alleviation in West Bengal (W.B.) with special reference to Purba and Paschim Medinipur districts.

ASPECT OF SELF HELP GROUP(SHG)

The SHG is the surer way in reaching the poor and assisting them in terms of credit, technology, market etc.The programme has in-built safeguards for the weaker sections. The programme insists that 50% of the SHGs must be formed exclusively by women and that 50% of the benefits should flow to Scheduled Castes(SCs) and Scheduled Tribes(STs). There is also a provision in disabled beneficiaries. The programme is credit driven and subsidy is back-ended.

SHGs are small groups of poor people. The ideal size of an SHG is 10 to 20 members.The group need not be registered. From one family ,only one person can become a member of an SHG. The group normally consists of either only men or of only women. Mixed groups are not generally preferred. The members should have the same social and financial background. In exceptional case 20% and in special case 30% of total members can be selected from above poverty line (APL) category. Some common factors for membership in SHG are (1) women or men from very poor households, (2) those who depend on moneylenders even for daily necessities, (3) those with a per capita income not exceeding Rs. 250 per month, and (4) those having dry land holding not exceeding 2.5 acres.The common living conditions for the group members are (1)living in kutcha houses,(2)having no access to safe drinking water, (3)having no sanitary latrine, (4)those who have only one or no one employed in the family, (5) presence of illiterate adults in the family, (6) presence of an alcoholic or drug addict in the family or a member suffering permanently from prolonged illness, (7) presence of children below five years in a family, (8) family eating two meals or less a day, (9)

Table 1

State/U.T. Wise Formation and Performances of SHGs(upto July 2006) in India

(Rs. In million)

State/U.T.	Total SHG Formed	No. of SHG Passed Grade-I	No. of SHG Passed Grade-II	Women SHG Formed	No. of SHGs Taken Eco Activities	% of Group Formation	% of Grade-I Passed	% of Grade-II Passed	% of Women SHG	% of SHGs Taken Eco Activities	Per Capita Credit Per SHG (as on 31st March 2005)
Andhra Pradesh	618603 (1)	48278	25115	137124	6347	31.55	7.8	4.06	22.17	1.03	55709.9
Arunachal Pradesh	357 (25)	35	32	29	56	0.02	9.8	8.96	8.12	15.69	4275
Assam	21373 (15)	17895	8514	11347	5146	1.09	83.73	39.84	53.09	24.08	
Bihar	21622 (14)	10101	4916	7805	2625	1.1	46.72	22.74	36.1	12.14	24339.1
Goa	795 (24)	164	80	90	80	0.04	20.63	10.06	11.32	10.06	7468.6
Gujarat	62567 (8)	3010	1383	822	1596	3.9	4.81	2.21	1.31	2.55	2777.5
Haryana	9429 (18)	1472	1158	873	1128	0.48	15.61	12.28	9.26	11.96	59871.6
Himachal Pradesh	6482 (21)	654	797	324	790	0.33	10.09	12.3	5	12.19	31746.8
Jammu and Kashmir	9320 (19)	463	164	289	244	0.47	4.97	1.76	3.1	2.62	34353.38

Contd.

State/U.T.	Total SHG Formed	No. of SHG Passed Grade-I	No. of SHG Passed Grade-II	Women SHG Formed	No. of SHGs Taken Eco Activities	% of Group Formation	% of Grade-I Passed	% of Grade-II Passed	% of Women SHG	% of SHGs Taken Eco Activities	Per Capita Credit Per SHG (as on 31st March 2005)
Karnataka	41240 (11)	5533	5443	4359	3636	2.1	13.42	13.2	10.57	8.82	33710.7
kerala	57109 (9)	5999	3452	5358	1598	2.91	10.5	6.04	9.38	2.8	41038.8
Madhya Pradesh	223981 (2)	12188	5946	4702	4896	11.42	5.44	2.65	2.1	2.19	24626.3
Maharashtra	161288 (4)	17472	8670	16757	6448	8.23	10.83	5.38	10.39	4	31401.7
Meghalaya	6611 (20)	632	156	435	75	0.34	9.56	2.36	6.58	1.13	31244.9
Orissa	153667 (5)	22659	9274	20225	5226	7.84	14.75	6.04	13.16	3.4	20428.5
Punjab	6322 (22)	485	225	556	313	0.32	7.67	3.56	8.79	4.95	47156.2
Rajasthan	26656 (12)	2924	1293	882	1083	1.36	10.97	4.85	3.31	4.06	23564.9
Sikkim	1149 (23)	141	116	223	116	0.06	12.27	10.1	19.41	10.1	32142.8
Tamil Nadu	162517 (3)	19893	6314	24220	4726	8.29	12.24	3.89	14.9	2.91	76026.9
Tripura	17891 (16)	3003	1007	1952	1794	0.91	16.78	5.63	10.91	10.03	12587.4

Contd.

State/U.T.	Total SHG Formed	No. of SHG Passed Grade-I	No. of SHG Passed Grade-II	Women SHG Formed	No. of SHGs Taken Eco Activities	% of Group Formation	% of Grade-I Passed	% of Grade-II Passed	% of Women SHG	% of SHGs Taken Eco Activities	Per Capita Credit Per SHG (as on 31st March 2005)
Uttar Pradesh	115210 (7)	20289	16945	4729	19416	5.88	17.61	14.71	40.1	16.85	26375.6
West Bengal	151953 (6)	26690	7586	31475	2241	7.75	17.56	4.99	20.71	1.47	13622.4
Lakshadeep	2 (26)	0	0	1	0	0	0	0	50	0	
Uttaranchal	13007 (17)	1462	1409	883	1249	0.66	11.24	10.83	6.79	9.6	41020.4
Chattisgarh	46988 (10)	2548	1294	941	1063	2.4	5.42	2.75	2	2.26	92605.7
Jharkhand	24744 (13)	3127	1207	0.3902	1554	1.26	12.64	4.88	15.77	6.28	33195.3
Total	1960883	227117	112496	280303	73446	100	11.58	5.74	14.29	3.75	1236338.7

Source: Ministry of Rural Development, GOI
Note: Figures in brackets indicate ranks.

SC/ST families. If a family has at least four of these nine conditions, it can be considered poor, and one member of that family can be encouraged to become a member of SHG. Locally important conditions may also be considered to decide whether a family is poor. A reasonably educated and helpful local person has to initially help the poor people to form groups. This person is called an animator or facilitator. Usually, the animator is a person who is well known locally. The members of an SHG face similar problems. They help each other to solve their problems.

SHGs promote small savings among their members. The savings are kept with the banks. This is the common fund in the name of the SHG.The SHG gives small loans to its members from its common fund. After six months, if the SHG satisfies the bank as per the check list for quality, bank can give loans to the SHG. The members of SHGs realize that like their savings, the bank loan is also their own money. The group as a whole commits repayment of the loan to the bank. Moral pressure is exerted on the borrowing members for repayment of loan. SHGs provide good business opportunities to banks. Reserve Bank of India(RBI) and National Bank for Agriculture and Rural Development(NABARD) have approved banking with SHGs. RBI has classified loans to SHGs as priority sector lending.

The group should meet regularly. Ideally, the meetings should be weekly, or at least monthly.The attendance in all the group meetings is compulsory. Membership Register ,Minutes Register, etc. are to be kept up to date by the group by making the entries regularly. Simple and clear books are to be maintained. Minutes Book, Savings and Loan Register, Weekly/Fortnightly/Monthly Register, Member's Passbooks are kept by SHG. The major functions of SHG are (a) savings and thrift, (b) internal lending, (c)discussing problems, and (d) taking bank loan. The linking of SHGs to bank has four steps: (1)opening of savings bank account, (2)internal lending by the SHG (3) assessment of the SHG, (4) checklist for assessment of SHG,(5) sanction of credit to SHG ,and (6)repayment of loan by the SHG. For purveying credit to the

SHGs, there are different models of SHG-Bank credit linkage. In the present paper, we have made a comparative study of panchayat-led and NGO-led SHGs.

Review of Existing Literature

In this section we shall make a brief review of existing literature on SHGs. Dasgupta (2001) has examined the different aspects of micro financing through informal groups like SHGs. Dutta and Raman (2001) have examined the co-existence of heterogeneity and social cohesion in SHGs and also the impact of SHGs on income level of members in Andhra Predesh. Namboodiri and Shiyani (2001) have examined the potential role of SHGs in term of reach, linkage with banks for savings and credit–for the weaker sections of rural households in Gujarat. Satish (2001) has made a study relating to some issues in the formation of SHGs in the states like Karnataka, Maharashtra and Uttar Predesh. Madheswaran and Dharamadhikary (2001) have highlighted the aspect of empowering rural women through SHGs in Maharashtra. Gurumoorthy (2000) has also discussed about the empowerment of rural women through SHGs. Ojha (2001) has highlighted the role of SHGs in rural employment generation. Mandal (2005) has made an assessment of SGSY and SHGs in India. Thakuria (2005) has highlighted about the growing mission of self-helping. Das (2003) has concluded that the micro credit–SHGs model has got tremendous attention in recent years and micro credit-SHGs integration could be the way out for overall rural development vis-à-vis poverty allevation. There also exists a large number of studies on SHGs, viz. Kulshresth and Gupta (2001,2002), Tripathy (2003), Singh (2003) Sarangi (2003), Chatterjee (2003. 2002), Rao (2002), Dogra (2002), Chowdhury (2005), Rao (2005), Dadhich (2001), Naithanj (2001), Malhotra (2005), etc.

From this brief review of existing literature on SHGs it may be said that there is a scope to conduct a comparative study of panchayat-led and NGO-led SHGs for analysing the progress, problems of SHG activities and impact of SHG activities on poverty alleviation in W.B. with special reference to Purba and PaschimMedinipur districts.

Objectives of the Study

The objectives of the present study are:

1. To examine the progress of different aspects of SHGs in India by states, W.B. by districts, blocks of Purba and Paschim Medinipur and Gram Panchayats (GPs) of Sahid Matangini block in Purba Medinipur.
2. To conduct a comparative study of Panchayat-led and NGO-led SHGs for analysing the impact of SHG activities on poverty alleviation through income and employment generation and problems of SHG activities in Sahid Matangini block in Purba Medinipur district of W.B.

Data Base & Methodology

The secondary data used for this study has been collected from various government sources, viz. Economic Survey of Government of India (GOI), Statistical Abstract of Government of W.B., Economic Review of Government of W.B., Office of Paschim and Purba Midnapore Zilla Parishad, Office of Sahid Matangini block. The progress of SHGs activities using secondary data has been observed for India by states, W.B. by districts, blocks of Purba and Paschim Medinipur, GPs of Sahid Matangini block. The field level data for different variables relating to SHGs activities has been collected from 20 SHGs (12 SHGs led by Panchayats and 8 SHGs led by NGOs) in Sahid Matangini block. The simple statistical techniques like percentages, growth rate, rank, mean, standard deviation (S.D.), etc have been used for this study. For measuring the progress of SHGs activities using secondary data, we have studied the factors like number of SHGs formed, credit -saving ratio, saving per SHG, cash credit per SHG, % of grade-I or grade-II passed, etc. Again, the field level study has considered the factors like, income and employment generated from SHG activities, condition of women members engaged in SHG activities, etc. to conduct a comparative study of Panchayat-led and NGO-led SHGs for measuring the impact and problems of SHG activities.

Progress of SHGs in India by States and W.B. by Districts

In this section, we shall highlight the progress of SHGs in India and districts of W.B. There is a positive growth rate of SHGs in states but in terms of growth of SHGs there is a wide variation among states. Linkages of Banks with SHGs are found impossible for this variation. States such as Andaman and Nicobar, Gujarat, Karnataka, Kerala, Orissa and Uttar Pradesh have comparatively lower growth whereas other states have higher growth of SHGs. The states with lower growth rates might have begun their SHG-bank linkage programme at an earlier stage so that it may already have sufficient linkages and further linking is quite difficult. Most of the states with lower growth rate will have a lower number of SHGs linked in the recent years compared to states that have a high growth rate (Soundarapandian, 2006). There are vast credit variations among the states and among the regions. Among the regions, southern region is the best region in financing SHGs. Next to that the performance of central region, eastern region and western region is moderate. The northern and north east region are comparatively poor. While considering the number of groups the southern region, central region, eastern region have enrolled more SHGs. Other regions enrolled less SHGs. Among the regions southern region distributed more credit and per capita credit per SHG are very high. While considering the states among the region Pondicherry and Tamil Nadu states are performing well and have distributed more credit. In central region Chattisgarh state distributed more credit and per capita credit. In western region Goa State's per capita credit is high and in northern region Haryana and Punjab states' per capita credit is very high. Eastern region and north eastern region's per capita credit per SHGs are up to the level and Mizoram, the only state in north eastern region, recorded 101428.5 rupees per capita distributed to the SHGs. It could be clear that the level of credit is increased and one can find a sign of development of SHGs and involved more economic activities (Loganathan & Asokan, 2006). As per GOI own information total SHGs formed in all India upto July 2006 has

Table 2
District wise Formation & Performances of SHGs in West Bengal by Districts

	Total No. of SHGs Formed					*G.R. (%) (No. of SHGs)*		*No. of Women SHGs G.R. (%)*			*R.W.SHGs*		
Districts	*2002 (upto Dec.)*	*2004 (upto Dec.)*	*2006 (upto July)*	*R'04*	*R'06*	*02-06*	*04-06*	*2002 (upto Dec.)*	*2004 (upto (Dec.)*	*2006 (upto July)*	*2004 (upto Dec.)*	*2006 (upto July)*	*02-06*
24 Parganas(N)	1824	9261	11270	3	5	517.87	21.693	1044	8301	2899	3	4	177.68
24 Parganas(S)	7365	8619	8937	4	9	21.344	3.6895	4640	5386	48	6	18	-98.97
Bankura	1206	4514	6940	11	12	475.46	53.744	764	3194	801	10	13	4.8429
Birbhum	835	2909	8173	14	10	878.8	180.96	475	1527	1488	16	7	213.26
Burdwan	3016	5923	10514	7	6	248.61	77.511	1307	3381	2341	9	5	79.112
Cooch Behar	1807	6170	9130	6	7	405.26	47.974	1699	5978	3782	4	3	122.6
Darjeeling	0	1814	1460	17	18	#####	-19.51	0	901	129	18	17	#DIV/0!
Hooghly	1925	5017	3312	9	15	72.052	-33.98	15	2799	444	11	16	2860
Howrah	1142	2323	3243	15	16	183.98	39.604	1127	2246	595	14	15	-47.2
Jalpaiguri	1327	7171	14044	5	2	958.33	95.844	1313	5856	6158	5	1	369
Malda	1222	3947	9053	12	8	640.83	129.36	1199	2483	2302	12	6	91.993
Murshidabad	2586	4760	7900	10	11	205.49	65.966	202	3999	1208	8	9	498.02
Nadia	981	3288	6664	13	13	579.31	102.68	695	2413	1038	13	11	49.353
Uttar Dinajpur	421	1633	4612	18	14	995.49	182.42	133	1114	1462	17	8	999.25
Purulia	991	5551	11331	8	4	1043.4	104.13	55	4376	3869	7	2	6934.5
Dakshin Dinajpur	1389	1897	3009	16	17	116.63	58.619	1134	1824	976	15	12	-13.93
East Midnapore	10547	11283	12572	2	3	19.2	11.424	8223	9469	728	2	14	-91.15
West Midnapore	13644	16771	18695	1	1	37.02	11.472	9957	12503	1170	1	10	-88.25
Siliguri	656	887	1094	19	19	66.768	23.337	265	758	46	19	19	-82.64
Tota	52884	103738	151953			187.33	46.478	34247	78508	31475			-8.094

Contd.

G.R. (%) Women SHGs	*% of Women SHGs*	*R% of Women SHGs*	*Gr. I Passed*		*G.R. (%) of Gr-1*	*%Gr-1 2006*	*R% of Gr-106*	*Grill Passed*	*Gr. (%) of Gr-11*	*% of Gr II*	*R% of Gr II*	*SHGs taken eco activities (2006)*		
04-06	*2006*		*2004*	*2006*	*(2004-06)*					*(2004-06)*	*2006*	*2006*	*No*	*%*
-65.076	25.7232	6	4806	3629	-24.49	32.2	1	675	452	-33.037	4.011	10	132	1.1713
-99.109	0.53709	19	6345	1696	-73.27	18.98	8	180	218	21.1111	2.439	13	38	0.4252
-74.922	11.5418	14	1454	1210	-16.781	17.44	9	129	78	-39.535	1.124	17	11	0.1585
-2.554	18.2063	10	1902	1151	-39.485	14.08	13	439	155	-64.692	1.896	15	160	1.9577
-30.76	22.2656	8	3533	2015	-42.966	19.16	7	884	692	-21.719	6.582	6	173	1.6454
-36.735	41.4239	2	3623	2506	-30.831	27.45	4	3623	654	-81.949	7.163	5	180	1.9715
-85.683	8.83562	15	717	344	-52.022	23.56	5	94	191	103.191	13.08	2	207	14.178
-84.137	13.4058	13	3188	387	-87.861	11.68	14	1380	304	-77.971	9.179	3	128	3.8647
-73.508	18.3472	9	1481	256	-82.714	7.894	17	861	256	-70.267	7.894	4	347	10.7
5.1571	43.8479	1	3012	2815	-6.5405	20.04	6	41	73	78.0488	0.52	18	25	0.178
-7.2896	25.428	7	1353	939	-30.599	10.37	16	211	170	-19.431	1.878	16	7	0.0773
-69.792	15.2911	12	2522	1144	-54.639	14.48	12	510	264	-48.235	3.342	12	114	1.443
-56.983	15.5762	11	1762	992	-43.7	14.89	11	531	247	-53.484	3.706	11	333	4.997
31.239	31.6999	5	502	725	44.422	15.72	10	82	111	35.3659	2.407	14	2	0.0434
-11.586	34.1453	3	1565	3225	106.07	28.46	3	471	0	-100	0	19	0	0
-46.491	32.436	4	1205	868	-27.967	28.85	2	243	163	-32.922	5.417	8	136	4.5198
-92.312	5.79065	17	7876	621	-92.115	4.94	19	2987	2499	-16.337	19.88	1	214	1.7022
-90.642	6.25836	16	8980	2093	-76.693	11.2	15	863	999	15.759	5.344	9	8	0.0428
-93.931	4.20475	18	417	74	-82.254	6.764	18	161	60	-62.733	5.484	7	26	2.3766
-59.909	20.7136		56243	26690	-52.545	17.56		11397	7586	-33.439	4.992		2241	1.4748

Notes: GR= growth rate, R= rank, W=women,Gr=grade

Source: Govt. of West Bengal.

been 19, 60, 883 (table-1). Andhra Predesh has ranked first either in case of total SHGs or in case of women SHGs. But Assam and Lakshadeep have ranked first and second respectively in case of % of women SHGs formed. It is found that 14.29% SHGs be women SHGs in India as a whole. On the other hand, 11.58% and 5.74% SHGs in all India have passed grade-I and II respectively. Assam and Bihar have ranked first and second respectively either in case of % of grade-I passed or in case of % of grade-II passed. The percentage of SHGs taken economic activities has been highest for Assam.

Let us examine the different aspects of SHGs in the districts of W.B. It is observed that the total number of SHGs formed in W.B. has increased from 52, 884 to 151963 during 2002-06 (table-2). The growth rate of total number of SHGs formed has been 187.33% for W.B. In 2006, Paschim Midnapore has ranked first in case of total number of SHGs formed. On the other hand, Jalpaiguri has ranked first in case of women SHGs formed. In July 2006, the percentage of women SHGs formed in W.B.has been 20.71. It has been maximum for Purulia. The number of SHGs passed grade-I or II has declined over years during 2004-06 for the districts. In W.B. 18% and 5% SHGs have passed grade-I and II respectively. The percentage of grade I passed has been maximum for North 24-parganas and that of grade-II passed become maximum for Purba Medinipur. On the other hand, 1.47% SHGs in W.B. has taken economic activities. This percentage share has become largest for Howrah.

Progress of SHGs in Blocks of Purba and Paschim Medinipur

In this section, we shall highlight the different aspects of SHGs in blocks of Purba and Paschim Medinipur.

Purba Medinipur

In Purba Medinipur, there exists 25 blocks. The total number of SHGs formed in Purba Medinipur has increased from 2109 to 12572 during 2001-06 (Table-3). The growth rate of number of SHGs formed has been 496.11%. 45.47% and 74.07% SHGs in Purba Medinipur have passed grade-I respectively in March 2001 and March 2006. On the other hand, the % of grade-II

Table 3

Purba Midnapore Block wise position on SHG of March 2001 and March 2006

(Amount in Rs. Lakh)

	Total No. of SHGs No.		G.R of S/SHG	Grade I passed CC/SHG		% of Grade I passed		Grade II passed		% Gr-II	GR	S/SHG	CC/SHG	CSR
Blocks	2001 Mar	2006 Mar	of SHGs	2001 Mar	2006 Mar.	2001 Mar.	2006 Mar.	2001 Mar.	2006 Mar.	2006 Mar.	of Gr-I (%)	2006	2006	2006
Tamluk	184	683	271.1957	131	542	71.19	79.36	0	232	34.55	313.74	0.07	0.18	2.8
	(2)	(4)				(5)	(8)		(16)	(7)				
Sahid Matangini	52	406	680.7692	21	313	40.38	77.09	0	145	35.71	1390.48	0.02	0.13	6.4
	(17)	(14)				(15)	(10)		(10)	(6)				
Panskura - I	153	637	316.3399	9	500	5.9	78.5	0	73	11.46	5455.56	0.02	0.11	5.9
	(3)	(7)			(21)	(9)		(17.5)	(22)					
Panskura - II	23	399	1634.783	8	253	34.78	63.41	0	64	16.04	3062.50	0.02	0.11	5.5
	(24)	(15)				(18)	(19)		(19)	(19)				
Mayna	49	847	1628.571	37	541	75.51	63.87	0	267	31.52	1362.16	0.07	0.12	1.7
	(18.5)	(1)				(4)	(18)		(4)	(9)				
Nandakumar - I	57	652	1043.86	48	551	84.21	84.51	0	309	47.4	1047.92	0.04	0.2	4.9
	(16)	(6)				(2)	(5)		(2)	(3)				
Sutahata	95	369	288.4211	0	190	0	51.49	0	48	13.01	0.00	0.05	7.3	155
	(10)	(21)				(24)	(22)		(21)	(21)				
Haldia	118	334	183.0508	117	287	99.15	85.63	0	88	26.35	145.30	0.04	0.09	2.1
	(5)	(24)				(1)	(3)		(10)	(14)				
Nandigram - I	83	717	763.8554	66	294	79.52	41.00	0	242	33.75	345.45	0.03	0.1	3.9
	(13)	(2)				(3)	(24)		(5)	(8)				
Nandigram - II	103	375	264.0777	63	303	61.16	80.8	0	170	45.33	380.95	0.06	0.15	2.4
	(7)	(20)				(7)	(7)		(8)	(4)				
Mahisadal	93	387	316.129	40	251	43.01	64.86	0	14	3.62	527.50	0.09	0.09	1.1
	(11)	(16)				(13)	(17)		(23)	(24)				
Contai - I	49	573	1069.388	16	417	32.65	72.77	0	273	47.64	2506.25	0.1	0.2	1.9
	(18.5)	(10)				(19)	(13)		(3)	(2)				

Contd.

	Total No. of SHGs No.		G.R of S/SHG	Grade I passed CC/SHG		% of Grade I passed		Grade II passed		% Gr-II	GR	S/SHG	CC/SHG	CSR
Blocks	2001 Mar	2006 Mar	of SHGs	2001 Mar	2006 Mar.	2001 Mar.	2006 Mar.	2001 Mar.	2006 Mar.	2006 Mar.	of Gr-I (%)	2006	2006	2006
Contai - II	39	383	882.0513	21	270	53.85	70.5	0	65	16.97	1185.71	0.09	0.33	3.9
	(19)	(18)				(9)	(14)		(18)	(18)				
Contai - III	77	654	749.3506	32	586	41.56	89.60	0	373	57	1731.25	0.1	0.11	1.1
	(14)	(5)				(14)	(22)		(1)	(1)				
Ramnagar - I	114	451	295.614	57	291	50	11.10	0	44	9.76	410.53	0.09	0.14	1.5
	(6)	(12)				(10)	(25)		(22)	(23)				
Ramnagar - II	131	612	367.1756	64	563	48.85	92	0	130	21.24	779.69	0.04	0.09	2.3
	(4)	(9)				(11)	(1)		(13)	(16)				
Bhagabanpur - I	100	384	284	4	287	4	74374	0	150	39.06	7075.00	0.02	0.1	4.6
	(8)	(17)				(22)	(11)		(9)	(5)				
Bhagabanpur - II	92	506	450	57	341	61.96	67.4	0	142	28.06	498.25	0.07	0.13	1.9
	(12)	(11)				(6)	(15)		(11)	(13)				
Pataspur - I	26	363	1296.154	15	225	57.7	61.98	0	52	14.33	1400.00	0.04	0.16	4
	(22)	(22.5)				(8)	(20)		(20)	(20)				
Pataspur - II	41	363	785.3659	20	206	48.78	56.75	0	111	30.58	930.00	0.09	0.2	2.1
	(19)	(22.5)				(12)	(21)		(14)	(10)				
Khajuri - I	2.5	378	1412	0	254	0	67.2	0	107	28.31	0.00	0.01	0.09	6.3
	(22)	(19)				(24)	(16)		(15)	(12)				
Khajuri - II	29	441	1420.69	0	378	0	85.71	0	133	30.16	0.00	0.09	0.16	1.8
	(21)	(13)				(24)	(4)		(12)	(11)				
Egra - I	99	617	523.2323	30	507	30.30	82.17	0	6	.9	1590.00	0.03	0.1	3.1
	(9)	(8)				(20)	(6)		(24)	(25)				
Egra - II	67	348	419.403	25	177	37.31	50.86	0	73	20.98	608.00	0.07	0.12	1.7
	(15)	(23)				(16)	(23)		(17.5)	(17)				
Nandigram - III	210	693	230	78	515	37.14	74.31	0	177	25.54	560.26	0.08	0.14	1.7
	(1)	(3)				(17)	(12)		(7)	(15)				
Total	2109	12572	496.1119	959	9312	45.47	74.07		3488	27.74	871.01	0.06	0.13	2.3

Notes: CC=cash credit, GR=growth rate, Gr=grade, S=saving, CSR=credit saving ratio.
Source: Purba Medinipur Zilla Parishad

passed has increased from zero to 27.74% during 2001 to 2006. The block level analysis shows that in case of number of SHGs formed Nandigram-III and Moyna have ranked first respectively inMarch 2001 and March 2006. Side by side, the % of grade-I passed has been highest for Haldia in March 2001 and for Ramnagar-II in March 2006. The % of grade-II passed has been maximum for Contai-III in March 2006. Again, the growth rate of grade-I passed in Purba Medinipur has been 871.01% during 2001-06. It has been highest for Panskura-I block. In Purba Medinipur the saving per SHG and cash credit per SHG has been Rs. 6000.00 and Rs. 13,000.00 respectively in March 2006. Again, the credit- saving ratio in the district as a whole has been 2.25. It has been highest for Sutahata block.

Paschim Medinipur

In Paschim Medinipur there exists 29 blocks. The number of SHGs formed in Paschim Medinipur has increased from 11,689 to 18441 during 2002-06 (Table-4). The growth rate has been 66.32%. 76.3% SHGs in Paschim Medinipur be women SHGs in March 2006. The growth rate of grade-I passed in Paschim Medinipur has been 83.30% during 2002-06. The % of grade-I passed has risen from 51.50% to 60% in the district as a whole. The number of SHGs formed has been highest for Garbeta-I in March 2002 and for Debra in February 2006. The growth rate of both the numbers of SHGs formed and grade-I passed is highest for Debra block during 2002-06. The % of grade-I passed has been highest for Keshpur in March 2002 and for Kharagpur-II in February 2006. On the other hand, 9.92% SHGs has passed grade-II in the districts as a whole during February 2006. The % of SHGs passed grade-II has been maximum for Debra block. In 2006 the credit saving ratio, saving per SHG and credit per SHG have been 1.58, Rs. 0.06 million, Rs. 0.09 million respectively for the district as a whole. The credit saving ratio has been highest for Garbeta-III block.

Progress of SHGs in G.P.s of Sahid Matangini Block

In Sahid Matangini block, the total number of SHGs formed has increased from 293 to 402 during 2002-06 (table-5). The %

Table 4

Paschim Midnapore Block wise position on SHG of April 2002 and Feb. 2006

(Amount in Rs. Lakh)

Blocks	*SHG formed*			*Women SHG*		*Passed Grade - I*			*Passed Grade - II*		*% of grade - I*		*% of Gr.II*	*TS*	*CC*	*CSR*	*S/SHG*	*CR/SHG*
	Mar-02	*Feb-06*	*Growth Rate (%)*	*Feb-06*	*%*	*Mar-02*	*Feb-06*	*Growth Rate (%)*	*Mar-02*	*Feb-06*	*Mar'02*	*Feb-06*	*2006*	*2006*	*2006*	*2006*	*2006*	*2006*
Grabeta - I	756 (1)	985 (4)	30.30	362.00	36.80	477(1)	693	45.3	0	84	63.1(10)	70.35(7)	8.25	60.61	93.82	1.5	0.06	0.095
Garbeta - II	396 (15)	619 (17)	51.30	325.00	52.50	255(9)	395	54.9	0	41	64.4(9)	63.8(14)	6.62	38.51	40.2	1	0.06	0.065
Garbeta - III	510 (8)	559 (18)	9.60	417.00	74.60	278(8)	393	41.4	0	109	54.51(14)	70.3(8)	19.5	26.83	93.4	3.5	0.05	0.167
Keshpur	524 (7)	1019 (2)	94.50	604.00	59.30	460(2)	747	62.4	0	80	87.8(1)	73.3(5)	7.85	67.98	157.8	2.3	0.07	0.155
Midnapore	430 (12)	691 (12)	60.70	232.00	33.60	302(6)	394	30.5	0	36	70.2(5)	57(17)	5.2	32.12	64.57	2	0.05	0.093
Salboni	461 (11)	707 (10)	53.50	595.00	98.30	179(16)	296	65.4	0	24	38.8(21)	41.4(26)	3.4	61.6	20.68	0.3	0.09	0.029
Dantan - I	246 (26)	388 (26)	57.70	388.00	100.00	117(21)	161	37.6	0	24	47.6(17)	41.5(25)	6.2	18.44	28.02	1.5	0.05	0.072
Dantan - II	253 (25)	409 (23)	61.70	407.00	99.40	175(17)	321	83.4	0	66	69.2(7)	78.5(2)	16.1	22.45	63	2.8	0.05	0.154
Debra	352 (18)	1058 (1)	200.60	1050.00	99.70	65(26)	775	1092.3	0	278	18.5(27)	73.2(6)	26.3	12.46	123.7	9.9	0.01	0.117
Keshiary	262 (24)	784 (8)	199.20	781.00	100.00	181(15)	470	159.7	0	58	69(8)	56(19)	7.4	34.46	45.25	1.3	0.04	0.058
Khargpur - I	627 (3)	655 (13)	5.50	655.00	100.00	340(4)	426	25.3	0	84	54.2(16)	65(12)	12.8	48.23	76.5	1.6	0.07	0.117
Khargpur - II	298 (21)	367 (27)	85.40	367.00	100.00	214(12)	347	62.1	0	62	71.81(2)	95(1)	16.9	27.5	32.3	1.2	0.07	0.088
Mohanpur	280 (22)	332 (28)	18.50	332.00	100.00	165(18)	203	22.3	0	48	58.9(12)	61.1(15)	14.5	28.98	49.35	1.7	0.09	0.149
Narayangarh	480 (10)	805 (7)	67.70	800.00	99.40	81(24)	456	463	0	75	17(28)	56.6(18)	9.3	38.6	46.9	1.2	0.05	0.058
Pingla	298 (21)	427 (22)	3.30	425.00	99.80	133(19)	213	60.2	0	40	44.6(19)	50(20)	9.4	25.5	36	1.4	0.06	0.084
Sabang	561 (5)	631 (16)	12.50	624.00	98.60	240(10)	442	84.2	0	91	43(20)	70(9)	4.4	51.75	39.95	0.8	0.08	0.063
Binpur - I	505 (9)	706 (11)	39.80	98.00	13.90	189(14)	329	74.1	0	28	37.4(22)	46.6(22)	3.4	19.16	34.96	1.8	0.03	0.05
Binpur - II	404 (14)	922 (5)	128.20	832.00	90.20	230(11)	591	157	0	133	57(13)	64.1(14)	14.4	91.03	86.48	1	0.1	0.094
Gopiballavpur - I	119 (28)	482 (19)	305.00	206.00	42.70	74(25)	239	223	0	11	62.2(11)	49.6(21)	2.3	5.67	12.15	2.1	0.01	0.025
Gopiballavpur - II	182 (27)	404 (24)	122.00	206.00	51.00	129(20)	263	103.9	0	76	70.9(4)	65.1(10)	18.8	50.54	28.7	0.6	0.13	0.071
Jamboni	290 (21)	318 (29)	9.70	105.00	33.00	57(27)	123	115.8	0	38	19.66(26)	38.7(27)	11.9	12.22	14.25	1.2	0.04	0.045
Jhargram	679 (2)	1010 (3)	48.70	514.00	50.10	318(5)	596	87.4	0	10	47(18)	59(16)	1	66.55	107	1.6	0.07	0.106
Nayagram	278 (23)	774 (9)	18.40	393.00	50.80	40(28)	192	380	0	3	14.4(20)	24.8(29)	1.03	17.2	18.75	1.1	0.02	0.024
Sankrial	542 (6)	808 (6)	49.10	788.00	97.50	198(14)	364	83.8	0	34	36.5(23)	45(24)	4.2	38.77	63.5	1.6	0.05	0.079

Contd.

	SHG formed			Women SHG		Passed Grade - I			Passed Grade - II		% of grade - I		% of Gr.II	TS	CC	CSR	S/SHG	CR/SHG
Blocks	Mar-02	Feb-06	Growth Rate (%)	Feb-06	%	Mar-02	Feb-06	Growth Rate (%)	Mar-02	Feb-06	Mar' 02	Feb-06	2006	2006	2006	2006	2006	2006
Chandrakona - I	369 (16)	435 (21)	17.90	435.00	100.00	201(13)	329	63.7	0	54	54.5(15)	76(4)	12.4	23.08	50.4	2.2	0.05	0.116
Chandrakona - II	355 (17)	399 (25)	12.4	384	96.2	91(23)	185	103.3	0	47	25.6(25)	46(23)	11.8	10.34	26.25	2.5	0.03	0.066
Daspur - I	417 (13)	637 (14)	52.8	629	98.7	296(7)	414	39.9	0	63	70.98(3)	65.01(11)	9.9	53.14	73.65	1.4	0.08	0.116
Daspur - II	616 (4)	635 (15)	3.1	625	98.4	431(3)	494	14.6	0	97	70.01(6)	77.8(3)	15.3	39.11	85.35	2.2	0.06	0.134
Ghatal	301 (19)	475 (20)	57.8	341	71.8	100(22)	172	72	0	30	33.2(24)	36.2(28)	6.3	10.87	19.85	1.8	0.02	0.042
Total	11689	18441		14022	14022	76.3	6017	1102783.30%		0	1829	51.50%	60%	9.92	1033.71633		1.6	0.06
0.089																		

Note: CSR= credit saving ratio, S/SHG= savimg/SHG, CR/SHG= credit/SHG, TS= total saving, CC= cash credit,

Source: Paschim Medinipur Zilla Parishad.

Table 5
Progress Report of Sahid Matangini Block (GP wise) on SGSY of April 2003 and January 2006

GPs	*SHG formed*		*GR(%)*	*Women SHG Formed*		*GR(%)*	*Grade-I passed*		*GR(%)*
	Apr-03	Jan-06		Apr-03	Jan-06		Apr-03	Jan-06	
Santipur-I	21(7)	24(7)	14.28(7)	18(6)((85.7))	24(8)((100))	33.33(10)	16(6)((76.15))	20(8)((83.33))	25(9)
Santipur-II	34(3.5)	56(3.5)	64.7(4)	34(2)((100))	56(3)((100))	64.7(6)	31(2)((91.17))	43(4)((76.8))	38.7(7)
Kharui-I	25(6)	19(8)	-40	9(?)((36))	19(9)((100))	111.11(4)	9(9)((36))	10(10)((52.6))	11.11(10)
Kharui-II	19(8)	33(5)	73.68(3)	12(8)((63.2))	33(6)((100))	175(1)	10(8)((52.63))	27(6)((81.82))	170(1)
Khakarda	48(1)	66(1)	37.5(5)	42(1)((87.5))	65(1)((98.5))	54.76(8)	33(1)((68.75))	56(1)((84.85))	69.69(4)
Balluk-I	15(9)	17(9)	13.33(8)	7(10)((46.71))	16(10)((94.1))	128.57(2)	7(10)((46.67))	11(9)((64.71))	57.14(5)
Balluk-II	33(4)	64(2)	93.9(2)	32(3)((97))	64(2)((100))	100(5)	30(3)((90.1))	53(2)((82.81))	77.66(3)
Raghunath pur-I	28(5)	56(3.5)	100(1)	23(5)((82.14))	50(4)((89.3))	117.39(3)	23(5)((82.14))	47(3)((83.93)	104.34(2)
Raghunath pur-II	36(2)	42(4)	16.66(6)	27(4)((75))	37(5)((88.1))	37.03(9)	28(4)((17.78))	36(5)((85.71))	28.57(8)
Dhalhara	34(3.5)	25(6)	-24.47	16(7)((47.1))	25(7)((100))	56.25(7)	15(7)((14.12))	21(7)((84))	40(6)
Total	293	402	37.2	220	389	76.83	202	324	60.4

Contd.

Grade-II passed		*GR(%)*	**Credit per SHG**		**Credit/Member**		**CSR**		*% of*	**MSEA**		**GR(%)**	**WSEA**		**GR(%)**
Apr-03	*Jan-06*		*Apr-03*	*Jan-06*	*Apr-03*	*Jan-06*	*Apr-03*	*April-03 Jan-06*	*recovery*	*Apr-03*	*Jan-06*		*Apr-08*	*Jan-06*	
1((4.76))	5((20.8))	400.00	6190.5(5)	1916.67(9)	722(2)	1917(1)	24.1(2)	1.6(2)	60	130	190	46.15	13	19	46.15
0	15((26.8))	0.00	8823.5(1)	1598.2(10)	880(1)	1598(3)	29.3(1)	1.7(1)	50	300	370	23.33	30	37	23.33
0	0	0.00	2400(10)	7894.7(7)	577(9)	652(10)	19.2(9)	.66(10)	50	60	60	0.00	6	6	0.00
2((10.53))	10((30.3))	400.00	3157.9(9)	7272.7(8)	366(10)	741(9)	12.2(10)	0.87(6)	50	60	90	50.00	6	9	50.00
4((8.33))	35((53))	775.00	6250(4)	18333.3(1)	664(6)	1721(2)	22.1(6)	1.3(4)	45	300	530	76.67	30	53	76.67
3((20))	5((29.4))	33.33	3333.3(8)	8529.5(6)	617(8)	792(8)	20.6(8)	0.86(7)	50	50	60	20.00	5	6	20.00
3((9.1))	23((35.94))	666.66	6969.7(2)	11953.1(4)	678(5)	1062(6)	22.6(5)	1.4(3)	50	230	320	39.13	23	32	39.13
5((17.86))	25((44.64))	400.00	6071.4(6)	9553.6(5)	688(4)	937(7)	22.9(4)	0.8(9)	52	150	330	120.00	14	22	57.14
3((8.33))	21((50))	600.00	6944.4(3)	16785.7(2)	661(7)	1183(5)	22.1(7)	1.1(5)	50	250	150	40.00	21	33	57.14
5((14.71))	6((24))	20.00	3823.5(7)	13800(3)	703(3)	1228(4)	23.4(3)	0.85(8)	55	130	320	146.15	13	15	15.38
26	145	457.69	5733.8	13557.2	680	1236	23	1.17	61.2	1660	2420	45.78	161	232	44.10

Note: figures in ( ) Indicate rank

WSEA= Women started economic activities GR(%) = Growth rate(%)

MSEA= Members started economic activities

figures in (( )) indicate percentage

Source: Sahid Matangini block office

of women SHGs has also risen from 75.08 to 96.77%. Khakarda G.P. has ranked first in case of either total SHGs formed or women SHGs formed during 2003-06. The growth rate of total SHGs formed has been highest for Raghunathpur-I. On the other hand, the growth rate of women SHGs formed has been maximum for Kharui-II. The percentage of either grade-I or grade-II passed has increased over years for the district as a whole and highest for Khakarda G.P.The credit-saving ratio has been highest for Santipur-II.It is to note that the credit - saving ratio has declined over years during 2003-06. In January 2006, the credit per member and credit per SHG have been maximum for Santipur-I and Khakarda respectively.

Impact and Problems of SHGs : A Micro Level Study

In this section, a micro level study has been conducted among 20 SHGs (12 Panchayat- led and 8 NGO -led SHGs) having 200 members selected randomly for highlighting a comparative analysis of impact and problems of Panchayat -led and NGO-led SHGs. The details regarding number of members from two types of SHGs are given in tables 6& 7. It is customary to present the demographic and social background of the group members as they exert tremendous influence on availing credit and its utilization.

Age Profile

The details of age profile show that in case of Panchayat-led SHGs 18% of the selected members belong to the age group 15-25 years and 72% of them to the age group 25-45 years. On the other hand, in case of NGO- led SHGs, 80% of the beneficiaries belong to the age group 15-45 years. This distribution reveals that 80-90% of the beneficiaries belongs to the economically active segment of the population.

Social Status

The distribution of beneficiaries according to their social groups reveals that in case of Panchayat-led SHGs 40% of the beneficiaries belong to weaker sections, i.e. SCs, STs and OBCs. But 30% of the beneficiaries belong to weaker sections in case of NGO- led SHGs.

Table 6
Details of SHG led by Panchayat

Name of the led Panchayat	*Total No. of SHGs*	*Total No. of Member*		*Total*
		Male	*Female*	
Dhalhara	3	0	29	29
Khakarda	5	0	51	51
Santipur - I	1	0	14	14
Santipur - II	3	12	20	32
Total	12	12	114	126

Source: Field Survey

Table 7
Details of NGO led SHGs

Name of the led Panchayat	*Total No. of NGO*	*Total No. of Member*		*Total*
		Male	*Female*	
Dhalhara	2	10	10	20
Khakarda	0	0	0	0
Santipur - I	4	10	25	35
Santipur - II	2		19	19
Total	8	20	54	74

Source: Field Survey

Literacy Status

It seems that the SHGs are giving equal importance to illiterate and literate people. These data shows that in case of Panchayat -led SHGs 70% of the members have educational level of class I-VII and in case of NGO -led SHGs 60% of the members belong to educational level of class I-VII. 30% & 40% of the members belong to educational level of class IX-XII respectively in case of Panchayat- led and NGO -led SHGs.

Family Size

The average size of the member's family is 6 members for both types of SHGs.

Land Holdings

No doubt the rural poor mostly belong to asset less groups or have marginal value of assets. An attempt is made in Table-8

Table 8
Distribution of Operational Holdings (Acress)

Panchayat								NGO									
Ownership of Land	*0-0.25*		*0.26-0.50*		*0.50 & above*	*Total*		*Ownership of Land*	*0-0.25*		*0.26-0.50*		*0.50 & Above*		*Total*		
	HHs	*land*	*HHs*	*land*	*land*	*land*	*average*		*HHs*	*land*	*HHs*	*land*	*HHs*	*land*	*HHs*	*land*	*average*
own land	80	18.5	12	5.5	3.1	28.1	0.3	Own land	25	7.8	15	6	6	1.1	46	15	0.62
leased in	13	3.2	15	1.8	0.6	4.7	0.15	leased in	17	3	10	0.5	1	0.9	28	4.4	0.16
leased out								leased out									
Total	93	21.7	27	7.3	3.7	32.8	0.26	Total	42	8.1	25	6.5	7	2	74	19	0.26

Source: Field Survey

to explain the land ownership of sampled members, as the primary asset in rural areas is agricultural land. The average size of the land holding is 0.26 acres for both types of SHGs (which shows that all the members are from marginal farmers category).

Let us now examine the scenario of provision of loans, purpose of loan and repayment of loan. It is found that the loans have been provided for the purposes of cloth business, dairy, tailoring, grossary shop, rice processing, poultry, cultivation of paddy, flower, oilseeds, betelvine in case of both types of SHGs. In case of panchayat -led SHGs the average amount of loans varies from Rs. 33,000.00 to Rs. 25,862.00. 60%, 30%, 10% of the members received loans respectively between Rs. 3000.00 to Rs. 15,000.00, between Rs. 15001.00 to Rs. 20,000.00 and Rs. 20,001.00 to Rs. 25,862.00. On the other hand, in case of NGO led SHGs the average amount of loans varies between Rs. 2000.00 to Rs. 15,000.00. 70% of the members received loans between Rs. 2000.00 to Rs. 10,000.00. Thus the average amount of loans has been larger in case of Panchayat-led SHGs. Again, the repayment performance is better in case of NGO-led SHGs. We have also calculated the coefficient of variation (C.V.) for the distribution of loans across the sample households of either Panchayat-led SHGs or NGO-led SHGs. It is found that the values of C.V. are 20.32 and 23.26 respectively for Panchayat-led SHGs and NGO-led SHGs. These values indicate that more consistency is found for the distribution of loans among the households in case of Panchayat-led SHGs compared to NGO-led SHGs.

Impact of SHG activities on Poverty Alleviation: A Comparative Study

Let us examine the impact of SHG activities on poverty alleviation through income and employment generation. It is observed from Table-9 that average income generated has been higher for Panchayat-led SHGs as compared to NGO-led SHGs. The share of income generated from the SHG activities in total family income has been higher in case of Panchayat-led SHGs as compared to NGO-led SHGs. Again, the contribution of

Table 9
Impact on Income Generation in the Year 2005

(Amount in Rs.)

Panchayat						*NGO*					
Financing Activities	*No of HHs*	*IGFP*	*TFI*	*Average Income from the Project*	*POIFP*	*Financing Activities*	*No of HHs*	*IGFP*	*TFI*	*Average Income*	*POIFP*
cloth business	17	110000	153000	6470.588	71.90	cloth business	12	70000	180000	5833.33	38.89
dairing	20	145000	180000	7250	80.56	dairing	8	42000	120000	5250.00	35.00
tailoring	18	85000	110000	4722.222	77.27	tailoring	5	30000	100000	6000.00	30.00
grossary shop	9	60000	75000	6666.667	80.00	grossary shop	21	90000	230000	4285.71	39.13
rice processing	15	90000	120000	6000	75.00	rice processing	8	52000	100000	6500.00	52.00
poultry	8	58000	75000	7250	77.33	poultry	2	12000	45000	6000.00	26.67
agriculture						agriculture					
paddy	12	50000	67000	4166.667	74.63	paddy	7	28500	56000	4071.43	50.89
flower	9	47000	62000	5222.222	75.81	flower	8	33500	76000	4187.50	44.08
oil seeds	10	43000	57000	4300	75.44	oil seeds	2	10000	50000	5000.00	20.00
betelvine	8	44500	62000	5562.5	71.77	betelvine	1	4001	18000	4001.00	22.23
Total	126	732500	961000	5813.492	76.22	*Total*	74	372001	975000	5027.04	38.15

Source: Field Survey

Note:

i. IGFP = Income genetated from the project

ii. POIFP = % of income from the project

iii. TFI = total family income

Panchayat-led SHGs in total family income has been substantial. Side by side, it is found that the C.V. for the distribution of income among the households be higher in case of Panchayat-led SHGs (18.61) as compared to NGO-led SHGs (15.61). It implies that more equal distribution of income among the sample households is observed in case of NGO-led SHGs. On the other hand, the Table-10 shows that the impact on employment generation is better in case of Panchayat-led SHGs. It is seen that higher income and employment have generated in case of non-farm activities.

Let us examine the problems faced by SHGs.

(a) After joining in the SHG activities the burden of work on women has increased for both types of SHGs. They are working for 12-17 hours per day during the post-SHG period. They have to participate not only in domestic works but also in different economic activities. It has made in some cases, an adverse impact on vital domestic functions, e.g., child care , etc. and health of women.

(b) It is seen that the meeting of sample SHGs are not held regularly. In some cases, the resolution books, etc. are not maintained properly. The factors behind these irregularities are lack of education/training (particularly in case of females), more responsibility for domestic functions in case of females, etc. As a result, the groups have become dependent on other persons having the required skill for completing these tasks.

(c) The main obstacle in the way of development of SHGs is the sale of their products. The theory behind the formation of SHGs is that there exists a large number of buyers and sellers in the product market, homogeneous product, full mobility of information, etc. But those characteristics do not seen in reality. Big companies have occupied almost the whole market. Products are not homogeneous. Perfect mobility of

Table 10
Impact on Employment Generation in the Year 2005

	Panchayat				NGO		
Financing Activities	*No of HHs*	*Total Employment Generated*	*Average Employment Generated*	*Finacing Activities*	*No of HHs*	*Total Employment*	*Average*
cloth business	17	1800	105.88	cloth business	12	810	67.50
dairing	20	6000	300.00	dairing	8	1840	230.00
tailoring	18	5960	331.11	tailoring	5	1170	234.00
grossary shop	9	2250	250.00	grossary shop	21	7350	350.00
rice processing	15	1800	120.00	rice processing	8	708	88.50
poultry	8	2560	320.00	poultry	2	440	220.00
agriculture				agriculture			
paddy	12	1080	90.00	paddy	7	530	75.71
flower	9	1530	170.00	flower	8	1040	130.00
oil seeds	10	1200	120.00	oil seeds	2	200	100.00
betelvine	8	2000	250.00	betelvine	1	200	200.00
Total	126	26180	207.78	*Total*	74	14288	193.08

Source: Field Survey

information is not found. Under these circumstances, it has become very difficult for weaker organizations like SHGs to compete in the market effectively. So this may also explain why the SHGs do not start economic activities.

(d) The principle of profit maximization has become an indicator of success for banks in the post-liberalization era. As a result, the social responsibility of banks has decreased. The banks are imposing different conditions for passing grade-I or II. These have made difficult for SHGs to pass even grade-I in some cases and lost the motivation of SHGs members. The factors like exorbitant service charge (imposed by banks), higher transaction costs, etc. are also the hindrances in the way of progress of SHGs.

(e) Similar mind of group members is a necessary element for the existence of SHGs in the liberalized era. But it is not seen in reality. The members are more interested in individual enterprise as compared to group efforts. Thus individualism, lack of homogeneity, solidarity and cohesiveness, etc. are acting as hindrances in the way of progress of SHGs in a country like India. As a result ,our sample NGOs have also started to finance some individual projects/ enterprises (in lieu of group projects) for generating self- employment.

(f) In case of NGO-led SHGs it is seen that the members have to pay an extra interest rate imposed by the groups (which is not found in case of panchayat-led SHGs) and this higher interest payment is a factor creating excess burden on the members and hence they are not able to borrow larger amount of loan. It creates an adverse effect on the expansion of activities of expansion of activities of members of NGO-led SHGs.

(g) Since there is a provision for getting revolving fund / credit linkage (i.e. subsidy) in case of panchayat -led SHGs, so the peoples, particularly people below poverty line (BPL) ,are more attracted to opt for the panchayat model as compared to NGO model. Again, since there are more opportunities to reach / motivate people through panchayat representatives and development programmes, hence there are greater scopes for forming SHGs led by panchayats as compared to SHGs led by NGOs. Side by side, since the panchayat is a mainstream or a part and parcel of the life of rural poor / people, so they make more trust upon panchayats as compared to NGOs. This factor may also act for more spread of panchayat-led SHGs in a country like India.

(h) The political problems often creates problems for the expansion of SHGs. The government rules and regulations sometimes do not able to include some peoples (who are not belonging to BPL category) to join in SHGs led by panchayats. Under this circumstance, there is a scope to participate in SHG activities through NGO-led SHGs. In this case NGO model is better.

Conclusions

In this section we shall first summarize the study and then give some policy prescriptions. It is observed that the programme of micro finance through SHGs has been making rapid strides in both India and W.B. Both Purba and Paschim Medinipur districts have played a significant role for spreading SHG activities in the districts of W.B. The block level / G. P. wise analysis also shows almost an optimistic scenario of progress of different aspects of SHG activities.

The Major Findings from the Field Level Study are as follows:

(1) The provision of loans is larger in case of panchayat – led SHGs and repayment performance is better in case of NGO-led SHGs. More consistency is seen for the distribution of loans among the households of panchayat -led SHGs

(2) The impact on poverty alleviation through employment and income generation has been better in case of panchayat –led SHGs.

(3) The SHGs activities have created an excess burden on the women members. There exists irregularities in office procedures, problem of selling the product ,exorbitant service charge & higher transaction costs for getting loans, lack of homogeneity, individualism, etc. which are acting as hindrances in the way of progress of SHGs.

(4) The panchayat -led SHGs are more acceptable to rural poor as compared to NGO-led SHGs. Thus, there is a more prospect for spread of panchayat -led SHGs in a country like India.

Despite the existence of many obstacles in the way of progress of SHGs, there is a good prospect for the progress of SHGs. The following measures may be taken for better functioning of SHGs.

(1) The greater emphasis should be given on (a) the unity, responsibility, awareness, etc. amog the members, (b) the utilization of local resources and the fulfillment of local demand for better progress of SHGs.

(2) More SHGs may be formed for the production of environment friendly products, which have a high domestic and foreign demand.

(3) The larger provision of cheap credit should be made not only for more progress of SHGs but also to bring poorest of the poor under SHG activities.

(4) The educational level & quality among members should be increased. The simplification of office procedure may be done for relieving the burden of work among the members (particularly women who find little time for rest).

(5) The SHG activities may be considered as a weapon for empowerment of women and social change in a country like India.

(6) Though it is observed from the micro level study that the panchayat-led SHGs are more suitable, but it is to be noted that the spread of both models be

emphasized for accelerating both social and economic development in India. It is also to note that the least political interference is essential for the way of functioning of SHGs.

To conclude, the organizations like SHGs may be considered as a model for both poverty alleviation and radical social transformation of less developed countries like India.

References

Annual Report (2002-2003), Ministry of Rural Development, GOI.

Antony, Valsamma (2006), 'Education and Empowerment- The Key to Women Empowerment', Kurukshetra, Vol. 54, No. 4, February

Chavan, P. and R. Ramakumar (2002), 'Micro-Credit & Rural Poverty: An Analysis of Empirical Evidence', Economic and Political Weekly (EPW), Vol. XXXVII, No. 10, March 9.

Chowdhury, S. (2005), 'Self-Help Group Formation through Frequently Asked questions', Kurukshetra, Vol. 53, No. 3, Jan.

Chatterjee, Dr. S. (2005), 'Networking SGSY, Banks and SHGs: Initiative in Uttar Pradesh', Kurukshetra, Vol. 51, No. 4, February.

Dasgupta, R. (2001), 'An Informal Journy Through Self- Help Groups', Indian Journal of Agricultural Economic (I.J.A.E). Vol. 56, No. 3, July-September.

Dutta, S. K. & M. Raman (2001), 'Can Heterogeneity and Social Cohesion Coexist in Self-Help Groups?' An Evidence From Group Lending in Andhra Pradesh in India, I.J.A.E, Vol. 56, No. 3, July-September.

Dadhichi, C.C. (2001), 'Micro Finance–A Panacea for Poverty Alleviation: A Case Study of Oriental Gramin Project in India'. I.J.A.E., Vol. 56, No. 3, July-September.

Das, S. (2003), 'Self-Help Groups & Micro Credit: Synergic Integration', Kurukshetra, Vol. 51, No. 10, August.

Dogra, V. M. (2002), 'Women Self –Help Groups: Profiles from Andhra Pradesh & Karnataka', Kurukshetra, Vol. 50, No. 6, April.

Economic Survey (2003–2004), GOI.

Gangaiah, C. B. Nagaraja & C. Vasudevulu Naidu (2006), 'Impact of Self–Help Groups on Income and Employment: A Case Study, Kurukshetra, Vol. 54, No. 5, March.

Gurumoorthy, T. R. (2000), 'Self- Help Groups Empower Rural Women', Kurukshetra, Vol. 48, No. 5, February.

Gupta, Dr. M. L. & Namita Gupta (2006), 'Economic Empowerment of Women through SHGs', Kurukshetra, Vol. 54, No. 4, February.

Ghosh, M. (2006), 'Bursting Balloons', The Sunday Statesman Magazine, October 22.

Ghosh, M. (1983), 'Bank Project Resucitates Rural Bangladesh', The Sunday Statesman, September 4.

Kulshrestha, Dr. L. R & A. Gupta (2001), 'Self-Help Group: Innovations in Financing the Poor', Kurukshetra, November.

Kulshrestha, Dr. L. R,and A. Gupta (2002), 'NGOs in Micro Financing: Partners in Rural Development', Kurukshetra , Vol. 53, No. 3, January.

Koutsoyannis, A. (1979), 'Theory of Econometrics', 2nd Edition.

Loganathan, Dr. P. R. Asokan (2006), 'Inter Regional Development of Self Help Groups in India', Kurukshetra, Vol. 54, No. 11, September.

Malhotra, R. (2005), 'Imperative Need for Fine-tuning The SGSY', Kurukshetra, Vol. 53, No. 8, June.

Mandal, A. (2005), 'Swarnajayanti Gram Swarozgar Yojana and and Self-Help Group: An Assessment', Kurukshtra, Vol. 53, No. 3, January.

Madheswaran, S. & A. Dharmadhikary (2001), 'Empowering Rural Women Through Self-Help Groups: Lessens from Maharashtra Rural Credit Project', I.J.A.E., Vol. 56, No. 3, July-September.

Haque, Mohammedul (2006), 'Dhubri Hatchery: Ray of Hope for Self Help Groups', Kurukshetra, Vol. 54, No. 11, September.

Namboodiri, N. V. & R. L. Shiyani (2001), 'Potential Role of Self-Help Groups in Rural Financial deepening', I.J.A.E., Vol. 56, No. 3, July-September.

Naithani, P. (2001), 'Micro-Financing The Self-Employment Activities: Sea-Saw of Ideas', Kurukshetra, Vol. 49, No. 10, July.

Ojha, R. K. (2001), 'Self -Help Groups and Rural Employment', Yojana, Vol. 45, May.

Pal, Dr. M. (2002), 'Swarnajayanti Gram Swarozgar Yojana: Evolution, Assessment and Future Prospect', Kurukshetra, June.

Rath, N. (1985), 'Garibi Hatao: Can IRDP Do it?' EPW, Vol. 20, No. 6, February 9.

Rao, R. (2005), 'Women's Groups Herold: A Wind of Change in Rural Uttaranchal', Kurukshetra, Vol. 53, No. 3, January.

Rao, V. M. (2002), 'Women's Self -Help Groups: Profiles from Andhra Pradesh & Karnataka', Kurukshetra, Vol. 50, No. 6, April.

Rao, C. A. (2003), 'Women Empowerment through SHG and DWCRA-A Study in Andhra Pradesh'. Indian Journal of Regional Science (I.J.R.S.), Vol. XXXV, No. 1.

Ray, S. K. & A. Das (2005), 'Self-Help Groups in West Bengal with Special Reference to Purba Medinipur District: Some Issues', Published in Seminar Volume on Self -Help Groups: A New Way of Rural Development, K. D. College of Commerce, Paschim Medinipur.

Sarangi, P. (2003), 'Self-Help Groups: An Experiment in Orissa', Kurukshetra, Vol. 51, No. 4, February.

Satish, P. (2001), 'Some Issues in The Formation of Self- Help Groups', I.J.A.E., Vol. 56, No. 3, July-September.

Singh, Dr. O. R. (2003), 'Role of NGOs in Fostering Self -Help Groups: A Case Study of MYRA DA', Kurukshetra, Vol. 51, No. 4, February.

Sau, S. (2006), 'Sasahayak Dal: Paschim Medinipur Zilla', (in bengali version), Aahawan (Paschim Medinipur)

Soundarapandian, Dr. M. (2006), 'Micro Finance for Rural Entrepreneurs: Issues and Strategies', Kurukshetra, Vol. 54, No. 11, September.

Sarkar, A. (2006), 'Arthanaitik Vikalpa Nai, Kintu Samaj Badaler Bara Astra', (in bengali version), Anandabazar Patrika, October 19.

Thoner, D. B. Kerblay & R. E. F. Smith (1966), 'Chayanov on the Theory of Peasant Economy', Homewood, Illinois, Richard D. Irwin.

Tenth Five Year Plan (2002-2007), GOI.

Thakuria, N. (2005), 'The Growing Mission of Self Helping', Kurukshetra, Vol. 53, No. 3, January.

Tripathi, O. M. (2003), 'Making Insurance Everybdy's Business, The SHG Way', Kurukshetra, Vol. 51, No. 4, Feb.

Tripathy, K. K. (2006), 'Micro-Credit Invention and Poverty Alleviation', Kurukshetra, Vol. 54, No. 11, September.

Yunus, M. (2004), 'Grameen Bank, Micro Credit and Millennium Development Goals', EPW, Vol. XXXIX, No. 36, September 4.

Yunus, M. (2000), 'Banker to the Poor: The Autobiography of Muhammad Yunus, Founder of the Grameen Bank', The University Press Ltd., Dhaka.

Yadav, S.S. (2006), 'Self-Help Group Movement in Rajastan: Bright Prospects', Kurukshetra, Vol. 54, No. 11, September.

CHAPTER–11

CHANGES IN DYNAMICS OF INDIAN TRADE UNION CONGRESS IN THE WAKE OF GLOBALISATION: AN OVERVIEW.

Kameshwar Pandit

The changing scenario due to Globalization and Economic Liberalization have causes significant inroads in the relationship between the State, Labour and Capital in India. The social dimension of this changed circumstances has serious implications on industrial relations. The most direct impact of the changed scene is increasing vulnerability of the workers ' interest in the labour–management power dynamics. Trade unions have to operate in the changed environment and curve out a new role for themselves of controlling and regulating the management for protecting the interest of workers. Trade unions have now to play an important role of cooperating with management, as the survival of the business itself in the increasing competitive environment would be at stake. The service conditions of employment would be determined by market forces hereafter rather than trade unions. With the liberalization of the economy, trade union power has come under severe threat (Singh and Mohanty, 2001). Industrial restructuring has led to retrenchment, employment loss, casualisation of employment and contract employment, etc., which in turn resulted in declining membership and weakening of the union power (Singh and Mohanty, 2001). Unions were earlier forced to check the unilateral power of management, but in the post-restructuring period they have lost their countervailing power (Sheth,1993, Multy,1993). Trade unions are losing not only their membership but also influence over the workforce as they have succumbed to the pressure of inter–union rivalry, political affiliation, lack of mature and internal leadership, and an antagonistic attitude towards management. Trade unions still have the legacy of protecting workers' interests. Without unions, management can become more powerful and exploit workers. Trade unions have not set their agenda beyond wage bargaining so far, and do not concentrate upon issues like retraining, technological up- gradation, skill-up gradation and professional growth (Pandit. K, 2006).

Globalization of business is having a significant impact on industrial relations practices to be followed by multi-national corporations. They have to decide as strategy whether labour relation systems are to be uniform at all locations or it may be tailored to each location. It is also imperative to orientation of multinational firms to organize labour, and also understand current issues and trends in managing global workforce. In the new economy resulting from globalization policies the concern for protectionism stands reduced to the minimum, and industry is increasingly exposed to the rationality of global competitive forces. Employees constantly face pressure to achieve higher standard of performance to survive in the competitive global environment. The focus on getting more or less in manufacturing sectors, generation of new knowledge, and global implications of business operations are necessary aspects of the economy. Capital, labour, raw materials, management, information, technology and markets are organized on global scale, either directly or through a network of linkage between economic agents (Debi S. Saini, 2003). These developments have fundamentally questioned the basic premises on which industry was working in most parts of the world before. But perhaps a greater area of concern all around in the fate of industrial relations frameworks that have been rooted in different types of protectionism in various parts of the world so far. It is not a case of simple shift in power from labour to employers especially because mortality of organizations in the new economic scenario is also in the rise. Power shift is taking place at several levels, both covert and overt. This shift has its casual roots in the changes in various contexts of industries working in the new economy (Debi S. Saini, 2003)

In the wake of globalization and its emerging issues and impact on various dimensions of working conditions with respect to labour- management relations , trade unions have not only to survive and bargain effectively but also to influence public policy in their favors and to mitigate its negative effects. Trade unions, commonly known as protest organizations, never take up any developmental activities. To quote, N. R. Seth Indian Journal of Industrial Relations (IJIR), Oct. 2001, *"Unions are at Crossroads. They are on divergent path. One wonders they would like to map the new path early. They have to redefine their social responsibilities in relation to unemployed, contract workers and displaced workers. They may like to explore ways for development of new leadership for new trade unionism appropriate for the global society in the years ahead."* In this context the trade unions have to play developmental role instead of their traditional role. Keeping in view of the above and to examine the visionary change of the trade unions, the author in this paper has selected *Indian National Trade Union Congress a* largest central federations as a case study and has tried to study the change of visionary approach and ideology since its inceptions and after the globalizations.

The Indian National Trade Union Congress: A Resume

The INTUC came in to existence on 4th May, 1948, as a result of the resolution passed on 17th November 1947., by the Central Board of the Hindustan Mazdoor Sevak Sangh , which was a labour organization working under the direction of National Congress–minded labour leaders on Gandhian Philosophy of

Sarvodaya. This resolution called upon its various members unions to affiliate themselves with the All India Trade Union Congress and to promote through that body the policy and programmes of the Congress party. Since, the AITUC was under the stronghold of the Communists, the Congress labour leaders thought of forming a new central trade union organization. To give effect to this idea, a conference was convened at New Delhi under the Chairmanship of Sardar Vallabhbhai Patel amongst the eminent socialist leaders having broader objectives. The INTUC, Partly with the support of the government both at the provincial and central levels and partly because of its earnest organizing activities, soon become the most dominant of the central federations in terms of numerical strength. In 1948, the Government of India recognizes it as the most representative amongst the central federations and gave to it the right to nominate the workers' delegation to ILO.

At present the INTUC is the most representative federations of India having the largest membership and largest nos of affiliated trade unions in comparison to other federations The number of affiliated unions of INTUC are1604 and their memberships are 2692 thousands as reported by Govt. of India, Ministry of Labour .

Vision of INTUC at the Time of Its Inception

Ideologically as well as administratively the blood stream of the INTUC flows from Ahmedabad being the Textile Labour Association provides it with a strong membership nucleus, a rich treasury and a cadre with long experience in labour work. The INTUC aim was at the *Sarvodaya* ideal and stands for gradual transformation of the existing social order . Its aims at establishing a socialist state in India. At its first conference the visions, aims and objectives of the INTUC were clearly formulated. The objects as stated in the Constitution are as under:

(a) (i) To establish an order of society which is free from hindrances in the way an all round development of its individual members, which fosters the growth of human personality in all its aspects and goes to the utmost limit in progressively eliminating social, political or economic exploitation and inequality, the profit motive in economic activity and organization of society and the anti-social concentration of power in any form.

(ii) to place industry under national ownership and control in suitable form in order to realize the aforesaid objective in the quickness of time.

(iii) to organize society in such a manner as to ensure full employment and the best utilization of its manpower and other resources.

(iv) to secure increasing association of the workers in the administration of industry and political interest of the working class.

(b) (i) To secure an effective and complete organization of all categories of workers including agricultural labour.

(ii) to guide and co-ordinate the activities of affiliated organizations.

(iii) to assist in the formation of trade unions.

(iv) to promote organization of workers of each industry on a nation wide basis.

(v) to assist in the formation of regional or provincial branches of federations.

(c) (i) To secure steady improvement of conditions of work and life and status of workers in industry and society.

(ii) to obtain for the workers various measures of social security including adequate provision in respect of accidents, maternity, sickness, oldage and unemployment.

(iii) to secure living wage for every workers in normal employment and to bring about a progressive improvement in his standard of life.

(iv) to regulate hours and other conditions of work in keeping with the requirements of the workers in the matter of health, recreation and cultural development .

(v) to secure suitable legislative enactments for ameliorating the condition of workers and to ensure proper enforcement of legislation for the protection and uplift of labour.

(d) (i) To establish just industrial relations.

(ii) to secure redress of grievances, without stoppage of work by means of negotiations and conciliation and failing these arbitration, adjudication.

(iii) Where adjudication is not applied and settlement of disputes within a reasonable time by arbitration is not available for redress of grievances to have recourse to other legitimate methods, including strikes or any suitable form of *satyagraha.*

(iv) to make necessary arrangement s for the efficient conduct and satisfactory and speedy conclusion of authorized strikes or satyagraha.

(e) (i) To foster the spirit of solidarity, service, brotherhood, cooperation and mutual help among workers.

(ii) to develop in the workers a sense of responsibility towards industry and community.

(iii) to raise the workers' standard of efficiency and discipline.

About the means to be used for achieving those aims the relevant clause states, " The means to be adopted for the furtherance of the above mentioned objectives are to be peaceful and consistent with truth." (A.S. Mathur)

Vision of INTUC after Globalization

The new Industrial Policy formulated by the Government of India in the light of global economy has created a big setback to the public sector industries in the Center and the State. The

Govt. of India and the State Governments are showing their helplessness to run the Public Sector more efficiently & profitably by taking necessary steps to modernize and introduce the new technology so that the public sector may be able to compete in the national and international market. Government of India and the State Governments are expressing that they do not have financial capability and also lacking technical personnel to administer properly to run the public sector industries.(G.Sanjeeva Reddy) . In a paper presented by G. Sanjeeva Reddy entitled *"INTUC Approach Papers for General Council"* as "The public sector is virtually controlled by bureaucrats without giving any attention towards the modernization. More over, the industries are also affecting badly due to red- tapism and non-professionals interference in day to day working. One of the most stumbling blocks for progressing the public sector is non-availability of required working capital and market strength to run the industry. The Board of Directors of Public Sector mostly comprised of IAS officers who are lacking technical and business knowledge.

The present state of affairs of public sector is mostly due to the bureaucratic control to run the public sector industries. *Now the time has come that this public sector should be liberalized from the hands of the bureaucrats and convert this public sector industry into peoples' sectors.* There is a strong feeling and desire that the ordinary people of India should be asked to purchase shares of the public sector undertakings so that the industry may be able to get the money directly from the common citizens of India and the public sector be controlled by such people of the country through their participation in the shares of the PSUs. The Government can keep 51% share in their hands and prohibit purchasing the public sector shares by monopoly houses in India or outside so that the majority shares go in hands of common people who would have their representative in the Board of Directors. This way the present public sector can be converted in to peoples' sector and efficiency and competitiveness can be increased . The INTUC, therefore , is not opposed to disinvestments in the public sector industry up to 49% so that the people may get an opportunity to participate in the company affairs. Some visionary change of INTUC as mentioned in the speech of the INTUC President in *Building Trade Unions into the 21st Century* may identify in the following areas are as under."

Industrial Relations in the light of Global Economy

Since independence the Indian industrialist as well as trade unions continued to enjoy protection from Government through various regulations and they become habituated to run the industry in such an environment only. As such protections has been disappeared and the market economy has become the order of the day and the number of Indian industries have gone out of gear and have not been able to stand the competitions with multinationals. In the light of the above situations new industrial relation culture is necessary to be evolve in the country leaving *the conventional approach* of the trade union movement INTUC have to *create intellectual collective bargaining* in the industrial relations and strengthen the forces by adopting constructive methods and in the manner suitable for the present situation and insuring protection of interest of the poor people and the workforce in the industry. Today the trade union has got a manifold responsibility to save the industry from becoming a sick. The following concentration and study is required for the trade union and keep continuous vigilance on the working of the industry. Control of production cost which plays dominant role in determining the price of goods produced by the company. Examination of optimum manpower cost element in the total cost of production. Control of non-productive expenditure.

The Modernization and Automation should be a continued process to enable the industry to stand in the competitive market. The expansion of the industry is required huge investments so that the industry may able to stand in the international market. The trade union leader should participate in the management for running the industry and its production process, including quality of production, so that the interest of the consumers be safeguarded by supplying the qualitative goods at reasonable price. That is only possible through competitive market. It is essential to build up mutual trust between the management and the trade union in the area of industrial relations. The INTUC unions should practice in building up mutual trust between both the parties pertaining to the industries and its functioning. The trade union should also formulate workers sharing in the profit of the company at reasonable level. For security of service and improvement of economic conditions of workers healthy and economic running of the industry, effective marketing network for its product is the need of hour. The trade union is required to change its present system of working in the light of above changed atmospheres

Labour Laws

The INTUC and the representatives of Ministry of Labour , Govt. of India agreed about the necessity to amend the labour laws in the light of new economic situation and stated that no committee would be able to bring about a unanimous report in the present juncture. Therefore, the Indian Trade Union Act and Industrial Disputes Act should be amended as per the unanimous recommendations of Ramanujam Committee. Setting up an Industrial Relations Committee in place of Industrial Tribunal. Proportionate representation of trade unions in the negotiations committee. Conducting the Secret Ballot elections over representation of the union . Introduction of check-off system.

The INTUC oppose in amendment or removal of the section 25(M.N&Q) of the Industrial Disputes Act. There should be a common definition to identify the workmen in all the laws relating to labour. The INTUC is interested in bringing the Agricultural Labour Act in the coming future.

Organizing the Unorganized Workers

More than 90% of the working population of the country is working in unorganized and informal sectors and no trade union center worth its name can ignore this vast majority of workers to be unionized. Considering the decline of membership in the organized sector it has become imperative for INTUC to put greater emphasis for organizing the unorganized workers spread over not only in rural and semi-urban areas but also in the urban areas. The INTUC has organize Bidi workers, Construction workers, Forest workers, Contract labour, Self employed persons , Power loom sectors , Agriculture and rural workers and so on.

Chronic Sick Public Sector Undertakings & Trade Unions Approach

It is estimated that approximately 1,20,000 industries are suffering with sickness in the Country, small, medium, and large including public sectors. All the traditions are under Confusion what to do and what not to do in regard to the workers problems of sick Industries. The INTUC vision is clear in this respect that;

(a) In a sick industry unions should extend over all cooperation with the management to reverse their industry from loss to profit.

(b) As far as possible the unions should avoid making any wage increase demands in the sick public sector industry till such time the financial position of the unit become better.

(c) The union should work together with the management to diversify the Industries production and also work out formula for making the units economically Viable.

(d) The unions should educate not to behave irresponsibly in the sick public sector Industries. There will be a serious implications against they may not get even gratuity, Provident fund and other terminal benefits.

After studying the Chinese line of action we cannot have a different type of approach to find out solutions of sick industry. We therefore, should consider taking the following steps:-

(i) In the sick industry we should have a united trade union movement and joint action committees with other trade union organization.

(ii) The sick industry which can not be brought back as economically viable, unit, then we should agree for closure of the industry with guarantee for payment of the terminal benefits such as gratuity, provident fund etc.

The trade unions should learn to talk to workers the truth in the prevailing situations and Guide them in a proper and correct line. No false hopes should be given under any circumstances.

Social Safety Net

INTUC firmly believes that the Social Safety net and Social Security legislations have their very limited applicability and are too inadequate to provide reasonable relief to the workers who are hard pressed in the present insurmountable economic crisis.

INTUC is of the view that in present economic crisis the retired employees need more Protection, as without proper earning and non-availability of adequate social security Benefits they are forced to face sufferings in their old age when they deserve more care. To tackle this grave situation and provide adequate protection INTUC feels that the coverage of existing Social Security legislation has to be expanded to bring under their preview all sections of workers and implementing machinery has to be equipped with authority and power to enforce the laws and deal with those responsible for even the least violation of any of them. INTUC, therefore, impress upon the Government to ensure-

(a) release all dues to the workers who have been rendered jobless due to sickness and closure to save them from starvation and for that create a special fund.

(b) enlarging the coverage of all Social Security legislations to encompass all sections of the workers including the self employed, and

(c) providing job at least to one of the dependents of the retiring employees in the establishment they served as they need more social protection in their old age.

Conclusions

Above comparative discussions presents clear picture in change of vision and visionary approach, attitude and positive thinking of trade unions like INTUC in the present global scenario. *INTUC has changed their traditional role and move towards developmental role.* As quoted by *N.R, Sheth , IJIR, oct. 2001* that, HRM- HRD provides a comprehensive leverage to management to feel responsive to the whole spectrum of workers' interests-psychological, social economic and organizational. Accordingly, unions are welcome as far as they exists, they should function essentially as partners in the pursuit of progress of the enterprise where their constituents work. The management emphasis is on development of workers as human capital. The key areas are to develop sense of participation and ownership, training, communication, information, understanding, security, compensation, multi-skilling, reaching out to the workers families, emotional intelligence, trust building and the like. Union should be adequately informed and involved in achieving excellent performance. Bipartite negotiations should lead to achievement of organizational goals.

All union leaders have accepted the positive role of unions in HRM-HRD and achievement of performance objectives. The emerging role of trade unions pulls unions progressively closer to the managerial functions of HRM- HRD. There seems to be a broad range of agreement between managers and union leaders on the direction of change in this regard. The INTUC has redefined their role as one of the developmental rather than protest institution in the organization. They have become *Agitator to Trainer, Blackmailer to Educator, Crisis dealer to Counselor, Grievance handler to Motivator, Coercive Bargainer to Facilitator, Productivity bargainer to Communicator.* The INTUC become more cooperative and playing an important role by cooperating with the management for their own survival as well as survival of organization under the competitive environment. As a social institution, trade union with new path has to play more positive role in Global environment keeping in view that most of the employment conditions would be determined by the market forces rather than the political and/ or member strength of trade unions

REFERENCES

Bhatia, S.K. (2002), International Practices in Industrial Relations, Deep and Deep Publications Pvt. Ltd. New Delhi.

Chamberlain and Kuhn (1993) , Collective Bargaining, Tata McGraw Hill Publishing Company, New Delhi.

Deshpandey, Lalit K & Alakh N. Sharma (2004), Liberalization and labour, Institute for Human Development, New Delhi.

Jha,Shiv Chandra (1970), The Indian Trade Union Movement) Firma K.L. Mukhopadhyay, Calcutta.

Karnik, V. B. Indian Trade Unions: A Survey. Cited in Jha S. C. , Calcutta.

Patnaik, P. (1998), "Some Indian Debates on Planning in Byres", Economic and Political weekly, Vol. 30, No. 47.

Pandit. K. (2006), "Emerging Issues of Globalisation and Changing Role of Trade Unions" GITAM Journal of Management , Vol. 4. January-June, Visakhapatnam.

Reddy, G, Sanjeeva, " Building Trade Unions into the 21st Century", Indian national Trade Union Congress, New Delhi.

Saini, Debi S. (2003) ,"Dynamics of New Industrial Relations and Postulates of industrial Justice", The Indian journal of Labour Economics, Vol. 46, No. 4, New Delhi.

Sen Gupta, Anil K. (2003) , "Decline of Trade Union Power in India," The Indian Journal of Labour Economics, Vol. 46, No. 4, New Delhi.

Sheth, N.R. (2001), "Unions are at Cross- roads" The Indian Journal of Industrial Relations, October.

Thakur, C.P. (2003), "Emerging Pattern on Industrial Relations from Reality Check to Some Speculation", The Indian Journal of Labour Economics, Vol. 46, No. 4 New Delhi.

Verman, Rahul and Manali Chakraborti (2003), "Workers ' Struggle in Times of Globalisation: A Critique of Trade Unions in Historical Perspective", The Indian Journal of Labour Economics, Vol. 46. No. 4. New Delhi.

Annual Reports of INTUC New Delhi.

CHAPTER–12

A BRIEF ANALYSIS OF SOME CHALLENGES FACED BY AGRIBUSINESS ALONG THE VALUE CHAIN

Vinodh K. Natarajan
J. Cyril Kanmony

INTRODUCTION

The global agribusiness is gradually being dominated by value chain relationships in which lead firms exercise vertical coordination. There is a startling variety of forms of such linkages in agribusiness value chains, including out grower schemes, contract farming, category management by supermarket suppliers, marketing contracts, etc. It is these linkages that small and medium enterprises can enter and add value to agricultural products. A number of strategies are available as a means of adding value to agricultural commodities. Strategies can involve certification or closer link with traders, producers, retailers or small farm producers. The adoption of these strategies by small producers in poor or developing countries is not very easy.

Meeting these challenges means organizing agribusiness value chains so that they are able to deliver what is required by global buyers and food safety regimes. As Van Roekel et al. (2002) state that integrated supply chain is a vital tool for competing in tool in today's globalizing business economy. Also it has been suggested that a defining characteristic of the agro-industrialization phenomenon is the growing number of complex contractual arrangements replacing spot markets (Cook and Chaddad, 2000).

Before we can explore the challenges faced by agribusiness, it is important to understand the various actors and relationship involved in the agribusiness value chain. Given below is a simplified agribusiness value chain diagram.

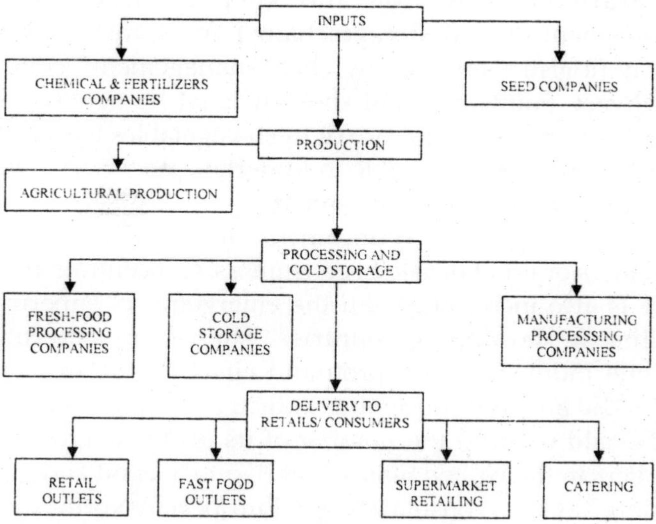

Figure 1: A Simple Agribusiness Value-chain Diagram

The above figure shows a simplified agribusiness value chain. Further it also shows the concentration of business activities at various stages in a value chain. Here at the first or input stage, concentration of chemical and seed companies are evident. The second stage or at the production stage there is concentration of agricultural producers. In this stage there are a large number of producers whose nature of concentration is based on the nature of products being produced. Climatic and soil conditions play a very important role in the nature of agricultural crops that can be cultivated in a particular region. For e.g., cultivation of cotton crop needs a dry climate, where as cultivation of rubber needs a rainy climate. This is an important criterion for emergence of agribusiness clusters among agricultural producers.

The third stage covers the processing industry. The processing industry covers a broad range of activities. At one end there are processors of fresh produce and at the other end, agricultural processing can involve the transformation of agricultural raw materials into a variety of processed products. In the processing stage value is added through packaging, preparation, innovation and keeping products fresh (involvement of cold storage chains) and transferring them quickly (logistics and supply chain management) from farm to delivery points or retail shelf. It must be noted that the benefits of processing in case of fresh vegetables has favoured large exporters who are able to undertake necessary levels of technical expertise and investment.

The last stage in the agribusiness value chain is the delivery to retailers or point of sale to consumers. Concentration in this space is also increasing with the emergence of supermarket retailing in developing countries. The rise of supermarket retailing indirectly has a profound effect on the structure of the production and processing industry. For e.g. in the 1970's Mc Donald reduced the number of its domestic ground-beef suppliers in the United States from 175 to 5. Food and grocery retailing has been consolidating in Europe and North America, where as in developing countries like, India China, and Brazil etc it is still in the evolving stage.

Concentration at the retail level is not only about size. It also changes the value-chain relationships as large buyers or supermarkets have transformed themselves from resellers of products made by others, into firms that find suppliers for the products they can sell under their brand to their customers. Increasingly they play an active role in branding, product development, supplier selection and distribution. The position of retailers within agribusiness is shown with the help of the table below.

Table 1
The Agricultural Supply Chain

Stage in Value Chain	*Number of Actors*
Consumers	160 million
Customers	89 million
Retail outlets	170,000
Supermarket formats	600
Buying desks	110
Manufactures	8,600
Semi-manufacturers	80,000
Suppliers	180,000
Farmers/Producers	3,200,000

Source: Grievink (2002)

The above table shows the different level of actors and the level of concentration prevailing in the food value chain in Europe. The above data clearly shows that the market power of key actors in agribusiness value chain comes from high levels of concentration at certain points in the chain. The consequence of these trends implies that there would be less income following to less concentrated parts of the value chain, mainly small farmers or producers. Therefore the need to look into the challenges faced by small producers and take steps to increase their incomes while adding value to their products must be given at most priority in the developing countries. If not the above value chain model will be replicated even in developing countries and the small producers will be marginalised.

The increasing influence of retail and branded markets as one of the main agents of globalisation was brought out by Gereffi (1994). He termed theses firms as manufactures without factories as they did not engage directly in manufacturing production themselves, but played an important role in product design, supplier selection and value chain coordination. A good example which highlights the role of firms participating through the global value chain can be seen through the way Nike conducts its business. It designs and markets footwear and clothing, but it does not own any footwear or clothing factories. It works with suppliers across various countries to deliver a rapidly changing range of products to shops and retailers spread across the world. Its core competences are design and branding, and not manufacturing. Logistics and supply chain management have been core competences, but these are increasingly outsourced to first-tier suppliers.

This type of business model is gaining prominence among agribusinesses and hence posing challenges as well as opportunities for small producers and farmers in developing and poor countries. The process of adding value along the value cum supply chain requires that the identity and distinctiveness of the product is established at the point of origin and maintained as it moves along the value as well as supply chain. Adding value need not involve physical transformation of the product. Global buyers such as supermarkets and large processors are not solely buying a physical product. They are buying a product that is bundled with a set of value-adding services. In other words, adding value to traditional agricultural export commodities often involves the same types of challenges as seen in the production and trade of non-traditional agricultural exports.

Value-chain analysis suggests a number of strategies for adding value. In particular, it emphasizes the opportunities for adding value through increasing "buyer service" elements of the total product package delivered to buyers. Increasing revenue streams from agribusiness by adding value should be the objective of any government policy. This challenge is one which has confronted policymakers not only in agriculture, but in export manufacturing as well.

THE IMPORTANCE OF AGRIBUSINESS ALONG THE VALUE CHAIN

The growth of agriculture sector is of primary importance for any country. Historical experience suggests that agricultural sector growth and increases in agricultural productivity may be a prerequisite to broader-based sustained economic growth and development (Department for International Development, 2002, UK Govt). Also many studies have documented the fact that agricultural growth is more effective in poverty eradication than growth of mining, manufacturing or services sector, since agriculture forms the backbone of any economic activity in rural areas. Moreover it can be said that agricultural growth provides a direct link to the poor as seen from the fact that forty to sixty per cent of the world's poor live in rural area (World Development Report 2000). Therefore, many economists have backed the agriculture sector as the engine for kick-starting growth among developing and poor countries

One opportunity for achieving higher agricultural growth lies in increasing export of agricultural products of poor countries in the global markets. The above argument is based on a theory which equates high economic growth with higher exports. Therefore for any country to achieve higher economic growth, the country must expand its export sector. Although this theory is debatable, many studies have brought out the fact that a higher export in any one sector accelerates economic growth. A major reason for articulating the idea that promoting agricultural exports will reduce poverty among developing and the poorest countries is based on the fact that the potential for export growth from the mining, manufacturing and service sectors is poor among developing and poor countries.

In short increasing the agricultural exports of poor and developing countries is not only important for economic growth but also a critical factor in reducing poverty. But, increasing exports by taking part in the global agricultural trade or being part of the global value chain, the agricultural sector provides both opportunities and challenges, which will be dealt later in the paper. The section below will bring out a brief outlook of the global agricultural scenario, which will be the basis on which some of the challenges faced by the agribusinesses will be dealt in detail.

The Global Agriculture Sector – An Overview

In the last decade or so there has been a rise in agricultural trade especially among developing countries. Improvements in transportation technology have played a vital role in promoting agricultural trade. Further the last quarter of a century has also seen large scale increase as well as transformation in global trade in agriculture sector. But it should be noted that not all sectors of agriculture provide the same opportunity for export led growth. This can be seen from the table given below.

Table 2
The Changing Structure of Agricultural Trade
(Percentage of Export Value)

	Total for Developing Countries	
Products	*1980-81*	*2000-01*
Traditional Tropical Products		
Coffee, Cocoa and Tea	18.3	8.5
Natural Fibres	8.0	3.3
Sugar and Confectionery	10.5	4.3
Nuts and Spices	2.4	2.8
Subtotal	39.2	18.9
Temperate Products		
Meats, Fresh and Processed	7.2	6.0
Dairy Products	0.3	1.1
Grains, Raw and Processed	9.3	7.0
Oilseeds and Edible Oil	4.6	5.5
Animal feed	7.5	8.5
Subtotal	28.8	28.1
Fish and Horticulture		
Fish, Fresh and Processed	6.9	19.4
Fruits, Vegetables and Flowers	14.7	21.5
Subtotal	21.6	40.9
Other Products		
Tobacco and Cigarettes	2.6	3.3
Beverages	1.1	3.6
Other Processed Food	6.7	5.2
Subtotal	10.4	12.1
Total	100	100

Source: Jaffee (2005)

From the above table it is clear that during the last two and half decades, there has been a substantial shift away from traditional tropical products and towards non traditional agricultural exports, particularly horticulture and fish (which includes seafood more generally). This is substantiated with the fact that in the early eighties, traditional tropical products accounted for 39.2 per cent of all food exports from developing countries, where as twenty years later this had fallen to 18.9 per cent. Conversely, during the same period, of the total food exports, the share of horticultural products rose from 14.7 per cent to 21.5 per cent and fish (seafood) rose from 6.9 to 19.4 per cent.

Overall, over the years the share of bulk commodities in total agricultural trade has gone down. Decreased demand for bulk commodities has been compensated by the growth in intermediate processed products, which are essentially processed bulk commodities. The consequences of this shift are also seen at the level of individual products. The rapid expansion of global demand for and trade in horticultural and seafood products created attractive export opportunities, while the relative decline of traditional tropical products, most notably coffee, created problems.

A deeper look at the reasons why this shift from traditional tropical products to fish and horticulture by small farmers in developing countries happened might as well provide us with some interesting facts useful for framing policies for reducing poverty in developing or poor countries.

The advantages which the small producers experienced in shifting to horticulture production were many folds. Firstly, it offered them favourable price and quantity trends. Secondly, the horticulture industry is highly labour-intensive. Often horticultural production requires twice as much, sometimes up to four times as much labour than the production of cereal crops. Therefore it is a sector which generates relatively high levels of employment (Weinberger et al. 2005). Thirdly, some types of horticultural production yield the same amount of production using just a fraction of an acre needed to grow other crops. This helped the small farmers experience economies of scale and provided them with relatively high incomes per hectare of land in use.

Therefore, it is not surprising that a lot of effort has been devoted to promoting the production and export of non-traditional agricultural products with particular emphasis given to horticulture and fresh and processed produce.

Moreover small farmers benefiting from huge increase in agricultural income do not shift their additional farm income on imported or capital intensive goods as done by large concerns. This is highlighted by the fact that reduction in poverty has been larger in countries where small and medium sized farms have driven agricultural growth.

As it has been said earlier that promoting agricultural exports is fundamental for reducing poverty, it is imperative that small and medium enterprises (SMEs) and poor producers being able to gain access to the value chains involved in the production, processing and distribution of these agricultural products. As poverty reduction depends on the economic growth of small producers it is very apt to look into some of the challenges faced by agribusiness in developing and underdeveloped countries and finding ways to overcome some of these challenges so as to benefit the people who are dependent on the agribusiness for their livelihood.

Global Trends in the Agribusiness

Global agricultural markets have become increasingly complex because of concentration at all points in the value chain. Many initiatives undertaken by many countries have been targeted to benefit the small producers as changes in agricultural trade have imposed new problems and challenges for agribusiness as a whole. Changes like growing disposable income of individuals, urbanization, consumer awareness regarding quality and safety are affecting the global agricultural trade. Therefore realizing the potential benefits of agricultural export growth for poverty reduction requires careful analysis of trends in global markets which are hindering the growth of agricultural exports of poor and developing countries. Some of the major changes that are impacting the global agricultural trade have been discussed below.

The Growth of Food Processing Sector

The faster growing categories in agricultural trade are non-bulk packaged processed food products, which are marketed under different brands. Developed countries have played an important role in promoting trade in processed food products. In developed countries, there is a demand for labour saving and better quality products, due to which the import of high value and processed foods products is more in these countries. On the other hand, in case of developing countries, due to increase in level of incomes and other factors the demand for processed food is slowly but steadily increasing, resulting in higher import as well as local production of these products. But still the share of developed countries in import of processed food products is more than developing countries, whereas in case of bulk commodities share of developing countries exceeds the import of developed countries. However the change in consumption pattern in developing countries caused by numerous factors is accelerating the growth of processed food industry.

Food Safety Initiatives-Standards

Food safety has emerged as an important issue in global agricultural trade. Moreover, increased consumer awareness, especially in developed countries has highlighted the important of food safety in agricultural trade. The importing as well as the exporting country are emphasizing hygiene and food safety issues in food production, processing, distribution and preparation. WHO is working closely with the Food and Agriculture Organization of the United Nations (FAO) to address food safety issues along the entire food production chain i.e. from production to consumption. Currently the WTO agreement, the Sanitary and Phytosanitory Measures Agreement (SPS) sets out the basic rules on food safety and animal and plant health standards. The SPS agreement allows countries to set their own standards and adopt different methods of inspecting products. But having different technical regulations and product standards makes life difficult for producers and exporters. Therefore adoption of international standards is a better option for exporters, but it certainly involves significant costs. The high costs involved may discourage manufactures from poor countries from trying to sell their agricultural produce abroad thus preventing access to taking part in the global market.

Growing Ethnic Influence

On the global level food consumption can no longer be confined to food being produced locally. Fast-food burgers, French fries, Chinese noodles and rice, Italian pasta and pizza, Indian curry, Japanese sushi, and many varieties of types of food have spread their reach to all parts of the world. This has lead to the availability of a wider choice of ethnic food. Due to increase in the number of working women, greater disposable household income, increased trade and above all the free movement of people across the boundaries the awareness and demand for and consumption of many ethnic foods is on the rise. The availability of different ethnic food locally has influenced the consumption pattern of people at the global level. This has led to new agricultural products being produced and exported from developed countries to developing countries and vice versa.

Food Retailing

The growth of Modern distribution outlets or retail chains in the wholesale and retail agribusiness are shifting customers from traditional traders to modern retail chains. The rise or modern distribution outlets are a significant gain for the packaged food industry. According to a survey by US Department of Agriculture, packaged food products account for large shares of total food expenditures among consumers in high-income countries where the demand for convenience is growing. The United States, the European Union, and Japan account for over half of total global sales of packaged products. In developing countries, intermediate products such as vegetable oils, dry pasta, and other dried products account for the bulk of retail sales. However, market trends indicate strong growth in sales of packaged food products among developing countries partly due to rapidly growing income levels created by the growth of the manufacturing and service sectors.

In order to safeguard the interests of small farmers it is important for the government, development agencies, as well as private players to undertake several initiatives to include them as part of this organised retailing. Being part of the retail chain business can help the small farmers to gain more income and reduce the poverty level on a larger scale.

Having seen some of the trends that confront the agribusiness, it is worthwhile to look in detail some of challenges affecting the Indian agribusiness taking part in the global value chain in lieu of the changing trends in agricultural trade.

THE GROWTH OF FOOD PROCESSING SECTOR AND FOOD RETAILING

Historically speaking, processing of fruit and vegetables in the simplest form like pickle making, sun drying and or making preserves has been practiced in the country from very ancient times almost in every home. It has generally been the exclusive domain of grandma's who developed their own fine recipes without any formal training except their age-old experience and conventional wisdom.

Worldwide, during the last half a century, the food processing industry has undergone massive changes. It has emerged as a big industry with major sub sectors like, Fruit and Vegetable Processing, Fish-processing, Milk Processing, Meat and Poultry Processing, Packaged/Convenience Foods, Alcoholic beverages and Soft drinks and Grain Processing. Also during the same period, from the age of famines and food importer, the Indian food and food processing sector has evidenced strong growth.

As of 2006 India ranks third in production of food grain (210 million tonnes), is the worlds second largest producer of fruits and vegetables (150 million tonnes) the largest producer of milk (91 million tonnes), the largest producer of tea (820 million tonnes) third largest producer of fish (6.3 million tonnes) has the worlds largest livestock (485 million) and produces 489 million poultry and 4.52 billion eggs annually. Further, during 1998-99 all varieties of spices worth over Rs. 3500 crores (US $ 900million) amounting to 25-30 per cent of world production was produced and processed for value-addition and export. It grows 22 million tonnes of oilseeds covering most of the varieties. In 1999 the total area under fruits and vegetables cultivation was estimated to be at 5.63 and 5.6 million hectares respectively (Annual Report 2006, Ministry of Food Processing Industries (MFPI), India).

India produces large variety of fruits and vegetables-tropical, sub-tropical or temperate. These include mango, banana, apple, orange, chikoo, and pomegranates, and vegetables like potato, tomato, onion, cauliflower, and cabbage. Moreover India is also one of the major producers of plantation products including tea, coffee, cocoa and cashew. Over the last few years, there has been a positive growth in ready to serve beverages, fruit juices and pulps, dehydrated and frozen fruits and vegetable products, tomato products, pickles, convenience veg-spice pastes, processed mushrooms and curried vegetables. The above statistics gives a small but significant picture about the importance of agriculture sector to the Indian sub continent.

Having looked at the agriculture sector as a whole, it is worthwhile to look at some statistics prevalent in the food processing sector. It was in the First World War that some mechanization and commercialisation entered into this industry mainly to meet the demand of the armed forces. The Second World War gave it a much-needed fillip. Since then it has been progressing fairly well and has been meeting the local demand and in a very limited way entered the exports market. It is, however, not a heavy weight industry but has the potential to develop into a Sunshine Industry of the country.

As per a recent study on the Indian food processing sector, during the year 1998-99, the turnover of the total food market is approximately Rs.250,000 crores (US $ 69.4 billion) out of which value-added food products comprise only Rs.80,000 crores (US $ 22.2 billion). During the year 2001 -2002 processed food exports were at around 17,09,813.84 (Million Tonnes) generating revenue of Rs.4381.57 crores. As of 2005-06 processed food exports rose to 19,05,819 (Million Tonnes) generating revenue of Rs.7539.43 crores. Out of these exports, processed fruits & vegetables accounted for 26.34 per cent, animal products accounted for 36.25 per cent and other processed foods accounted for 37.41 per cent. The average growth rate of food processing industry during five years preceding 2003-04 has been 7.15 per cent.

In meat & meat processing sector, poultry meat is the fastest growing animal protein in India India's livestock population is largest in the world with 50 per cent of world's buffaloes and 20 per cent of cattles. As the Indian consumer prefers to buy freshly cut meat from the wet market, rather than processed or frozen meat only 6 per cent of production of poultry meat is sold in processed form. Of this, only about 1per cent undergoes processing into value added products. The total processing capacity in India is over 1 (Million Tonnes) per annum, of which 40-50 per cent is utilized. India is the 5th largest exporter of bovine meat in the world. Indian buffalo meat exports have the potential to grow significantly. The estimated production is 1,500 thousand tones growing at CAGR (compound annual growth rate) of 13 per cent through 1991-2005. Per capita consumption has grown from 870 grams in 2000 to about 1.68 kg in 2005. This is expected to grow to 2 Kg in 2009.

India is the largest milk producer in the world with a production of 91 million tones growing at a CAGR (compound annual growth rate) of 4 per cent. About 35 per cent of milk produced in India is processed. The organized sector (large scale dairy plants) processes about 13 million tonnes annually, while the unorganized sector processes about 22 million tonnes per annum. The quantum of marine products processed and exported during the year 2004-05 was around 4,61,329 (Million Tonnes) generating revenue of Rs. 6647 crores. Size of the semi-processed and ready to eat packaged food industry is over Rs. 4000 crores (US$ 1 billion) and is growing at over 20 per cent.

Primary food processing is a major industry with lakhs of rice-mills/hullers, flour mills, pulse mills and oil-seed mills. There are several thousands of bakeries, traditional food units and fruit/vegetable/spice processing units in unorganised sector. In the organised sector, there are over 820 flour mills, 418 fish processing units, 5198 fruit/vegetable processing units, and 171 meat processing units. India's agricultural production base is quite strong but at the same time wastage of agricultural produce is massive. Processing level is very low i.e. around 2 per cent for fruits & vegetables, 26 per cent for marine, 6 per cent for poultry and 20 per cent for buffalo meat, as against 60-70 per cent in developed countries.

The statistics mentioned above show that Indian food processing sector is in for some tasty times. India can emerge as a leader in the Food Processing Industry in terms of production, consumption, exports and growth prospects due to various factors. Some of the factors which are in favour of India emerging as a leader in the food processing industry are stated below.

- Due to its diverse agro-climatic conditions, it has a wide-ranging and large raw material base suitable for food processing industries.
- It is one of the biggest emerging markets, with over a billion in population.
- Rapid urbanisation, increased literacy and rising per capita income, have all caused a rapid growth of 250 million strong middle class leading to changes in demand patterns, providing tremendous new opportunities for exploiting the large latent market. It is said that an average Indian spends about 50 per cent of his household expenditure on food items.
- Liberalised overall policy regimes, with specific incentives for high priority food processing sector, provide a very conducive environment for investments and exports in the sector.
- Very good investment opportunities exist in many areas of food processing industries like fruit and vegetable processing, meat, fish and poultry processing, packaged, convenience food and drinks, and milk products.

Although the above factors are important for the growth of the food processing industry (FPI), it is imperative that government also frames policies and action plans which facilitate this growth. Having understood the importance of food processing sector, for the economic growth of India, the Indian government has accorded the food processing industry a high priority, with a number of fiscal relief and incentives, to encourage commercialisation and value addition to agricultural produce; for minimising pre/post harvest wastage, generating employment and export growth. Currently the state governments in India have been responsive at the policy level by amending certain sections of the Agricultural Produce Market Committees Act, 1966 to allow effective implementation of contract farming.

As a result of several policy initiatives undertaken since liberalisation in August 1991, the industry has witnessed fast growth in most of the segments. Since liberalisation in Aug 1991 and till Feb 2000 over Rs.53,800 crores (US$ 13.4 billion) of projects have been proposed in various segments of the food and agro-processing industry by the central government of India. Besides this, the Indian government has also approved proposals for joint ventures, foreign collaboration, industrial licenses and 100 per cent export oriented units envisaging an investment of Rs.19,100 crores (US$ 4.80 billion) during the same period. The total inflow of FDI in FPI sector up to 2006-07 (upto December 2006) was Rs.2500.65 crore. In order to give fresh impetus to processing of Fruit and Vegetables, Government in 2004-05 has allowed under I.T. Act, 100 per cent deduction of profit for first five year and 25 per cent deduction for another five years for new upcoming Fruits & Vegetables Processing units. A Vision 2015 on Food Processing Industries has been finalized by the food processing Ministry for giving boost to growth of food processing Sector which envisages increasing the size of the processed food sector by increasing the level of processing of perishables from 6 per cent to 20 per cent, value addition from 20 per cent to 35 per cent and share in global food trade from 1.5 per cent to 3 per cent by 2015. To achieve this the thrust areas identified for strategic intervention are-establishing Mega Food Parks, Modernization of Abattoirs, Cold Chain/Value Addition and Preservation Infrastructure, Upgrading Safety and Quality of

Street Food and Establishment/Upgradation of Quality Control Laboratories.

The above statistics and government initiatives speak volumes about the growth rate experienced by the agricultural sector and more importantly the food processing industry. Despite all this bounty, two challenges confront the agricultural sector. One challenge stems from the projected increase in household demand for goods and services in tune with anticipated population growth. The second challenge which is very important from the agribusiness point of view is that despite all world class status achieved among different agri-products less than two per cent of the food produced is processed in any way. This can be attributed to a number of reasons. The reasons for the domestic consumption of value added fruits and vegetable products being low as compared to the primary processed food in general and fresh fruits and vegetables in particular can be attributed to higher incidence of tax and duties including that on packaging material, lower capacity utilisation, non-adoption of cost effective technology, high cost of finance, infrastructural constraints, inadequate farmers-processors linkage leading to dependence upon intermediaries. The smallness of units and their inability for market promotion is also other main reasons for inadequate expansion of the domestic market.

On the whole the food processing industry is facing constraints like non-availability of adequate critical infrastructural facilities like cold chain, packing and grading centres, etc. lack of adequate quality control and testing infrastructure, inefficient supply chain, lack of processable varieties of farm produce, seasonality of raw material, high inventory carrying cost, high taxation, high packaging cost, affordability and cultural preference of fresh food.

The implication is that the Indian agribusiness experiences a huge loss of potential revenue for producers, since processed food generally commands premium rates. Also in India where so much of food is produced, bulk of it gets wasted due to lack of transportation, cold storage and processing facilities (like sorting, cleaning, and freezing and basic preservation methods.). Therefore the food processing is not a luxury but a necessity and this industry provides a huge potential which is waiting to be tapped.

The Indian consumers by and large very much prefer fresh fruit and vegetables. The high cost of packaging pushes up the cost of the processed items and thereby makes them out of reach of the common man. Because of the varied agro climatic conditions some fresh fruit and vegetable are available throughout the year. The fruits like bananas are non seasonal and apples, oranges, and potatoes etc. are put in the cold stores thus prolonging their shelf life and making them available in the off-season. Some fruits like guavas, oranges have two seasons so they are available in fresh form for four to five months in a year. Therefore it can be seen that domestic consumption of processed items is quite meagre because of economic reasons and also as a matter of habit.

In spite of the fact that India, is the second largest producer of fruit and also of vegetables in the world yet the commercial processing of fruit and vegetables is estimated at 2.20 per cent of the total production. The installed capacity of fruits and vegetables processing industry has increased form 11.08 lakh tons on 01.01.1993 to 21.18 lakh tones as on 01.01.2006 and 24.74 lakh tones as on 01.01.2007. Therefore the food processing industry has abundant investment opportunities in the expanding domestic market and export arena. Further increasing acceptance of new products with market development efforts along with changes in export-import policies and exchange rate adjustments have helped improving the export potential of processed foods.

There is a good international demand for certain fresh fruits as well as processed fruits products. Fresh fruits identified as having good export potential are: mango, grapes, banana, lichee and exotic fruits like sapota, ber, pomegranate, custard apple and other tropical fruits. Among vegetables, the items identified as having good export potential are: onion, potato and green traditional vegetables like: okra, bitter gourd, green chillies and other seasonal vegetables. Many non-traditional vegetables mainly processed mushrooms and gherkins, and other like: asparagus, celery, bell pepper, sweet corn, green and lima beans and organically grown vegetables are also increasingly being exported.

Also with its over 8000 km. of coastline, 3 million hectares of reservoirs and 1.4 million hectares of brackish water, India has vast potential for fishes from both inland and marine resources. Units mostly exist in the small scale sector as proprietary/partnership firms or fishermen co-operatives. Over the last decade, the organized corporate sector has become increasingly involved in preservation, processing and export of coastal fish. But the wide variety of fish resources found in Indian inland waters, coastal areas and deep seas comprising India's Exclusive Economic Zone, still remain grossly underutilized.

In developed countries farming cooperatives harvest, grade and preserve their own produce. This not only helps them to limit wastage but also provide them with time to negotiate profitable deals to sell their produce to large food processing companies, whereas in India the farmers have as little as twenty-four hours to strike a deal because of the perishable nature of the produce. In fact the farmer looses out as the day wears on, since fresh produce commands a higher price in the morning. This wastage can be estimated to be as high as 40 per cent. The annual total value loss arising from such wastage can be estimated to be around Rs 50,000 crores. To bring about more value out of the food industry it is imperative that there is a very effective infrastructure and supply chain setup which helps in tapping the value available in the food processing industry.

Although many strategies can be used to improve agricultural infrastructure in the value chain, contract farming is one strategy which can be used in the Indian market especially in the food processing sector. The benefit of contract farming can be seen if contracts are well designed and implemented. On the one hand the farmers and small producers (Small and Medium Enterprises) benefit from guaranteed prices, technical assistance and funding for cold chain infrastructure. On the other hand the big corporates benefit from assured raw materials. Therefore it is a win-win situation for the local farmers as well as big retail corporate or super markets. In India the multinational dairy sector has been one of the largest users of contract farming model which allows many actors to participate in the value chain.

Many big industrial corporates like ITC, Reliance, Birla, and RPG Group, are setting up huge network of retail chains and supermarkets across the country. Retail chains in agricultural products are expected to drive the growth of contract farming, especially in fruits and vegetables. This provides a huge potential for the food processing industry as contract farming helps in solving some of the problems faced by the local farmers through backward integration of business processes. A very good example of a successful contract farming business in India is the Suguna Chicken Company.

Due to massive increase in number of big retail stores, the demand for cold storage chains is increasing. This is another problem faced by agribusiness in India. The current cold chain storage infrastructure in India is fragmented. The major reasons why cold chain storage is not very prevalent in India are high capital and power costs, low utilisation and lack of support structure including human capital, quality benchmarks and food protocols. There are a very few players who operate in the integrated logistics management namely, Snowman, Frick India, Chitanya Cold Storage, Fresh Express and Kausar.

The annual demand for frozen food by organised retail chains is estimated to be around Rs 1500 crore, which presents a huge opportunity for growth. Currently the back end creation investment by all retail players is estimated at Rs 20.5 lakh crore. The government has also initiated action on this front by planning to implement the scheme for infrastructure development comprising the following components to address different aspects of food related infrastructure, like Mega Food Parks, Packaging Centres, Integrated Cold Chain Facility, Value Added Centres, Irradiation Facilities, and Modernized Abattoir across the country. The MFPI has so far approved 54 food parks for assistance out of which 29 are operational as on date. The food parks are based on public-private partnerships with private partners expected to bring in around Rs.400-450 crores for each project.

Because of the liberal government and other developmental measures being taken, to some extent cold chain storage is being provided, which will help in retaining quality, freshness and reduce post-harvest losses. With the new hybrid varieties being added the production season is also being extended. If the above mentioned challenges are looked into and measures are taken to implement them, then it shall result in the greater availability of quality raw materials to the industry. This will result in better capacity utilisation and producing a wider range of products and of international quality and in effect enhancing the success of the Indian agribusiness. With the rise in the per capita income particularly of the middle class accompanied by drastic change in the food habits the processed foodstuff seems to be the winner.

THE NEED FOR QUALITY INFRASTRUCTURE IN AGRIBUSINESS

The presence of quality infrastructure, for conducting agribusiness, is very important for ensuring continued market access and supporting improved competitiveness. The term infrastructure is widely used and if detailed it aims to cover three broad areas that need development for the growth of agribusiness trade. Three broad areas identified within this quality infrastructure requirement are: logistics capability development, inspection and testing infrastructure which are accredited according to international standards and certification agencies.

There is a need for physical and informational infrastructure, visible at airports, seaports, and inland storage centres to support coordination between enterprises and the rapid shipment of products. The speed of product transport and supply-chain coordination depends on effective communication which requires investment in relatively simple, cheap, and reliable Information, Communication and Technology (ICT) infrastructures. The communication infrastructure helps the suppliers to coordinate their activities with buyers. In short, the above requirements call for a sound logistics capability development within a country.

The importance of quality products with increasing control on the number of substances that can be used in production processes has put a strong demand for the setting up of inspection and physical testing infrastructure. This infrastructure provides a dual function: it provides assurances to producers about the quality of inputs they use and the safety of the products they sell, while at the same time providing assurances to buyers through regular inspections of producers and products. Thirdly, given the increasing importance of standards, governments need to support the development of local certification companies that will provide services at a reasonable cost.

The need for provision of this quality infrastructure by a government is important as there is an increasing importance placed on "buyer service requirements" such as food safety, quality and speed and reliability of delivery in agribusiness trade. Further developing countries like China, Brazil and India are expected to increase their food exports, which face non-tariff barriers such as stringent sanitary and phytosanitory norms.

The area of standards has been dealt elaborately in this paper as it is the area of non-tariff barriers wherein developing countries will be facing the biggest challenge in increasing their agricultural exports in the coming years.

Food Safety Initiatives-Standards

Standards today encompass much more than technical product standards. Hawkins states standards as 'external points of reference', by which a product or service's performance, its technical and physical characteristics, and/or the process and conditions under which it has been produced or delivered can be assessed" (Nadvi and Wältring, 2004).

The standards environment for agribusiness has exhibited some important trends that are important for the structuring of value chains in the agribusiness sector. Increasing awareness of the health risks has led to increasing stringency of public mandatory standards relating to food safety. Tightening of control in areas like pesticide residues, colouring and purity in foods have been seen in the Europe Union.

Satisfying food safety requirements of importing countries have become more complex. This is due to the fact that the range of items as well as the stringency of standards covered by mandatory standards have increased. Not only the agribusiness sector is facing increasing mandatory standards and stringency of standards but also the sector is facing complications in demonstrating compliances with standards because of a shift from product standards towards process standards (i.e. the way products are grown, harvested, processed and transported). Product standards merely define particular outcomes to be achieved; process standards indicate particular procedures that need to be put in place. The shift towards process based standards will require new systems to be established and verified, which imposes additional costs.

With the adoption of Hazard Analysis and Critical Control Point (HACCP) norms in food processing sector many countries have shown a commitment to transit from product standards to process standards controls. Hazard Analysis and Critical Control Point is an important quality assurance system. HACCP is an important requirement for ensuring the quality of products from health and safety aspects and is crucial for exports. This system ensures that the products are safe and of good quality. For e.g. the US has made HACCP mandatory in plants processing meat, poultry, fish and fruit juices. Canada has made HACCP mandatory in the fish processing sector and the EU has made HACCP mandatory for dairy, meat and fish products. The shift towards a process-control approach to food safety is clearly expressed in the law establishing the European Food Safety Authority.

Standards in Agribusiness Value Chain

Standards in agribusiness value chains operate, at multiple points. There are controls by different agents carried out in different ways at different points along the value chain in response to the requirements of private sector companies, coalitions of private-sector standards setters and public agencies. The development of public and private standards involves interventions at multiple points along the value chain. The need and importance of public and private standards can be best explained with an illustration.

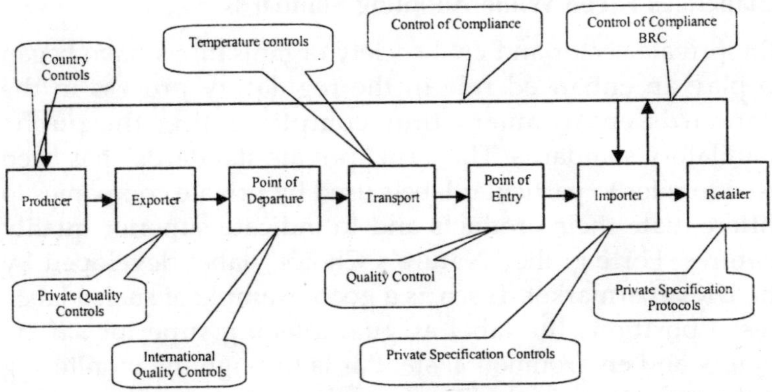

Source: Author

Figure 2: Food Safety and Quality Control in an Agribusiness Supply Chain

The figure above highlights the various points wherein public and private standards in agribusiness value chain are needed. It illustrates that standards are created, adopted, applied and verified by different actors (enterprises and institutions) at different points in the value chain. Although the above value-chain highlights the range of options available for the enforcement of standards the requirements for public enforcement of standards vary according to the nature of the value chain. On the one hand, when the export sector is fragmented, or when the outputs of the export sector are relatively standardized and sourced through arms-length market relationships, governments can enforce standards through inspection, testing, and certification of producers. In contrast, when products are highly customized and relationships between buyers and sellers are information-intensive, then much of the task of ensuring buyer confidence is achieved through the buyer-seller relationship.

Food safety is viewed as a product of the value chain as a whole, "from primary production to delivery to the consumer", and as a consequence risks have to be managed at all points and traceability guaranteed so that a particular product's chain history can be reconstructed.

Challenges Faced While Adopting Standards

The private sector and civil society organisations have began to play an enhanced role in the regulatory process in the standards environment thus complimenting the public mandatory standards. The term "private standards" has been used to refer to particular labels used by private companies to differentiate their products and to indicate superior quality features. For e.g. the "Nature's Choice" label developed by the UK supermarket, Tesco, is a good example of such a label. Tesco positions the label as guaranteeing superior safety, quality and environmental standards through the monitoring and certification of suppliers. Less visible, but more important, are the collective private standards developed by groups of firms and business associations. In the European food industry, these standards include the EurepGAP standard, developed by EUREP (an association of European fresh produce importers and retailers), the UK British Retail Consortium standard for food processing and the Franco-German International Food Standard.

The consequences of the rapid development of public and private standards have created many challenges and problems for producers in the agribusiness. Firstly producers in developing countries face more standards, more stringent standards and multiple standards developed by different agencies addressing the same issue. The magnitude of this challenge faced by the food industry is evident when we take a look at the list of certification offered by a single company in Switzerland. The table below illustrated the list of certification offered by a Swiss company called ProCert.

Secondly certificates have become indispensable marketing instruments, whether they are visible to the consumer, or required on principle by western retail chains for imported

Table 3
Certification Offered by a Swiss Company called ProCert

Standard	*Title*	*Accreditation*
ISO 9001:2000	Quality management system	SCES 039
ISO 14001:2004	Environmental management system	SCES 039
ISO 22000:2005	Food safety management system	SCES 039
OHSAS 18001:1999	Management System for Occupational Health and Safety	SCES 039
FSIO-DI 2000 (Swiss)	Quality management system for Institutions for the disabled	SCES 039
BRC Global Standard-Food	Food safety management system	SCES 038
IFS (International Food Standard)	Food safety management system	SCES 038
DS 3027	Food safety management system	SCES 039
ELOT 1416	Food safety management system	SCES 039
eduQua	Swiss quality certification for continuous training institutions	SCES 039
EUREPGAP	Euro Retail Produce Working Group for GoodAgricultural Practice	SCES 038
Programms AOC (Swiss)	Appelation d'origine contrôlée (AOC) Sbrinz,Rheintaler Ribelmais, Cardon épineux genevois	SCES 038
Programms IGP (Swiss)	Indication géographique protégée (IGP) - Viande desgrisons, Saucisson vaudois, Saucisson aux choux vaudoise	SCES 038
Feed Safety (Swiss)	Feed Safety Management system	SCES 038
Naturane (Spain)	Integrated Production	SCES 038
Fontestad (Spain)	Integrated Production for citrus fruits	SCES 038
Natursense (Spain)	Integrated Production for citrus fruits	SCES 038

Source: http://www.procert.ch/zertifizierungen

fruit and vegetables. Certification by international agencies can be costly for developing country producers. For this reason development of local certification agencies is needed in most developing countries. Another question may arise is whether the certification by local certification agencies in developing countries will be acceptable to the authorities in developed countries. Further, developing a different domestic market standard creates the problem of proliferation of standards for companies that wish to produce for both markets. However, it should be noted that governments have a difficult choice to make; particularly when they seek to develop standards for agricultural produce sold domestically as well as exported. If a government decides to apply the same standard prevailing in key export markets to its domestic market, it could place the small producers at a disadvantage. This is due to high costs involved in adapting to international standards as the market for their produce is primarily domestic which is price competitive. A very good example to counter the above stated argument can be seen from the success of AfriCert, the first Nairobi based Certification Company in Eastern Africa. AfriCert has now gained accreditation according to the international ISO 65 standard. AfriCert's seal of approval confirms that producers subscribe to good agricultural practices, namely resource conservation, safe use of pesticides, good post-harvest protection, hygiene, and occupational health and safety. AfriCert now offers growers in Kenya and the region affordable certification in line with internationally recognized standards. "The company has enabled us to close a considerable gap in the value chain of agricultural products. Previously, exclusively European companies offered certification - a costly process that only major growers could afford. Without the EurepGAP certificate, growers are unable to export their goods to European supermarkets as powerful retailers in Europe have begun demanding the EurepGAP certificate from their suppliers. The advantages especially for small and medium-sized fruit and vegetable growers are obvious, rather than spending a lot of time and money on European companies coming here to assess and certify them, the growers are now able to receive the same service at much lower cost from a local company.

Thirdly another challenge posed by standards relates to providing the type of support for achieving certification that is appropriate for small producers. Certification agencies both private as well as public tend to be more focussed on the large enterprises than those of small enterprises or small farmers. This problem arises as small farmers might be unable to bear the costs of obtaining knowledge about standards and certification. Another reason for small farmers in developing or poor countries not willing to obtain certification is that small farmers or producers know that they have limited or no opportunity for exporting their products. So the produces are mainly for local consumption. As the local consumers are not that particular about certified products, due to their poor standard of living conditions, small farmers do not go in for certification. Lastly the challenge facing small farmers relates to the cost of adjusting production systems to the new requirements, so that they comply with the new standards.

Although the necessary quality infrastructure can be built the benefits arising from them might not pass on to small producers living in rural areas. Therefore it is necessary that challenges faced by small producers need to be taken into consideration while building up the quality infrastructure of a country. The analysis of standards pointed out the importance of business associations in collaboration with governments for establishing sector-wide practices and ensuring the overall reputation of the export sector.

CONCLUSION

The issues outlined so far have focused on the trends and changes seen in the global agribusiness which shows the need for governments and development agencies to support agribusiness producers and exporters taking part in the agribusiness value chain. It is important to understand the various actors and relationship involved in the agribusiness value chain so as to have an easy understanding about the problems faced by agricultural businesses.

It was argued that export agribusiness, and in particular non-traditional agricultural exports, had been identified as having an important part to play in poverty-eradication strategies because of their ability to make a difference to the incomes of poor people in rural areas. It is hence suggested that framings of pro-poor policies for agriculture should be equated to pro-poor agricultural growth with improvements in the ability of small farmers to access export markets.

The increasing complexity of the global agricultural trade environment, which creates new risks for buyers, and increasing requirements for traceability do not provide the coordination and control needed by global buyers. Furthermore, there are economies of scale in coordination and control, which work against small farmers. In this context, the top priority for policy is to be realistic, particularly with respect to the opportunities open to small farmers. The poverty reduction goal should not lead to policy interventions that lack sustainable business logic.

Also, more attention needs to be given to the potential of domestic and regional markets in developing countries. This potential has been somewhat overshadowed by the priority given to export markets, and in particular developed-country markets.

Moreover, the assumption of small farms being a more effective route to poverty eradication in rural areas than large-scale farming needs to be re-examined. This type of analysis needs to be extended to see if the conclusions are valid for other sectors and other countries.

There are many difficulties as well as opportunities facing Indian producers and exporters in the food processing and food retailing sector. It is evident that the food processing industry is a sunrise industry having a huge potential in generating revenue. Many suggestions were provided as how to integrate the small farmers into the food processing industry value chain.

Another important aspect discussed is that the provision of quality infrastructure. It is evident that there is an urgent need by the government for speeding up various projects and programs involved in providing quality infrastructure. It is evident that the impact of standards varies from sector to sector. In the food processing sector the impact is felt more strongly in the area of costs. One possible way of increasing the cost-effectiveness of local certification may be through the development of national equivalent standards that are a subset of international standards. This will be beneficial to domestic companies as these standards can act as a stepping-stone for companies wanting to take part in the global trade. This will happen as meeting the domestic standard becomes a partial fulfilment of the export market standard.

Overall, the paper has tried to identify some challenges faced by small producers who wish to take part in the global value chain. The analysis of agribusiness exports along the value chain highlights the increasing challenges facing developing-country farmers' taking part in global markets. Linking farmers to global markets has usually involved the bulking of produce, often through local markets for commodities and state marketing boards. Markets are becoming more complex, more demanding and more differentiated. In this context, policy interventions to support farmers and exporters must be grounded in realistic appraisals of the needs of the market, the capacities of the export sector and competitors in global markets. It will be then only small farmers will be able to take part in the global food trade and the economic benefit arising out of exports will be experienced by small farmers and poverty will decline on strong agricultural growth. Otherwise even though developing countries like India experience huge agricultural growth, poverty reduction will still be a vocal call.

REFERENCE

Bain, Carmen, James Deaton, and Lawrence Busch (2005), "Reshaping the Agri-food System: the Role of Standards, Standards Makers and Third-party Certifiers", in Vaughan Higgins (ed.), Agricultural Governance: Globalisation and the New Politics of Regulation (London: Routledge),pp. 71-83.

Cook, Michael, and Fabio Chaddad (2000), "Agroindustrialization of the Global Agrifood Economy: Bridging Development Economics and Agribusiness Research", Agricultural Economics 23 (3), pp. 207-218.

DFID (2002), Better Livelihoods for Poor People: The Role of Agriculture, (London: DFID).

Donaghu, Michael, and Richard Barff (1990), "Nike Just Did It: International Subcontracting and Flexibility in Athletic Footwear Production", Regional Studies 24 (6), pp. 537-552.

Eastwood, Robert, and Michael Lipton (2000), "Pro-poor Growth and Pro-growth Poverty Reduction: Meaning, Evidence, and Policy Implications", Asian Development Review 18 (2), pp. 22-58.

EUREP (2001), "EUREPGAP Protocol for Fresh Fruit and Vegetables", Available online at http://www.eurep.org/

FAO (1998), Food Quality and Safety Systems - A Training Manual on Food Hygiene and the Hazard Analysis and Critical Control Point (HACCP) System, (Rome: FAO). Available online at http://www.fao.org/

Grievink, J.-W. (2002), "The Changing Face of the Global Food Industry", Presentation at OECD Conference, The Hague, February.

Gereffi, Gary (1994), "The Organisation of Buyer-Driven Global Commodity Chains: How U.S. Retailers Shape Overseas Production Networks", in Gary Gereffi and Miguel Korzeniewicz (eds), Commodity Chains and Global Capitalism, (Westport: Praeger) pp. 95-122.

Goldman, Robert, and Stephen Papson (1998), Nike Culture, (London: Sage).

Hendrickson, Mary, and William Heffernan, (2005), "Concentration of Agricultural Markets", Columbia, MO: University of Missouri, Department of Rural Sociology, 2005.

Humphrey, John, and Olga Memedovic (2006), "Global Value Chains in the Agrifood Sector". UNIDO.

Jaffee, Steven (2005), "Food Safety and Agricultural Health Standards: Challenge and Opportunities for Developing Country Exports". Report 31207, (Washington D.C.: The World Bank, Poverty Reduction and Economic Management Trade Unit).

Jebaraj, Priscilla (2007), "Supply Chain Infrastructure Needed to Propel Agri-business Boom" The Hindu, December 2nd.

Manarungsan, Sompop, Jocelyn O. Naewbanij, and Tanapat Rerngjakrabhet (2004), "Costs of Compliance with SPS Standards: Thailand Case Studies of Shrimp, Fresh Asparagus, and Frozen Green Soybeans", Agriculture and Rural Development Discussion Paper, Washington DC: World Bank, Accessed April 2005.

Nadvi, Khalid, and Frank Wältring (2004), "Making Sense of Global Standards", in Hubert Schmitz (ed.), Local Enterprises in the Global Economy, (Cheltenham: Edward Elgar), pp. 33-94.

Swinnen, Johan (2004), Dynamics of Agri-food Supply Chains in Transition Countries, (Sarajevo).

Unnevehr, Laurian (2000), "Food Safety Issues and Fresh Food Product Exports from LDCs", Agricultural Economics 23 (3), pp. 231-240.

Van Roekel, Jan, Ron Kopicki, Carry Broekmans, and Dave Boselie (2002), "Building Agri Supply Chains: Issues and Guidelines", Available online at http://www.agrichaincompetence.org/.

Vorley, Bill (2003), "Food, Inc.: Corporate Concentration from Farm to Consumer". London: International Institute for Environment and Development and UK Food Group,

Weinberger, Katinka, and Thomas Lumpkin (2005), "Horticulture for Poverty Alleviation: The Unfunded Revolution", Working Paper 15, (Shanhua, Taiwan: AVRDC).

Willems, Sabine, Eva Roth, and Jan van Roekel (2005), "Changing European Public and Private Food Safety and Quality Requirements Challenges for Developing Country Fresh Produce and Fish Exporters", Agriculture and Rural Development Discussion Paper, Washington DC: World Bank.

Young, Linda and Jill Hobbs (2002), "Vertical Linkages in Agri-Food Supply Chains: Changing Roles for Producers, Commodity Groups, and Government Policy", Review of Agricultural Economics 24 (2), pp. 428-41.

Websites

http://www.gtz.de/en/

http://www.eurep.org/

http://www.procert.ch/zertifizierungen

http://www.fao.org/

http://www.wto.org/

Reports

Annual Report (2005-06), Ministry of Food Processing Industry, Government of India.

CHAPTER–13

IMPACT OF WTO ON AGRICULTURAL MARKETING

R. B. Dhande
G. D. Kharat

Introduction

The world agricultural trading system has been experienced a tremendous change during the second half of the 20th century. The tread on agriculture was signed at the ministerial meet on 15th April 1994 by 125 nations and the agreements of agriculture (AOA) become effective from 1st Jan 1995 with the establishment of WTO.

The WTO agreements are a milestone in the development of International trade in agricultural commodities; agriculture has been brought under international discipline. It is very difficult to foresee that exact outcome of WTO.

Agriculture marketing was tilled recently, not fully accepted as an essential element in agricultural development in the countries of Asia Agricultural marketing occupies as fairly low place in agricultural development policies of developing countries. Agricultural development means not only enough to produce a crop but also we must see it to be satisfactorily marketed. The present paper has been described the need for better agricultural marketing. Foreign customers demand quality products. The challenges left before the agriculturists providing them an opportunity for making some heroic efforts to capture the world market. Traditionally, plantation & fiber crops occupied primary position in agricultural exports of our nation.

Objectives of the Study

The present study is an attempt to -

1. Examining an impact of AOA on Indian Economy.
2. Identifying the need for better agricultural marketing.

Hypothesis

The marketing (both domestic and export) of agriculture is a decisive issue & hence requires an intensive strategy with structural & infrastructural facilities for the development of well built marketing system.

Methodology

The methodology is designed with an intention to make a critical appraisal of the present day agriculture & identify the challenges. The study is based on secondary source of data.

Agreement of Agriculture (AOA)

Agreement of agriculture (AOA) is related to reforms in agricultural trade over time. Accordingly member countries have to formulate market oriented policies. The commodities under AOA are to be fulfilled through–

(a) Providing market access

(b) Reducing domestic support

(c) Containing export subsidies

The member countries have to provide market for agricultural products to the extent of 3% of domestic consumption by end of implementation period i.e. 2000 & 5% latter on. In order to move towards free trade, member countries have to reduce tariffs. Developed countries have to reduce import tariffs by 36% for all products (at least 15% per product) whereas developing countries 24% of all products (at least 10% per product) from present level. Under WTO these have been replaced by tariffs that provide equivalent levels of protection. If the domestic prices were 25% higher than the prices prevailing in International Market, now import tariff called tariffication could be 25%

As a part of AOA, subsidies & other form of support to agriculture including minimum support prices & procurement prices have to be used less intensively by the member countries, to promote agriculture sector in their respective economies.

WTO categorized the domestic support in terms of trade distorting called as 'amber box', 'green box' & 'blue box'.

'Amber box' includes the domestic support policy induce farmers to produce more than the domestic requirement. The presence of over production forces the Govt. to provide subsidies to clear it out. The trade distorting domestic support is measured in terms of Aggregate Measure of Support (AMS). It means the difference between minimum support price & external price quoted in the International Market.

'Green box' includes minimal trade distorting domestic support toward scientific research, disease control, development of infrastructure & to ensure food security (to maintain PDS). It also includes the direct payment made by Govt. to sustain incomes of farmers on the one hand & other to discourage farmers to cultivate certain crops & to limit the production through declaring crop holiday.

The domestic support in the form of direct income payments to farmers is called as *'Blue box'*. The members can continue other domestic support on small scale, called as *'Special & differential box'*.

The other major issue related to agriculture is containing export subsidies. The member countries have to contain the quantity of subsidized export as well as the amount earmarked towards exported subsidy. The developed and developing countries agreed to cut the subsidized quantity & amount of money they spend on export subsidies.

Impact of AOA on Indian Economy

Agreement of Agriculture is biased in-favor of developed nations. Provision of marked access clause adversely affects the developing nations particularly India. It is fact that, there is huge market for agricultural products in developing nations and at the same time, there is surplus food production in developed nations. In the guise of AOA & its market access clause, the developed nations will dump their surplus food grains in developing countries.

Market Access Clause

India has reached to stage of self sufficiency in food grains. We do not need impact of food grains. But under this clause, we have to provide market access for agricultural products to the extent of 3% by spending precious foreign exchange. AOA has been structured in such away to deny increased market access to developing nations. India could not derive any advantage from market access clause. Being a member of WTO & a party of AOA, India has to fulfill its commitments by allowing impacts of agricultural products in the presence of adequate domestic supply of agricultural products. The import of agricultural products even in the presence of glut of output has adverse impact on Indian economy in terms of fall in prices of agricultural products & income levels of farm community.

Domestic Support

The second major issue under AOA is related to containing domestic support especially subsidies to agriculture sector. AOA stipulated that total subsidies to agriculture should not exceed 10% of the value of GDP of agriculture sector.

The developed nations providing subsidies to agriculture well beyond stipulated limits. USA spends more than 1/3rd of GDP from agriculture, Japan 1/4th of the GDP from agriculture, Canada & European Union around 10% of GDP from agriculture towards green box subsidies.

In India, the amount of subsidies extended to agriculture sector constitutes less than 10% (near about 6%) of GDP from agriculture. In our economy the adverse impact of weather, defective seeds & rise in fertilizers prices on overall crop yields. Under these conditions, the government has to provide subsidies to protect farm sector & to ensure food security. If the Indian Government under AOA in near future, agricultural output may fall due to lack of incentives to farmers & focus our millions of people to look at developed countries to satisfy their hunger. This is the final outcome that the developed nations aim to achieve under AOA. Though we are a party of AOA, we should not fall in the trap of developed nations.

Export Subsidies

Regulation of export subsidy is a major factor that adversely affects the performance of agriculture sector. Under AOA, the government has to regulate export subsidy in terms of duty drawbacks, cash compensatory support, etc. The aim of developed nations, under the guise of AOA, is to make the exports of agricultural products from developing nations less competitive in the international market through regulation of export support. The provision of market access, containing domestic support & regulation of export subsidies clearly indicates that, developed nations have to clever vision in terms of expecting a huge market for their agricultural products in developing economies. According to the clause of "technical barriers to trade "also prepared in favor of developed nations. Under this clause, developed nations can effectively prevent imports of agriculture & allied product from India, on health grounds, environmental issues & citing violation of human rights in the form of employing child labor.

Need for Better Agricultural Marketing

Agricultural marketing plays an important role not only in stimulating production & consumption but in accelerating pace of economic development. Marketing of agricultural produce is complex phenomenon. It requires special treatment at all levels with government & institutional support.

Indian farmers are poor and illiterate; consequently do not acknowledge the new technology in pre harvest operations. All sort of pre-harvest operations are not market oriented &

sustainable. Quality of production also annoyed due to natural calamities & climatic conditions. Crop protections measures are becoming costly. Cost of input also remains high. There is no guarantee of prices to be paid for farmers produce. The producer's share in consumer rupee is tremendously less in India. All the lacunars deserve to have Institutional and infrastructural facilities to be made available to the farmers by government authorities. The government has taken various steps to improve the conditions of the agricultural marketing, but these steps are not meeting the required demands. In the wake of globalization, the farmers have to face lot of challenges ahead to market his product. Some of the initiatives needed for tomorrow's better marketing are as follows ....

Expansion of Co-operative Marketing & Processing

Expansion of co-operative marketing facilities for all commodities assures reasonable prices so as to remove all exploitation of the farmers by the middlemen. A network co-operative at the national level, state level & primary level needed to help farm producers to get best markets & best prices for their product. These markets have their own storage & warehousing facilities which results in better control over the flow of supplies & influence the prices.

Electronic Trading

It may facilitate the direct interaction between buyers & sellers. Agricultural market committee can also set up the special information kiosks for this purpose. The issue in the concept calls for the dual role of farmers as producers & seller. With the present infrastructural facilities can we justify it?

Information Network System

The ministry of agriculture has recently implemented an I T based central sector scheme to link 710 important regulated markets spread all over the country including the state Agricultural Marketing Board & Directories. Under this scheme, an agricultural information system network is being set up to computerize 27 major commodities with online data of daily market arrivals, prices, storages, dispatches with destination cost, sold & unsold stocks, infrastructural facilities, etc with this advances the world has become a small place and a larger market at one can go.

Forward & Future Markets

In the wake of WTO, the government has withdrawn its intervention from commodity sector to ensure that the demand & supply forces will determine the market prices in the new economic environment. The Forward Markets Commission (FMC) performs the functions of advisory, monitoring, supervise & regulating in future and forward trading. In the century, currently future controls are traded for nine commodities in twenty commodity exchange. The linkage between spot & future markets seem to be poor due to domination of speculators. The government therefore has to continue its efforts to strengthen traders. Efforts have also to be made to extend the role of exchange in other traders and other services like warehousing, financing, investments and market intelligence which could improve the existence of the future markets.

Creation of Cold Storage Facility

In India, presently, the total warehousing in both urban & rural areas which accounts to 35 million tones (2000-2001) capacity. Now, the need of the hour ahead is creation of cold storage facilities to growing demands of fruits & vegetables, where we have to convert our comparative advantage in the production & process of fruits & vegetables, to competitive advantage which is still untapped potential. Very merger efforts have been made in a form location specific Agri-Export Zone [AEZ] in this area which could not sufficient. It may be noted that plantation crops like tea, coffee, spices, coconut, cashew, dairy products require storage facilities. Efforts will have to create crop-specific storage capacity during the 11th five year plan.

Linkage of Roads

As compared to railway, the road transport system has definite advantages. Road development in India was neglected in past years for various reasons. In the first place, central & state governments did not appreciate the importance of developing the road system. During the next three plans, the planning commission provided for a total outlay of Rs.8600 corers on road programs & for road transport. One of the most ambitious projects launched in independent India is the National Highway Development Project (NHDP), which is expected to go a long way in promoting economic development of the country & integrating remote regions with the main stream economic activity and ensuring connectively of the rural roads.

Private Investment

The decline in the share of Investment in Agriculture as percentage of GDP has been an area of continued concern. This decline was attributed mainly to near stagnation or fail of public investment in agriculture. For the development of agricultural marketing, private sector must invest their share in agriculture in the coming years.

Price Support Policy

Food grain marketing has been a subject of considerable debate in the recent past. The government intervention in food grain market in case of rice & wheat in a farm price support, buffer stocking & PDS helped a lot in reaching the rural poor. Today food security is one of the prime importances of the nation. There are only 24 agricultural commodities which are covered under minimum price support policy & have regulated markets throughout the country. There are several other commodities which of high economic significance that need urgent coverage through comprehensive price stabilization as well as establishment of regulated markets in the respective agro climatic regions. There is a need for policy which should have high market intervention and it should increase the operational efficiency of purchasing agencies in the context of cost efficient purchases vis-à-vis competitive sales as to avoid or reduce loss. There is a need for bringing uniformity in the state level tax structured for better efficiency.

The infrastructure under government ownership & management has, however, proved thoroughly inefficient and corrupt. The demand for infrastructure facilities & services has always out paced supply, besides the quality of the existing supply is extremely poor. The widening gap between demand and supply of infrastructure & the extremely poor quality of the existing supply raises important questions concerning the sustainability of economic growth of the country in the coming years.

After considering the above issues, it is sure that we are able to develop well built marketing system.

References

Acharya, S. S and Agrawal, N. L. (2004), "Agricultural Marketing in India" Oxford and IBH Publishing Co. Pvt. Ltd.

Arunachalam, R. (2002), "An Analysis of India's Steucture and direction of foreign Trade' 'Agricultural Growth & Economic reforms' p: 215-225.

Mercia Selva Malar, S. (2005), 'WTO in Support of Agriculture Trade'- Kisan World p: 63

Prasad (2005), "Encyclopedia of Agricultural Marketing–Vol XI"

FAO (2005), The State of Food and Agriculture, Rome, Italy.

Josling, T and S Tangermann (1999), Implementation of the WTO Agreement on Agriculture and Developments for Next Round of Negotiations. European Review of Agricultural Economics, 26 (3): 371-388.

Dr. A. Nakula Reddy (2006), Multilateral Trade Agreement on Agriculture–Impact on Indian Economy, Osmania Journal of International Business Studies, July-December. p: 51-56.

CHAPTER–14

PERFORMANCE OF DAIRY INDUSTRY IN TUMKUR DISTRICT– A CASE STUDY

K. Sivachithappa

Introduction

Dairying is one of the animal husbandry enterprises, which provide employment, and income not only at the stage of rearing of cattle but also at the stage of production of milk products and cattle feed industry. Dairy is the place where handling of milk and milk products is done and technology refers to the application of scientific knowledge for practical purposes. Dairy technology has been defined as that branch of dairy science, which deals with the processing of milk and manufacture of milk products on the industrial scale. But, dairy is an economic activity, which adds income to households. It provides indirect insurance against risks from crops, such as crop failure due to drought or pests. It is pertinent to study how for dairying helps the farm families to get gainful employment. In the light of the above study of the economics of dairying services shall be appropriate.

A micro investigation in Tumkur district shall be made to review the existing structure, growth trend in milk production competitiveness of dairy industry, cost of production and level of efficiency in dairying. Study shall also cover income generation capacity of dairying in rural areas and marketing problems of dairying in the district.

The existing literature unfolds, interesting dimensions of the new trends and patterns of dairy development since 1980s. The new market oriented policy regimes since 1991, and concomitant process of integration of the Indian economy in to the world economy through trade, investment and technology transfer is bound to have a major influence on the dairy sector. Because of liberalization dairy cooperatives have already come in conflict with the corporate business in the area of milk collection and processing. Now it is very pertinent to look into the competitiveness and efficiency of dairy industry. And it is therefore high time that a proper assessment and evaluation were made on role of dairy cooperatives in the development of weaker sections in the district in the light of the needs of the fast changing and growing Indian economy.

The present study examines the progress and working evaluation of dairy co-operatives in Tumkur district. The main focus is on analyzing the growth and performance of the dairy co-operatives. It is because of the dominant role-played by the dairy co-operatives in the total co-operative sector in the district. Dairying in Tumkur district is one of the major side activities of agricultural farmers in income and employment generation. Among the co-operatives, generally, dairy co-operatives growth is gradually increasing in every taluks of Tumkur district.

The dairy co-operatives in Tumkur have strong organizational set up. Tumkur District Milk Producer Union is the first largest Union in the milk production in Karnataka State. Hence the study analyses the growth and performance of dairy co-operatives particularly organizational structure, membership growth, milk procurement, turn over, profit, service extension programmes etc. The study also intended to analyses the saga of its growth and, reasons for poor performance of the societies.

Review of Previous Studies

In order to create a foundation for the study, to understand the various nuances and dimensions of the topic of study as well as to prepare a proper methodology and framework for the study, elaborate efforts have been made to review the available literature on the topic. There are several studies by different scholars dealing with either the economic aspect or the social aspect or both. These studies have come out with divergent conclusions. Some studies have shown that modern dairy activity has benefited all sections of the rural population. While some other have concluded that the dairy population, while some other has concluded that the dairy benefits has gone mostly to the upper castes and classes. Some of the significant literature and their points of view are presented here below;

Somjee and *Geetha Somjee* in their work, "Co-operative Dairying and Profiles of Social Change in India," brought out the fact that "the milk co-operative had become an instrument of social justice at the hands of the socially oppressed group."

D.S. Thakur as aptly puts the role of dairy co-operatives, "The milk co-operatives has in it the seeds of an entire social revolution. Besides serving as an effective instrument for milk production and marketing. These co-operatives help to break down the barriers of caste, class and sex and to stimulate interest in all worthy social services including literacy drives and family planning."

While emphasizing the role of dairy co-operatives *Dr. V. Kurien* pointed out that "dairy as an industry-but its development must also serve rural and semi- rural population. Our dairying must develop in such as to contribute to the solution of rural poverty." [Dr. V. Kurien, The Larger Dimensions of Dairy Development in India. New Delhi ICAR 191 P.U Mimeographed]" *Raghbir Singh* in his "Milk and Milk Products industry in India [Indian Dairyman. Vol.39. April 1987.] Pointed out while analysing the role of dairy co-operatives, "it attracts various agricultural operations including irrigation, transport and also manure for the fields. It is also important as a supplementary source of income being a subsidiary occupation to small and marginal farmers. Besides it also creates substational employment opportunities".

Prof. Manubhai. M.Shah emphasizes the dimensions of social impact of dairy co-operatives as follows- "Above all, a unique ethos in society grew. There was general stimulation all round among the people. There were attitudinal and conceptional changes. There was spread of understanding and cooperation among the masses. The barriers of illiteracy, caste, communities, social status, political creeds, age, sex brackets, traditional habits–beliefs–customs-values began to breakdown slowly but steadily ...and the entire value system began to change."

*Sivachithappa. K,(*2002) in his study on "Dairy Cooperative Scocieties on Rural Prosperity", observed that the dairy deelopment activities are being extended further to touch every nook and corner of the country ushering in a white revolution and making an impact on the socio-economic front of the rural scene. The economic order is being transformed by the totally integrated operations".

Ilangovan.D,(2002) in his study on "Performance of agricultural credit cooperatives in Tamil Nadu" analysed the agricultural credit cooperatives in detail and he further observed that the short term and long term institutions also more or less trying to present an equal level of performance as compared to long term ones. As and when efforts succeed in reduction of overdues, the agricultural credit cooperatives in Tamilnadu may break records to achieve summits at National levels. Of course, that is need of hour at national level, so as to bring about best results in the agricultural front."

Suriyamurthy (2001) in his study on cooperative dairies in Tamilnadu observed that " Dairy cooperatives having put in enormous efforts to increase milk production and having spread message of organizing themselves in to a cooperative union. Which is financially viable, it now appears that private venders are coming forward to lap up profits in this business what is really happening is that private operators are offering a better price for milk to ensure that milk supply is diverted from cooperatives to private collection center.

The *World Bank* on the "Impact of Dairy Development in India" clearly establishes "the dairy former families in villages with milk societies earn more money then non- dairy farmer families. The income from dairying has myriad of multiplier effects having for reaching impact on socio-economic fabric of the village.

The National Commission on Agriculture in its interim Report (1971:1) observes that "the experience of Anand milk scheme reveals that small farmers derive many benefits by taking to milk production as a subsidiary occupation for example, additional income, better nutrition and more employment opportunities to the farm family labour".

While explaining why the Kheda district dairy Cooperatives in Gujarat were so successful Baviskar and Attwood (1984 : 93) recognizes that "the dairy farmers of this district have profited from a number of economic, political, social and historical advantages which may not be available elsewhere much of the district has good soil and irrigation. Long before the dairy co-operatives were organized, the district was noted for its high levels of dairy production. Thus it was successful dairy farming which led to successful co-operatives and not vice versa (George 1983).

Shanti George (1983) argues that the planners have created a fictitious image of the Anand dairy co-operatives and are thus attempting to replicate an imaginary model rather than a real one. For example the real Anand co-operatives are based on buffalo milk production (an indigenous technology) whereas, the replication efforts are directed at promoting the use of crossbred cows with the help of foreign high yielding genetic material. Whatever the advantages of crossbred cows, these were not essential in the successful prototype, and we wonder about them utility in the replication efforts (quoted in Baviskar and Attwood 1984:93:94).

Shanti George asserts that "the milk production and marketing technology associated with western society may be appropriate and effective in the temperate climes and thinly populated affluent societies where this technology is found, but when transported across the world to a very different agricultural economy in India can engender a number of inefficient or undesirable effects"

A comparative study of two villages in Uttar Pradesh (Madan and Dasgupta: 1968) clearly shows the association of factors like caste, leadership, and attitudes of people with levels of agricultural development.

According to Katz (1961) "it is unthinkable to study diffusion without some knowledge of the social structure in which potential adopters are located (Cited in Raghava Rao 1979 : 281).

Avatar Singh observes that Communities with widespread intersectional networks , effective and locally well - recognized leadership, a distinctive local ethos tend to have higher adoption rates than those in which most such characteristics are lacking" (1973 : 381).

Danda and Danda (1971) in their study find that apart from inter-village variations in farm practice, adoption rate differences in adoption level are found among different communities within a village.

Raghava Rao (1979-279-360) in his study on modern farm technology in Kolar district of Karnataka, examines two villages having similar infrastructural base but showing varying levels of adoption to understand why the adoption level varies across villages and across castes within the same village. He finds that the stratified village with nine castes with Brahmins at the top of the social hierarchy and Scheduled Castes at the bottom.

Studies on milk co-operatives have shown that certain co-operatives functioned free of caste and functional politics while certain other societies have become the arena of power struggle and caste politics.

Kamat (1972) points out that the milk co-operative union at Anand had become a successful venture providing a model for many other similar units not only within the country but perhaps in other developing Countries as well.

The study of Amul, conducted by Singh and Kelly shows that the most important factors contributing for the success of the kaira co-operative milk producers union were the presence of outstanding local tendership, highly efficient and dedicated management and consistent commitment of the villages to the came of improving their human conditions (1981 : 143).

Somjee and Somjee (1978 : 577-590) conducted three case studies of milk cooperative societies in Kaira district. They have shown that milk co-operatives had become effective instruments for enhancing the income of rural people, particularly the ex-untouchables. The caste systems and the power structure in the villages had not impeded the growth of dairy co-operative movement in these areas. They further stated that the villages had made a clear distinction between the village panchayat and milk co-operative which catered to the divergent needs of the people.

The scholars like Bhattacharya (1973) Chawla and Khanna (1974) Vyas and Jodha (1973) and Dev (1981) argue that scientific development of dairying would go a long way in the socio–economic transformation of rural areas, particularly its weaker sections.

Sohal (1978) states that development of agriculture on small and scattered holdings required greets efforts, time and costly inputs, whereas, dairy development with adequate infrastructural facilities helps in the development of the rural poor in a shorts span of time.

Kulandaiswamy (1982:234) states that "the social dimension of the benefits of co-operative dairying is intangible and long term in nature. It is the social dimension, which renders the dairy co-operatives more relevant to rural transformation than even the economic dimension.

Katar Singh and Mukunda Rao's (1984) study shows that the average milk yield per milch animal, the average price received by milk producers, the level of employment in dairying the average per capita protein intake and the receptivity to the innovations introduced under Operation Flood I are all substantially higher in the co-operative villages than in the control villages.

Marty Chen et .al (1986) assert that although dairy development has made significant strides in the country in recent years, it has largely by passed the women who do most of the work of cattle maintenance. Since women do not go returns in economic terms, there if no improvement in their status inspite of their work inputs.

Problems of poverty and unemployment also have been shaking our domestic tranquility and peace. The low absorptive power of the industry has lead to increased pressure of unemployed rural masses on agriculture and allied activities. Owing to seasonally in operations, selective mechanization and large percentage of cultivated area being dry lands, crop production as its innate problem in absorbing the unemployed rural masses and generating income for their sustenance. Live stock farming; particularly dairy farming assumes a special significance in this context.

Realizing its importance, a large member of empirical studies was carried out to look into the potential of dairy enterprise in providing employment and income to the rural people. According to Saini and others (1977) dairying was an ideal alternative to diversity of the crop enterprise for getting more, stable and continuous farm income and high employment opportunities. Study by Dutt (1990) indicated that dairying offers a vast scope for increasing the income, employment and purchasing power and in turn reduces poverty in rural facilities. Another study by Mishra (1978-79) revealed that the rate of participation in dairying was the highest for the marginal and small farmers, but income from dairying was higher for the large farmers mainly from dominant caste.

The National Commission on Agriculture (1971) in its Interim Report concluded that small farmers derived many benefits such as additional income, better nutrition and employment opportunities from dairying compared to large farmers. Thus dairying is , by and large , small man's business. Biradar (1988) opined that dairy development in India should be the basic strategy for eradicating rural poverty and bringing rural poor above the poverty line. Many researchers have found out that dairying played a vital role in the socio-economic transformation. Moore (1978), Varma and Park (1978), Grewall and Rangi (1980) , Saini and Singh (1985), Apte

(1989), Acharya (1990), Rajendran (19991), Bhat and Taneja (1998) , Paroda (1998) highlighted the need to expand the non crop sector like live stock sector, particularly dairy enterprise to generate gainful employment and substainable income.

R.C. Mascarenhas said the dairy development project in Karnataka on the 'Anand' type of co-operative structure combines commercial approach milk active producer participation. Thus dairying provides an alternative occupation in addition to other form of Agriculture enterprises, Though income generates from dairying reflect the existing socio-economic inequalities.

Journal of "Rural Development Vo.1 No.7 by A.C.Jena in his article told about the dairy development. According to him" The increasing pressure on land, agriculture alone cannot provide gainful employment to all in the rural areas. Therefore, allied activates like animal husbandry, dairying have to be viewed as effective instruments of social change for supplementary the income and providing employment to weaker sections of the people in rural areas.

Debey Singh and Bhupal Singh in their case study the dairy entrepreneurship observed that per day milk production was found to be highest in case of medium size of farmers followed by landless labourers and large holders. Marginal farmers produced least quantity of milk.

Vijayalakshmi in her article "Role of Dairy co-operatives in Augmenting Milk Production" A case study of Karnataka. According to her "on the scope of milk consumption in India commented that the decision of a consumer price of milk, availability of milk and its products purchasing power of money in country. Purchasing power of the person, range of substitutes and knowledge about usefulness of milk knowledge about the utility of milk push-up the per capita consumption of milk.

S.K. Bhanja and S. Venkatadri in their article "Profiles of Dairy Cattle Beneficiaries" stated like this: distrubution of milch animals is the most popular and single major weapon in the armory of I.R.D.P against its frontal attack as the rural poverty.

The review of literature reveals that the dairying plays a crucial role in the socio-economic upliftment of the people. The studies have also pointed out that in the development of dairying, the role of dairy co-operatives is immense. Further the studies also pointed out the dairy co-operatives in the generation of income, employment and the working of dairy co-operatives.

Thus, several studies have been conducted on dairy co-operatives and its role in the rural development of the economy. But so far no such attempt has been made to analyse the role of dairy co-operatives and its performance evaluation regarding the growth of dairy co-operatives and its activities in Tumkur district of Kamataka State. Therefore, the present study is a humble beginning to study the role of dairy co-operatives and its performance evaluation in Tumkur district. At present this district is the largest milk-producing district in the state. To fulfill this research gap the present study is undertaken.

Objectives of the Study

It is generally felt that there have been perceptible changes in the living conditions of the weaker sections mainly on economic side and relatively on social side owing to the role of dairy cooperatives. It is with this perceptional background that the detailed study has been undertaken to find out the economic impact of dairy cooperatives on the weaker sections. Impact assessment in this context implies questions about outreach and effectiveness in meeting development objectives. In the light of this, the following are the main objectives of the study.

(a) To analyze the performance of dairy co-operatives in Tumkur District in terms of growth in number, membership, financial operations and working results.

(b) To study the factors responsible for successful working of the societies and find out the reasons for poor performance of the societies.

(c) To identity the specific problems faced by the dairy co-operatives in Tumkur district and

(d) To make suggestions for the further development of dairy cooperatives on the basis of the findings of the study.

Dairy Development in Tumkur District

Tumkur district is purposively selected for the present study. Since it is the district with dairy development is one of the most important aspects. Nearly 90 percent of the total populations of the district are engaged in agriculture since agriculture is a basic occupation. There is a lot of importance for dairy development in the district, because of the large extent of availability of livestock in Tumkur district.

Dairy development programme is one of the important phenomena with the cattle development. The Government dairies and the rural dairy centers in the district. Milk products in the rural areas and marketing facilities for the milk producers, are important aspects to serve milk and its products to the city in a whole year. There are 3 chilling centers (Yediyur, Sira and Kibbanahalli) under the control of the K.M.F. Bangalore. Almost all districts dairies are engaged in the Procurement of all the available milk from the producers in the rural areas. The managing capacity of Dairies is to be increased from the present level of 3 chilling centers with a capacity of 70,000 liters per day in a development programme.

There are 3 chilling centers in rural dairies working at Yediur, Sira, and Kibbanahalli each with a processing capacity these chilling units provide chilling facilities to the producers in the rural areas. They have engaged themselves information of milk producer's co-operative societies, arranging their institutional finances for dairy farming. With wealth coverage for the successful management of the dairy cattle and the guiding assured marketing services including the source of cattle foods, feed green fodder in their field etc. dairy development for the welfare of the farmers engaged in dairy activities.

The K.M.F. Ltd Tumkur Dairy was started Govt. Order No.AAH:155:KDC83:DATE 20 March 1987 from Bangalore Milk Union. The project scales to development an integrated programme for increasing milk production in the rural areas through 7th year action plan of procuring on quality cross breeding animals health and development facilities of milk collection, processing and marketing in the formation and operation of 620 village dairy co-operative societies (DCS). This will be beneficial to 1,50,737 farmers contributing to the full utilization of farming labour force in the rural areas village dairy co-operative societies at village level, co-operative milk producers societies union (CMPSU) at the union level.

Tumkur has the level best cattle populaion in the state. The production per capita of milk is extremely high. Milk cattle population is mostly distributed the details of each category of livestock are furnished in taluks. The taluk that has registered the highest increase of milk cows and buffaloes is Sira, Second place is kunigal. The taluk that has registered the highest increase of milk cows and buffaloes are Sira, second place is Kunigal, The taluk that has shown the lowest increase in madhugiri which accounted for total livestock population in the districts shown below table.

Table 1
DCS Producer Membership, and Milch Animals in Tumkur District (2006-07)

Taluks	*Dairy Farming People*	*Milch Animals*		
		Cows	*Buffaloes*	*Total Animals*
C.N.Halli	7552	387	770	1156
Gubbi	14889	365	795	1160
Koratagere	20020	388	723	1111
Kunigal	10024	841	1109	1950
Madhugiri	35560	249	235	484
Sira	11207	968	1452	2420
Tiptur	7794	111	437	548
Tumkur	18343	133	640	773
Turuvekere	9872	275	1123	1398
Total	1,39,220	3,717	7,284	11,001

Source: Tumkur Milk Union Limted, Mallasandra –Progress Report – January 2006-07.

Dairy Farming People in Tumkur District

The total population of the district was 23,05,819 about 19,23,656 of people live in rural areas and remaining 3,82,163 in towns. Scheduled Caste Population 4,08,524 and Scheduled Tribes population 1,67,632 remaining population belongs to other caste communities.

The above table majority of people depend upon dairy activities. The total dairy farming population is 1,39,220. The total increase of population of the taluk has dairy activities is the highest increase of people Madhugiri (35,560) second list in the dairy farming is Koratagere (20,020) and taluk that has shown the lowest increase Tipur (7794) respectively which accounted for total dairy farming population in the district.

Regions of Dairy Development in Tumkur District

Calculation of a combined index of dairy development reveals clearly the disparity in the level of dairy development in Tumkur district. The three regions were Highly Developed Group. Moderately Developed Group, and low Level Developed Group marked on the table can be described as follows;

Table 2
Regions of Dairy Development

Taluks		*Dairy Farming People*	*Milk Production (in liters)*
	Highly Developed		
Madhugiri		35,560	25,161
Gubbi		14,889	12,975
Koratagere		10,024	12,232
	Moderately Developed		
Tumkur		18,343	11,458
Tiptur		7,794	8,299
Kunigal		10,024	7,895
C.N.Halli		7,752	7,426
	Low Level Developed		
Turuvekere		9,872	6,517
Sira		11,207	3,475
Pavagada		3,959	3,051

Source: Tumkur Dairy Background Report 2006-07.

Taluk Wise Dairy Farming of Tumkur District

Tumkur District consists of ten taluks and these taluks have some similarities, basically all they differ due to the difference in existing infrastructure, facilities food, fodder, milk producers DCS Memberships, and transport, dairy and also differ in surface water resources. Because of these differences the existing condition of dairy industry based activities in each spinning based units etc.,

Herein the following talukwise comparative study is undertaken which just highlights the taluk in position in generating dairy development in brief and mentioned the dairy developments.

Tumkur

Tumkur is the center for all dairy industrial activities. Tumkur stands 4th place for dairy farming activities. This taluk milk procurement 11,458 kgs in 2006-07 and 57 DCS functioning. Textiles, sericulture, Pasturelands and Transport in all those dairy acivities are progress.

Madhugiri

Madhugiri is most important taluk of Tumkur District. This taluk is leading in the product vegetable and were good opportunity for dairy industry. The number of existing dairy activities milk production, milk society member, grassland and other dairy activities. It is producing more dairy development activities. 2006-07 milk production 35,560 Kgs. This taluk 1st place for dairy production activities.

Gubbi

Gubbi is another important taluk of Tumkur District. This taluk in the dairy production activities take a second place. In 2006-07 milk procurement 12,975 Kgs. The cattle feeding have an important role in the dairy development in this taluk. In the point of view of developing dairies and increasing in the production of milk. Cattle feeding unit is established in Gubbi in the year of 1984-85

Koratagere

Koratagere is the most important taluk in the district. In this taluk DCS Registered 52 and also DCS functioning 52. Milk procurement 12,235 Kgs functioning village covering in 2006-07 154. This taluk closely related Tumkur District or taluk. Dairy development activities. This taluk good transportation facilities dairy development.

Tiptur

Tiptur is another important taluk of Tumkur District. Tiptur is moderately developed in dairy activities. This taluk good transportation facilities dairy development.

Kunigal

Kunigal taluk also is one among the progressive taluks. Water resource is available and good soil. And good transportation facilities dairy development highly developed in this taluk. Because of the facilities the taluk is getting much progress in the field of agriculture and dairy based industries. In 2006-07 milk procurement 7,896 Kgs per day.

C.N.Halli

C.N.Halli is one of taluks in Tumkur District. Agriculture and dairy are main occupations of the taluk. But not much developed when compared to other taluks of the district. Coconut is the important crop of the taluk. And dairy farming is normally developed in the taluk.

Turuvekere

Turuvekere is another important taluk in Tumkur District. This taluk has low developed in Dairy activities among other taluks in the district. 2006-07 milk procurement 6,517 Kg per day.

Sira

Sira is one of the taluks in Tumkur District. Agriculture and dairy are main occupations of the taluk but not much developed in dairy development. This taluk having one chilling center 20,000 LPD. Groundnut is the important crop of the taluk.

Pavagada

Out of the ten taluks in Tumkur district pavagada is most backward taluk. It stands least and no way it can be compared to other taluks. This taluk basically lacks in infrastructure. Even land is less fertile after adding to this surface water resources are very much limited as a result is taluk remains backward. In dairy activities is very low progress in 2006-07 milk procurement only 3051 Kgs/day.

Major Findings of the Study

Based on the analysis and discussion in the study of performance evaluation of dairy cooperative societies in Tumkur district, the following findings have been drawn:

The important findings of the study were as follows:

1. High percentage of rural people is engaged in the dairy farming.
2. In this district the high percentage of people having low income so, there are many upliftment programmes for low-income people.
3. Almost equal number of dairy farm labour was found in the high medium and low overall knowledge.
4. Large majority of farm labour adopted the practices like maintenance of separate cattle shed, location of the cattle shed type of flour for the cattle shed, feeding colostraum to the calf within six hours, artificial insemination dairying period of the pregnant animals frequency of milking the animal green grasses grown keeping the sick animals separately method of controlling diarrhea, method of controlling sicks and lice and burying the dead animals.
5. Nearly 50 percent above farm labour were illiterate. Their education level ranged from primary to high school, none of the farm labour were graduate.

6. Very little dairy farm labour participated in extension activities like meeting and training programme.
7. The main problems of this study is regarding the dairying most of the people have not utilised this facilities due to the lack of education and landless labourers.
8. Among the economic problems majority of the farmers, experienced the lack of loan facilities high cost of milch animals, high In the existing situation in Kolar district there is no alternative other than Dairy Co-operatives to serve and protect the interests of dairy farmers. The Dairy Co-operatives may continue to have their relevance under economic reforms. It is imperative induct cost and quality consciousness, strengthening of internal financial resources modernization of management, human resource development, perspective planning etc. the competitive strength of the Dairy Co-operatives to encounter their counter part in market should increased.
9. Over the last five years the Dairy Industry in Tumkur district as progressed from scarcity to one of plenty making. Tumkur is the largest producer of milk in Karnataka state.
10. It is observed that dairy industry is relatively inefficient and unproductive with yields per cow. And in Tumkur 90% of the dairy co-operatives are not adopted computers in the process of billing system and milk collection. The adoption of computers increases efficiency and productivity and minimises the strain. It increases transference creates a basis for improving the quality of the milk produced.

Policy Implications

In the light of our findings and observations some suggestions are made about effective functioning of dairy cooperatives in Tumkur district. The suggestions are listed as follows

1. The dairy farmers are in need of term loans for the dairy developmental activities. The provisions should be made to provide loans by the dairy co-operatives.
2. The dairy co-operatives at the grass root level need regular assistance from the unions in the form of health care services. This is far from satisfactory. For this, Union should appoint a doctor and technical staff to assist the dairy farmers covering three or four co-operatives.
3. On an average 1/3 of the dairy co-operatives in the district are very small in size (less than 30 active members) and per member day collection of milk is quite meager. Such societies should be amalgamated with other societies or measures should be under taken to increase the per member milk collection.
4. District unions should make proper arrangements for the milk collection by the use of computers (Automatic Milk Collection Centers).
5. In order to reduce the spoilage of milk during the time of transportation from the collection centers to chilling centers vehicles having cooler systems shall be used. By this way quality of the milk can be maintained.
6. Milk conservation facilities should be established in the corner point of the unions or chilling centers.
7. A very serious organisational constraint of the dairy co-operatives emanates from unduly long tenure of the secretary of the societies. The same persons holding the position since the inception of the society. They should be transferred locally.
8. The dairy societies should ensure regular feed and fodder supply to the members.
9. Training and awareness programs regarding quality milk production, low cost operations to be organised by the dairy co-operatives. In addition to this consumers are to be educated how they are unhygienic and adulterated milk, through a bit of cheaper in its price, may cause serious health hazards to them.

10. To develop the standard of living among small and marginal farmers and landless through the intensive dairy development programme by providing financial assistance.
11. As average small and marginal farmers have little interest in terms of input, it suggested that the more community irrigation schemes such as lift irrigation scheme should be brought into operation.
12. By ploughing back fund for dairy development activities infrastructural facilities can built agricultural development of rural people can take place an improvement in the standard of rural poor can be turned.
13. The bank has to sanction long term financial facilities to the rural people for the development of dairying.

Conclusion

Dairy is not only represented area of the basic agricultural industry but a pleasant satisfying was of people so many people engaged in producing milk and its products. Dairying is the subsidiary occupation for the peasantry. As we know in rural area, poverty is spread over haunts of the masses. For eradicating rural poverty, dairying is a means of the benefits for dairying penetrates deeply. A large magnitude of the rural population gets substantial extra income from dairying and women folk finds employment in dairying a gainfully to utilize their time productivity and profitability. No doubt Tumkur Dairy Development Corporation achieved better result. But the project is only meant for the rich and influential classes of the people with that pre- conceived nation the poor class of the people in the district do not even come forward to know to avail of the facilities offered by the government agencies.

References

Acharya R.M. (1990), Dairy India 1992, Indian Context of Agriculture Research New Delhi.

Ananthakrishna C.P. & Padmanabhan P.A. (1992), Dairy Farming and Milk Production Shri Lakshmi Publishers.

Benjamin Thomas P. (1982), Management of Dairy Developmen Factors for Increasing Milk Production under Co-operatives.

Crooty.R Cattle (1980), Economic and Development Common Wealth Agriculture Bearue London.

Dr. Manob & Bandyopadhyan Dairy Co-operative and Rural Development in India.

Khurody D.N. Operation Flood-Progress and Potentials, Vo 1.2 Anand Published by NDDB.

Ganguli B.K. (1974), Dairying in India Asia Publication House Bombay.

Olson T.M. (1938), Elements of Dairying The Macmillan Company New York.

Palakashappa T.C. Social and Economic Implication of Dairy Development New Zealand, University of Waikato.

Patrick John (1975), Economics of Dairy Development in India: Published byKarnataka State.

Somjee A.H. & Somjee (1978), Co-Operative Dairying and the Profiles of Social Change in Indian Economic Development and SocialChange. Vo 1.26.

CHAPTER–15

DEVELOPMENT OF RURAL INFRASTRUCTURE FOR POVERTY ALLEVIATION IN INDIA–ISSUES AND CONCERNS

V. Basil Hans

INTRODUCTION

Fifty *plus* years of development planning in India has been unable to eradicate poverty or ensure a Marshallian well-being for a large number of people residing in the six lakh villages of the country. A gleeful account of the many rural development schemes may be given, but the woeful problem of rural poverty makes people ascribe adjectives to it like "cruel" "grinding" "painful" "vicious", "disturbing", "dehumanising"," destabilising" and so on. This calls for a thorough analysis of the causes and consequences of rural poverty. There are several constraints to economic progress in the countryside; chief of them is lack of basic infrastructure, both physical and social. Given that the rate of rural-urban transformation has been slow in India and that more than 70 per cent of people still lve in rural areas, more attention has not so far been given to the provision of rural infrastructure.[1] Even the economic reforms since the last decade have not been able to remove the obstacle. Inadequacy of infrastructure has made life miserable for numerous rural people in terms of consumption as well as production. While technology and technology-based services are the driving forces of modern growth–even in developing countries like India–the ubiquitous absence of sound infrastructure is driving away even the private and foreign private investors.

Public policy and programmes always reiterate that provision of basic needs and inputs is the prime agenda of our development and the primary concern of every government. The uncertainties and delays involved in realising the objectives linger and poverty meanwhile is unabated. Several projects of power, road and house construction and irrigation development have been started with much paraphernalia of publicity but the critical needs are the same - electricity, sanitation, drinking water, roads and housing. There seems to be an indifference in accepting the truth in rural development viz., infrastructure development in the rural areas is not an "either or option". Such indifference not only affects the potential of development but also the future prospects in the rural areas. This paper, therefore, seeks to address the pertinent issues in building and managing infrastructure for rural development with the basic objective of amelioration of poverty.

IDENTIFICATION OF RURAL POOR

Poverty is a multi-faceted phenomenon, defined/explained as a situation in which a person lacks the necessary capabilities and entitlements to satisfy his or her basic needs and aspirations. The rural poor are all people who a) live in a rural area at or below subsistence level; b) are dedicated full- or part-time to agriculture, forestry, fisheries, handicrafts and/or related occupations; and c) are over-dependent for work and livelihood on others with more power and means of production.

It is a misconception that all who live in a poor or backward area are poor.[2] The rural populace also has a rich component -

those having abundance of means of production, largely private and also better access to infrastructural facilities created for the public at large. There are various ways of classifying the rural poor. One categorisation is as: small and marginal owner-farmers, tenants, sharecroppers, landless labourers, small fishermen, forestry workers, and part of the rural artisans, of tribal people as well as of nomads and refugees. Uphoff has classified the rural poor into four categories: 1) the middle class having secure and sufficient access to income and assets; 2) subsistence producers having some access to income and assets; 3) the very poor having very little access (labourers, hawkers, etc.); and 4) the destitute including the handicapped who are not able for whatever reason to help themselves. Yet another way of classifying the rural poor or disadvantaged people is as follows: 1) the marginally poor (small farmers), 2) the poor (small farmers-part-time labourers), 3) the very poor (labourers and part-time micro farmer-labourers), and 4) the destitute (i.e., those without an economic base).

The broad contours of rural poverty outlined in the preceding paragraphs clearly indicate that the poorest of the poor in the rural areas belong to the families of small and marginal farmers, agricultural labourers, rural artisans, SCs, and STs. For a successful implementation of any programme for the rural poor it is necessary that these categories of rural poor have to be the target groups.[3] Economic justice (for the poor in general) and social justice (for the above sections in particular) are therefore, on the top of the national agenda since independence. Moreover, it is the central theme of India's welfare economics, in theory and practice.[4]

The Planning Commission of India in 1977 defined the rural poor as those whose per capita consumption expenditure was below the midpoint of the monthly per capita expenditure class having a per capita daily calorie intake of 2400, compared with urban poor's 2100 calories. This was the poverty line.[5] In rupee terms the cut-off point turned out to be Rs.107 and Rs.122 for rural and urban areas respectively at 1984-85 prices.[6] For a household of five members, the poverty line was fixed at an annual income of Rs.6,400 in rural areas and Rs.7,200 in urban areas. Later based on the recommendations of a study group on poverty line, the private consumption deflator from national accounts statistics was selected to update the poverty line in 1978, 1983 and 1987-88. Subsequently the expert group under the Chairmanship of Lakdawala examined the issue. While it accepted the definition and base figures of the poverty, it suggested an alternative methodology to calculate poverty line. It recommended the use of consumption index for agriculture to update rural poverty line. This was accepted by the Planning Commission.

At 1992-93 prices, the poverty line for the rural areas was estimated at a monthly consumption expenditure of Rs.181.50 (urban: Rs.209.50). For a family of five members it was fixed at an annual income of Rs.10,890 (urban: 12,570). The Eighth Five Year Plan (1992-97) stipulated poverty line be defined as annual income of Rs.11,000 at the period's prices. In the next decade the Government of India defined poverty line at Rs.300 per person per month while the minimum wages was determined at Rs.1250 per month. The 55th round (1999-2000) of the National Sample Survey (NSS) has used a different methodology from all previous rounds, to take into account both higher income and higher expenditure by the rural sector.

Thus, it is clear that there is relativity and dynamism in the concept of poverty line.[7] Discerning the dynamics of poverty is difficult. But the poverty line choice has important bearing on matters such as inter state allocation of anti poverty resources as well as the measurement of the impact of the use of such resources in terms of availability, accessibility and affordability. In India the generally accepted definition of poverty emphasises the minimum level of living, because many people are far from the stage of a reasonable living. Both absolute and relative poverty are evident in rural India. Starvation deaths of bygone days seem to be replaced by suicides (of the farmers). The cliché term "vicious circle of poverty" or "poverty breeds poverty" may have become less relevant but is still prevalent. Severe poverty in many villages and tribal areas of the country has manifested itself not only in under nourishment but also utter inadequacy of other basic amenities of life such as healthcare, housing, schooling etc. Lack of these facilities has undermined people's productivity and earnings. The infrastructural inadequacies by themselves lend force to finding India's grinding poverty. Absolute poverty and absolute low productivity are like the two sides of the same coin. The concept of relative poverty goes beyond the basic needs.[8] It is associated not only with low productivity but also low productive work and gross inequalities of assets such as land in case of rural poor. Disparities in resources other than natural have accentuated despite economic growth. The decline in the share of rural sector in the national income in India in recent years is the foremost indication of this.[9]

INCIDENCE OF RURAL POVERTY

The total number of the poor in India was estimated at 211million in 1989-90. Of these more than 80 per cent were in the rural areas. Their number was 169 million, constituting 28 per cent of the rural population. Aptly India's poverty is described as rural poverty. Over the years, however, rural poverty has declined (see Table 1).

As observed from Table 1, the proportion of rural population below the poverty line was more than 50 per cent till the end of the Fifth Plan. This has to be weighed against the successes of planning itself. It is well known that the achievement through planned development till almost the early 50s, i.e., during the Third Plan, was commendable, relative if not to what the contemporary fast growing less developed countries achieved, but certainly to the country's the growth rate during the colonial period.

In the 70s poverty eradication became the trump card of major political parties and "garibi hatao" their clarion call. Despite the populism of promise the proportion of rural poverty remained high. In the 80s the platitudes and programmes to abrogate poverty were invigorated. The percentage of rural population below poverty line did climb down somewhat, but, not again, commensurate with the efforts and the hype. In 1983 the number of rural poor remained as high as 252 million even as the poverty ratio declined to about

46 per cent. With further reduction in the ratio to 39 per cent in 1987-88 and 37 per cent in 1993-94, one could talk of a 'secular' decline in the incidence of poverty.[10]

Table 1
Rural Poverty in India, 1956-2006

		Rural Poor	
Year	*Number (millions)*	*Per cent*	*Sen's Index*
1956-57	182	54.1	0.23
1966-67	231	56.6	0.24
1977-78	264.353.1	0.14	
1983	252.045.7	n/a	
1987-88	231.939.1	n/a	
1989-90		33.4	
1992		43.0	
1993-94	244.037.3	n/a	
1996-97	n/a	30.55	n/a
1999-2000	193.227.1*	n/a	
		24**	
2004-05	n a	28.3	n/a
2006-07ä	170.5	21.1	n/a

Note: * 30-day recall, ** 7-day recall, ä projection, n/a not available

Source: P.R. Brahmanand and V.R. Panchamukhi (ed.), *Development Process of Indian* Economy, Bombay: Himalaya Publishing House, 1987; John Mellor and G.M. Desai (ed) *Agricultural Change and Rural Poverty*, Delhi: Oxford University Press, 1986; Ninth Plan (1997-2002) and Tenth Plan (2002-07), Planning Commission, GOI; *Economic Survey 2000-01*, GOI and 'Poverty in India', from Wikepedia , May 7, 2008. Retrieved on 16-6-2008.

As per the NSS 55th round of survey, during 1999-2000 the poverty ratio for rural India has been estimated at about 27 per cent (based on 30 day recall) or at 24 per cent (based on 7 day recall). While the results of these estimates are still debated particularly with reference to its innovative methodology, we also have poverty figures coming out from international organisations such as the World Bank. As per the available data by the World Bank, with a GNP per capita of 440 dollars in 1999 India continued to have the highest concentration of poverty with more that 360 million people (about 36 per cent of its total – both rural and urban – population), living below the official poverty line. The decade of economic reforms (1991-

2001) has not been a period of comfort either as far as poverty eradication is concerned. It has been established that the 90s have hardly done anything for the rural poor in India. Leave alone secular decline in poverty, in fact 70 million people were added to the poor category between 1989-90 and 1997. During 1983 to 1990-91 the GDP growth rate was 5.6 per cent and poverty decline was 3.1 per cent per annum, during 1991 to 1996-97 GDP growth accelerated but poverty ratio increased.[11]

During the planning period the annual average rate of growth in GNP has increased from 3 per cent in 50s to 4 per cent in 60s, 5-6 per cent during 1980-81 to 1990-91, and from 6.6 per cent in 1991-92 to 6.8 per cent in 1998-99. During 1994-2000 it was 6-8 per cent.[12] The inference is that income inequality, for rural India has more or less remained stable. So from "poverty in the midst of plenty" to "inequality with growth" has been the journey for over five decades. The urban-bias syndrome seems to have reappeared in the LPG era. For some this is the accentuation of the 'rural-urban income disparities'[13, 14], for others it is the increase in regional inequality in the incidence of poverty'[15]. Even while poverty declined at the macro level, rural-urban disparity was visible.[16] Disparities between and discrimination within socio-economic groups leading to deprivation are manifestations of bias in development.[17] Government has admitted that while the ratio of general poverty did fall since 70s, the number of rural poor has more or less remained the same. Hence rural poverty is quite a serious problem even today.

Added to income poverty there are also the phenomena of capability poverty (a measure of poverty that links economic growth with employment and economic well being) and human poverty (an index of poverty which is the opposite of human development index) in rural India. According to one estimate the capability poverty in India is more than 60 per cent.[18] Recent researches related to poverty are studies based on Living Standards Measurement Survey (LSMS) that provide a more detailed picture of infrastructure access and consumption by the poorest households across countries and within countries.

The NCAER study for Rural Infrastructure Report highlights that nine-tenths of rural households do not own telephones, half do not have domestic power connections and even the connected households are without power because of outages for almost 17 hours a day in monsoon months and 13 hours a day in other months. The report also says that half of all people living in habitations away from a main village do not have access to all-weather roads and although almost all rural households are covered by a source of drinking water, the quality and quantity of water actually available is often low because of poor maintenance and operation,

Almost eight-tenths of rural households have no access to sanitation facilities, it says, adding that as many households have no access to sanitation facilities.[19]

It can be argued, therefore, that poverty in some form exists during planning as well during reforms. Once it was criticised as failure of "trickle down effect". Now it is blamed on the lacklustre performance of reforms - "failure to reduce vast economic and social inequalities and to empower the poor" as Bhiku Parekh puts it.[20] Then it was lack of percolation effect, now it is the inadequacy of factors to 'pull' the poor up. What is the best option today? A combination of 'down' 'up' and 'spread' effects. Access to infrastructure seems to have an answer.

POVERTY ALLEVIATION–WHAT INFRASTRUCTURE CAN DO

India has for long been referred to as "a rich country with poor people". While this meant that there was a mismatch between natural resources and capital resources–the latter being scarce–the inference is that there is a population explosion in which poverty plays a double role as a cause and an effect. But while remedies were spelt out by everyone concerned with the problem there was too much emphasis on population control measures to the neglect of measures to build and develop infrastructural facilities. While infrastructural facilities (including health care, education etc) are growth inducing factors it has to be admitted that economic growth is the best contraceptive. Improved infrastructural facilities such as good schools, hospitals, houses, irrigation etc when present in a particular region may enhance the potential of the natural endowments. Growth becomes effective with infrastructure as the framework.

In the 80s and 90s creation of social and economic overheads (the other name for infrastructure) figured in the national scheme of things, largely as employment generating activities. Construction of wells, godowns, etc was given priority in the rural development programmes. Here also the importance of infrastructural facilities was seen as limited to generating immediate income. The activities were hardly perennial and so were the gains. Most of the activities related to social and economic capital were in the nature of public works programme. Rural works programme and labour based infrastructure activities are closely related. The people involved in the creation of assets were sometimes labourers and other times beneficiaries, rarely both at the same time. Even the socio-economic security that these assets seemed to have provided was superficial. Ad hoc benefits got more acclaim. Sans migration the fall in rural poverty was marginal. All in all something vital was missing. That something was a thrust on infrastructure.

With the coming of the era of globalisation the doors of the economy were wide opened for foreign investment and MNCs, and the need for strong and wide net work of infrastructural facilities was felt more than ever before. Under economic reforms the concept of "global village" became a reality. But villages had to wait. All through the First Generation Reforms it was urban infrastructure that got all the attention–in transport, housing, marketing, energy etc. Urban poverty did fall significantly because of infrastructure development but rural poverty still remained high. This became a worrisome feature particularly because globalisation was on the threshold of rural India. Agricultural transformation and rural resurgence could not wait. Agriculture faced a fiscal compression. Welfare activities in the rural areas suffered from various constraints including lower sectoral spending, in the changed scenario.[21]

The Second Generation Reforms set to put things in order. At the macro level our policy suggested the following.

- Further lowering of tariffs
- Making labour laws flexible
- More conducive investment climate
- Move towards unified goods and services tax
- Thrust on Infrastructure

Under the changed circumstances and from the lessons learnt from the past, the renewed focus on rural infrastructure development means not only a different priority but also a different pattern in building and developing the infrastructural facilities–not in a quick fix grandiose fashion but giving attention to all its aspects such as availability, adequacy, accessibility and affordability. New discourses on rural development consider rural infrastructure as the nucleus of regional/local development programme. The new Economics of Rural Infrastructure spells out in clear terms that rural areas need–

- Infrastructure in general and agriculture-specific infrastructure (agri-infrastructure)
- Equal development of infrastructure in all regions
- Better access and affordability
- Avoiding the over use and misutilisation of infrastructure (e.g. avoid the urban-type problems like pollution)
- Managing rural infrastructure with a participatory approach by the people, government and private enterprise.

In short, in the new environment development of rural infrastructure is seen not as some form of charity that we can give to the rural people or only as a final output of rural labour. Rather it is seen in a wider perspective of overall development of the rural areas and improvement of the rural livelihood. It is akin to primary wants of man. If food, clothing and shelter are something you cannot do without so are the infrastructural facilities like rural schools, village health centres, rural markets etc without which no village can have healthy development. Putting it plainly, "it is normal and nothing special". Only the interest about it is something special. There is a new manner of thinking and doing activities for rural development. For some this is a revelation if not a revolution. The missing link in rural resources and rural development is now put in place.

It is realised that infrastructure links rural communities with goods and services found elsewhere, and that a healthy rural economy depends on rural infrastructure for market access and personal mobility.[22] Definite links of infrastructure to economic growth have been identified. Many studies regarding impact of infrastructure on development show very high returns in a time-series analysis of GDP growth. For instance studies in the US, China and Taiwan suggest that the impact of infrastructure investments on economic growth represent 60 to 77 per cent rates of return.[23] Studies conducted by Singh; Barnes and Binsanger; Binswanger, Khandelkar and Rosenzwieg; Fan, Hazell and Thorat; Chand and Sonia; Roller, Hendrik and Waverman; Songco; and Gosh ; and surveys by World Bank in 1995 and 2002 point out the beneficial effects of better rural infrastructure on economic growth and poverty alleviation.[24] A study conducted by UNESCAP states that one of the causes of persistent rural poverty in Asia is inadequate investment in human capital, agricultural technology and infrastructure.

Rural infrastructure investments benefit the rural poor through increased incomes and improved consumption patterns revealed in lower costs of basic goods, lower expenditures on energy (because of new energy sources), greater uses of social and extension services, etc. These concrete benefits lend strong support to the argument for more infrastructure investments. In the language of econometrics, investing in infrastructure can help in wiping out poverty treating each variable, (i.e. facility) as an independent variable.

A study conducted by the World Bank reveals that fifty per cent of poor Ecuadorian families see improvements in basic infrastructure provision as the way to alleviate poverty. For instance the Bank's experiences of operations in rural electrification projects in Asia (and India) tells that the use of electric pumps in well irrigation was promoted in place of diesel pumps, and led to increased agricultural productivity through greater land use, less reliance on rainfall, and a change in crop pattern to higher-yield crops. Diesel pumps continued to be used to supplement electric pumps, yet the new energy source was cited as the likely catalyst for the farmers' move to more productive irrigated farming. Advances in irrigation due to rural electrification were shown to reduce significantly the incidence of absolute poverty.

In Bihar a World Bank project aimed to alleviate rural poverty by increasing production and market access; strengthening local capacities; involving project beneficiaries; and incorporating environment-friendly economic activities. The project succeeded not only in increasing the area of irrigated land available for farming (which should increase incomes) but also made for improved rural roads and bridges providing greater market accessibility. Another success was in the provisions of drinking water to significantly more households thereby minimising water-borne diseases. The whole experience of implementing the project has strengthened local capacities. Similarly in Kerala land values have increased five times following rural water supply improvements and in Karnataka the decline in inter-regional imbalances in growth right from 1980s is largely attributed to the improved use of infrastructure.[25]

Thus, it can be said that rural infrastructure development mitigates poverty effectively in at least five ways: 1) creating better access to existing and new employment and providing further earning opportunities; 2) increasing efficiency in production (e.g. creating value-added centres); 3) creating access to previously inaccessible commodities and services by enlarged time and space dimensions (the rural-urban, local-global linkage perspective); 4) saving time, which can be better utilised in productive activities; and 5) improving the quality of human capital through better health and physical conditions as well as social relations of the rural population (e.g. gender mainstreaming).

The uniqueness of rural infrastructure is that it helps overcome three types of vulnerability in the rural areas–economic vulnerability, social vulnerability, and personal vulnerability–at the same time too.

MANAGING RURAL INFRASTRUCTURE–TASKS AHEAD

Any attempt to highlight the role of infrastructural development in the rural economy is going to be inadequate unless the stakeholders of development are informed about its implications for a futuristic policy. Creation of any infrastructural facility in a village does not end the matter. In the context of poverty therefore, it means that infrastructure is a tool with which we can take on the challenge of poverty. Much depends on how we handle this tool. Builders, financiers, buyers, owners and facilitators are the various parties involved in matter. The operative principle is the 'involvement' of these parties in managing infrastructure. Problems are bound to arise not only with regard to the nature and amount of infrastructure and investment for it, but also with regard to pricing and policy interventions. The private/public participation can pose challenges given the heterogeneity and multi-dimensional nature of the infrastructural projects.[26, 27] At this juncture India needs to give thought to the following aspects.

1. Overcoming financial constraints–because as the India Rural Infrastructure Report (released in December 2006), says infrastructure development suffers on the one hand from the fact that while infrastructure in villages is largely owned and run by the government, its funds are constrained, and on the other hand, private funds are attracted to areas where rates of return are at least reasonable.[27]
2. Better spatial distribution of infrastructural facilities considering equity. Rural people must put great pressure on their organisations to make sure this is happening. It is because infrastructure decisions can so easily be biased to providing better services to some at the cost of some services for all, that it is important that these decisions be made at the level of government

closest to the people. Panchayats and other organisations need to play a pro-active role here.

3. Encouraging rural people to invest on goods such as vehicles, telephones and other equipment when their incomes permit for even such demands spur infrastructural investments.
4. Enhance the quality of services from rural infrastructure while also being cost effective.

Modalities should be worked out for each facility and for each village or locality where the infrastructure is to be built and/or developed. Adaptability to the given environment - local and global - should never be ignored. In the context of WTO system, for instance, measures should be taken to strengthen the competitive capability of agriculture by providing suitable infrastructural support and incentives for inducting change.[28] The success of any infrastructural development programme will largely depend upon adaptation-continuously-according to the changing circumstances of power, economics and culture.

CONCLUSION

It is now a well established fact that there can be no meaningful rural growth without rural infrastructure. Eleventh Plan aims at "faster and more inclusive growth" This should include rural growth too. An employment-intensive economic growth policy does reduce poverty in the long run. However, this strategy needs to be complemented with a focus on provision of basic facilities or infrastructure.[29] The job at hand is enormous but a beginning is already done with initiatives such as Rural Infrastructure Development Fund, Bharat Nirman Programme, new rural employment programmes like Jawahar Gram Swarozgar Yojana (JGSY), Swarnajayanti Gram Swarozgar Yojana (SGSY), Rural Women's Development and Employment programme (RWDEP), Samagra Awaas Yojana (SAY), Pradhan Mantri Gramodaya Yojana (PMGY), Integrating New and Sustainable Technologies for Elimination of Poverty (INSTEP) etc. We also have a built-in capacity combined in the forms of cooperatives, decentralised institutions, Self-Help Groups, micro finance institutions etc, many of which have strengths of success and stability. These can help in building and managing rural infrastructure effectively for people's empowerment and rural development. Such efforts make infrastructure grows faster; social justice easier. Higher growth and increasing revenue will enable the government spend more on rural infrastructure.[30] The state can help in creating an enabling environment through general political, legal and administrative framework that supports civil society initiatives.

The investment on infrastructure has to be stepped up from 4.0 per cent to at least 7 per cent of GDP in the next few years. Government subsidy for encouraging private players to invest in rural infrastructure development requires a whopping Rs.1,58,313 crore. Rural India requires Rs.92,690 crore (at 2002-03 prices) for providing telecom connectivity, Rs.55,243 crore for power supply, Rs.5,892 crore roads and transport and Rs.4,488 crore for water and sanitation. Not only the centre and the states but also the local governments have to make provision the basic infrastructure facilities in their annual budgets.[31] Funds can be mobilised. What matters is how infrastructural projects will be managed in the future. Meanwhile efforts to eradicate rural poverty should continue with added vigour so that the people in India's 638,589 villages will have a better tomorrow. Yes, India still lives in its villages.[32] To reiterate, infrastructure development in the rural areas enables the government and the people to make frontal attack poverty directly and empowers the people to develop with unleashed ability.

NOTES AND REFERENCES

1. Rakesh Mohan (2006), Foreword to the *India Rural Infrastructure Report*, 2007 (NCAER), New Delhi: Sage Publications India Pvt Ltd.
2. This misconception arises mainly due to the fact that most of the income/poverty studies do not make a distinction between area based poverty and family level poverty. A clear distinction

between the two will help bring out the dimensions of poverty as also the endogenous and exogenous factors leading to poverty and deprivation of the masses.

3. For a detail on the characteristics of these groups see Patel, Shah, D'Mello (1984), *Rural Economics*, Bombay: Himalaya Publishing House.
4. D.Venkateshwaralu (2001), "Eradication of Poverty through People's Participatory Approach-An Evaluation of 'Janmabhoomi' Programme in Andhra Pradesh", *Samaja Shodhana*, Vol.10, No.1-2, p.1.
5. Poverty line was earlier known as "starvation line". It is the most common measure of poverty. The number of persons living below this line is counted as poor, i.e., below poverty line (BPL) and the number is expressed as a percentage of total population in the country (or region). This is also known as the head count measure of poverty. Although simple, this measure has a weakness in that it gives equal weight to all irrespective of their distance from the poverty line. This problem can be overcome by using an alternative measure suggested by Amartya Sen. Sen's index takes into account both the number of poor and the intensity of poverty (poverty gap); it is the difference between the poverty line and the income of the poor. Sen's index is a weighted sum of the poverty gaps of all the poor, the weights being such that less poor persons get lower weight than those who are more poor. The index is on an ascending scale between 0 and 1. A higher Sen's index implies a higher incidence of poverty.
6. This figure takes into account expenditure on minimum necessary foods only and ignores non-food necessities like clothing. In the USA poverty line means not having enough money to pay rent also. The distribution of services also needs to be taken into account while preparing a 'measure' of poverty. See Ravi Batra (1987), *The Great Depression of 1990*, New York: Simon and Schuster, and A.M. Khusro (1988), "Poverty of Poverty Analysis", in Institute of Economic Growth, *Development Perspectives*, B R: New Delhi. Even the per capita aggregates for food consumption mask the inherently unequal distribution of that consumption, just as GNP figures often mask the magnitude of absolute poverty [Michael P. Todaro (1987), *Economic Development in the Third World*, Hyderabad: Orient Longman, p. 290].

7. In the workshop on measurement and evaluation of poverty held on 11-12 January 2001 at New Delhi (organised by the World Bank and the Planning Commission of India) one of the views expressed was that India's poverty line itself is low by international standards, and hence it needs to be reviewed and revised.

8. In a sense relative poverty is more an index of inequality than of poverty. It is used to compare some individuals or groups within a country or between countries. That way relative poverty will always be there. In recent years it is the poverty in the absolute sense that is aimed to be overcome.

9. One of the changes is the replacement of the existing National Accounts (NAS) series by a new series (base 1993-94) in 1999. It includes 30-day food recall and 365-day recall for clothing etc. But the 55th round itself has generated lot of discussions regarding comparability or otherwise with the previous rounds, overestimation of poverty decline, inclusion of non food spending (ala Deaton's assumption of stable relationship between poverty and non food spending) and so on. Just as poverty is alive, so is the debate on its estimate criteria. For a discussion on the methodology of the 55th round see Abhijit Sen and Himanshu, 2004, "Poverty and Inequality in India - I", *Economic and Political Weekly*, 39(38), pp. 4247-63.

10. Aditya Raj Das (2001), "Economic Reforms and the Poor', *Deccan Herald*, March 3, at *http://www.deccanherald.com/deccanherald/mar04/spotlite1.htm.*

11. Keshab Das (2001), 'Issues in Promoting Rural Infrastructure in India'. Available at http://econpapers.repec.org/paper/monceddtr/67.htm and http://ged.u-bordeaux4.fr/ceddt67.pdf

12. See Chapter 6 Economic Performance @ http://lawmin.nic.in

13. See Amit Bhandari and Deepak Nair (1996), *The Intelligent Person's Guide to Liberalization*, New Delhi: Penguin Books.

14. For a detailed analysis of the definition and degree of disparity see D. Rajasekhar and Gagan Bihari Sahu (2004), *The Growing Rural Urban Disparity: Some Issues*, Working Paper 156, Bangalore: ISEC. The authors, among other things, suggest that income is not a sufficient indicator to capture the magnitude of disparities at any level, and therefore, some other indicators representing human resource development and *infrastructure facility* needs to be developed. [Emphasis authors'].

15. See R. Nagaraj (2000), "Indian Economy since 1980: Virtuous Growth or Polarisation?" *Economic and Political Weekly*, 35 (32), pp. 2831-9.
16. See for instance Government of India (2001-02), *Economic Survey*, New Delhi: Ministry of Finance, GOI.
17. V. Basil Hans (2008), Marginalization in the Midst of Modernization–Women's Health Empowerment'. In L. Rathakrishnan (ed.) *Empowerment of Women through Entrepreneurship*, New Delhi: Gyan Publishing House.
18. V.B. Hans (1997), *Nature and Scope of Health Economics*, unpublished M.Phil Dissertation. Mangalore University, Mangalagangothri, p. 305.
19. *http://timesofindia.indiatimes.com* (17 Dec 2006), 'PM releases report on rural infrastructure'. The report, among other things suggests a Public-Private Partnership model to resolve the contradiction of public-private investment on infrastructure. In the model Government provides subsidies to the private players commensurate to the level of development required in particular rural area. Compare this with Public-Farmers-Private Partnership (PFPP) model for Special Agricultural Regions (SARs) proposed under 'Agriculture Vision 2020' by the India Liberal Group (Project for Economic Education). See for details India Liberal Group (2006), *Taking Reforms to the Poor – The Liberal Budget 2007-08*, Mumbai: Indian Liberal Group p.20. Whatever the model, the crux of the issue is to fill the visible and viable gap in funding, keeping in view the nature and need of rural development.
20. Quoted in Shridar Pande (2002), "Liberalisation, Globalisation and the State in Indian Economy", in K.R. Gupta (ed.), *Liberalisation and Globalisation of Indian Economy*, Vol. V, New Delhi: Atlantic Publishers and Distributors, p.29.
21. D. Rudrappan (2003), "Globalisation and Agricultural Crisis in India". In Y.K. Alagh (ed.), *Globalisation and Agricultural Crisis in India*, New Delhi: Deep & Deep Publications, p.47.
22. Richard Reeder (2005), 'Infrastructure and rural development policy', Economic Research Service, United States Department of Agriculture. ERS/USDA, @ *http://www.ers.usda.gov*
23. V. Basil Hans (2007), "Problems and Prospects of Rural Infrastructure - Showcasing Karnataka" in Jayasheela and V. Basil Hans (ed.), *Rural Karnataka*, New Delhi: Serials Publications, p. 231-33.

24. *ibid.*
25. *ibid.*
26. For a discussion on emerging rules and strategies in managing infrastructural projects see Manoranjan Sharma, "Infrastructure Development–Road Map for the future" in K.R. Gupta op.cit. pp. 95-125.
27. In a seminar organised by the Bangalore Chamber of Commerce and Industry (BCIC) at Bangalore on August 7, 2008 the evolution and impact of PPP model was discussed in detail. Devesh Agarwal (chairman, Infrastructure Committee of BCIC), and A. Ravindra (chairman, Centre for Sustainable Development), hailed PPP as "innovative mechanism", a "mantra in recent years". But Somak Ghosh (Group President, CF&DB, Yes Bank), cautioned that PPPs need not be treated "as a panacea" for soving all the infrastructure-related problems. According to him infrastructure needs to be considered as a "public good" prior to the entry of the private sector, actively in the sector, and there is need to hedge the foreign exchage component of infrastructure projects to avoild disasters (see *The Hindu*, Friday, August 8, 2008, p. 6, "PPPs not panacea for all infrastructure related problems").
28. Talwar Sabanna and M.S. Kallur (2003), "World Trade Organisation: Implications on Indian Agriculture. In R.V. Dadibhavi and S.T. Bagalkoti (ed.), *World Trade Organisation – Implications on India,* Dharwad: Karnataka University, p. 195.
29. Parveen Gill and Pushpinder Gill (2003), "Economic Reforms and Poverty in India: An Overview". In P.P.Arya and B.B. Tandon (ed.), *Economic Reforms in India – From First Generation and Beyond,* New Delhi: Deep & Deep Publications Pvt. Ltd., p.157.
30. See *The Economic Times* Monday January 1, 2007, Editorial p. 4, "Grow faster – It makes Social Justice Easier".
31. Keynote Address by Dr. G.V. Joshi, Professor of Economics & Dean, faculty of Arts, Mangalore University at the State Level Conference on 'Development of Coastal Karnataka: Possibilities and Problems' organised by St Aloysius College Mangalore (Autonomous) and Mangalore University Economics Association, held in the college on February 16, 2008.
32. John (2008), 'Infrastructure Development and Economic Growth in India', *chillibreeze,* July. Available at http://www.chillibreeze.com/articles/Infrastructure-Development-and-Economic-Growth.asp#a.

CHAPTER–16

INDIAN AGRICULTURE IN THE NEW GLOBAL SCENARIO

U. Thirunavukarasu

INTRODUCTION

Neo-classical economists are the champions of the free trade/ lassaize faire policy who developed various economic models and provided policy prescriptions during 1700-1930, but at the time of world depression, all the prescriptions of classical economists were proved frivolous. This is how Keynes postulations were invoked. Subsequently, interventionist policies were come in to existence. Again in the name of macro economic stabilization/structural adjustment programs, the World Bank economists have switched back to the neo-liberal philosophy of free market economy and free trade calling for change in the policies which has led to withdrawal support to agriculture.

The new 1991 economic policy was initiated with the objective of LPG of the economy and later in 1994, accordingly GATT agreement signed by 125 countries including India. This accord aims at substantial progressive reduction in support and protection so as to prevent restrictions and distortions in the world market. It includes establishment of WTO which came in to force on 1st Jan 1995 including other proposals relating to agriculture such as market access, domestic support and export subsidies, removal of quantitative restrictions.

ROLE OF INTERNATIONAL INSTITUTIONS IN THE AGRICULTURAL SECTOR:

Some important questions which arise as a result of globalization are

1. Why are international institutions entering in to the matters related to agriculture sector?
2. Is it to protect the agriculture sector or to establish corporatism in the primary sector?
3. Do WTO agreements really offer a helping hand to the farming community consisting of 91% small farmers and 8% of medium farmers? Or does it protect the interest of only 1% large farmers in India.

In the view of above questions, in this paper an attempt has been made to examine the impact of WTO agreements on agriculture development in India.

PLAN ALLOCATIONS

Plan outlays on Agriculture and allied activities have been gradually declining during the plan period from 14.9 percent in the first plan to 5.2 percent by the tenth plan. This clearly shows Government withdrawal from the agriculture sector development. (Table -1)

Table 1
Plan Outlay in Agriculture and Allied Sectors

(Rs. in Crores)

Plan	*Total Outlay*	*Agri & Allied Sectors*	*% of Agri & Allied Sectors*
i plan	2378	354	14.9
ii plan	4500	501	11.3
iii plan	8577	1089	12.7
iv plan	15779	2320	14.7

Contd.

Plan	*Total Outlay*	*Agri & Allied Sectors*	*% of Agri & Allied Sectors*
v plan	39426	4865	12.3
vi plan	97500	5695	5.8
vii plan	180000	10525′	5.9
viii plan	434100	22467	5.2
ix plan	859200	42462	4.9
x plan	398890	20668	5.2

Source: Tenth Five Year Plan: 2002-2007

AGRICULTURE GROWTH

Agriculture production has two components - food grains and non-food grains. The former contributes approximately two-thirds of total agricultural production. Agricultural growth analysis presents the fact that there has been a decline in average annual growth rate during pre-reform and post-reform period i.e., from 3.9 percent per annum to 3.6 percent. Growth rate in Food grains during 1980-1990 was 2.9 percent and it has declined to 2.0 percent during 1992-2000. Similarly there was a decline in the growth rate of non-food grains from 4.3 percent to 2.4 percent during the same period i.e pre-reform and post-reform periods as shown in Table-2.

Table 2
Pre & Post Globalisation Growth in Agriculture Sector
(Average Growth Rate)

Crop	*1980-1991(%)*	*1991-2000(%)*
Agriculture and Allied activities		
a. Agriculture	3.6	3.9
b. Forestry	4.2	3.7
c. Fishing	-0.1	0.8
Crop		
a. Food grains	2.9	2.0
b. Cereals	3.1	2.1
c. Rice	3.7	2.2
d. Wheat	3.6	3.6
e. Coarse cereals	0.0	-1.6
f. Pulses	1.4	0.8
g. Non-food grains	4.3	2.4

Source: Economic Survey–2001.

CAPITAL FORMATION

Gross domestic capital formatting in agriculture has been undergone a secular decline due to steady erosion in the share of public investment. The increasing private capital formation has been concentrated in inputs like power and other inputs are available uninterruptedly and with large subsidy. In fact more and more investment must be fueled into farm sector in the fields of research, extension, infrastructure development, marketing etc. to attain higher production and productivity. It would raise the income position of rural population.

Table 3
Gross Capital Formation in Agricultural Sector

(at 1993-94 prices)

	Gross Capital Formation			
Year	*Public Sector*	*Private Sector*	*Total*	*Investment in Agri as % of GDP*
1993-94	33.0%	67.0	7.47	1.6
1994-95	33.0%	67.0	6.51	1.6
1995-96	28.9%	69.1	5.56	1.6
1996-97	28.9%	71.1	6.51	1.5
1997-98	25.0%	75.0	4.77	1.4
1998-99	26.0%	74.0	6.18	1.3
1999-00	24.8%	75.2	6.18	1.3
2000-01	24.2%	75.8	6.02	1.3

Source: Central Statistical Organization, New Delhi.

But Public investment in agriculture was at higher levels in the initial years of the planning while, in the later years it had been declining in particular after 1980's. Investment in agriculture as a percentage of GDP has remained at 1.6 percent during 1993-1996 after that it has gradually decline to 1.3 percent by 1999 and same level has continued up to 2001. This fall is due to the decline in Public Investment from Rs. 4467 crores in 1993-94 to Rs. 3869 crores in 1998-99 (Table- 3). Since private investment seems to be compensating for decline in public investment in agriculture, voices are being raised in some circles that there is no need to expand public investment in agriculture. But public investment and private investment cannot be considered to be mutual substitutes in view of their current composition. Public investment in mainly made in medium and major irrigation projects, rural roads etc. in contrast private investment is essentially taking place for short term asset building, ground leveling etc.

In the name of macro economic stabilization of the economy, many measures have been introduced, though these liberalization measures would do nothing to raise the level of investment. And the present rate of capital formation is fart below the rate that is required to transform India's low-level agricultural economy into high-level agricultural economy. Instead to raise the investment in agriculture sector, Government itself -withdrawing from the sector.

RURAL EMPLOYMENT

Agricultural un-employment that may be classified into- seasonal, disguised, chronic and usual status unemployment. According to the NSS, current daily status rural unemployment rate for male workers was 4.58 percent in 1987-88. Since then un-employment among rural male workers has been 7.2 percent in 1999-00 as against 5.64 percent in 1993-94. Table–4 depicts that the agricultural employment has declined from 2.17 to 0.18 in between 1987-94 and 1994-2000 and total employment also has shown a decline to 0.66 from 2.14 during the same time period. Therefore we can conclude that the globalization has failed even in improving employment position in agriculture sector.

Table 4
Rural Employment Growth

Employment	*1987-88 to 1993-94*	*1993-94 to 1999-00*
Total Employment (PS+SS)	2.14	0.66
Agriculture Employment (PS+SS)	2.17	0.18
Non-Agricultural Employment (PS+SS)	2.02	2.34

Source: Human Development South Asia 2002, Sarvekshana various issues

AGRICULTURAL EXPORTS

The share of agricultural exports in total exports was 44.2 percent in 1960-61 which was declined to 19.4 percent in 1990-

91 and by 2000-01 it has further declined to 13.5 percent. The information in Table-5 clearly shows that especially since 1995-96, the share of agricultural exports gradually declined till the end of 2000-02 (Table-5). It is clear that though agriculture provides almost 25 percent of India's GDP, agricultural exports are insignificant.

Table 5
Agriculture Exports ($ million)

Year	*Agricultural Exports*	*Total Exports*	*Agri. Exports as % of Total Exports*
1960-61	596	1346	44.2
1970-71	644	2031	31.7
1980-81	2601	8486	30.6
1990-91	3521	18143	19.4
1995-96	6320	31797	19.8
1997-98	6840	35006	18.5
1998-99	6205	33218	18.2
1999-00	5773	36822	15.2
2000-01	6246	44560	13.5

Source: Economic Survey of Various Issues.

India had expected that with dismantling of domestic support in developed countries and widespread reduction in export subsidies by these countries, market access for Indian agricultural products in developed countries would expand. The developed countries have played their cards very cleverly and have taken effective steps to block agricultural exports from developing countries including India behind various loopholes in AOA and allied agreements.

SECTORAL DISTRIBUTION OF GDP – POST LIBERLIZATION PERIOD

Table-6 shows the data of the shares of all the three sectors (agriculture, industry and services) in GDP of India for post liberalization period.

If we look at the data, it shows that the share of agriculture in GDP has registered a downfall of almost 14% from 33.54% in 1993-94 to 19.90% in 2005-06.The share of industrial sector in GDP has also registered a decrease of almost 4% from 23.69% to 19.90% during the period of analysis. The services sector, however, has increased its share in GDP from 42.77% in 1993-94 to 60.70% in 2005-06.

Table 6
Sectoral Distribution of GDP–Post Liberlization Period

Year	*Agriculture*	*Industry*	*Service*
1993-94	33.54%	23.69%	42.77%
1994-95	32.94%	24.35%	42.70%
1995-96	30.59%	25.47%	43.94%
1996-97	30.87%	25.45%	43.68%
1997-98	29.02%	25.19%	45.78%
1998-99	28.86%	24.56%	46.57%
1999-00	27.36%	24.30%	48.33%
2000-01	26.24%	24.90%	48.85%
2001-02	26.28%	24.41%	49.30%
2002-03	29.86%	24.97%	51.17%
2003-04	24.86%	24.53%	51.43%
2004-05	19.50%	19.50%	59.70%
2005-06	19.90%	19.90%	60.70%

Source: Economic survey –various issues

It shows that the agriculture sector, which used to make a major contribution to the GDP in the pre-reforms period, has slowed down during post-reforms period, as the contribution of agriculture to GDP was around 57.41% in 1950-51.The gradual rise in the share of the services sector in the GDP, has been a result of the new economic policy.

CONCLUDING REMARKS

Indian farm sector is on one side neglected by reducing plan allocations by Government itself and on the other side globalization had led to declining share of agricultural exports in total exports and a fall in capital formation, and decline in rural employment . Subsidies have been withdrawn. In the case of agricultural exports no subsides were offered in India. But developed countries have been providing higher level of subsidies. Contribution of agricultural sector to GDP has also come down. The quantitative restrictions on imports have been withdrawn. Due to globalization of international trade has proved to be beneficial to the developed economies rather than developing economies like India.

However, it is clear from the detailed discussion above; the developed countries have played their cards very cleverly and have taken effective steps to block agricultural exports from developing countries including India behind various loopholes in AOA and allied agreements. Therefore to protect the Indian agriculture and Indian farmers from evils of globalization, the Indian agricultural policy needs to be built-up with adequate "safety-nets". This is possible only under interventionist policies of the Government.

REFERENCES

Gulati Ashok and Narayan Sadhu (1999), Indian Agriculture in the Global Economy.

Chada O.K (2000), Indian Economy Under WTO Regime: Happenings and Missing Links, IEA Conference (83rd) volume of the millennium 2000.

Chand Ramesh (2000), Trade Liberalization WTO and Indian Agriculture, EPW March 10th.

CHAPTER–17

INDIAN ORGANIZED RETAILING: EYEING THE FUTURE

T. Ravikumar

Retail–The Industry

India has been called a nation of *dukandaars* (shopkeepers) due to the huge number of its retail enterprises, which totaled over 23 million in 2003. About 78 percent of these are small family business utilizing only household labour, bulk of them too using less than three workers (Source: Report on Retailing in India, www.the-infoshop.com).

Retailers today will have to support the large retail infrastructure in terms of malls and superstores that are being created. The challenge for leading retailers shall therefore shift from diverting demand to creating demand. With all the modern stores offering convenience in terms of an assortment of products, ambience, service and innovative products, the paradigm shall shift from competing with the kirana stores to in-house demand aeration.

Even though India has well over 12 million retail outlets of all sizes and styles (or non-styles), the country sorely lacks anything that can resemble a retailing industry in the modern sense of the term. This presents international retailing specialists with a great opportunity.

Unorganized Sector in Retail

Retailing in India is thoroughly unorganized. There is no supply chain management perspective. According to a survey by AT Kearney, an overwhelming proportion of the Rs. 4,00,000 crore retail market is UNORGANIZED. In fact, only a Rs. 20,000 crore segment of the market is organized. About96 percent of the 5 million-plus outlets are smaller than 500 square feet in area. This means that India per capita retailing space is about 2 square feet (compared to 16 square feet in the United States). India's per capita retailing space is actually the lowest in the world (source: KSA Technopak (I) Pvt Ltd, the India operation of the US-based Kurt Salmon Associates).

Organized Retailing in India

A tremendous opportunity exists in the Indian market and organized retail will prevail as in other parts of the world. Since, it's only a matter of time, this is the right time to invest and reap profits in around 5-7 years.

Organized retail is transforming the neighborhood grocery store (commonly known as Kirana store); gone are the days of dust-coated, cluttered shelf-displays and actualization of buying power is now in the hands of the consumer. Modern retail in India, in the last decade has been characterized by a shift from traditional channels to few formats including department stores, hypermarkets, supermarkets and specialty stores across a range of categories. Modern retail formats with sprawling shopping centers, multi-storied malls offering shopping, entertainment and food all under one big, comfortable roof have mushroomed in metros and mini-metros. In the last few years modern retail has also established its presence in the second rung cities thus, exposing the residents of these cities to shopping options like they have never experienced before. It has been forecasted that the share of modern retail will increase from 2 percent currently, to about 15-20 percent over the next decade.

According to consultants KSA Technopak; the organized retailing is expected to be worth a whopping Rs. 1, 80,000–2, 00,000 crore by 2010. It means that the organized retail pie will move up from the current 2 percent (Rs. 22,500crore) to 10-12 percent in another six years. High growth projections are being translated into frenetic activity on the ground. It is estimated that by 2007-08 over 300 malls spread across 50 million sq. ft. of retail space will come up. Over 600 malls with an area of 100 million sq. ft. will spring up on the Indian landscape by 2010.

A consumer revaluation is on its way as organized retail is uniquely positioned to take care of the convenience and aspiration needs of Indian consumers. Even as modern retailers garner share from traditional channels, there is a larger role that they would be required to play in boosting the overall consumption levels of the Indian economy. The retail arena is today is very different–the opportunities are incredible but exploiting them calls for being in the know. One has to be constantly on the move, keeping tabs on the shifting trends in the marketplace and maneuvering one's strategy to stay on top.

However retailers will have to strive hard to meet the tough expectations of today's super smart shoppers who instantly lap a good buy and dismiss a bad product. Today's consumers demand superior quality at an affordable price and they want it instantly. For retailers aiming to make a big sale, there is not much of a choice but to find ways to win customers over and keep them permanently happy, which is a tough ask in a restrictive Indian business environment that too lacking infrastructure

Change Accelerators

The following factors will be significant in driving growth in the retail sector:

Consumer factors

- Increase in income
- Working women

- Changes in lifestyle–demand for "global" trends.

Supply side factors

- Growing importance of retailing in political and economic agenda
- Real estate reforms
- Major restructuring of the manufacturing sector easing product supply constraints for efficient retailing.
- Reduction in import duties-offering mire global sourcing.

Segments of Organized Retailing in India

Retail trade is represented by large segments of food, clothing, consumer durables and books & music. Other segments include gold ornaments, furniture and footwear.

Food and Groceries: This segment is worth upwards of Rs. 6, 00,000 crore per annum. The biggest player in food retailing–Food World–is no bigger than Rs. 400 crore. The opportunity is huge for new entrants. The food and grocery segment accounts for 14 per cent of the market.

Clothing & Textiles: Textiles are a Rs. 85, 000 crore business (including clothing, home furnishing, lingerie, sleepwear, etc.). The largest supplier–Madura Garments–is only around Rs. 400 crore. Even Shoppers' Stop, which gets about 60 to 70 per cent of its turnover from textiles, is a Rs. 404 crore company. In comparison, Japanese retail firm Aeon is $20-billion (Rs. 92, 00-crore) firm. For textile companies in India, the retail opportunity is one way of beating the dismantling of quota system in 2005.

Consumer Durables: Retailing of consumer durable continues to be a fragmented marker except in the south where organized retail has a strong foothold. Viveks and VGP are the large players here. While there are several single large stores in the metros, the chain stores are yet to make a significant impact. Vijay Sales and Akbarallys are the main players in Mumbai. A new trend has been sale of consumer durables through stores like Big Bazaar. Shoppers' Stop too has added consumer durables to its portfolio in certain outlets.

Every city has several large one-store retailers who can be classified as organized due to the size of their business and the implementation of several management practices by these players.

Books & Music: The books and music market saw several new entrants recently. Fountainhead in books and planet M, Music World, Fast Forward and Groove in music are shaking up the market. Established stores like Crossword, taken over by Shopper's stop, Higginbotham's and Landmark are expanding rapidly. There has been an increasing focus on the retailing of books. Landmark, for instance, is credited to be the first ISO 9000 certified bookstores in the country. In recent times, publishing, majors have started to focus to a greater extent on the kids segment. Consequently, the segment is witnessing the advent of sophisticated packaging and they are also supplementing it with aggressive marketing efforts. With the establishment of malls and large department stores, any players are experimenting with setting up book and music corners in high traffic locations within these premises–like planet M in several department stores and Crossword in Shoppers' stop.

Size of Organized Retail Market – Indian Bazaar (Crore Rs.)

Category	*Format*	*2001-02*	*2007*	*CAGR (%)*
Food	Chain Stores	1500	6726	35
	Single large stores & others	300	746	20
	Sub-total	1800	7473	33
Clothing	Manufacturer Retailers	1350	2715	15
	Chain Stores	1450	3919	22
	Single large stores	2150	3789	12
	Sub - total	4950	10423	16
Consumer durables	Manufacturer Retailers	650	1307	15
	Chain Stores	450	1373	25
	Single large stores	550	1106	15
	Sub - total	1650	3787	18
Books & Music	Chain stores	250	928	30
	Single large stores	200	498	20
	Sub-total	450	1426	26
Others	All formats	7150	14107	
Total organized retail		16000	37216	18

Source: ORG-Marg, The Economic Times

Big Players in the the Retail Market

Some of the India's biggest Corporations like ITC, Bombay Dyeing, Reliance and Godrej are climbing onto the organized retail bandwagon. They are setting up malls, hypermarkets, supermarkets, and specialty stores.

Table- The key players in Indian retail space and their future plans

Player	*Plans*
Tatas	After stabilizing operations of their Westside chain of lifestyle stores, the Tatas are launching a chain of hypermarkets called *Start India Bazaar*. Each hypermarket will be around 50,000 sq. ft.,
Reliance	Into telecom and broadband-driven retailing through their Web Worlds, 200 of them. Petroleum retail outlets -could also have food and groceries stores, *Web Worlds and Java Green coffee shops.*
ITC	Embraced the rural retail model and plans to put up stores called Chaupal Sagars, each catering to 100 villages. The first Chaupal Sagar in Sehore (MP) is already operational. ITC plans to have 1, 000 of such Chaupal Sagars, with 50 of them scheduled to be set up in the first year itself at *an investment of Rs. 150 crore.*
HLL	In the retail space with its *Lakme Beauty Salons* and Ayush Therapy centres. Currently have 65 Lakme salons and 12 Ayush Therapy centres. Plans to expand to 100 Lakme salons and 30 Ayush Therapy centres in one year.
HERO Group	Creating a chain of 7-11 type of *convenience retail stores,* for which the Munjals will tie up with companies and banks. From the current level of 700 -odd stores, the group plans to have 10,000 outlets spread across the country over the next three years.
Bharti	Foraying into *broadband retailing,* with scope to offer video conferencing, high-speed internet and virtual gaming.
Wadias Singhanias Godrej	In various stages of evaluation of different models. Wadias will probably set up a chain of life style stores, Raymond is evaluating various models including *hyper markets* and Godrej has embarked on an environment scanning process.
RPG Group	One of the few conglomerates to venture relatively early into retail, the group is aggressively expanding its

Contd.

Player	*Plans*
	beauty centers (Health and Glow), music stores (Music World) and Hyper markets, Spencer's Daily. The largest organized retailed has invested Rs. 140 crore over the last three years.
Ajay Piramal	Another early entrant, Piramal is expanding its life style stores (with supermarkets), Piramyd, for three to sixteen in three years, at cost of Rs. 320 crore.

Current State of Organized Players in Indian Retail Industry

Retailer	*Format*	*Status*
Pantaloon Retail (I) Ltd	Value and lifestyle retailing	Already in
BATA India Ltd	Footwear	Already in
RPG Retail	Value and lifestyle retailing	Already in
Shoppers Stop	Lifestyle retailing	Already in
Vivek Ltd	Consumer electronics	Already in
Trent Ltd	Value and lifestyle retailing	Already in
Subiksha Trading	Discount retailing –F&G	Already in
Margin Free	Discount retailing –F&G	Already in
Trinethra	Value retailing –F&G	Already in
Nilgiri's	Value retailing –F&G	Already in
Raymond Ltd	Lifestyle retailing	Already in
Piramyd Merchandising & Retail Ltd	Value and lifestyle retailing	Already in
Vijay Sales	Consumer electronics	Already in
Globus Stores	Lifestyle retailing	Already in
Nalli	Specialty saree retailing	Already in
Ebony	Lifestyle retailing	Already in
ITC	Lifestyle retailing	Already in
Madura Garments	Apparel brand retailing	Already in
Aravind Brands	Apparel brand retailing	Already in
Levi Strauss India	Apparel brand retailing	Already in
Times Retail	Music retailing	Already in
Barista	Coffee beverage retailing	Already in
Café Coffee Day	Coffee beverage retailing	Already in
McDonald's	Food service retailing	Already in
Pizza Hut	Food service retailing	Already in
Crossroads	Mall retailing	Already in
In-Orbit	Mall retailing	Already in
Forum Mall	Mall retailing	Already in
Spencer's Plaza	Mall retailing	Already in
Nirmal Lifestyles	Mall retailing	Already in
J.C.Penny	Multi Format	Evaluating
Reliance	Multi Format	Already in
Tesco	Multi Format	Evaluating

Contd.

Retailer	*Format*	*Status*
Woolsworth	Specialized stores	J.V.with Tata's infinity retail
WalMart	Hypermarket	50:50 JV with Bharathi
Marks & Spencer	Single Brand Store	Franchise
Espirit	Specialized stores	Franchise
Landmark Group	Lifestyle retailing	NRI / OCB route
Carrefour	Multi Format	Awaiting approval
Lifestyle International	Lifestyle retailing	Lifestyle retailing

Source: Survey of Indian Industry – 2006.

Growth of Organised Retail Sector

The organized retail industry is estimated at over $ 7 billion and is slatted to grow to $ 30 billion over the next four years.

Growth of Organized Retail Sector

Particulars	*2005*	*2006*	*2007*	*2008*	*2009*	*2010*
Retail Sales	215.3	226	241.8	259.3	278.7	300
Organized Retail	7.3	7.8	12.1	18.2	22.3	30

(Billion $) Source: Enam Securities.

Organised Retailers Stores Location

Forty percentages of organized retail stores are located in tier 1 city, 59% in tier 2 cities and 1% in tier 3 cities.

Organized Retailers' Stores Location

Cities	*Percentage*
Tier 1	40
Tier 2	59
Tier 3	01

The contribution of smaller cities to total organized retailing sales was 15% in 2005 and was expected to grow to 25% by the end of 2006. Organized retailing in small towns is growing at 50% to 60% per year compared to 35% to 40% in the large cities. The striking point is that it is the big names in the organized retail business that are eyeing these new opportunities.

Reason for Retail Boom

Liberalization and Economic growth have mainly driven a vast change in India. Till few years ago, Indian consumers were happy with one TV channel, few retail stores and only one footwear chain-Bata. The scenario is totally different today. People are experienced with malls, lifestyle stores, Pizza hut, Hybermarkets etc. Reason for such changes would be

1. Change in Individual income
2. Brand Consciousness
3. Change in Market structure
4. Change in Lifestyle
5. Change in Buying behavior and
6. Regional Preferences.

Change in Individual Income

- Growth of the urban middle class which demands value for money, has led to a lot of changes on the retail front.
- There is a substantial increase e in the number of youth who are beginning to earn early. According to NRS, there is a 20% increase in the number of persons between the age of 15 to 19 who have started earning.
- This is largely due to the growth opportunities for urban youth in the BPO, Call centre and Software sector.

Increase in the Disposable Income and Rise in the Middle Class

Classification	*Household Millions (% of population)*					
(Annual Household Income)	*1995–96*		*2001-02*		*2006-07*	
Very Rich (> INR 360,0001)	1.2	0.8%	2.6	1.5%	5.2	2.7%
Consuming Class (INR 80,001 - 360,0000)	32.5	20.1%	46.4	25.9%	75.5	39.5%
Climbers (INR 40,000- 80,000)	54.1	33.7%	74.4	41.9%	81.7	43.1%
Aspirants (INR 28,001 - 40,000)	44.0	27.4%	33.1	18.8%	20.2	10.7%
Destitute (< 28,000)	33.0	20.5%	24.1	13.7%	16.5	8.7%

Source: NCAER

- The increase in the double income households has also led to change in spending habits across the urban India.

Brand Consciousness

Indian men are highly price conscious but also Brand Conscious. They like to buy branded products and flaunt them.

Brand Consciousness in India-City Wise

Delhi	*Kolkata*	*Mumbai*	*Chennai*	*Bangalore*	*Hydera-bad*	*Ahmeda-bad*	*Pune*
52%	37%	32%	71%	38%	41%	33%	39%

Source: Business today December 30, 2007.

- Chennai comes first by emerging as the most brand conscious city.
- North and South are brand conscious a contrast to East and West.
- Less than 10% of men don't care too much about brands. For the others, brand name matters.

Changing Indian Market Structure

The media burst, growing popularity of internet has brought the Generation Y closer to all developed economies. The young 15 to 30 years old are technology savvy, discerning shoppers, believe in self gratification, have money, and are spoilt for choice, look out for differentiation that adds " fun " to the experience of consuming that product.

The table below captures the extent of change in socio-cultural aspects and attitude from 60s / 70s.

The changes in the nation social structure like improvement of Indian Economy, Consumerism, Urbani-zation, and Profusion of plans have been the main causal factor for the development of modern formats.

Effect of Lifestyle Changes on Buying Behaviour

The rise in income level of Indian households shows a direct relationship with the increased spending habits.

Three Consumer Types Across Three Generations of India

Parameter	*Traditionalist (60s / 70s)* *Pre-liberalization*	*Transient (80s/90s)* *liberalization*	*Millennium (2000s)* *Post-liberalization*
Mindset	Security Conformity Family Obligation Discipline Risk avoidance Moderation	Freedom Individuality Work Entitlement Self-indulgence Risk taking Excesses	Meaning Personal style Personal pleasure Accountable Self-control Risk Management Balance
Motto	I want my children to be better off than mine.	I want to be better off than my parents.	I want to enjoy.
Accomplishment	What I have done for my family?	What I have and own?	What I do?
Obsession	My country	My self	My society
Purchase behaviour	Functionality Is it good for my family?	Statement Is it good for me?	Enjoyment Is it good for me and my society?
Key driver	Information	Enticement	Entertainment

Source: Madhukar Sabnavis, Indian Management.

Asset Acquisition Rate

Asset	*1999*	*2001*	*Increase (%)*
Own House	40164	42883	7
Receive FM	8204	10215	25
Colour TV	16758	21527	28
Cable and Television households	22348	27216	22
Hi-fi CD	577	982	70
Motor Cycle	4465	5441	22
Refrigerator	6580	7199	9
Microwave	251	358	43
Camera	5044	5810	15
Mobile	567	661	17
Vacuum cleaner	796	856	8
Air conditioner	557	762	37
Water Purifier	1082	1466	35
Washing Machine	1175	1627	38
PC	380	1089	187
Computer Printer	186	376	102
Fax Machine	72	78	8
Video Camera	81	172	112
No. of Servant	47213	50459	7

(Number of Households)

Source: NRS 2002

From the above table, the following inferences can be made about the asset acquisition rate of urban Indian consumers:

- The acquisition of the assets is increasing fast with rising income levels.
- Lifestyle assets figure top among the purchases by the consumers.
- Although regular assets like scooters, radios have seen flat or negative growth rates, the second rung lifestyles assets like ovens, vacuum cleaners and air conditioners which previously had negligible market potential are witnessing double digit growth rates.
- This depicts that urban households, with rising composition of both husband and wife working, try to improve their lifestyle relaying on gadgets to reduce household work.
- The table also reveals the fact that the number of urban households without a domestic help has risen by 7%, thus increasing the demand for lifestyle products.

Priority List of Spending on Various Segments by Indian Consumers

Taking a look at the table, the following inferences can be made about the spending habits of the Indian consumers.

Year-On-Year Spending Across Segments

Segment	*2000*	*2001*
Grocery	47.8	48.0
Personal care items	7.5	7.1
Books and Music	7.8	6.7
Home Appliances	0.7	2.0
Home Textiles	1.0	1.5
Savings & Investments	6.1	6.4
Clothing	6.5	4.7
Consumer Durables/electronics	4.8	5.5
Vacation	3.3	3.1
Eating out	7.9	8.8
Footwear	2.0	2.2
Movies/Theatres	2.7	2.6
Entertainment	3.0	3.0

Source: KSA Consumer Outlook 2002 (% of total wallet)

- Buying food is the top priority of the Indian consumer and 48% of their total income goes in buying food.
- Another factor that has gained prominence is eating out.
- Spending on consumer durables and electronics has shown increment.
- To sum up, all in all, food is the top of the purchase list for consumers.

Sector Wise Indian Consumer Expenditure

A study by KSA Technopak India Private Ltd (See the above Table) has revealed that food & beverage sector gets the major chunk (52%) of the total consumer spending in India followed by clothing and footwear. It reveals that Food retailing and Home improvement stores are going to flourish in Indian retail industry.

Sector wise Indian Consumer Expenditure

Sector	*Share of Customer spending in India*
Food & beverage	52%
Cloth & footwear	11%
Entertainment	3%
Consumer durables & furniture	7%
Healthcare	2%
Housing	9%
Others	16%

Source: www.economictimes.com march 6, 2004

Regional Preferences

The fast changing profile of Indian consumers is affecting their shopping patterns and practices. The differences between the spending habits of high end consumers who come in A category and B category is narrowing down, however, there is a need to look at segmentation criteria, that is "regional segmentation". The retailers need to carefully analyze the money spending priorities of the consumers by the region of their living.

Across Borders

Money spending priorities by region			
West	*North*	*South*	*East*
Grocery	Grocery	Grocery	Grocery
Eating out	Personal care	Eating out	Apparel
Books & Music	Eating out	Apparel	Savings
Personal care	Books & Music	Books & Music	Personal care
Savings	Savings	Savings	Eating out

It can be observed that eating out ranks as number two for western and southern part of India as these regions have large number of restaurants and eating together that are affordable and hygienic and also because these regions have maximum number working women.

On the other hand, North Indians are more fashion conscious; hence personal care is the second most important area of spending for them.

People living in the eastern region like spending more of their income on apparel. It is primarily clothing that drives consumers in Kolkata.

Consumers living in Metros like Mumbai and Delhi spend more time and money buying and reading books and listening to music, this is simply due to the fact that most of the people spend about 2-3 hours each day while traveling.

The Challences of Indian Retail Industry

The journey of Indian retailing in India is not free from road blocks. Major barriers are discussed below.

Manpower Management

Managing manpower will be the toughest challenge for organized retail players in this fast growing and intensely competitive industry. The retail industry is booming and with an expected Compounded Average Growth Rate (CAGR) OF 30-35% for the next few years, finding expert manpower, especially at the senior and middle management levels will be a difficult task. A study on domestic retail sector by Enam estimates that 5-6 lakh employees will be needed in the organized retail sector.(Refer the below Table).

Expected Retail Headcpimt

Company	*Headcount 2010 E**
Reliance	2.0
Pantaloon	1.0
Bharathi–Walmart	0.6
A B Group	0.5
Shopper's Stop	0.2
Trent	0.1
Total organized sector jobs	6.0

(Lash)* Rough Estimates
Source: Enam Securities/ETIG Analysis

Space Jam

With some 350–odd malls expected to come up in the next three years, availability of retail space is another major area of concern. New malls are springing up in the country every other day. If the expansion drives of new entrants go as per plans, the total operational retail space will touch around 100 million sq. ft. by 2008 with about 500 malls across the country.

However, availability of land and rising rentals could come in the way of retails' mega plans.

The following table represents the occupied and needed space till 2010.

Occupied and Needed Space of Retail Sector

Particulars	*As on Dec. 06**	*FY' 20 10*
Pantaloon	3.4	30
Shoppers' stop	1.06	5-6
Trent	0.6	105-2
Reliance	N.A	100
A B Group	N.A	12-15
Bharti	N.A	15-18
Provogue	0.1	1.5
Max Retail	0.12	1
Brand House (S Kumars)	0.053	0.2
Spencers (RPG)	0.5	1

*Million Sq. ft.
Source: ET Survey

Lack of Adequate Infrastructure

There is a lack of storage equipment such as racks, fixtures and shelves. Lack of adequacy of infrastructure in terms of supply chain and logistics is a big challenge for organized retailing in India. Logistics, which is a very fragmented market today, is going through consolidation stage. There is going to be a major change. Players are forced to set up their own infrastructure, as there are few independent logistics solution providers. Entrepreneurs who could invest in infrastructure development for different stages of the supply chain are also limited.

Lack of a Uniform Tax System

The country requires a uniform tax system for organized retailing. The lack of uniform tax system stands as on obstruction to the setting up of a truly national chain. The present chains, in spite of claiming to be national chains, are restricted to certain regions of the country. Players working in 28 states face 28 types of legislation and are confined to state barriers. Since retailing is essentially a business of supplying commodities to locations far from production units, a different tax system in different states is surely turning to be a hindrance to faster development of this industry.

Dominance of the Unorganised Sector

The unorganized sector has dominance over the organized sector in India, especially because of the low investment needs. In India, organized retailing is only 2% of total retailing worth $ 180 billion. This is playing at multiple levels. For instance, the reason for low number of discount stores in India is an effect of the dominance of the unorganized sector. The manufactures have high bargaining power in the pricing of products due to this small scale of operation of retailers. The lobbying by the unorganized sector is also the main reason for the Government of Indian's restrictions on 100% FDI in retailing in the country.

Status of Organized Retail Industry Internationally

Country/Region	*Organized Retail Sector as on Approx % of Retail Sales*
USA	80 %
Western Europe	70%
Brazil	40%
Argentina	40%
Korea	35%
Taiwan	35%
Malaysia	20%
Thailand	20%
China	20%
India	02%

Low Operational Size

The number of retail outlets in India is more than the number of outlets in most of the other countries. Small size retail outlets dominate the Indian scene. 96% of the outlets are lesser than 500 sq. ft. The retail chains of India are also smaller than those in the developed countries. For instance, the superstore food chain, Food World, is having only 52 outlets whereas

Carrefour-Promodes' has 8800 stores in 26 countries. The volume of sales in Indian retailing is very low, which is only $180 billion. Even the largest players have a turnover of only $ 140 million which is very small by the global standards. India, with the second largest population in the world and fast growing economy, has huge untapped potential of organized retailing which is not given its due weightage by the government.

Government Restriction on FDI

Organized retailing in India is yet to get an industry status. The consequence is quite obvious. 100% FDI is not permitted in retailing in India. Without the FDI, the sector is deprived of access to foreign technology that is imperative for faster growth. Retailing is a 'technology-intensive' industry. Under the liberalized regime of the WTO, the 'Protected Nature' of an industry may do more harm than good. In the short-run, the Government may succeed in protecting the domestic industry but in the long run we would be losing too many opportunities and technological innovations. This in addition, would also block any attempt by the domestic industry to become competitive internationally.

Political and Emotional Issue

The unorganized Indian retail sector has been in existence for centuries. With the coming of the new organized retail format-irrespective of whether it is domestic of foreign–the neighborhood retailers have become anxious about their very existence. Now, this issue has become cause of concern to policy makers as well, who are worried about the economic and political consequences of small retailers being forced to shut shop. Voices against organized retailing are coming from wholesalers and traders across the country. The leftists have clearly articulated their objection to organized retailing stating that with fails the three tests that are germane to the issue whether the investment augments productive capacity, leads to upgradation technology and generates employment.

Suggestions

Some suggestions are as follows to deal with multi dimensional challenges.

- A central tax system becomes more imperative in a country like India where the regional disparity in production of commodities is high. Government should introduce uniform taxation all over the country to replace the laws that are restricting the inter-state flow of goods.
- Government should consider providing incentives and amending labour laws etc., Shortage and high cost of real estate, tenancy legislation and high property tax etc., are other areas to be reviewed by the Government. Government should Single Window System.
- The big challenge for the Indian retailing industry is the heterogeneity of the market. Therefore, retailer should be able to predict where and what consumers will spend the highest share of their wallet and use this last leg of economic chain to build India.
- Every country goes through a demographic boom when a majority of the population enters the earning and spending bracket. India is currently going through this and we should utilize it to help the country to grow rather than gift - wrap it and allow others to grow their revenues, profits and market capitalization. If, with organized retail at 3%, India is attractive, at 10% it will be more so. Hence Indian retailers must be allowed first to gain size for preparing a level playing field and then market should be opened for foreign players in a phased manner.
- Significant investment in restructuring of the supply chain management should be done.
- Small Indian retailers should be convinced properly that organized retailing will not prove to be a threat to them. They can get a large benefit by reconfiguring

their business model, reinventing themselves, adopting the concept of franchising as their new way forward and thus can keep up with the dynamics of a changed landscape.

References

James R. Ogden and Denise T. Ogden (2005), Integrated Retail Management, Biztantra Publication, New Delhi.

www.ksa-technopak.com

(2002), Retail Industry- Witnessing a Paradigm Ahift by Pradeep K. Singh, Saket Industrial Digest, November, volume 8, issue 11.

(2002), Case Studies on Retailing Sector, edited by Senthil Ganeshan and Published by ICFAI, Hyderabad.

www.economictimes.com March 6, 2004.

(2007), Business Today December 30.

(2005), Retailing–Roundtable, Business India, November 21 to December 17, pp 46-50.

(2007), Retail Segment- Small Vs Mall, Franchising World, March.

Bhat U R (2007), Reinventing the Kirana shop, The Economic Times, March 12.

Rao Srinivasa M.V.S. (2006), Foreign Direct Investment in Indian Retail Business, The Indian Journal of Commerce, volume 59, April- June, pp. 8-18.

CHAPTER–18

WTO AGREEMENT ON AGRICULTURE: IMPLICATIONS AND CHALLENGES

Kiran Kumar P
Jayasheela

Introduction

Agricultural sector is the mainstay of the rural Indian economy around which socio-economic privileges and deprivations revolve and any change in its structure is likely to have a corresponding impact on the existing pattern of social equity. The Agreement on Agriculture forms a part of the Final Act of the Uruguay Round of Multilateral Trade Negotiations, which was signed by the member countries in April 1994 at Marrakesh, Morocco and came into force on 1st January 1995. The Uruguay Round marked a significant turning point in world trade in agriculture. For the first time, agriculture featured in a major way in the GATT round of multilateral trade negotiations. Although the original GATT–the predecessor of the World Trade Organization (WTO)–applied to trade in agriculture, various exceptions to the disciplines on the use of non-tariff measures and subsidy meant that it did not do so effectively. The Uruguay Round agreement sought to bring order and fair competition to this highly distorted sector of world trade by establishment of a fair and market oriented agricultural trading sector.

The root cause of distortion of international trade in agriculture has been the massive domestic subsidies given by the industrialized countries to their agricultural sector over many years. This in turn led to excessive production and it's dumping in international markets as well as import restrictions to keep out foreign agricultural products from their domestic markets. Hence, the starting point for the establishment of a fair agricultural trade regime has to be the reduction of domestic production subsidies given by industrialized countries, reduction in the volume of subsidized exports and minimum market access opportunities for agricultural producers world-wide. The first important condition in the WTO agreement on agriculture is - get rid of the license-permit system in imports and exports. During the socialist era in India, almost all imports were banned under the guise of saving foreign exchange. Imports were totally controlled by bureaucrats doling out import licenses and permits.

The Agreement on Agriculture contains provisions in the following three broad areas of agriculture and trade policy:

Market Access

On market access, the Agreement has two basic elements:

(i) Tariffication of all non-tariff barriers. That is to say, non-tariff barriers such as quantitative restrictions and export and import licensing etc. are to be replaced by tariffs to provide the same level of protection. Tariffs, resulting from this "tariffication" process together with other tariffs on agricultural products, are to be reduced by a simple average of 36% over 6 years in the case of developed countries and 24% over 10 years in the case of developing countries. With India being under balance of payments cover (which is a GATT-consistent measure), we had not undertaken any commitments with regard to market access and this has been clearly stated in our schedule filed under

GATT. The only commitment India has undertaken is to bind its tariffs on primary agricultural products at 100%; processed foods at 150%; and edible oils at 300%.

(ii) The second element relates to setting up of a minimum level for imports of agricultural products by member countries as a share of domestic consumption. Countries are required to maintain current levels (1986-88) of access for each individual product. Where the current level of import is negligible, the minimum access should not be less than 3% of the domestic consumption, during the base period and tariff quotas are to be established when imports constitute less than 3% of domestic consumption. This minimum level is to rise to 5% by the year 2000 in the case of developed countries and by 2004 in the case of developing countries. However, special Safeguards Provisions allow for the application of additional duties when shipments are made at prices below certain reference levels or when there is a sudden import surge. The market access provision, however, does not apply when the commodity in question is a 'traditional staple' of a developing country.

Domestic Support

Provisions of the Agreement regarding domestic support have two main objectives–first to identify acceptable measures that support farmers and second, to deny unacceptable, trade distorting support to the farmers. These provisions are aimed largely at the developed countries where the levels of domestic agricultural support have risen to extremely high levels in recent decades.

All domestic support is quantified through the mechanism of total Aggregate Measurement of Support (AMS). AMS is a means of quantifying the aggregate value of domestic support or subsidy given to each category of agricultural product. Each WTO member country has made calculations to determine its AMS wherever applicable. Commitment made requires a 20%

reduction in total AMS for developed countries over 6 years. For developing countries, this percentage is 13% and no reduction is required for the least developed countries.

AMS consists of two parts -- product-specific subsidies and non-product specific subsidies. Product-specific subsidy refers to the total level of support provided for each individual agricultural commodity, essentially signified by procurement price in India. Non-product specific subsidy, on the other hand, refers to the total level of support for the agricultural sector as a whole, i.e., subsidies on inputs such as fertilizers, electricity, irrigation, seeds, credit etc.

Export Subsidies

The Agreement on Agriculture lists several types of subsidies to which reduction commitments apply. However, such subsidies are virtually non-existent in India as exporters of agricultural commodities do not get direct subsidy. Even exemption of export profits from income tax under Section 80-HHC of the Income Tax Act is not among the listed subsidies. It is also worth noting that developing countries are free to provide three of the listed subsidies, namely, reduction of export marketing costs, internal and international transport and freight charges.

In general, it may be noted that the virtual explosion of export subsidies in the industrialized countries in the years leading to the Uruguay Round was one of the key issues addressed in the agricultural negotiations. Export subsidies also became a major factor in depressing or destabilizing world market prices for many agricultural commodities. The Uruguay Round marked a radical departure from the earlier GATT disciplines in the areas of agricultural export subsidies. Members are required to reduce the value of direct export subsidies to a level of 36% below the 1986-90 base period level over a six year implementation period. The quantity of subsidized export is to be reduced by 21% over the same period. In the case of developing countries, the reductions are two-thirds those of the developed countries over a ten-year period and there are no reductions for least developed countries. Under the Agreement, export subsidies are defined as "subsidies contingent on export performance" and the list covers export subsidy practices such as direct export subsidies contingent on export performance; sales of non-commercial stocks of agricultural products for export at prices lower than comparable prices for such goods in the domestic markets; producer-financed subsidies such as government programmes which require a levy on production which is then used to subsidize the export of the product; cost-reduction measures such as subsidies to reduce marketing costs for exports including handling costs and costs of international freight; internal transport subsidies applying only to exports; subsidies on incorporated products i.e., subsidies on agricultural products such as wheat contingent on their incorporation in export products made of wheat etc. All such export subsidies are subject to reduction commitments in terms of both the volume of subsidized export and budgetary outlays for such subsidies. As indicated earlier, such measures are virtually non-existent in India and, hence, the issue of reduction of export subsidy on agricultural products is not of particular relevance for India.

Product Coverage Under the Act

The Agreement defines agricultural products by reference to the harmonized system of product classification. The definition covers not only basic agricultural products such as wheat, milk and live animals, but the products derived from them such as bread, butter, other dairy products and meat, as well as all processed agricultural products such as chocolates and sausages. The coverage includes wines, spirits and tobacco products, fibres such as cotton, wool and silk, and raw animal skins destined for leather production. Fish and fish products are not included nor are forestry products.

Peace Clause

The Agreement on Agriculture contains a "due restraint" or "peace clause" (Article 13), which regulates the application of other WTO agreements on subsidies in respect of agricultural products. The Article provides that Green Box domestic support measures cannot be the subject of countervailing duty action or other subsidy action under the WTO Agreement on Subsidies and Countervailing Measures, nor can they be subject to actions based on nullification or impairment of tariff concessions under the GATT. Other domestic support measures which are in conformity with the provisions of the Agreement on Agriculture may be the subject of countervailing duty actions, but due restraint is to be exercised by Members in initiating such investigations. Further, in so far as the support provided to individual products does not exceed that decided in the 1992 marketing year, these measures are exempt from other subsidy action or nullification or impairment action. Export subsidies conforming to the Agreement on Agriculture are subject to countervailing duty actions, but here also due restraint is to be exercised by Members in initiating such investigations. The peace clause remains in effect for a period of nine years from 1995, i.e., the entry into force of the WTO Agreement.

Implications of the Agreement

Implications of the Agreement would differ from country to country and would depend largely on the overall agricultural scenario in the country. Indian agriculture is characterized by a preponderant majority of small and marginal farmers holding less than two hectares of land, less than 35.7% of the land, is under any assured irrigation system and for the large majority of farmers, the gains from the application of the science & technology in agriculture are yet to be realized. Farmers, therefore, require support in terms of development of infrastructure as well as extension of improved technologies and provisions of requisite inputs at reasonable cost. India's share of world's agricultural trade is of the order of 1%. There is no doubt that during the last 30 years, Indian agriculture has grown at a reasonable pace, but with stagnant and declining net cropped area it is indeed going to be a formidable task to maintain the growth in agricultural production. The implications of the Agreement would thus have to be examined in the light of the food demand and supply situation. The size of the country, the level of overall development, balance of payments position, realistic future outlook for agricultural development, structure of land holdings etc. are the other relevant factors that would have a bearing on India's trade policy in agriculture.

Short Term Implications

Opening of markets and impact on trade in agriculture is concerned, it may be noted that the share of developing countries in world exports of food remained at 44% and of agricultural raw materials increased insignificantly from 32% in 1994 to 34% in 1996, that is the post-Agreement period. The average growth of developed countries imports of agricultural products increased by just 1% during 1994-96. Nearer home, agricultural exports of ten Asian developing countries increased from US $ 49252 million in 1994 to US $ 55902 million in 1996. India's share in total agricultural exports from developing Asia is 8%, behind China's 19%, Thailand's 17%, Malaysia's 14% and Indonesia's 10%. India's exports of agricultural products have increased from US $ 4151 million in 1993-94 to US $ 7054 million in 1997-98. No tangible opening up of the markets has thus been noticed in the post-Agreement period so far. However, it may be premature on this basis to assess the long-term impact of the Agreement on opening up of markets.

Regarding freedom to pursue our domestic policies, it is quite evident that in the short term India will not be affected by the WTO Agreement on Agriculture. The safeguards provided for developing countries give enough manoeuvre to insulate ourselves from any major impact of trade liberalization in agricultural commodities.

In India, for the present, the minimum support price provided to commodities is less than the fixed external reference price determined under the Agreement. Therefore, the AMS is negative. Theoretically, therefore, we could increase the product-specific support up to 10%, the only restraint being the fiscal sustainability in the country's context.

Long Term Implications

Regarding the impact of liberalization of trade in agriculture in the long term, Indian agriculture enjoys the advantage of cheap labour. Therefore, despite the lower productivity, a comparison with world prices of agricultural commodities would reveal that domestic prices in India are considerably less with the exceptions of a few commodities (notably oilseeds). Hence, imports to India would not be attractive in the case of rice, tea, sunflower oil and cotton. On the whole, large-scale import of agricultural commodities as a result of trade liberalization is ruled out. Even the exports of those food grains, which are cheaper in the domestic market, but are sensitive from the point of view of consumption by the economically weaker sections are not likely to rise to unacceptable levels because of high inland transportation cost and inadequate export infrastructure in India. Through proper tariffication, however, we will have to strike a balance between the competing interest of 10% farmers who generate marketable surpluses and consumers belonging to the economically poor sections of the society.

For a large majority of farmers in different parts of the country, the gains from the application of science and technology in agriculture are yet to be realized which would require infrastructural support, improved technologies and provision of inputs at reasonable cost. The Agreement on Agriculture thus recognized this and developing countries have been given the freedom to implement such policies under Article 6 relating to differential treatment, but any attempt in future to dilute provisions relating to differential treatment for developing countries could affect us adversely. The rise in domestic prices would put pressure on the public distribution system and accentuate the problem of food subsidy. Furthermore, freedom to export agricultural products without restrictions will also need shedding the long-nurtured inhibition against their imports. The nature and character of State intervention and State support will have to undergo qualitative changes in order not only to realize the opportunities for exports, but also to cope with the implications of our agriculture coming into increasing alignment with the international market place.

Freeing Indian Agriculture from State Control

Laws and by-laws, rules and regulations, red-tapeism, and inefficiency of governmental machinery have strait-jacketed Indian agriculture. Ousting the State from agriculture and privatization of the agriculture sector are the most important measures. At present, land is owned by the State. It is leased to farmers for cultivation. The State, at its whim, can acquire land on the pretext of public purpose and dislodge farmers. Understandably, farmers are not willing to undertake sizeable investment on their land. The State controls all farm inputs like fertilizers, pesticides and farm equipment, etc. Disposal of the produce is also under comprehensive State control.

Unifying the Indian Market

The entire world is getting unified as a market, but India itself is not a unified market. State barriers like district bans, state bans, zoning and levy have fragmented the domestic market. On the other hand, different countries in Europe, with different languages, faiths and cultures, and despite a history of two world wars have come together and developed a unified common market (The European Economic Community or the EEC). In India, it has become imperative to scrap the Essential Commodities Act and other restrictive measures emanating from it and to create a unified market when we are on the threshold of globalization. A unified Indian market will increase the demand for agricultural produce; besides, the market will facilitate cropping patterns consistent with agro-climatic realities and comparative advantage.

Agriculture Subsidies

Due to the Agreement on Agriculture (AOA), India can no longer remain aloof from the rest of the world. It had to join the WTO. This AOA has established a number of generally applicable rules with regard to agriculture and trade related matters. Most of the developed countries are providing huge subsidies to the agricultural sector. In these countries not more than 10% of the population is dependent on agriculture. The below table gives the information about the subsidies that are being given to agriculture by different countries and the percentage of the population depending on agriculture

India provides only 2.33% subsidy to agriculture. It is very small when compared with other countries. The Aggregate Measure of Support (AMS) to agriculture will be 10 percent in India as against 5% in the developed world. The total subsidy on agriculture in the developed world works out to $150 billion and in the developing world $19 Billion. If the AMS exceeds 10 percent in any country, it has to reduce by 13% by 2004. According to the WTO the AMS in India, product subsidies is 7.5% and subsidy on non-product is minus 38.5%. So there is no question of losing any thing in our agriculture by accepting the AOA.

Subsidies to Agriculture

Country	*Subsidy Per Hectare*	*% Subsidies*	*Population Dependent on Agriculture*
USA	$32	26%	5%
Japan	$35	72%	4%
China	$30	34%	24%
South Africa	$24	60.67%	18%
India	$14	2.33%	60%

Source: WTO reports

Tariffs

The tariffs on agricultural commodities have been considerably restructured to comply with WTO requirements. India is committed to reduce tariffs on 686 agricultural products. The average tariff on agricultural commodities was 115% before the agreement. After the agreement it has been reduced to 35%. Along with 686 commodities the tariff on 587 other commodities is on an average 50% less than the negotiated tariff. Only on 10 commodities is the tariff rate more than the negotiated tariff rate. Pulses were imported under OGL (Open General License) at zero interest rates. In July 1999 the Government of India sought to renegotiate the tariff on pulses. But the international community has not yielded.

The Challenge

(a) *Investment:* Indian agriculture needs a lot of investment to have large-scale production. By this we can reduce production costs. But the problem is that large scale agriculture displaces persons who are dependent on agriculture. Instead of criticising WTO we have to think of an alternative system. Corporatisation of agriculture is seen to be inimical to social justice. Redistribution of land to the landless poor through the various land ceiling acts leads to fragmentation which will be a hurdle to improved production as well as productivity.

(b) *Patent System:* Plants such as neem, turmeric and products such as Basmati (scented rice) are patented or about to be patented by American companies. It is strange that in India these have been household plants used in cooking and for medicinal purposes since ancient times. The system of Ayurveda has existed since times immemorial. All medicinal products based on plants and plant products must be patented by Indian companies. Conceding the patent rights to an American based company is ridiculous and we have to take this up with the WTO's Dispute Settlement Board (DSB) at Geneva.

Conclusion

India is a marginally efficient producer of agricultural products. The problem lies with the employment of people who are displaced in agriculture. In this Situation instead of finding fault with international law we have to think how best to apply that law in our interests. When imports have caused problems they have followed either leaden-footed decision-making or the Government placing the interests of the consumers above that of the farmers. Both were evident in the setting of tariffs for edible oils which were raised only recently. The larger problems that Indian farmers face are the result of high costs, low productivity, falling public investment, poor market development and ultimately limited purchasing power among one billion people. The problem identified in the existing agreement on patents, anti-dumping duties, subsidies, trade and textiles indicate that the developing countries are waking up to the need to ensure that India has to take the lead in ensuring the WTO regime is used to maximum advantage to protect the interests of developing countries.

Reference

Agricultural News (2006), *Financing Agriculture*, 38 (2), April-May, pp. 40-42.

(2005-06), Government of India, Economic Survey.

Jayasheela, Vishwanatha and Ali (2005), "Co-operative Credit for Sustainable Agricultural Development in the Post WTO period", in Talwar Sabanna (Ed), WTO and the Agriculture, Serials Publications New Delhi. pp. 10-18

Mahendra, Dev S. (2006), "Half-hearted Attention to Agriculture", *Economic and Political Weekly*, 41(14) April, pp. 1327-29.

Minakshi, Garg (2005), Economic Reforms and Indian Agriculture. In R. K. Uppal (ed.), Economic Reforms in India, New Delhi: New Century Publications.

Narayan, Subash (2007), "Farm Sector awaits 11th plan bonanza", *The Economic Times*, ET Finance, Tuesday, 8 May, p.1.

Revathy (2008), "Indian Agriculture-Major Challenges and Tasks Ahead", *Kisan World*,

Vol 35 (6) pp. 20.

Satya, Sundaram I. (2003), Agricultural Exports, Untapped Potential, *Facts for You*, vol 24 (3), pp. 9-11.

Sunil, Phougat (2006), "Economic Reforms and WTO implications for farmers", *Kurukshetra*, 54 (5), March, pp. 26-29.

Tushar, K. Mahanti (2006), "Yield, Not an Acreage Holds Key to Higher Agricultural Production", *The Economic Times*, Wednesday, 26 July, p. 23.

Vasudevachary, A. K. (2006), Indian Agriculture in the New Global Scenario, *Southern Economist*, 44 (17), January, pp. 7-9.

Footnotes

1. Research Scholar, Department of Economics, Mangalore University. Mangalagangothri-574199 Karnataka, India, Email: kinni_p4u@yahoo.com

2. Reader, Department of Economics, Mangalore University. Mangalagangothri, Email: Jayasheela_mu@yahoo.com

CHAPTER–19

WTO: INDUSTRIALIZATION AND GLOBAL ENVIRONMENTAL DEGRADATION

B.R. Honparkhe

Introduction

Industrialization has two sides, positive and negative. Positive side is useful and essential for society's welfare or to lift the standard of living. Industrialization is necessary for utilization of natural resources for production activities to provide different types of goods and services for society. But the negative side of the industrialization is harmful to human health and life because of rapid unplanned industrial progress creates many more different types of pollution problems, such as air, water, noise and soil.

Objectives

The present paper has been prepared with the following objectives.

1. To know the different types and causes of environmental pollution.
2. To know the nature and indicators of environmental degradations.

3. To know the ways to prevent industrial pollution.
4. To study the current issue global warming.

Types of Environmental Pollution

The different types of environmental pollutions are given below:-

1. Air pollution.
2. Water pollution.
3. Thermal pollution.
4. Noise pollution.
5. Soil pollution.

Reasons for Environmental Pollution

The reasons are given below:-

1. Natural pollution.
2. Population Explosion.
3. Standard of living.
4. Deforestation.
5. Vehicular traffic.
6. Heavy Irrigation.
7. Agriculture.
8. Industry the scapegoat.

Nature of Environmental Degradation

In many parts of the world, environmental degradation the deterioration of the natural environment, including the atmosphere, bodies of water, soil, and forest is an important cause of poverty. Environmental problems have led to shortage of food, clean water, materials for shelter, and other essential resources. As forests, land, air and water are degraded.

Ways of Preventing Industrial Pollution

There are basically three ways of preventing pollution.

1. Self Realization.

2. Environmental Movement.
3. Govt. Interference.

Global Pollution and the WTO

As Jagdish Bhagwati carefully explains, much of the analysis so far has been addressing what I called the domestic pollution problems. But something must be said about global problems such as global warming, ozone layer, depletion, acid rain, and other causes where there are externalities for other countries effects on them from what one country does within its own jurisdiction or in the global commons where no country has jurisdiction.

Global Warming

Troposphere the lower most layer of the atmosphere, traps heat by a natural process due to the presence of certain gases. This effect is called green house effect as it is similar to the warming effect observed in the horticultural green house made of glass.

Concluding Remark

Concluding the subject of industrialization and its positive and negative effects on society and atmosphere would be something like this, to meet the ever-growing demand of the people because of continuous increase in population, sufficient steps should be taken on industrial ground which should be properly planned taking into consideration of safety, pollution free atmosphere so that the climate/atmosphere shall be without pollution which is the basic need of mankind..

Dignitaries engaged in the various fields, scientists and world leaders are worried about the global warming which is increasing with a super fast speed because of the negligence of the industrialists for taking proper action and to a great extent of govt. machinery which are not emphasizing the law connected to environmental technology.

References

Madhu Raj, Dictionary of Environmental Economics, published by Ivy Publishing House, Delhi-110095; page no. 115.

Madhu Raj, Dictionary of Environmental Economics, published by Ivy Publishing House, Delhi-110095, page no. 104.

Prof. Anubha Kaushik and Prof C.P. Kaushik, Perspectives in Environmental Studies (2nd edition), New Age International Pvt. Ltd., Publishers (formerly WILEY Eastern Ltd) New Delhi, Bangalore, Chennai, Cochin, Guwahati, Hyderabad, Jallandhar, Calcutta, Lucknow, Mumbai, Ranchi; page no. 123.

S.P. Misra, Environmental Pollution, Avishkar Publishers & Distributors, Jaipur-302003 (Raj), India; page no. 27, 28, 32, 33, 39, 41.

P.R. Trivedi, Encyclopedia of Environment, Pollution, Planning and Conservation (A set of 6 volumes) (Environmental Education Volume 5); page no. 154.

K. Aswathappa, Essentials of Business Environment, Himalaya Publishing House, Mumbai, Delhi, Nagpur, Bangalore, Hyderabad (8th edition); pages 618-623.

K. Aswathappa, Essentials of Business Environment; page nos. 627-629.

Abhijit Dutta, Sunita Dutta and P.N. Pandey, Environmental Economics, Published by Kulbhushan Nangia, APH Publishing Corporation, 5, Ansari Road, Daryaganj, New Delhi-110002; page nos. 144-95.

Jagdish Bhagwati, In Defence of Globalization, Published by Manzar Khan, Oxford University Press, YMCA Library Building, Jaysingh Road, New Delhi-110001; pages 158-159.

Prof. Anubha Kaushik and Prof C.P. Kaushik, Perspectives in Environmental Studies; pages 179-180.

Pramod Chaudhari-an article on 'The bio-fuel option', Business India, April 20, 2008; page no. 122.

CHAPTER–20

MACROECONOMIC ENVIRONMENT AND AGRICULTURAL SECTOR GROWTH IN NIGERIA

Emmanuel O. Eyo

Introduction

In Nigeria, the agricultural sector has been invaluable in supporting economic growth and development since 1960. In fact before the discovery and exploration of petroleum, the Nigerian economy depended on funds generated from agricultural export expansion for the development of other sectors of the economy. Due to its important rôle in nation building, the agricultural sector has continued to be a target of government policies overtime.

Efforts to fortify the Nigerian agricultural sector have a long history. At independence in 1960, the first task of government was the development of high level manpower resources, (Wells 1970). This was in addition to funding agricultural research and extension activities, farm settlement schemes, plantation agriculture, cattle ranches and irrigation project. In 1971, government established the agricultural research council, and introduced the National Accelerated

Food Production Program in 1973. Between 1974 and 1980 government embraced the direct food production policy, introduced the model farms, the Nigerian Grains Production Company, the Nigeria Root Crop Production Company, the Naiwa Mechanized Farm Limited, the Nigerian Dairy Company Limited and the Nigerian Poultry Production Company. Also, government established the Department of Agricultural Cooperatives, provided support to the small farmers and commenced the pilot phases of the Agricultural Development Project, established the Agricultural Project Monitoring and Evaluation Unit to monitor agricultural project of government and established new research institutes. Other programmes introduced to fortify the sector were the Strategic Grains Reserve Program, the Operation Feed the Nation, the River Basin and Rural Development Authorities, the Land Use Act, the Green revolution program, and the Federal Agricultural Coordinating Unit (Eyo 2005). By 1986 government deemphasized the direct food production policy and adopted an integrated approach that combined agricultural with rural development. As a result of this new Agricultural development thrust, government established the Directorate for Food, Road and Rural Infrastructure to construct and maintain feeder road. However, by 1988 government agricultural policy thrust was directed at providing support services while all aspects of agricultural production and marketing including input supply as well as agricultural mechanization were to be handled by the private sector, (Eyo 2005). To enhance the provision of the support services in all parts of the country, government established the Agricultural Development Projects in all state of the federation and established the National Agricultural Land Development Authority. With the growth in the number of government agricultural development programmes, one expected meaningful agricultural output growth, positive change in farm sizes and general development in the sector over time. Unfortunate the index of real agricultural sector GDP shows complete absence of any substantial growth. For example, the growth rate in real GDP of agriculture between

1981 and the year 2005 fluctuated between -13 and 65.13. Table 1.0 shows the growth rate in real agriculture GDP. According to this table, the growth rate in real GDP agriculture was positive in 1982, between 1987 and 2003 and negative by 1983 to 1986, as well as 2004 and 2005.

Table 1
Growth Rate of Real GDP-Agriculture

Year	*Index of Real GDP Agric*	*Growth Rate*
1981	100.00	
1982	103.85	3.85
1983	96.20	-3.80
1984	90.59	-9.41
1985	100.13	-0.13
1986	98.44	-1.56
1987	136.35	36.45
1988	136.35	36.35
1989	105.30	5.30
1990	118.43	18.43
1991	122.71	22.71
1992	128.07	28.07
1993	132.39	32.39
1994	127.60	27.66
1995	131.19	31.19
1996	137.68	37.68
1997	143.18	43.18
1998	143.76	43.76
1999	143.33	43.76
2000	141.37	41.37
2001	159.08	59.08
2002	163.39	63.39
2003	165.13	65.13
2004	69.52	-30.48
2005	71.79	-28.21

Source: CBN Statistical Bulletin (Various issues)

On the other hand, the index of real GDP for agriculture fluctuated from 100 in the base year to 98.44 in 1986, from 136.35 in 1987 to 141.37 in the year 2000, increased steadily to 165.13 in the year 2003 and then dropped to 71.79 by the year 2005.

Usually several factors can be said to be responsible for the dismal performance of the Nigerian agricultural sector. Pre-eminent among these factors is the macroeconomic environment. The macroeconomic environment comprises fiscal, monetary, exchange rate, income and other policies that are used to regulate production activities not only in the agricultural sector but in the other sectors of the economy. Unfortunately, macroeconomic policy outcomes vary greatly depending in part on the policy targets and instruments used, (Agu, 2007). However, several authors (Binswanger, 1989; Kwanashie et al 1998; and Killick 1990) agree that agricultural production marketing and financing decisions are influenced by the macroeconomic environment. More so, Garba, (2000) and Akpokodje (2000) confirm that major macroeconomic policy shifts heighten agricultural policy instability. This paper assesses the macroeconomic environment in Nigeria. and analysis the effect of the macroeconomic policies on agricultural output growth over time.

Methodology

The Study Area: The study area is Nigeria. It has an area of 923,769 square kilometers and a population of about 88 million people. It is bounded on the West by the republic of Benin and the republic of Niger; on the East by the republic of Cameroon; on the north by Niger and Chad republics and on the South by the Gulf of Guinea. The climate is equatorial and semi-equatorial. There are two seasons; the wet and the dry season and agriculture is a major employer of labour.

Source of Data and Data Analysis

This study uses principally secondary data obtained from the Central Bank of Nigeria the Nigerian National Planning Commission. Existing literature indicate that prices, government expenditure in agriculture, volume of credit to the agricultural sector, nominal interest rate and exchange rate which are indicators of monetary, exchange rate and price policies determine activities in the agricultural sector, (Fosu, 1992; and Garba, 2000). Consequently, in this study, data on exchange rate, nominal interest rate, world prices, credit to the agricultural sector, and government expenditure on the agricultural sector, inflation rate, and foreign private investment in agriculture were obtained between 1970 and 2005 and used as indicators of the macroeconomic environment. The method of data analysis is the multiple regression analytical technique (Ordinary Least Square Procedure). The problem of autocorrelation and multi-collinearity were aborted by the use of relevant econometric tests, namely; the Durbin Watson test, the F-test, the t-test and the coefficient of multiple determination.

The structural response function used by Fosu (1992), Amin (1995), Kwanashie et.al (1998), and Umoh (2003) were adapted and used in this study.

Consequently, the model postulates that the index of agricultural production is a function of the indicators of the macro economic environment, namely; foreign exchange rate (F), nominal interest rate (N), credit to the agricultural sector (A), world prices (W), government expenditure on agriculture (G), rate of inflation (L), foreign private investment in agriculture (P) and time (T).

Consequently, $Y = f(F, N, A, W, G, L, P, T)$

The Implicit Form of the Model is given as:

$$Y = a+b_1 F + b_2 N + b_3 A + b_4 W + b_5 G + b_6 L + b_7 P + b_8 T + u$$

Where

Y = Index of agricultural production

F = Foreign exchange Rate

N = Nominal Interest rate on loans

A = Credit to Agricultural sector n Naira.

W = World Prices of agricultural produce in Naira per tone

G = Government Expenditure in Naira

L = Inflation Rate in Percentage

P = Foreign private Investment in Naira

T = Time trend representing technological change overtime.

a = intercept; b_1-b_8 = coefficients, u = stochastic disturbance term.

Results and Discussion

Many macroeconomic policy strategies have been tried in Nigeria in an attempt to meet the objectives of diversifying the production and support base away from dependence on petroleum, among other things. In particular several efforts are identifiable in the area of exchange rate, fiscal, income and monetary policies. For instance, the exchange rate policy adopted as many as three strategies, namely; pegging of the Naira exchange rate to the Dollar; the dual exchange rate regime of 1995 to 1999 and allowing the exchange rate to be determined by forces of demand and supply. The fiscal policy strategies adopted in Nigeria so far included the introduction of value added tax to replace sales tax, the abolition of excise duties, regulation of custom and excise tariff from time to time, and the retention of tariff concession granted to the transport sector, among others. Similarly, the strategies of the income policy have included wage freeze of 1976/77, 7% wage increase of 1977/78, increase in minimum wage and allowances of 1980, among others. Apart from these, the Structural Adjustment Policy (SAP) introduced in 1986 set in motion a stream of reforms that completely reversed the effect of the macroeconomic environment on many sectors of the economy. The reforms of the SAP used several policy instruments. First, there was a recall of Naira counterpart of outstanding external payment arrears to the Central Bank of Nigeria, second, there was increase in permissible credit expansion in 1988, third, there was increase in commercial bank cash ratio requirement which started in 1989, fourth, there was also the introduction of cash ratio requirements for merchant banks and raising of the liquidity ratio of commercial banks from 25 to 30%, fifth, there was the lifting of credit ceiling for healthy banks and increase of minimum cash reserve requirements of banks from 3 to 6% in September 1992. On the whole, during SAP, efforts were made to strengthen bank supervision, and new banking standards were introduced minimum capital was increased, special interest on agricultural loans was abolished and subsidy on agricultural inputs were removed. In the post SAP period, more macroeconomic policies were introduced which brought about more financial reforms. As a consequence of the new policies a number of micro credit programmes have been introduced, government merged the Nigeria Agricultural Cooperative bank, the Peoples bank and the Family Economic Advancement Program to form the Nigerian Agricultural Cooperative and Rural Development Bank in the year 2000. By the year 2004 the minimum capitalization of banks was raised to twenty five billion Naira, all public sector funds were withdrawn from commercial banks, and mergers as well as acquisitions were allowed as a means of consolidation of banking institutions. Also, community banks were converted to micro finance banks, and their minimum capitalization was raised to a minimum of twenty million Naira of shareholders fund unimpaired by losses (Imala, 2005).

Table 2
Percentage of Agriculture in Total Export

Year	*% Agric Export*	*Other Export*
1982	2,03	97.97
1983	3.58	96.42
1984	2.62	97.38
1985	2.08	97.92
1986	4.90	95.10
1987	2.95	97.05
1988	6.35	93.65
1989	2.11	97.89
1990	1.71	98.29
1991	1.31	98.69
1992	1.20	98.80
1993	1.7	98.30
Mean Exchange	2.71	97.29

Source: CBN Statistical Bulletin (various issues)

Unfortunately, existing data suggest that the macro-economic environment created by the macroeconomic policy strategies were not agricultural sector friendly. For example, the exchange rate regime has not resulted in any meaningful export of agricultural produce over time. For example, Table 2 shows that between 1982 and 1993 agricultural export was only 2.71 percent of the total export, on the average; the yearly percentage of agricultural output in the entire export was highest in 1988 (6.3%) and lowest in 1992 (1.2%).

The proportion of agricultural export in the entire export increased from 2.02% in 1982 to 3.58% in 1983, and then declined to 2.08% by 1985. In 1986 when SAP was introduced the percentage of agriculture in the entire Nigerian export increased to 4.90% and then gyrated to 6.35% by 1988 and then declined steadily to 1.20% and 1.70% in 1992 and 1993, respectively.

Table 3
Maturity Structure of Commercial Bank Loans (1980-1996)

Year	*Percentage of Loans that Mature in One Year*	*Percentage of Loan that Mature After Five Years*
1980	78.38	4.86
1981	68.59	6.01
1982	78.70	5.70
1983	81.40	2.00
1984	79.36	5.51
1985	82.08	5.00
1986	81.96	4.70
1987	80.82	4.50
1988	83.31	3.90
1989	46.92	2.33
1990	82.01	5.30
1991	82.31	4.87
1992	82.66	5.84
1993	83.11	5.33
1994	84.40	4.59
1995	83.96	4.72
1996	83.00	5.00

Source: CBN Stat. Bulletin 2005

More so, the macroeconomic environment culminates in the financial sector giving mostly short term loans. This is evident from the distribution of loan maturities in the economy. According, to Table 3, over 68% of the commercial bank loans had loan maturities of one year or less between 1980 and 1988. By 1989, only 46.92% of the loans had maturities of one year and less, but beginning 1990, over 80 percent of commercial bank loan to the economy had maturity of within one year. Loans with short maturities are mostly operating loans, which are inadequate for the acquisition of intermediate and fixed assets that are invaluable in improving the capital base of the sector.

Besides, an assessment of credit to the agricultural sector in Table 4 shows that between 1970 and year 2005 the real credit to agriculture was consistently low.

Table 4
Mean Volume of Credit to Agricultural Sector in Real Terms

Year	*Mean Volume of Credit to Agricultural (Millions Naira)*
1970-1974	1.25
1975-1999	4.91
1980-1984	12.34
1985-1989	16.21
1990-1994	14.72
1995-1999	15.45
2000-2005	42.45

Source: CBN Statistical Bulletin (various issues)

It was 1.25 million on the average between 1970 and 1974, 4.19 million Naira on the average in 1975 – 1979; 12.34 million on the average from 1980 to 1984; 16.21 million Naira in 1985 to 1980; it was 14.72 million on the average in 1990-1994; 15.45 on the average in 1995-1999 and moved to 42.45 million in the year 2000-2005.

Effect of the Macro Economic Policies on Agricultural Output Growth

The effect of these macroeconomic policy strategies on the agricultural sector is captured in the following regression equation.

$$Y = 70.06 - 0.14\,ER + 1.11\,NR + 9.89\,AC + 4.23E - 03WP + 9.02\,E - 05GE$$

t = 6.38* t = - 1.86*** t = 2.52** t = 0.19 t = 2.841* t = 2.241**

- 0.155INFR + 3.38E – 02 FPN – 0.45T

t = - 1.26 t = 3.672* t = 0.90

R^2 = 96%; Adjusted R^2 = 94%

ST. Error 9.68; F. Value 72.043* Durbin Watson = 1.741.

This result shows that the explanatory variables explained 94 percent of the total variables in the index of agricultural production, all the explanatory variables were collectively relevant as evident in the F-statistic being significant 1% level and the Durbin Watson statistic is plausible. However, credit to the agricultural sector, inflation rate and technology changes were not significant in their effect on the index of agricultural output whereas the exchange rate regime, nominal interest rate, world prices, government expenditure and foreign private investment in agricultural were significant in their effect on the index of agricultural output. It is also clear from the regression analysis that exchange rate is negatively related to the index of agricultural production. Consequently, at favorable exchange rates, more agricultural outputs would be produced.

Against the apriori expectation, the nominal interest rate is positively related to the index of agricultural production. This implies that at higher nominal interest rate, more credit facilities are made available to the operators of the Nigerian agricultural sector; but at lower nominal interest rate, credit facilities are no more widely available. The index of agricultural production is also positively related to world prices of Nigerian major agricultural commodities. This implies that better world prices would enhance agricultural output growth. Similarly, the index of agricultural production was positively related to government expenditure on agriculture and had no significant effect on agricultural output growth. Consequently, more government investment would greatly enhance agricultural output growth. The index of agricultural production is negatively related to the level of inflation, implying that the higher the rate of inflation the lower the index of agricultural production. Foreign private investment in agriculture is positively related to the index of agricultural production whereas technology is inversely related. This confirms that the level of technology used in the Nigerian agricultural sector has been grossly inadequate.

Conclusion

An intuitive appeal of the salient points of the theories of economic growth clearly indicates that sustained growth in per capita agricultural output is possible through capital accumulation and technical progress, among other things. More so, the theories of agricultural development, particularly, the high pay-off input theory emphasizes that sustained agricultural output growth can be achieved by applying high pay-off inputs as well as new technologies like improved planting materials, fertilizer, irrigation facilities, improved livestock species and motorized equipment. This research confirms that the technological progress is limiting, as well as credit to the agricultural sector. Invariably the macroeconomic environment has not been able to support the operators of the agricultural sector to acquire high pay-off inputs that are invaluable in improving the capital base of the agricultural sector. Intermediate and fixed assets make up the capital base of the farm business and contribute significantly to the size of the farming operation. Therefore their acquisition is important to the growth and development of the agricultural sector and access to external financing would be invaluable in accelerating the growth process. In view of these, macroeconomic policies that enhance favorable exchange rates, make agricultural credit widely available at low interest rate, reduce the rate of inflation, increase foreign private investment in agriculture, would not only fortify government investment in the sector but would be invaluable in supporting agricultural output growth in Nigeria.

References

Akpokodje, G. (2000), The Effect of Export Earnings Fluctuations on Capital Formation in Nigeria. African Economic Research Consortium. Research paper RP103 October 2000, Nairobi, Kenya.

Agu, C. (2007), What does the Central Bank of Nigeria Target? An Analysis of Monetary Policy Reaction Function in Nigeria. Final report submitted to the African Economic Research Consortium, Nairobi, Kenya, December 2007.

Amin A. A. (1996), The Effect of Exchange Rate Policy on Cameroon's Agricultural Competitiveness. AERC Research Paper 42. Initiative Publishers. Nairobi.

Binswanger H. (1989), The Policy Response of Agriculture: In: Stanley F. and D. de Tray eds. Proceedings of the World Bank Conference on Development Economics. Washington DC pp. 121-53.

CBN (2005), Statistical Bulletin Volume 16, December 2005.

CBN (1994), Statistical Bulletin Volume 5 no 2, December 1994.

Eyo, E. O. (2005), Agricultural Development in Nigeria: Plan, Policies and Programmes. Best Print Business Press, Uyo-Nigeria.

Fosu, K. F. (1992), The Real Exchange rate and Ghanas Agricultural Export AERC Research Paper 9. Kenya, Nairobi.

Garba, P. K. (2000), An Analysis of the Implementation and Stability of Nigerian Agricultural Policies. 1970–1993 African Economic Research Consortium Research Paper 101. Nairobi, Kenya.

Killick, T. (1990), Markets and Government in Agricultural and Industrial Adjustment. ODI Working Paper 3, London.

Kwanashie, M., Garba, A. and I. Ajilima (1997), Policy Modelling in Agriculture: Testing the Response of Agriculture to Adjustment Policies in Nigeria. AERC Research Paper RP 57.

Umoh, G. S. (2003), Nigeria: Macroeconomic Environment and the Perennial Crops. Global Journal of Agricultural Science. Vol. 2, No. 1, 2003: 53-61.

Wells, J. C. (1970), Issues in Agricultural Development Policy During 1962-68. Nigerian Development Plan. *In Growth and Development of the Nigerian Economy*. Edited by Carl K. Eicher and Liedhorim. Michigan State University Press.

CHAPTER–21

IMPACT OF GLOBALIZATION ON INDIAN SUGAR INDUSTRY

J.P.Bhosale

Introduction

We are all aware of the recently emerging information technology and its impact created on individual , organizational and social activities. The advancement in sophisticated information technology resulted in devising a number of electronic devices which have been rendering value added services and increase in socio-economic status ot the people worldwide, These are the days of information revolution, new economic order information oriented society and the age of global communication, instantly accurately at faster rate over video, audio, graphics, across the boundaries of the world.

Explosion in information technology in recent years is to a great extent is attributed to a new vistas opened up from space observation platform and rapid advancement in remote sensing technologies which are based on the silicon chip, fiber optics, coaxial cable, laser, satellite etc. Information technology has been changing and reshaping the dreams of business organizations, individuals etc., and many of them are proffering modern technologies today corporation have been giving top priority and spending substantial amount on information technology.

India is second largest sugarcane sugar producer in the world ,Since 1991. During the year 1999-2000 it has produce over 18.20 million tonnes of sugar, contributed nearly 15 percent of the world sugar production. the yearly turnover of the industry exceeds Rs. 20000 crores & play the annual wage bill more than Rs. 10000 crore. Over 45 million farmers are involved in sugarcane production and its, allied activities and the receive Rs. 5500 crores in the form of sugarcane prices. The area under sugarcane cultivation is nearly 40.76 lakh hectares. It is just 2.8 percent of the total area of the cultivation land in the country. Though there are more than 700 registered sugar mill in the country but presently some 450 plus sugar mills are in operation in different part of the country.

If we concentrate on the qualitative progress of the industry, it is observed that the sugarcane yield per hectare has been increased from 32 m. tonnes per hectare in 1950-51 to 72.6 m. tonnes in 1999-2000 but the sugar recovery is hovering around 10 per cent only during the same period .

ClIITGnt Scenario

India is the leader in the world sugar production after Brazil. But its position in the world sugar market has become very vertical. At present it carries a huge stocks of 12 million tonnes which represents almost 38 % (percent) of the world inventory. Globalization of the world sugar economy has been already started but the extent of it remains limited as compared to the manufactured goods. Historically sugar has been regarded as one of the most regulated agro industries in the world . Now the globalization has created obvious challenges for those whose cost of production is higher & benefiting to those cost of production is low. India stand third (increasing order) in the cost of sugar production. Thailand, Australia and Brail are the low cost sugar production in the world. On this background Indian sugar industry has to rearrange & strengthen its position very carefully so as to make it more competitive in the world market.

The world sugar market is now open under the regime of WTO. Millions of farmers are anxious to know the impact of WTO on Indian sugar industry in general and their income levels, levels of living and quality of life in particular .

Feature of World Sugar Trade

The main feature of the WTO Agreement on Agriculture is the opening up of world market for agriculture products. Under this competition is bound of increase. The enforced competition will have two fold effects on the sugar industry.

1. That will increase domestic competition between different sugar factories .
2. The commitment to improve will make them globally competitive in the world sugar trade scenario the major importers of raw refined sugar are developed countries like European Union, U.S.A., Japan & Russia. IZach of these countries has heavily protected their sugar market through (1) reduces consumption, (2) encourage domestic production & (3) restrict trade. It shows that these countries have shield their producer from world mnrket prices through.
   (a) Import protection
   (b) Higher support prices to domestic producer &
   (c) Export—subsides particularly in Ruropean union.

Ultimately it leads to huge export subsides, large scale domestic support of producers, high tariff wall & selective little market access to developing countries.

Export of sugar from the E.U. have contributed 15% of the world exports over the past five years. Most of these exports are produced under price support management and are subsidized. The heavily subsidized export of E.U. sugar stimulated surplus production and contributed directly to lower the world sugar prices.

European union under common Agricultural policy , USA with its tariff rates & highly protected industry of Japan are mainly responsible for the distortion in the world sugar trade. Owing to this protec'ive tariff policies the India could not export its sugar to the traditional markets. At the same time it has become a dumping ground fui uilnjio. If we ^ce the comparison between domestic & international prices, it is observed that not only for sugar but for major Agriculture products the extent of protection enjoyed by domestic producers in E.U. is quite substantial. For sugar this gap is highest. This can be seen with the help of following table .

Comparative Prices of Various Food Items in E.U. World During 1999-2000

	Items	*E.U.*	*World Average %*
Wheat	133	188	13
Maize	140	92	52
Rice	600	300	100
Sugar	650	250	160
Bananas	660	360	83
Tomato's	787	633	24
Butter	2954	1307	126

Source: EU's Everything but Arms proposal for LDCs Likely

Impact for India's Sugar Industry by chetan Bijesure

The above table indicates that the high cost producers of sugar (E.U.) are dominating the world sugar market at the cost of effective producers of sugar in the world . It is also observed that most of the developed countries, mainly offer two types of subsidies to their domestic producers namely.

1. Transparent subsidies &
2. Veiled Subsidies

To Protect the home sugar industry the developed countries like European Union, U.S.A., Japan & Russia charge duties 250 percent & above on imported sugar, naturally it checks the import of sugar from developed countries, this is called as transparent or direct subsidies. While in the from of veiled subsides particularly Thailand, Australia & Brazil Government offer interest free loans of their sugar industries for modernization of sugar mills. They also give the exemption to their sugar mills from certain long tern loans. Ultimately it helps to bring down the cost of sugar production in these countries & indirectly help to their sugar industries to become more competitive in the world market.

Impact of Globalization on Indian Sugar Industry

The Indian sugar industry is required to concentrate on number of important areas so as to make it more cost effective as well as more competitive at the global level.

Need to Bring Down the Cost of Sugar Production

The world average production cost of sugar exceeds prices. Costs tend to exceed prices because many producers benefit from Government protection enable them to survive despite their costs exceed world price level .year after year the sugar price has shown a downward trend approximately 1.5% . This trend has clear posed a serious challenge before the sugar producer around the word.

A study of Dr. James Fray, managing Director of LMC reveals that in

1. Field Cost : It is lowest in India followed by Australia, Thailand, world average & China increasing order.
2. Factory Cost: It is lowest in Thailand followed by Australia, India world average & China Increasing order.
3. Total Cost of sugar Manufacturing: Shows that it is lowest in Thailand, followed by Australia, India world average & China, It shows that though, India has an advantage of lowest field cost in the world but when the field + factory cost considered together, Indian sugar industry stand third (increasing order) It means the Indian sugar industries not able to exploit the benefits of lowest field cost in bringing down the final or total cost of sugar production. Thus Thailand & Australia sugar industries are more cost effective as compared to Indian sugar industry . In Thailand the average crushing capacity per day is 15000 M. Tonnes

where as it is just 2500 + TCD in India . Naturally it items the industry ability to exploit economies of scale in capacity has been started in number of sugar mills in the country, so that it will help to bring down the final of sugar manufacturing.

Need to Rationalize the Sugarcane Prices

When we see the proportion of various cost components in the total cost of sugar manufacturing, it is observed that a single component i.e.. Cost of sugar cane alone contributes more than 75 percent in the total cost of sugar production. Therefore to check the total cost of sugar production there is need to concentrate more on i.e. cost of sugarcane (Raw material) & its quality. At present the central government decides the minimum statutory prices per ton to each factory , below which no sugar mill can pay the sugarcane price to their sugarcane growers. Again state Govt. comes in & decides the prices for each sugar mill, which are always higher than the statutory minimum prices decided by the central Govt. really this is the central crux the problem. It is observed that during the last 7 tears in U.h*., the state Advised prices have been increased by 55 percent practice of arbitrarily determining a state Advised price (SAP) invariably far higher than the M.S.P. fixed by the central Govt. In southern states, this proportion is comparatively lower than the northern state of India. Ultimately this leads to increase the cost of sugar manufacturing.

Therefore to rationalize the sugarcane price is the most important task before the industry for bringing down the total cost of sugar production. Ultimately that will help to make it more competitive at the international level .

Need to Concentrate on High Sugar Contents and High Yielding Varieties of Sugarcane

India is second largest producer of cane sugar in the world after Brazil. It contributes over 15% of the world sugar production. But even after this if we take a review of sugarcane yield per hectare & the quality of sugarcane produced the picture is grim. In spite of introduction of early mid & late maturing varieties , better technology in processing of cane juice, reduction in total losses, the sucrose recovery is rotating just around 10 percent during the last 50 years.

In this connection it can be mentioned that the Australian Sugar Industry Which boats of 14.25 percent sugar recovery is making extensive use of varieties which were originally developed at coimbtoor. Among many sugarcane varieties NCO 310 is the most preferred for higher sugar recovery in some Australian Sugar factories. The Burdkin district of Australia gets sugarcane with as much as 16 percent sucrose in cane resulting into average recovery of 14.25 percent on cane. This is Highest in the world. Secondly, it is also observed that the average productivity of cane ia also much lower as compared to number of countries in the world.

This can be easily seen with the help the help of following table. Yield of sugarcane & sucrose Recovery

Year	*Yield of Sugarcane Tonnes/per ha*	*Averages Sucrose Recovery %*
1930-1931	30.9 tonnes/pha	8.96
1960-1961	45.5 tonnes/pha	9.92
1997-1998	66.5 tonnes/pha	10.00
1999-2000	70.8 tonnes/pha	10.20

Where as the Sugarcane yield in Kenya 100.2 MT/P/ha, Egypt 100.3, Colombia 83.5 Australia 74.5 & Hawaii 150 M.T. per ha for the period of 24months crop & the recovery in these countries is always more than 12 per cent.

Therefore, it is the need of the time the Indian sugar industry should concentrate on to development the high sugar content & higher yielding varieties of sugarcane which play a key role in the sugar industry.

Need to the Promote the Promotion & Export of Raw Sugar

The cost of producing raw sugar in fairly low as compared to white sugar. It is because of less use of chemicals & utilization of higher crushing capacity. At present 55 % of the world sugar trade is in raw sugar. Asia itself imports about 8 million tones of raw sugar perineum. Indian sugar industry can use this opportunity & should promote the production of raw sugar for international market.

Since raw sugar is generally exported in bulk, there can be considerable saving in the handling expenses such as bagging and allied costs etc. If large scale export of raw sugar is undertaken on a regular basis India can switch over to mechanical handing, which will accelerate the rate of loading & thus can earn additional amount of foreign exchange.

Indian raw sugar has an edge over the raw sugar of other countries as its sugarcane has no dextrose content which makes it easy for refining.

The Country can built up a very big clientele in Russia, Japan, South Korea, Malaysia China, Indonesia along with European union. Here, the porting raw sugar to these countries. This will also help to stabilize the domestic market.

Need to Improve the Quality of Sugar

The international sugar trade is based on certain quality norms prescribes by ICUMSA (International Commission for uniform method of sugar Analysis) The sugar importing countries usually insist on co lour value less than 100 ICUMSA unit. In India the sugar quality is assessed by crystal size & luster s. The co lour is judged by visual comparison with Indian sugar standards supplied by National Sugar Institute Kanpur.

The colour of sugar is judged in the foreign countries by ICUMSA units. The codex commission judging the quality norm of sugar production now announced that method 10 would be the new testing mechanism for solving any international trade disputes in sugar. Till now the codex was using method 9 which was disadvantageous for Indian sugar because it consistently showed to have more than 150 ICUMA level.

According to experts, method 9, is a flaw because it is designed for testing beet sugar produced by the European union & not cane sugar produced by countries like India. Cuba, Brazil. Colombia, Thailand & Australia. It was nothing but a anomaly in testing norms which shows the poor quality of sugar. The newly adopted Method 10 is designed especially for cane sugar which will help to increase the marketability of Indian sugar. Now the sugar mills in India are required to make necessary changes in the quality norms of their sugar manufacturing which will help them to become more competitive in the international market.

Challenge Before Sugar Industry

Challenge are not new to sugar industry. tracing a little back, we come to know that the private sugar factory was powerful not only in maharashtra but Bihar & Uttar pradesh. But the government passed the shilling act and imposed rest ruction on holding land. It adversary affected the private sugar industry which was based on the cultivation sugarcane of a thousands acres of land. This created the first big challenge of supplying sugar to the ever increasing population before the co- operative sector. However the first co-operative sugar industry was lunched at Pravaranagr in Ahamadnagar District of Maharashtra. Statistically speaking there are 465 sugar factories functioning all over the country. But of these, there are 140 factories in Maharashtra done and 180 are functioning with their full capacity.

Co-operative sugar Industry was served to organize thousands of laborers. It has created cheerful and promising future for the Farmers and has contributed immensely to change the face of the rural Maharashtra. It has built the hospitals, opened educational & trailing units, & prepared roads to make the life in the rural area more developed and prosperous. The sugar industry with its beneficial approach to the member terms and customers, has also efficiently attended on cultivating sugar can & producing quality sugar. The following date would convince the efficiency and work of the sugar industry. The investment of the annual turnover is around 4000 crores. Near about 700 to 1000 laborers get wages on permanent on contractual basis. Around 5000 other benefic ions are there which include can-cuting labours cane transferred and sugar exchange business. the government has invested around 220 crores in the state co-operative sugar industry. Around 1590 crores deposits are owned by the sugar industry and the share of Maharashtra is 1/3 of the national sugar production, but presently the sugar industry has been tracing a big challenge today in the spate of new economic reforms. the scarcity of water, draught and invariability of resources also add to the complexity of the situation.

Along side the conventional problems like party-politics, inefficient administration, weak management, and mal-functioning factories, the new challenges knock the sugar industry in the new millennium. Following are some of the major challenges:

1. Without of government capital under the pretext of globalisation
2. The indifference of credit-societies in providing financial assistance to the sugar industry .
3. the sugar Industry has ceased to have share in the stock market.
4. The increase in state government restrictions on the sugar industry.
5. Renewed exposure of the industry to newly imposed tare policies.
6. Least distance between tow sugar factories thereby shooting cut-throat competition.
7. The advent of multi- national companies has created shortage of sugarcane production . this may result into the increase of the production cost.
8. The cane-cutting laborers may lose their wages with the introduction of operative machines in the sugar factories.
9. The skilled and unskilled human power engaged in the sugar industry is the sugar industry is facing the problem of up gradation in technology and advance training.
10. There is need to pay attention to human resource development and financial management.

11. There is rapid increase in the membership of the non-sugar-cane producers
12. The young generation of the cane-cutting laborers is willing to be free from the manual hard work
13. There is a cut-throat competition between sugar factories on allotting good tares to farmers.
14. There is need to give emphasis on research and new technology. 15. Co-operative bank in the state do not seem to be extending their helping hands to the sugar industry. 16. Mechanism of sugar industry can severely affect the employment sector. IT.Enormous increase in electricity and water charges, increase in salary, in the chemicals have added to the problems in sugar industry.

Conclusion

Economy liberalization, privatization on one hand have created big challenges before sugar industry and natural calamities on the other hand add to the severity of the situation. The industry needs strict economic discipline, high efficiency, managerial skill, clean leadership and sincere efforts to overcome the problems and to survive the challenges successfully.

In short, the path of development lies in competition and sugar industry has to prove its competence in the newly changing scenario.

References

Dr. G. A. Nikam, "WTO and It's Impact on Indian Sugar Industry Research paper published in the special Edition of "International Conference" namely" Globalization and Indiar. Economy". Apratim Publication Aurangabad.

Dr. G. S. Nikam, Management of Co-operative Sugar Factories in Maharashtra.

Dr. P.R. Dubhashi (2001), Perestroika in Co-operation and Other Essays.

Dr. J. P. Sing (2001), iodays Sugar Industry's need More Sugar content High Yielding Varieties of Sugarcane". Co-operativ Sugar,

February, Vol. 32 No. 6 P. 465, Editorial 'Indian Sugar Industry unbound' Co-operative Sugar, June 2001 Vol. 9 P .689, Editorial "Bitter Sugar Policy" The Economic Times, New Delhi.

Editorial Diabetic Suger Policy "Co-operative Sugar Press News, October 11, 2001 Vol. 32 No. 37 p. 20 & 21.

J M. R. Desai (2000), 'Regional Sugar Policies and Its Impact on Sugar Industry in Asian Countries " Co-operative Sugar September, Vol. 32 No. 1 pp. 29-33

N. N. Shrinivas (2001), "India Scores A Win as WTO Set New Sugar Testing Norms. Co-operative Sugar Press News, July 19, Vol. 32, No. 25. p. 36, 37

Ranvir Nayar (2001), "India to Take up Sugar Quota with E.U." 'Economic Times.'

INDEX